IMAGINING GERONIMO

IMAGINING GERONIMO

An Apache Icon in Popular Culture

WILLIAM M. CLEMENTS

University of New Mexico Press ◆ Albuquerque

LIBRARY OF CONGRESS CATALOGING-IN-PUBLICATION DATA
Clements, William M., 1945–
  Imagining Geronimo : an Apache icon in popular culture / William M. Clements.
    p. cm.
  Includes bibliographical references and index.
    ISBN 978-0-8263-5322-1 (cloth : alk. paper) — ISBN 978-0-8263-5323-8 (electronic)
  1. Geronimo, 1829–1909.
  2. Apache Indians—Kings and rulers—Biography.
  3. Indians in popular culture.
  I. Title.
  E99.A6G473 2013
  979.004'97250092—dc23
  [B]

                    2012037469

Book design and composition by Lila Sanchez

For Larry D. Ball

colleague, collaborator, friend

Contents

Illustrations

Acknowledgments

MANY PEOPLE DESERVE MY GRATITUDE FOR THEIR HELP IN COMPLET-ing this project. I begin, though, with an institution, Arkansas State University, where I taught first literature and folklore studies and later cultural anthropology and American Indian studies for forty years. Students, colleagues, and administrators helped to shape the direction my efforts have taken. Particularly, I want to acknowledge the Faculty Leave Committee, which granted me a semester to work on this project at the time when it was finally coming together. Individuals at ASU who deserve notice include Charles R. Carr, who served as chair of the Department of English and Philosophy throughout most of the time I was trying to pin down Geronimo's image, and Gloria J. Gibson, who was dean of the College of Humanities and Social Sciences during that same period. Their successors—Jerry Ball as chair and Carol O'Connor as dean—also deserve acknowledgment. I am especially grateful to two staff members at the Dean B. Ellis Library at ASU: Linda Keller and Michael Sheppard of the Inter-Library Loan Department. No research in the humanities at ASU can go forward without their assistance, and they have located and made available materials that I had feared I would never be able to access.

In addition to these representatives of Arkansas State, I am indebted to Evelyn Clements, Elizabeth Stafford, and Norman Stafford, who accompanied me on some of the travels involved in this undertaking; Mary Donaghy, who assisted in preparing the illustrations; Michael K. Hudson, who alerted me to the drama troupe 1491 and their moving and important articulation of what Geronimo continues to mean for Native North Americans; Southwestern scholar Alan Radbourne, who supplied me with a copy of the watershed film *Geronimo!* and offered some fine suggestions of other vehicles of the famous Chiricahua's image; and Marty Scarbrough, program director at KASU radio, who identified several musical treatments of Geronimo and copied them onto a CD for me. At the University of New Mexico Press, I am grateful to Elizabeth Ann Albright, the acquisitions editor who encouraged my submission of the manuscript and supported its publication; the anonymous readers who evaluated the manuscript and made suggestions that, even if I did not always follow them, helped me to see where I needed to develop points more completely and fully; copyeditor Sarah Soliz; production editors Amanda Piell and Felicia Cedillos; designer Lila Sanchez; marketing specialists Katherine MacGilvray and Nadya Guerrero-Pezzano; and managing editor Elise McHugh. Of course, none of these individuals should be held responsible for any of this study's shortcomings. They contributed importantly and saved me from many infelicities, but I fear I have persisted, either stubbornly or carelessly, in holding on to interpretations that they may not be comfortable with. I am also grateful to the Louisiana State University Press for allowing quotations from Rawdon Tomlinson's *Geronimo after Kas-ki-yeh*.

My most significant obligations go to two people. I have known Larry D. Ball, a noted historian of the Southwest of Geronimo's time, since 1971. During those forty years, we have been friends and collaborators. And his assistance and advice have been central to this project. He made available to me his vast collection of material on the Southwest, took notice of references to Geronimo for me as he was doing his own research, and talked with me about Geronimo and others who played their roles in the Southwest of the 1870s and 1880s. I hope he will accept the dedication of this book, which does not pretend to the historical rigor that marks his own scholarship. The other person to whom I owe a special debt is Frances M. Malpezzi, with whom I have shared ideas about Geronimo for the past decade and much else for a much longer time. She has read the manuscript several times and been supportive of the project throughout its development.

INTRODUCTION

WHO WAS GERONIMO?

GERONIMO AS THE KING OF SPADES IN A DECK OF "NATIVE AMERICAN" playing cards; a liquor store in Pensacola, Florida, called Geronimo's Spirits; the steel cable on an oil derrick that provides a rapid escape device for a derrickman in case of impending disaster known as the "Geronimo line"; an Australian company marketing Geronimo Jerky in six flavors, including Spicy Shaman; a Geronimo Heritage Blanket designed by Pendleton (fig. 0.1); a board game titled *Geronimo* published in 1995, which pits players representing various Indian tribes against the U.S. Army; postage stamps featuring Geronimo issued by the Marshall Islands, Angola, and the Gambia; a character named Geronimo from "the Cherokee Reservation" in a manga series; the eastern Ozarks town of Pocahontas, Arkansas, which included Geronimo among the hundred "famous individuals" on a Century Wall at the turn of the millennium (Davis-Baltz 2005, 264; fig. 0.2); Geronimo cited—with tongue in cheek—as a potential candidate for *Time* magazine's 2011 Person of the Year (Hopkins 2012): these are some of the ways that a Chiricahua Apache shaman and war leader, not even a chief, has remained a subtext in the mainstream American imagination and beyond as well as in the lore localized in the places where he spent his life, especially southern Arizona and New Mexico, northern Mexico, and southwestern Oklahoma.[1] This situation is not something new. Although journalistically upstaged by a devastating earthquake that struck Charleston, South Carolina, and by the assassination of the king of Bulgaria, Geronimo's

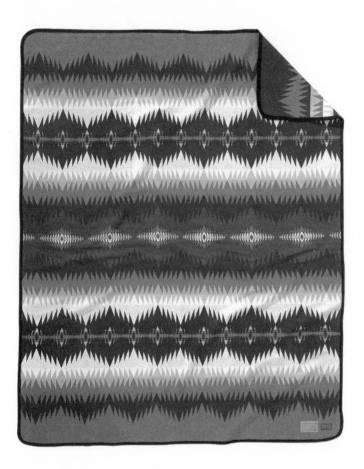

Fig. 0.1. The Geronimo blanket is part of Pendleton's Heritage Collection. According to the company's 2004 holiday catalog, "A tribute to the famed Apache medicine man, seer and spiritual leader, Geronimo. He was single-minded in his determination to preserve his people's land and culture through any means necessary." *Copyright Pendleton Woolen Mills. Used by permission.*

surrender to General Nelson A. Miles at Skeleton Canyon, Arizona Territory, in September 1886 was noted even in the international press, and for the remainder of his life accounts of his activities as a prisoner of war provided a reliable source of soft news to the newspaper-reading public. He appeared at three world's fairs and rode in Theodore Roosevelt's inauguration parade. His death in February 1909 produced scores of obituaries in newspapers across the United States as well as abroad in the *Times* of London and other prestigious dailies.

FIG. 0.2. Will Rogers, Ernest Hemingway, and Charles Lindbergh join Geronimo as the honorees whose visages appear on the Century Wall, a project celebrating the beginning of the twenty-first century in Pocahontas, Arkansas. *Photograph by William M. Clements.*

Geronimo inspired poetry, fiction, and drama during his lifetime and after. Tarzan creator Edgar Rice Burroughs used him as a character in two novels, and poets such as California and Southwest regionalist Charles F. Lummis and recent U.S. poet laureate Ted Kooser have employed him as a poetic focus. A recurrent figure in films, where actors such as Jay Silverheels, Chuck Connors, and Wes Studi have impersonated him, he served as the primary threat to the last stage to Lordsburg in John Ford's classic western *Stagecoach* in 1939, one of the genre's defining films. He appeared in episodes of western television series during their heyday in the 1950s. A photograph of Geronimo taken by Frank Randall in 1884 provided the model for a U.S. postage stamp and a painting by Andy Warhol. He has been the subject of several documentaries. A British high-tech firm has used the alleged gift of a Cadillac to him during his prisoner-of-war days as an exemplum to show the vanity of extending cutting-edge technology to unprepared recipients. His face has appeared on T-shirts, jigsaw puzzles, posters, and an action figure of a Chiricahua warrior. And these are not the only ways in which people have been imagining Geronimo for well over a century (fig. 0.3).

FIG. 0.3. The Geronimo Springs Museum in Truth or Consequences, New Mexico, devotes a room to artifacts associated with the famous Chiricahua, whose image appears on the museum's facade. Included in the museum's Geronimo collection is a life-size wax figure of Geronimo. *Photograph by William M. Clements.*

The process of that imagining has evolved in many ways since Geronimo was first coming to local attention in the Mexico of the 1850s and the southwestern United States of the 1870s. C. L. Sonnichsen first explored that evolution in 1986. Yet Sonnichsen's suggestive essay offers a too simplistic developmental contour of the ways in which the image of Geronimo has changed, and—intended only as a periodical article—it does not cover more than a superficial sampling of instances of that evolving image. More recently, Paul Andrew Hutton has surveyed Geronimo's evolving image in an article published in *True West* (2011). Hutton offers many more specific instances of the appearance of Geronimo in various media and in disparate contexts than did Sonnichsen, but he does not have space to address any of them thoroughly. Moreover, he insists that the development of Geronimo's image has been unidirectional. This project should be taken as an extension of the work by these eminent historians. Following their leads, I stress that the image of Geronimo has been far from static since the mid-1870s when he was first becoming known to the world outside the American Southwest and northern Mexico. But—unlike

Sonnichsen and Hutton—I also emphasize that changes in Geronimo's image have not followed a single-stranded line of development. Instead, they have wavered between extremes: highly negative portrayals that cast him as the consummate incarnation of savagism, a "red devil" who represents what it means to be "Indian" in the popular imagination in the starkest terms; and positive depictions that present Geronimo as the embodiment of freedom, courageous resistance, and principled defiance of overwhelming odds.

Surprisingly little is known about the first fifty or so years of the life of the man who inspired this imagery, particularly when we take into account his later widespread name recognition and prevalence in the inventory of Native Americana cultivated by various sources, Indian and non-Indian, during the twentieth century. A book-length biography for adults did not appear until 1971 (Adams 1971), and that work dealt more with the Apache wars than with the individual known as Geronimo. In 1976—sixty-seven years after his death—a fully developed biography did appear, and though historians of the Southwest have quibbled with some of her details and interpretations, Angie Debo's *Geronimo: The Man, His Time, His Place* (1976) remains a standard source. Debo based much of her work on the "autobiography" that Lawton, Oklahoma, educator S. M. Barrett (1996) constructed out of a series of interviews he had done with Geronimo using Daklugie—Geronimo's nephew, the son of his sister and Geronimo's friend and colleague Juh—as interpreter in 1905. Other works have confirmed, challenged, or adjusted what is related in that autobiography, and Debo takes into consideration many of those works as well as contemporary accounts of the Apache wars written, for the most part, by members of the U.S. Army. Geronimo did not enter significantly into the mainstream Anglo consciousness until the mid-1870s, and newspaper reports that mention him remained sketchy, contradictory, and downright inaccurate even after his name had become a household word a decade later. Much of what we know about Geronimo's life remains speculative, but before we can examine how Americans (and occasionally others) have imagined him, we should survey the "facts" of his life as far as they can be determined.[2]

Authorities hold that the Apache who later became known as Geronimo was born in 1829 either near the headwaters of the Gila River in what is now western New Mexico or farther west on the Gila near what is now Clifton, Arizona. Several commentators have argued that his birth year was actually earlier in the 1820s. This earlier date—often 1823—for Geronimo's birth makes more plausible the earliest reliably datable event in his life, the killing of his mother, wife, and children through what Geronimo believed to be Mexican treachery near Janos, Chihuahua, in 1851. Geronimo himself states that he was born in No-Doyohn Canyon, Arizona Territory, in 1829 (Barrett 1996, 58). We know with a fair amount of certainty that his father was Taklishim, a Bedonkohe, and his mother is referred to by the Spanish name Juana, though that does not necessarily mean she was other than a full-blood Apache. Reflecting the period's ethnic and racial hierarchies, early newspaper biographies of Geronimo erroneously claimed that he was Mexican or half Mexican.

Anthropologists and historians have tried to straighten out the interconnections among various Apache bands and tribes during the first half of the nineteenth century without complete success. However, the Bedonkohe were affiliated politically and through kinship with the Chokonen, Chihenne, and Nednhi bands, which many believe formed a larger unit, the Chiricahuas. By the time Geronimo attained celebrity, the Bedonkohe had all but disappeared as a distinct Apache community, apparently absorbed into the Chihenne. Geronimo was usually referred to simply as a Chiricahua.

Geronimo—whose name as a child was Goyaałé (also rendered as Goyahkla or Gokliya in other Anglicized orthographies), which is usually interpreted to mean "one who yawns"—probably had a conventional Apache childhood, interrupted only by the death of his father when the boy was still quite young, an event that may have thrust him into adult responsibilities at a relatively early age since his mother did not remarry. Although biographers, including Debo, usually deal with his childhood to some degree, only that material which appears in the autobiography can be considered anything but speculative. Supplementary information about his childhood has often been extrapolated from accounts of precontact enculturation practices recorded by anthropologist Morris Edward Opler ([1941] 1996) from Chiricahua consultants in the early 1930s, from memoirs such as those of Jason Betzinez ([1959] 1987) and James Kaykwala (Ball 1970), and from oral history interviews conducted by Eve Ball (1980) and others. Most of these sources, however, involve individuals who were at least a generation younger than Geronimo and grew up at a time when contact with Mexicans and North Americans had become much more commonplace. Moreover, they were looking back to that time of life that for many people is idyllic and in the cases of these sources made even more so if they were dissatisfied with the toll that forced assimilation had taken on them in the interim.

Presumably, Geronimo went through the requisite stages of attaining warrior status. At some time, most likely in the 1840s, he married Alope, a Nednhi. Not following the Apache custom of matrilocality, they set up housekeeping near his mother among the Bedonkohe (who were becoming integrated into the Chihenne), now led by the famous Mangas Coloradas. Geronimo was actively involved in male economic activities, including raiding Mexican communities in Sonora and perhaps Chihuahua. Although we have no confirmation other than his own account of his life, in which he is vague especially about dates, he may have distinguished himself in some of these forays enough to achieve notoriety among his own people by 1851. In March of that year, the event that came to define the rest of his life occurred. The Bedonkohe and other Chiricahua bands regularly traded at the town of Janos in northern Chihuahua. During one of these visits, which usually involved the entire band, a Sonoran military force led by Colonel José Maria Carrasco attacked the women and children who had been left in camp at a site known as Kaskiyeh while the men were trading in town. Alope, Geronimo's mother, and the couple's three children were among those who died. Geronimo attributed his lifelong hatred of Mexicans to this massacre, and it laid the foundation for much of his later hostility toward Anglos, which increased as he suffered perceived wrongs done by representatives of the United States.

For the next several years, Geronimo instigated and led revenge raids against Mexican communities. One of these may have been the occasion when he received the name by which he became most well known. Not all authorities agree, but most sources suggest that Goyaałé became Geronimo during the summer of 1852, when the Bedonkohe raided the town of Arispe, Sonora. Mexican soldiers lured from the town's protection confronted the raging Goyaałé and spontaneously invoked the aid of Saint Jerome, their cries of "Geronimo!" attaching to the man who was so vehemently attacking them. For the next decade Geronimo was especially active in raiding Mexican settlements, though, as he admits in his autobiography, not always with success.

Geronimo participated in the hostilities that developed during the 1860s after a botched attempt by an American officer, 2nd Lieutenant George N. Bascom, to locate Felix Ward, a mixed-blood boy who had been kidnapped by Apaches. Bascom accused the Chiricahua leader Cochise of involvement in the kidnapping and held several of his relatives hostage until the boy could be returned. Young Ward (who later attained notoriety during the Apache wars of the 1880s as a scout called "Mickey Free") was not in Cochise's camp, and the Chiricahua retaliated by taking hostages himself. The ensuing standoff resulted in the deaths of most of the hostages on both sides and enmity between Cochise and the Anglos that lasted for a decade. Geronimo may have been present at the famous Battle of Apache Pass in 1862. He was certainly affected by the death by treachery of Mangas Coloradas, leader of Geronimo's own band, the following year. Although he was probably involved in some of the attacks that Cochise and his Chiricahuas made against Anglos during the 1860s, Geronimo seems to have been more interested in raiding into Mexico, where he could satisfy his desire for vengeance while reaping economic rewards.

When General O. O. Howard created the Chiricahua Reservation after negotiating a treaty with Cochise in 1871, Geronimo continued to lead raiding parties into Mexico and was partially responsible for dissolution of the reservation and assignment of the Chiricahuas to the much less suitable facilities at San Carlos on the Gila River in 1876. When John P. Clum moved the Chiricahuas to San Carlos, Geronimo used trickery to lead a band into Mexico instead of making the trek to a new home. Clum, who retained a grudge against Geronimo for what he considered to be Geronimo's dishonesty for the rest of his life and whose own appetite for self-promotion contributed to Geronimo's emergence into the limelight (Shapard 2010, 93), enjoyed some revenge when he arrested Geronimo, employing some trickery of his own to do so, at the Ojo Caliente Reservation in New Mexico Territory in 1877. Geronimo went in chains to San Carlos and remained incarcerated for several months.

Life at San Carlos and later at nearby Turkey Creek on the Fort Apache Reservation did not suit Geronimo, and he led three "breakouts" during the next several years. He first left San Carlos in April 1878 and returned in December 1879 or January 1880. In connection with the death of the prophet Nock-ay-del-klinne, who inspired what might have turned into a full-fledged revitalization movement had he survived, Geronimo again crossed reservation boundaries in September 1881. This breakout led to the appointment of General George C. Crook, who had already served in Arizona in the early 1870s, as the region's military commander. Crook pursued Geronimo into his stronghold in the Sierra Madre of northern Mexico and negotiated a surrender that brought the Chiricahua warrior back to the reservation in February 1884. Geronimo's final departure from the reservation occurred in May 1885. The reasons for the dissatisfaction that led to this breakout remain controversial, but they included his chafing under the restrictions that reservation life placed upon traditional Apache lifeways as well as harassment particularly by Apaches who had sided with reservation authorities.

Though the hysterical press of Arizona and New Mexico attributed many atrocities north of the border to Geronimo during the next few months, he probably went more or less directly back to the Sierra Madre. From there he periodically led or instigated raids against Mexican communities and occasionally into the United States. Meanwhile, Crook's forces, consisting largely of Apache scouts, tried to ferret him out, every now and then reducing the population of his already small band. Geronimo met with Crook at Cañon de los Embudos not far from the international border in March 1886 to negotiate a surrender. While Crook assumed that their negotiations had been successful, Geronimo, under the influence of liquor that had been provided him by an unscrupulous trader, did not cross over into the United States afterward as planned. The resulting disappointment forced Crook's resignation and his replacement by General Nelson A. Miles. Relentless pursuit by forces led by Henry W. Lawton contributed to Geronimo's decision to accept terms of surrender offered to him by Lieutenant Charles Gatewood under Miles's authority. In September 1886 he surrendered to the general at Skeleton Canyon in Arizona, thus ending— at least symbolically—the Indian wars of the West.

Geronimo understood that he had agreed to be sent to Fort Marion, Florida, where he would be reunited with his family. After two years, he believed, they would be repatriated to Arizona. He went first, though, to Fort Sam Houston in San Antonio, Texas, where he awaited President Grover Cleveland's decision regarding his disposition. Finally, after about six weeks he and the other males who had been a part of his band were routed to Fort Pickens on Santa Rosa Island in the Gulf of Mexico near Pensacola, Florida, while the women and children went on to Fort Marion on Florida's Atlantic coast. Though some family members joined Geronimo and his comrades at Fort Pickens in 1887, it was not until the following year that the entire Chiricahua community was reunited. This reunion occurred at Mount Vernon Barracks, Alabama, rather than in Arizona. The Chiricahuas remained in Alabama until 1894, when they were removed to Fort Sill, Indian Territory. Geronimo lived there the rest of his life.

During the next fifteen years Geronimo became a celebrity. He attended world's fairs in Omaha, Nebraska, in 1898; Buffalo, New York, in 1901; and Saint Louis, Missouri, in 1904. He participated in Theodore Roosevelt's inauguration in 1905 and was courted by Wild West show entrepreneur Gordon Lillie (Pawnee Bill). He was a tourist attraction and provided good copy for journalists who speculated that he had gone mad, that his much heralded conversion to Christianity was only a sham, and that he was ever plotting an escape. Newspapers sought his opinions on such topics as the Filipino resistance to the American presence following the Spanish-American War and the education of Apache children. Geronimo died in March 1909 from pneumonia that he contracted after lying out all night after one of his periodic drinking bouts. He was buried in the Apache cemetery northeast of Fort Sill.

Why did this particular Chiricahua capture the imaginations of his contemporaries? Even more importantly, why has he continued to figure into the imaginations of their descendants? Many commentators, those contemporary with Geronimo and historians looking back at his life and times, have questioned whether he has deserved the attention that he has received. Often they cite contemporary opinion, both Indian and non-Indian, that denigrates Geronimo. Ross Santee, who devotes most of his treatment of Geronimo to showing that he was a consummate liar, notes, "It is ironical that Geronimo, who was without honor or integrity, even among his own people, is the one Apache who is best known today" (1947, 176). Writing in 1906, Norman Wood called Geronimo "the best advertised Indian on earth" (1906, 534). Some commentators propose that other Apaches from Geronimo's era deserve to be remembered more than he. Edwin R. Sweeney, author of the standard biography of Cochise, the Chiricahua chief who led his people through ten years of warfare before settling on a reservation in the southeastern corner of Arizona Territory, argues that this figure deserves more recognition than does Geronimo. He characterizes Geronimo as "a far lesser man" who could "not compare with Cochise by any logical measurement, either in his own day or in history" (1991, xiv). Sweeney has also made a case for Chatto, who assisted in the U.S. Army's pursuit of Geronimo during the time leading up to his final surrender. Chatto, Sweeney (2007) suggests, represented a more realistic alternative to the Euro-American presence in the Apaches' ancestral homeland than that favored by Geronimo. Dan L. Thrapp, who wrote several book-length treatments of the Southwest during the years of the Apache wars, opts for Juh as "well above Geronimo in accomplishment" (1973, 5). Leader of the Nednhi band, Juh seemed to be the appropriate successor to the Chihenne leader Victorio after the latter's death in 1880. In fact, Thrapp argues, Juh engineered a daring raid from Mexico's Sierra Madre into Arizona and New Mexico for which Geronimo is usually given credit (1973, 29–33; 1988, 547–49). He asserts that unlike Juh, who had the ability to lead the Apaches in outright war, Geronimo "never became more than a minor guerrilla chieftain" (1973, 39). Scholars often dismiss Geronimo as a much more minor figure in

Apache affairs than his public image seems to suggest. He is assigned fewer supporters among his fellow Chiricahuas than other figures had and is sometimes accused of being motivated by selfishness and pettiness rather than by patriotic concern for the welfare of his people. A recent exhibit at the Heard Museum in Phoenix has tried to bring several of Geronimo's contemporaries, including Naiche, Lozen, and Daklugie, out of his shadow (Cantley 2012).

So the arguments that Cochise or Chatto or Juh or perhaps some other luminary should represent the various qualities that Geronimo has come to epitomize in the popular imagination have some support and perhaps some grounding. However, these often represent opinions of non-Apaches who are basing their perspectives largely on non-Apache sources, even when they purport to reflect Apache points of view. Even those few Apache viewpoints that have survived, we must remember, are available only through the mediation of Euro-American editors and publishers. For an outsider to assess one person as a "better Indian" than another certainly risks the ethnocentric imposition of alien values. It probably does not matter anyway who *should* be recognized as the consummate embodiment of American Indian resistance since Geronimo, deserving or not, has come to fill that role. Media influence, which sensationalized the "atrocities" that Geronimo and his band were supposed to have committed; lack of a significant U.S. military presence anywhere else at the time of the Apache wars because of the relative calm among other American Indian communities; contemporary controversy over how that military was using its resources, including significant financial appropriations and the cream of military talent, in pursuing Geronimo; and later Geronimo's ability to manipulate his image and exploit his notoriety partially explain why his celebrity continues. And certainly the perception that his was a "last stand" of Native American resistance to Euro-American invasion accounted for much of his contemporary notoriety and his later emergence as a symbolic entity. He was the ultimate renegade, a "freedom-loving American" struggling against overwhelming odds to maintain a value that most Americans endorse.

How has Geronimo been imagined? The answer to that question has required a book-length study, which remains incomplete and already needs updating even before it sees print. He remains a nebulous figure from American history who, despite the somewhat limited nature of his accomplishments, has spoken to a range of opinions and mindsets. Presumably he will continue to do so.

This study, while far from exhaustive, examines Geronimo's image from a number of perspectives, in a range of media, and in terms of several disciplinary protocols. I begin by noting that the image that Geronimo has attained in the twenty-first century—at least in many quarters, including the *Congressional Record*—contrasts markedly with that which appeared in most sources during the time he was at war with the United States and Mexico and which continues to figure in the work of some historians. Instead of the "red devil" portrayed by newspapers ranging from those published near the scene of his activities to the national press, Geronimo often but not invariably comes across these days as a heroic freedom fighter and patriot. The first chapter looks at the demonization of Geronimo that once characterized his image and examines his later positive status. It suggests that his current identity reflects traditional patterns—some intercultural (e.g., trickster, social bandit), some pan-Indian (e.g., patriot chief, sage elder), and some specific to his cultural heritage (e.g., culture hero).

Although we have no contemporary oral documentation of stories told about Geronimo, indications of a flourishing tradition of such stories abound. Most likely, narratives about his exploits figured into storytelling repertoires of other Apaches, but most of the available records come from Anglo sources, especially newspapers. Some themes and specific stories recur in the published record, and many fall under two broad rubrics: atrocities and narrow escapes. But other themes, especially grudgingly admiring accounts of Geronimo's resourcefulness and daring, appear in Geronimo stories. Moreover, many narrators convert their experiences into "Geronimo stories" merely by attaching his name to their own tales of personal experience in the Southwest in the 1880s. The book's second chapter samples the repertoire of Geronimo stories.

Chapter 3 assumes a more historically oriented approach. From the time of his breakout from the San Carlos Reservation in 1881 and perhaps even earlier, Geronimo had been a public figure. His status increased after his final breakout in 1885. Between May of that year and September 1886, his name appeared in newspapers in the Southwest, nationally, and even abroad on an almost daily basis. Even after Geronimo surrendered and was sent first to Florida, then to Alabama, and finally to Oklahoma, he remained in the public eye. During his more than twenty years as a prisoner of war, he tried with mixed results to take some control of the image that he projected. This chapter examines that process, focusing particularly on Geronimo's presence at three world's fairs and at Roosevelt's inauguration.

Turning to a persistent question about Geronimo's image, the fourth chapter concerns his ostensible conversion to Christianity. Not only was there controversy in the contemporary press about the "sincerity" of his acceptance of the new religion, but the issue continues to resurface—for example, in a recent issue of *Wild West* magazine (Banks 2009). This chapter explores the historical record and the public response to news of Geronimo's conversion and suggests that Geronimo, like many other American Indians who accepted Christianity, viewed the "truth" of religion, Christianity as well as his ancestral faith, in "pragmatic" terms—that is, whether it offered a useful approach to making sense of and coping with the world where he found himself. This chapter assumes that Geronimo was indeed "sincere" in both his assumption of Christianity in the early twentieth century and his continued and contemporaneous devotion to the old-time religion.

Interest in Geronimo's physical appearance surfaced during the newspaper coverage of the Apache wars of the 1880s. Descriptions that supported the idea that he represented savagery frequently appeared in stories about atrocities credited to him or his warriors. The first photograph of Geronimo was taken in 1884, and he probably had become the most frequently photographed Indian in history by the time of his death in 1909. What these photographs show is a figure who represents both abstract savagery and a specific, easily recognizable individuality. Moreover, even the earliest visual representations show a subject exerting some control over his image. Never evincing the passivity that some commentators on photographs of American Indians have imputed to the subjects, Geronimo sat for the camera and the palette assertively and managed as far as he could the image that would result. Chapter 5 explores photographic and other visual representations of Geronimo.

By the time the nineteenth century had ended, Geronimo had appeared in a range of literary genres. The 1880s witnessed the publication of some newspaper verse about him, and poetic treatments, including book-length series of related poems, have continued into the twenty-first century. Geronimo was represented dramatically by about 1890, and though he has not flourished as much on stage as in other literary and performance venues, he has occasionally appeared in dramatic works since then. Both short stories and novels that featured him as a character were in print by the 1890s, and he has been a staple in western pulp fiction as well as in more ambitious fictional works since then. Even comic books and graphic novels have treated Geronimo. Though the development has been more circuitous than unilinear, his image has generally undergone improvement over the years, and he has moved from a supporting role in many early works to the center of attention, though rarely the protagonist even in more recent novels and short stories. Chapter 6 treats the literary image of Geronimo.

As Chapter 7 shows, visual images of Geronimo were not confined to still photography or other static arts. As early as 1912, but beginning especially with the 1940 feature film *Geronimo!*, this Apache has been the focal character in several cinematic treatments. Moreover, he has been a supporting character in many classic westerns, including *Stagecoach* and *Broken Arrow*. He has also appeared in several television programs, especially the westerns that flourished during the 1950s. Like his portrayals in literature, Geronimo on film and videotape has changed from arch exemplar of villainy to heroic patriot with occasional characterizations as buffoon, especially in television episodes.

Some evidence suggests that as early as the 1910s, rumors circulated that Geronimo's grave had been violated and that his skull had been removed. Those rumors later focused on the role of several graduates of Yale University, including Prescott Bush, father and grandfather of presidents, who were at Fort Sill during the run-up to World War I. Claims have been made that these soldiers, all members of the senior society at Yale known as Skull and Bones, deposited Geronimo's skull at their clubhouse in New Haven, where they employed it in initiation rituals. The rumor has resurfaced periodically—especially when a Bush has been in the news and quite recently when, in association with the centennial of his death, Geronimo's descendants sued to have his remains repatriated to the Southwest. This rumor, along with the use of Geronimo's name in the military operation that located and killed Osama bin Laden in 2011, reminds us that the story of Geronimo's image is far from complete. Presumably new chapters will be added as long as the American imagination requires someone who can represent both utter savagery and patriotic heroism as well as other components of the ever-dynamic American myth.

CHAPTER 1

TOWARD THE CANONIZATION OF GERONIMO

SEVERAL COMMENTATORS ON GERONIMO'S CAREER HAVE NOTED THE transformation in his image that has occurred since his first press notices in the mid-1870s. Odie B. Faulk indicates that while the U.S. military figures who participated in the Apache wars have been largely forgotten by the general public, Geronimo, as the years since his surrender passed, "gradually came to symbolize the brave fight of a brave people for independence and ownership of their homeland" and remains a household name (1969, 218). In a pioneering study of Geronimo's evolving image, C. L. Sonnichsen suggests that "Geronimo has undergone a desert change and become a symbol of heroic resistance" (1986, 6). Unlike Faulk, Sonnichsen recognizes that the evolution of Geronimo's image has not been strictly chronological, developing more or less in a single strand from the negativity of Geronimo's contemporaries to positive assessments that emerged with temporal distancing from the bloody events of the 1880s: "The two Geronimos have existed side by side almost from the beginning, and they still do exist, but Geronimo the Wicked is barely alive in the second half of the twentieth century, and Geronimo the Good is having things pretty much his own way" (1986, 6). Sonnichsen perceives a general pattern of development that allows only for polar opposites in Geronimo's image. Moreover, his treatment of how Geronimo's image has changed is impressionistic and based on too little concrete data to demonstrate his point fully. Paul Andrew Hutton has also addressed Geronimo's changing image. His essay in *True West*, published shortly after Geronimo had come again to public attention when his name was associated with the U.S. military operation that resulted in the death of Osama bin Laden, identifies many appearances by Geronimo in various media. While his illustrations are more extensive than those cited by Sonnichsen, Hutton does not have space to analyze them. He also reiterates contentions that changes in Geronimo's reputation have followed a unidirectional and binary contour "from bloodthirsty terrorist to patriot chief" (Hutton 2011, 23), and he asserts, "From a renegade warrior, hated by settlers on both sides of the international border and finally tracked down by his own people, Geronimo has morphed into a patriot leader who led the final resistance to preserve his land and culture" (24). Moreover, the evolution from negative to positive in Geronimo's image "is complete" (31).

Sonnichsen's dichotomy and Hutton's suggestion of single-stranded progression are too simplistic. Between the "wicked" Geronimo who dominated but did not have exclusive claim on early characterizations and the "good" Geronimo who became more prominent after his death exists a more human figure that some commentators have either discovered or manufactured. Moreover, even in the twenty-first century naysayers—perhaps including Hutton himself, who attributes Geronimo's positive depictions to "historical amnesia" (2011, 24)—are still promulgating their view of Geronimo. The evolution of Geronimo's image requires a more complex response than that encouraged by the question asked by the editor of *Wild West* magazine: "Was Geronimo a butcher of men, women and children and so mean-spirited that he would even scalp a little girl's favorite doll? Or was he a freedom-loving shaman struggling heroically to resist attempts by the United States and Mexico to exterminate him and his people?" (Lalire 2001, 6).

From the mid-1880s until his death in 1909 and even afterward, Geronimo provided regular copy for journalists. His final "breakout" from the Fort Apache Reservation in May 1885 generated an almost constant stream of stories, especially in newspapers in Arizona and New Mexico Territories. That event also received coverage on a national level, and during the fifteen months that culminated in his surrender to General Nelson A. Miles in September 1886, stories about Geronimo appeared frequently in newspapers throughout the country. Most journalists joined their Arizona peers in what one commentator has characterized as "a long and bitter verbal campaign against the red men" in which "the press utilized to the fullest extent all its editorial resources of impassioned rhetoric and blistering invective" (Turcheneske 1973, 133).

Edwin R. Sweeney has found an English reference to Geronimo dating from June 1873 (2010, 24), but most likely Geronimo's earliest significant press notices appeared locally in the mid-1870s when he refused to move to San Carlos after John Clum closed the Chiricahua Reservation. Clum, whose role in Geronimo's career at the time helped to shape his own self-image as well as that of Geronimo for the rest of both their lives, released a statement, which appeared in papers in various parts of the country in May 1877, about his arrest of Geronimo at Ojo Caliente, New Mexico. Datelined San Diego, 3 May, the story (as published on the front page of the *Morning Oregonian* in Portland for 5 May) quoted a telegram sent by Clum on 20 April from Fort Craig near the Ojo Caliente reservation: "I have Geronimo, Ponica, Girmo and 14 other prisoners. The worst are chained." The report of this event in Santa Fe's *Daily New Mexican* on 28 April 1877 does not mention Geronimo at all, even though the paper had made notice of a cattle raid that Geronimo had allegedly conducted several weeks earlier (4 April 1877).

Geronimo first came to the general attention of the national press a couple of years after Clum's press release. An article in the *New York Times* for 29 December 1879 reports a dispatch from Tucson saying that Geronimo, "an Apache chief," had surrendered at Camp Rucker with eighty-three others. "This is the band which has been depredating for some months past along the border, and did much of the work credited to Victoria's [*sic*] band," the *Times* noted. In its 4 June 1880 issue, the same paper published a report, datelined Tucson, that the Indian hostilities in Arizona Territory had now diminished. The report noted, "Until last December a large band of Apaches, who had refused to go on to the reservation, roamed about on the Mexican border, committing frequent murders, and robbing the settlers, both in Arizona, New-Mexico, and Mexico. Their leaders were Juh and Johronimo, and they were noted for their courage and daring." The *Times* related that the terms of surrender that had ended the threat posed by these Apaches the previous December had occasioned an act of brutality by "Johronimo," who summarily shot the "third in command" of the band for opposing those terms.

Geronimo's initial notices on the national level, brief as they were, conveyed several recurrent components of the image that would dominate, though not to the total exclusion of other views, in the many depictions of him during his lifetime: that he was a "chief"; that he bore responsibility for most of the hostility that characterized the borderlands during the period that began even before the death of Victorio in 1880 and continued through September 1886; and that he was utterly ruthless, even with members of his own community, when it came to getting what he wanted. These descriptions, which were reinforced by other features attributed to him as well as by outright direct declarations about him and other Apaches, especially Chiricahuas, amounted to a process of demonization, vestiges of which still endure. The *Times*, which sometimes noted that hostilities that broke out between Native Americans and whites were often the fault of the latter, nevertheless was unrelenting in its negative characterizations of Geronimo. Among noted American Indians in the latter half of the nineteenth century, only Sitting Bull was treated with more opprobrium, and that arose from his having spent more time on the national stage than Geronimo (Hays 1997, 7, 96). Consistently, Geronimo and his "bucks"—"no better than wild beasts"—were vilified for their "depravity" (Hays 1997, 122). In fact, *Times* editorialists tended to regard Indians of the Southwest in general as "of a low type, having plenty of cunning and audacity, and naturally predatory and murderous" (Hays 1997, 117).

The demonization of Geronimo in the press dominated depictions of him, especially after he left the Fort Apache Reservation in May 1885. Local and regional newspapers consistently characterized the "renegade" Apaches as "red devils"—long a commonplace term of opprobrium for those Natives who opposed European and Euro-American expansionism. For example, the *Silver City (NM) Enterprise* for 22 May 1885 portrayed Geronimo as "that murderous red devil" whose presence in the neighborhood—a couple of hundred miles east of the reservation he had left—would result, the newspaper boasted, in "a number of good [i.e., dead] Indians for the government to bury." Meanwhile, the *Las Vegas (NM) Daily Optic* headlined two of its early accounts of the breakout: "The Red Devils Again" (21 May 1885), which reported 150 Indians near Malone, Arizona Territory, and heading northeastward, and "Red Devils Across the Line" (23 May 1885), which located "Chief Geronimo and his band" near Hillsboro in southern New Mexico Territory. Members of the group were still "Red Devils" in the *Optic*'s issue for 29 May 1885. The *Tucson (AZ) Weekly Star* for 4 June 1885 published a report headlined "The Apache Fiend." Therein, Geronimo is characterized as "the Apache cutthroat." The piece rehearsed the routes of his "bloody and destructive" trails in the 1870s and earlier in the 1880s: "All human consideration for this ferocious fiend and his diabolical band has been exhausted and nothing short of total extermination will be tolerated by the people of Arizona." Meanwhile, across the border, according to the *Atlanta (GA) Constitution* for 11 September 1886, "the peasantry of Chihuahua and Sonora ... believed [him] to be the devil sent to punish the people for their sins." General George Crook's adjutant John Gregory Bourke had opined much the same in his memoir of the U.S. Army's expedition into the Sierra Madre in 1883, basing his views as much on his attitudes toward superstitious Mexicans as on anything he might have actually heard from them regarding Geronimo ([1886] 1958, 108). During the Battle of Alisos Creek, which occurred in Chihuahua in April 1882, Mexican soldiers received encouragement from their commander Lorenzo García to kill Geronimo, "the devil himself" (Sweeney 2010, 225).

The *Weekly New Mexican Review and Live Stock Journal*, published in Santa Fe, took up the imagery, calling Geronimo and his group "savage villains," "fiends," and "red devils" in its 4 June 1885 issue; "butchering barbarians" in its 25 June 1885 issue; "monsters" and "wretches" on 9 July 1885; and "skulking curs" on 16 July 1885. The *Las Vegas Daily Optic*, which often republished stories that had appeared in newspapers in southern New Mexico, unrelentingly continued its name-calling through the month of June: "red devils" again and again (6 June, 9 June, 11 June, 13 June), "red-handed hyenas" on 6 June, "coterie of cross-eyed tramps" on 12 June, "blood-thirsty redskins" on 13 June, "murderous wretches" on 16 June, "cruel, treacherous, filthy, and hopelessly savage beasts" on 18 June, and "worse than wolves or coyotes" on 27 June.

Despite occasional claims in the Southwest that the eastern establishment did not truly understand how diabolical Geronimo and his followers were, the national press often took up the banner of demonization. On 23 May 1885, the *Chicago Tribune* headlined the story "A Trail of Blood—Geronimo and His Band of Chiricahua Bucks Begin the Work of Murder—Half a Dozen Miners and Settlers Already Massacred by the Fleeing Indians—Capt. Smith and His Scouts Sight the Fugitives—Fears That They Will Be Ambushed." The Chiricahuas were "red devils" possessed of the "well-known treacherous nature of the Apachés." The story characterized Geronimo, a lieutenant of Victorio, as having led "almost as bloody a career" as his mentor. He and Juh were "apt pupils at pillage and murder." Already, only a week after the breakout, "the depredations of the savages have been of the most shocking description." Meanwhile, the *Atlanta Constitution* on 29 May 1885 headlined a story on the unrest in the Southwest, "The Red Devils," and held that a "more worthless and insolent lot of ruffians can not be found" on 2 June 1885. The *New York Times* joined the chorus of abuse. The Chiricahuas were "inhuman wretches" and "brutes" who were "committing the most horrible and shocking crimes," according to its 1 June 1885 issue, and a story the following day characterized them as "red-handed murderers." Meanwhile, a west coast perspective came from Charles F. Lummis, who was on assignment in the Southwest from the *Los Angeles Times*. In a 30 March 1886 dispatch, which was datelined Fort Bowie, Arizona Territory, he characterized Geronimo as "the gory Chiricahua" (Thrapp 1979, 17). A week or so later (9 April) Lummis described Apaches in general as "BORN BUTCHERS—and hereditary slayers." An Apache, he averred, was "a pirate by profession, a robber to whom blood was sweeter than booty" (Thrapp 1979, 49).

The language of demonization continued to appear in what purported to be straightforward dispatches from the field as well as editorial comments throughout the fifteen months of Geronimo's final resistance. Many military figures who wrote their memoirs of participation in the Apache wars continued to demonize Geronimo even years after his death, perhaps to counter the increasing tendency by some to treat him sympathetically. Britton Davis, who had charge of the reservation from which Geronimo broke out in 1885 and who participated in his pursuit, published his account of military operations in the Southwest in 1929. Therein, he consistently depicts Geronimo as "the trouble maker" (1929, 71), insisting that he was even "feared and disliked by the great majority of the Indians" (113). In response to Geronimo's failure to finalize his surrender to Crook at Cañon de los Embudos, Davis wrote, "This Indian was a thoroughly vicious, intractable, and treacherous man. His only redeeming traits were courage and determination. His word, no matter how earnestly pledged, was worthless. His history past and to follow was a series of broken pledges and incitements to outbreaks" (143). Davis's superior, General George Crook, dismissed Geronimo as "such a liar that I can't believe a word he says. I don't want to have anything to do with him." Crook was repudiating Geronimo's attempts to interact with him when the general paid a visit to the Chiricahua prisoner-of-war camp at Mount Vernon Barracks, Alabama, in 1890 (Schmitt 1960, 293). Meanwhile, James Parker, who had served at Fort Apache and other sites in the Southwest during the Apache wars, had Geronimo differing from "a common murderer only by the fact that he was an Indian and assassin on a large scale" (1929, 187).

Many people in the Southwest, especially those with access to printing presses, were considerably rankled by the arrangements that Crook had made with the Chiricahuas during his Sierra Madre campaign in 1883. He had allowed those who had left the San Carlos Reservation in September 1881 to return with impunity. Geronimo, who had assumed a leadership role, did not return to the reservation until February 1884, and he brought with him some three hundred head of Mexican cattle, which Davis had helped him to spirit across the border (Davis 1929, 82–101). The lack of punishment for the Indians following the breakout had incensed the local press, who seldom passed up the opportunity to berate Crook for his failure to exact retribution from the "renegades." The *Las Vegas Daily Optic*, for example, reprinted an editorial from the *Denver (CO) Times* in its 27 May 1885 issue, which noted the irony of the way in which Crook had handled these Indians versus the punishment meted out to Anglo rustlers, who suffered death or imprisonment. Responding to the breakout that had occurred less than two weeks earlier, the editorial noted, "If the Indians had been treated as the rustlers were, Geronimo would not now be turning the southwest settlements into butchers' shambles." Less extreme in its views but nevertheless suggesting that responsibility for the persistence of the Apache "problem" in the Southwest lay with Crook's policies, the *Tucson Weekly Star* for 26 May 1885 argued, "Had Geronimo and his band been taken to Indian Territory [i.e., part of what is now Oklahoma] after they were returned to the San Carlos reservation, they would not have been on the war path. This was the demand made by the press of Arizona, but the policy was not adopted, and the redskins are out again."

Opinions—some directly from the newspapers themselves and some attributed to particular individuals—about what should be done with the "red devils" once they were inevitably apprehended reinforced the demonic image of Geronimo and his cohorts. Crook's perceived mishandling of the aftermath of the breakout of 1881 colored opinions articulated during Geronimo's time off-reservation beginning in 1885. For example, during this last breakout the local press regularly published suggestions, often couched as threats, about what should be done once the renegades were captured. Sometimes the threats were cloaked in the vague terms of a piece republished by the *Optic* from the *Deming (NM) Headlight* on 29 May 1885: "The question has been asked, 'What will be done with the Indians in case they are captured?' They are not captured yet, and if they are, we would suggest that they be turned over to the citizens of Deming in order to save the government any trouble in the matter. We think our citizens could devise means of caring for them in about five minutes." The *Tucson Weekly Star* for 4 June 1885 also hinted at the extreme measures, perhaps at the hands of vigilantes, that should await Geronimo upon capture: "All human consideration for this ferocious fiend and his diabolical band has been exhausted and nothing short of total extermination will be tolerated by the people of Arizona." Vague threats continued to fill the pages of some newspapers as the Geronimo campaign was winding down. The *Optic*, for example, on 2 September 1886 (a couple of days before Geronimo surrendered) responded to the possibility that the Apaches would be allowed to return to San Carlos by suggesting, "They had better not be kept that way long for fear of accidents. This part of New Mexico is the wealthiest, best settled and most civilized, and such a nest of rattlesnakes in our midst as nearly two hundred of the meanest Apaches in the world, will not be endured for a great while."

Specific recommendations for how the Apaches should be dealt with after their capture stressed two options, both of which were actually considered by officials all the way up to President Grover Cleveland. One position called for their trial in the civil courts of Arizona Territory, while the other emphasized the necessity of their removal somewhere to the east. The *Silver City Enterprise* for 10 July 1885 articulated these options in a list of citizen demands: "That the scouts [Apaches who were assisting Crook in pursuit of Geronimo] be discharged; that every hostile or Indian found off the reservation and captured be turned over to civil authorities; that the Indians at San Carlos be completely disarmed, or that the reservation be abandoned. If these demands are accorded to well and good. If not, the San Carlos reservation will be raided and thousands of good Indians made" (Mullane 1968, 34).

The same newspaper might argue for both solutions to the Apache "problem." For example, the *Weekly New Mexican Review and Live Stock Journal* strongly asserted the need to remove the Apaches, apparently not just Chiricahuas, from the Southwest. An editorial called for closing the San Carlos Reservation and transferring its inhabitants to Indian Territory: "The annual outbreaks will happen as long as there is a San Carlos reservation." While this sentiment appeared on page 1 of the paper's 4 June 1885 issue, the second page presented an argument for a more final and inclusive solution: "An Indian, Chiricahua, Mescalero or Navajo, caught on a raiding or stealing expedition should be sent to the happy hunting grounds, and that quickly and through the agency of a rope.... [T]he sooner the Chiricahuas are killed off the better for New Mexico and Arizona." A month later on 9 July 1885, the same newspaper proposed executing a reservation

Indian for every Chiricahua who had left San Carlos and recommended abolishing the reservation altogether.

Articulations of these sentiments often addressed the perceived incompetence of the U.S. Army under Crook's command and might include threats of violence if steps to deal with the recurrent Apache "problem" were not implemented. For instance, in its 1 June 1885 issue, the *New York Times* published a letter to the "Press of New-York City" from the proprietors of the "Black Range Stage Line," purportedly representing citizens in Sierra, Socorro, Grant, and Doña Ana Counties in New Mexico. "Unless the Government at once takes steps to put down the present Indian outbreak and hunt to death every participant in it, our people will no longer consent to the restraint which has thus far prevented their marching upon the San Carlos Reservation and wiping it out of existence," the letter threatened.

The *New York Times* endorsed subjecting Apaches to the civil judicial process in its 2 June issue by asserting, "They should be punished for their horrible crimes, and their punishment should be either execution or imprisonment for life." Months before Geronimo's surrender to General Miles in September 1886, local sentiment was supporting the Apaches' trial by civil authorities should they surrender or be captured. The *Times* published a story datelined El Paso, Texas, in its 5 February 1886 issue, which noted that opinion in the Southwest favored "the summary execution of Geronimo." Petitions insisted that Apaches "be tried for murder under the local laws of the Territories." The *Times* had no doubt about the outcome of such trials: "If the people of New-Mexico and Arizona are permitted to have their way Geronimo and his fellows will be hanged." Local newspapers vehemently endorsed trying the Apaches in courts, already knowing how the courts would decide. Note these sentiments from the *Las Vegas Daily Optic* in September 1886:

> The people of New Mexico and Arizona are in favor of hanging Geronimo and his fellow murderers. That they deserve death no one will deny. [6 September]

> He [Geronimo] has been indicted for murder in several counties in New Mexico and Arizona, and the civil authorities should take charge of him, try him and hang him, and never let him go east to be lionized by the silly sentimentalists of that section. [11 September] [1]

Opinions about the ultimate disposition of the Apaches became a major topic of press coverage following their surrender to General Miles in September 1886. Those who favored trying them in civil courts believed that "sufficient evidence was obtainable to convict Geronimo and his braves of murder," as the district attorney of Arizona was reported to have claimed in the *Times* for 22 October 1886. Support for the trial and execution of the Apache prisoners had been "fervent and relentless" in Arizona Territory, the *Times* had noted a week earlier (15 October 1886). The soldiers who had been pursuing him, the same paper noted in its 23 September 1886 issue, "are anxious for the death of Geronimo, and would interpose no obstacle if the entire band were summarily disposed of. The people here too would be glad to see him shot or hanged or handed over to a few picked residents of New Mexico or Arizona."

As Geronimo and his band remained at large through the remainder of 1885 and into 1886, press coverage abated somewhat. It revived when news of Captain Emmet Crawford's death at the hands of a Mexican sharpshooter became known and even more so when Crook relinquished command after his meeting with Geronimo in March 1886 failed to bring an end to hostilities. Though Mexicans deservedly received most of the opprobrium resulting from Crawford's death, that event did bring the Apache problem to public attention again and encouraged rumors that Geronimo's capture or surrender was imminent. Consequently, the *Weekly New Mexican Review and Live Stock Journal* hastened on 4 February 1886 to urge Crook to allow civil justice to take its course, no matter what military arrangements he might have to make with Geronimo: "The civil authorities of New Mexico claim the right to try them [the Chiricahuas] for the cold blooded murders they have committed. We believe a few legal hangings would have a beneficial effect in the future. Every one of Geronimo's murderous gang that surrenders to the military ought to be arrested and tried in our territorial courts, and if found guilty of murder, arson or theft, ought to be given the extreme penalty of the law." On 18 February, the paper emphasized potential conflicts between local opinion and the federal government: "It is to be hoped that the old butcher will be turned over to the civil authorities, and then the interior department won't be called on to issue him socks, ammunition or any other commodity. A three-quarter inch rope will constitute his earthly needs." The *Tucson Weekly Star* was equally committed to subjecting Apaches to civil jurisdiction. Noting in its 25 March 1886 issue that they had committed their crimes off the reservation, the *Star* pointed out, "There is an adequate and speedy punishment prescribed by the statutes of both New Mexico and Arizona. These murderers are subject to these laws. They should be indicted for murder and tried before a competent jury, and if found guilty, they should suffer the death penalty. Such is the law for the white man, and it is the law applicable to these murdering Apaches." Some believed that sentiments such as these accounted for Geronimo's failure to comply with the agreement he had made with Crook at Cañon de los Embudos. As the *Atlanta Constitution* noted on 2 April 1886, that Geronimo did not then accompany Crook to Fort Bowie "is ascribed to the fact that having so much bloodshed to answer for, he could expect no clemency, and therefore prepared [preferred?] to live in the mountains to the prospect of hanging at the hands of the authorities." Miles is reported to have said, "So intense was the feeling against the Indians in that Territory [Arizona] that it was even suggested that the braces of the railroad bridges be destroyed in order to wreck the train conveying them to Florida" (Hatfield 1998, 112).

The issue of what to do with Geronimo climaxed with his surrender in September 1886 (fig. 1.1). Now much more than speculation or vague threats, concerns about how to handle these individuals who had become so demonized by the local press that a fair trial was probably impossible reached the highest levels of the federal bureaucracy. Although the terms of the surrender were not clear at the time, most commentators agree that Miles did violate his instructions to accept only unconditional surrender. Instead, he probably promised Geronimo that he and his band would be immediately shipped to Florida, where they would be reunited with their families, many of whom were already at Fort Marion or were en route. The Chiricahuas would remain in the east for two years, after which time they would be repatriated to their Arizona homelands. Miles's motivations for proposing this immediate solution primarily derived from his desire that the Apache conflict end satisfactorily on his watch, but he realized also that not getting Geronimo out of Arizona and New Mexico immediately could result in vigilantism by local citizens. The secrecy and haste with which the removal was effected and questions about whether Miles had sufficient authority to do it generated considerable press response, especially since Geronimo and his band remained about six weeks at Fort Sam Houston in San Antonio, Texas, out of the reach of Arizona and New Mexico territorial justice, while a decision about what to do with him was being made.

If they read the newspapers, those making that decision had plenty of outside input—most of which reiterated what had already been proposed.

FIG. 1.1. The *St. Louis Post-Dispatch* for 13 February 1886 published a line drawing of Geronimo, based probably on a photograph taken a couple of years earlier by Frank Randall. The caption notes that despite rumors of Geronimo's surrender (which finally did occur in September 1886), the "wily Apache is still at large."

The immediate response and apparent expectation of the local press was that Geronimo and his band would fall under the jurisdiction of territorial civil courts and, as a speaker at a meeting of the Society of Arizona Pioneers held, "would be treated with a wholesome dose of hemp" (*Tucson Weekly Star*, 9 September). The always forceful *Las Vegas Daily Optic* crowed upon receiving news of his surrender in its 9 September edition, "We should welcome Geronimo with eager hands to a hospitable scaffold. If ever any human being on earth needed hanging without delay it is this same Geronimo." The *Santa Fe New Mexican* for 13 September argued that once Geronimo and his band were turned over to civil authorities, "The effect of said action would be the certain and expeditious hanging of the offenders in question. . . . Their guilt is not to be doubted for a moment." A statement in the *Chicago Tribune* for 10 September—"There is no doubt that the public sentiment of the country demands the death of Geronimo"—demonstrated that support for Geronimo's speedy execution transcended local interest.

The *Tribune*, though, noted that the process of effecting that death might not be so simple as was being suggested, and the *Kansas City (MO) Evening Star* for 11 September 1886 spelled out the principal judicial options. A trial in civil court, which may have been rendered impossible anyway if the Chiricahuas were considered prisoners of war, would not be successful because of lack of witnesses to particular crimes. Meanwhile, a court-martial would not have sufficient scope to respond to the "atrocities of these prisoners, terrible as they were." The *Star*, consequently, argued for a trial by military commission and cited a precedent in how the losers of the Modoc War of 1872 had been dealt with. The *New York Times* cited the same precedent and noted that even if the Chiricahuas were considered prisoners of war, their "crimes against humanity committed in defiance of the laws of war" made them liable for prosecution. This editorial, published on 6 October 1886, noted, "It would hardly be denied that the atrocities of Geronimo have been worthy of hanging."

Some commentators suggested that the *Star*'s concerns that civil courts could not try Geronimo because of lack of witnesses who could testify to his actually having committed specific atrocities received some answer in the legal fortunes of the "Chicago anarchists," those tried in the Haymarket Affair. The *Santa Fe New Mexican* for 13 September noted that even if Geronimo could not be shown to have personally committed murder, the precedent of the "Chicago anarchists" would assure his execution. The paper's weekly edition for 16 September reiterated that "the rules of law applied in the trial of the Chicago anarchists would satisfactorily terminate the worst gang of fiendish and bloodthirsty marauders known to history."

The proposal for a special military commission to certify Geronimo's guilt and legitimate his execution received press support at several levels. Citing the *Army and Navy Register*, Denver's *Rocky Mountain News* for 11 September endorsed the idea: "If public opinion in and out of the army has weight in deciding the fate of Geronimo and his band they will be tried by military commission, speedily convicted and executed without undue delay." The judicial response to the Sioux Outbreak of 1862, which resulted in the largest mass execution in U.S. history, provided a model.

Finally, though, the federal government decided to treat the Chiricahuas as prisoners of war—"not ordinary marauders" as the *New York Times* for 23 October put it—and to confine them to Fort Marion and Fort Pickens in Florida. As President Cleveland was still weighing options regarding the disposition of Geronimo and his band, the *Times* had noted that exile to Florida would ultimately be more practical and satisfying than civil trial and inevitable execution of the leaders: "Hitherto in this region cries for the trial and execution of Apache prisoners have been fervent and relentless, but to be rid at one swoop of such a collection of pests of the frontier must for them dwarf in importance the question of whether the chief hostiles shall be exiled or executed" (15 October). So by mid-October 1886, Geronimo began gradually to fade from the public eye. Occasionally, though—especially with some new development in his situation such as the move to Fort Sill in 1894 or his appearance at exhibitions in 1898, 1901, and 1904—he would again become subject to press coverage, and while journalists might regard him with less distaste than they had in the 1880s, demonization remained a dominant trope in their characterizations of him. Though distance in time and space gradually mitigated some of the most extreme expressions of anti-Geronimo sentiment, strong feelings persisted as long as Geronimo was alive. For many he remained the "wickedest Indian that ever lived," as stressed by a story that appeared in the *Frederick (MD) News* for 7 December 1901, which dealt with Geronimo's daughter Anna's having been incarcerated at Lawton, Oklahoma, for the alleged murder of her lover.[2]

Memories of atrocities attributed to Geronimo and his band remained one of the staples in press accounts about him. For example, on 21 July 1912 the *New York Times* ran a story on the imminent release of the Chiricahuas from prisoner-of-war status. Images of Geronimo, "the Late Chief of the Captured Apaches," and his daughter, Lenna, dominate the page, while the copy reminds readers of the atrocities that he and his cohorts were accused of committing: "crimes against the whites which exceed in ferocity anything in the annals of Indian warfare in this country." Moreover, the Apache was "a murderer and a robber, a torturer. . . . [B]lood ran in rivers where his heel touched and death and destruction followed in his wake."

Occasionally, the public would be reminded of Geronimo's demonic character in response to changes (both real and rumored) in his postsurrender situation. Prior to the Chiricahuas' move from Mount Vernon Barracks to Fort Sill, the *Atlanta Constitution* responded vehemently to the rumor that the group, including Geronimo, was about to be released altogether. An editorial in the paper's 16 September 1894 issue held,

> Indians of the Geronimo stripe cannot be civilized. To get out of prison they will promise anything and behave like a class of Sunday school scholars, but when they find themselves again on their native plains there will be trouble. Geronimo will go back to his old business of raising Cain. His nature revolts against work of any kind. He has spent his whole life in a crusade of murder and pillage, and his imprisonment has not caused him to fall in love with his old enemies, the whites.

Even when Geronimo received some praise for adapting to his situation, reporters reminded their readers of his heinous past. While granting that

Geronimo was leading a "quiet and peaceful life" at Fort Sill in 1901, William R. Draper recalled that he was "once the meanest and most bloodthirsty Indian chief that ever fought the government" and retained "a deep-set bred-in-the-bone taste for murder" (1901, A1).

On 18 February 1907, two years before Geronimo's death, the *New York Times* quoted the enduring opinion of "the old soldiers who followed his last war trail": "If all of the redskins who have ever given the white man hell were bunched together, their combined deviltry wouldn't equal the record of Geronimo! If ever Satan himself was in an Indian you would have found him in that man!" The opprobrium heaped on Geronimo did not end with his death, for many obituary writers did not spare his memory. The issue of the *Times* for 18 February 1909, the day after Geronimo's death, had two pieces relating to that event. A news story, datelined Lawton, Oklahoma, reminded readers that Geronimo had "gained a reputation for cruelty and cunning never surpassed by that of any other American Indian chief." An editorial characterized him as "crafty, bloodthirsty, incredibly cruel and ferocious." Geronimo "was the worst type of aboriginal American savage." The obituary in the New Orleans, Louisiana, *Daily Picayune* for the same date held that "to the last Geronimo has been full of bitter hatred for the white man." The page 1 story in the Memphis, Tennessee, *Commercial Appeal* recapitulated some of the rumors about Geronimo's ancestry that had circulated since he first came to general public attention: "This half-breed Mexican, who was captured with the Apaches during one of their raids and was adopted by them, learned to fight when he was 16 years old and later proved the cruelest and most bloodthirsty chief of the tribe." On 19 February, the *Washington Post* editorialized, "No pity need be wasted on his end as a captive in the midst of his enemies, for in his life the old chief gave no pity. His soul drank blood." The *Post* concluded, "Geronimo was emphatically a bad Indian." The *Nebraska State Journal* (Lincoln) for 19 February quoted Miles regarding atrocities committed or suborned by Geronimo: "Hanging little girls by the under jaw to a great meat hook to suffer slow death, and men by their feet with their faces over a slow fire, is congenial pastime for" Apaches under his influence. The obituary in the *Army and Navy Journal* for 20 February 1909 characterized the decedent as "bloodthirsty, cruel and cunning." Various newspapers, including the *Boston Herald* and the *Philadelphia Inquirer*, stated that Geronimo had finally become a "good Indian" as a result of his death. The *Mansfield (OH) News* headlined its obituary notice on 17 February "A Good Indian at Last," and the *Nebraska State Journal* ran the notice of his death under the heading "Geronimo Is Good Indian." For the *Galveston (TX) Daily News* (22 February), Geronimo remained "the terrible warrior"; for the *Daily Kennebec (ME) Journal* (20 February), he was "the greatest rascal unhung"; for the *Reno (NV) Evening Gazette* (24 February), he was simply a "Bad Indian." Even the *Times* of London for 19 February 1909 reminded its readers that Geronimo had made the name Apache a "synonym for unmentionable atrocities" and cited Miles's description of him as "the lowest and most cruel of all the Indian savages on the continent." Obituaries from closer to Geronimo's bailiwick were particularly strong in their continuing demonization of the warrior. The Lawton, Oklahoma, *Daily News Republican*, published in the town nearest to Fort Sill, characterized him as the "most cruel and bloodthirsty brave that ever scalped a victim" (Turcheneske 1997, 105). The same city's *Constitution Democrat* averred that "even to the hour of his death he could not forget the great pleasures and excitement of the warpath." Several years after his death, the same paper recalled the response to his burial by women mourners who wailed in "the strange Chiricahua dialect": "Everybody hated you: white men hated you, Mexicans hated you, Apaches hated you; all of them hated you" (Turcheneske 1997, 106). Meanwhile, the *Arizona Daily Star* in Tucson reported that Geronimo "died ripe in years, full of Sunday school literature and with as much deviltry as the fiend incarnate to whom he has just gone." Describing Geronimo as a "craftsmaster in the art of human deviltry," the *Star* compared him to Torquemada, the notorious torturer of the Inquisition (Turcheneske 1997, 106).

A half century after Geronimo's final surrender, the erection of a monument commemorating that event revived negative opinion. According to *Winners of the West*, a monthly newspaper issued by the National Indian War Veterans Association, the attempt to erect a similar monument some fifteen years earlier in Yuma County, Arizona, had generated violent action. After the foundation for the monument had been laid, someone dynamited the site. In a story published in its August 1937 issue, the paper reported that a centenarian residing in the Arizona Pioneers' Home had declared vociferously while shaking his fist, "We'll blow up any statue of Geronimo you try to build. We ain't gonna see our state make a fool of itself, statuing any murdering thief like that redskin was!" The more recent monument, erected near Douglas, Arizona, in 1934, had no statue of the still-hated Geronimo, and its inscription focuses on events that led to his surrender, singling out Charles B. Gatewood for his role as negotiator. Nevertheless, the return of

Geronimo to the attention especially of old-timers in the Southwest occasioned reiterations of his reputation as "red devil." One person illustrated his animosity with an atrocity story like those that figured significantly in the narrative repertoires of the region's storytellers: "Might as well erect a monument to John Dillinger or Al Capone, only they wasn't half as bad as Geronimo. I saw that Indian's band burn a farmer's home. Geronimo took the woman. He bashed out the brains of her little uns, and had a fire dance around her husband, who had fought as long as he could." As the writer for the *Winners of the West* article points out, "During the early years the very name Apache was a symbol of terror and all things evil in the southwest and Geronimo was one of the greatest feared leaders." Two years later, the death of R. A. Brown, who had participated in the Apache wars, recalled the Dillinger/Capone comparison when the issue of *Winners of the West* for June 1939 characterized Geronimo as "one of America's earliest 'Public Enemies No. 1.'"

Assessing Native American opinion regarding Geronimo is not as easy as surveying perceptions of Anglos and other Euro-Americans. For one thing, early reports of what Indians were thinking come to us, of course, from writings by non-Indians, who may have been speculating as much as representing what their purported sources had actually thought and said. Moreover, as some postcolonial historians have noted, even opinions directly quoted from Native sources may reflect a "colonized mentality" and represent, as Elizabeth Cook-Lynn puts it, the "interiorizing of contrived histories imbued with defeat and under conditions of coercive assimilation" (2011, 46). In other words, Native Americans may have been saying what they thought their Euro-American audience wanted to hear. The negative opinions about Geronimo that figured in the reported outlooks of many of his contemporaries also contributed to the larger demonization of Geronimo and may have been presented to lend support to Euro-American attitudes toward him while they contributed to isolating him even from other Indians. A retired Philadelphia policeman who had served in the army in Arizona Territory in 1885, for example, claimed, "His tribe, the Apaches, were the cruelest and most heartless of all the Indians. And Geronimo was feared and shunned even by his own people" (Greene 2007, 4).

Nevertheless, longstanding enmity seems to have existed between many Chihenne (or Ojo Caliente or Warm Springs Apaches) and Geronimo. The group's leader, Loco, believed Geronimo was "untrustworthy, dangerous, and quite unhinged" (Shapard 2010, 144). That hostility lasted through the incarceration at Fort Sill, with Geronimo supposedly feeling increasingly isolated because of the legacy of that distrust (Shapard 2010, 185). Some, including Sam Haozous, blamed Geronimo for all the troubles experienced by the Chiricahuas after the 1870s, when he became a major figure in their community (Sweeney 2010, 78). Sherman Curley, an Aravaipa Apache who had served as scout for the U.S. Army, summarily stated in an interview a half century after Geronimo had surrendered, "He was the one who was responsible for all this trouble" (Goodwin ca. 1930s, 7). Some Chiricahuas who had been exiled to Fort Marion disliked being called "Geronimo Apaches," and many were none too enthusiastic when he joined them after they were moved to Mount Vernon Barracks. An interview with Blossom Haozous, who had been born after the Chiricahuas had moved on to Fort Sill, suggested a reluctance among his contemporaries to embrace Geronimo's memory: "What do we want to bring him among us for? He's a warrior man. . . . We never did kill nobody, never caused trouble to anyone. He's going to give us a name" (Turcheneske 1997, 3). Sam Kenoi, who provided anthropologist Morris Edward Opler with a Chiricahua perspective on the Apache wars, was dismissive of Geronimo, though he did not demonize him. He was, according to Kenoi, "nothing but . . . an old troublemaker." Moreover, he was a coward who allowed others to do all the fighting while he "stayed behind like a woman" (Opler 1938, 367). In addition, Kenoi blamed Geronimo for the troubles that beset the Chiricahuas after the 1886 surrender: "I know that he and a few others like him were the cause of the death of my mother and many of my relatives who have been pushed around the country as prisoners of war. . . . I know that we would not be in our present trouble if it was not for men like him" (Opler 1938, 367–68). The reported consensus among many of Kenoi's contemporaries was that Geronimo's role, especially in the events leading up to the May 1885 breakout, contributed to divisions among the Chiricahuas that endured for decades thereafter (Sweeney 2010, 396). Some Chiricahuas at the time that Geronimo was figuring so prominently in their affairs developed such enmity against him that they considered assassinating him: Fun (who later joined Geronimo in captivity in Florida and Alabama) for Geronimo's alleged cowardice (a charge that some modern historians question) at the Battle of Alisos Creek (Sweeney 2010, 226) and Chihuahua for Geronimo's alleged plot to kill Lieutenant Britton Davis in May 1885 (Sweeney 2010, 410). Non-Chiricahua Apaches such as Bylas hated Geronimo for specific actions he had taken— in this case, the massacre that had occurred at the Stevens sheep camp in 1882 (Sweeney 2010, 440). Many years later at Fort Sill, Geronimo continued to generate negative reactions from his fellow Chiricahuas, some of whom believed that he was using his shamanic power to prolong his own life at the expense of others in the community, even his own family members.

Cosel with Geronimo on His Last Raid: The Story of an Indian Boy, published in 1938 by Therese O. Deming, purports to be the true account of a boy of seven who left the Fort Apache Reservation with Geronimo in May 1885. Cosel supposedly lived with the author's family for a year while a student at Carlisle in the 1880s and perhaps later. Deming in her preface admits, "Cosel, no doubt, made several mistakes in his version of the story, but it is set down exactly as he told it" (1938, vii). The principal focus of the narrative is Cosel's attitude toward what he had believed would be a great adventure—returning to the Sierra Madre homeland—but which, in fact, became a miserable experience especially for the women and children, who subsisted on meager rations, endured long periods without rest, and faced relentless pursuit by U.S. troops.

The narrative is definitely anti-Geronimo, suggesting that he was a foolish strategist and a coward. Cosel attributes the 1885 breakout to Geronimo's heeding rumors spread by "trouble-makers" who speculated that the entire community would be moved to "a barren, desolate country, many miles away" while their leaders were made prisoners of war (Deming 1938, 10–11). "Natchez" is perceived as a "weak fellow and easily led by the cunning Geronimo, who was a wonderful speaker" (12). The only major dissenter from Geronimo's plans for the breakout was Chatto, whom the book consistently calls "the good Chatto." The narrator suggests that Geronimo's relentless driving of the escapees to the Sierra Madre was cruelly unnecessary: "Had Geronimo known in what a terrible condition the soldiers were, he would have rested his band more often" (37). Cosel also wonders if Geronimo had underestimated the number of troops that would join the pursuit (72).

Geronimo's leadership and character come in for considerable criticism. At one point when the pursuit by the troops and scouts led by "the good Chatto" seemed particularly relentless, "the warriors were dissatisfied. They had lost their faith in Geronimo. They knew he was not brave. When the last attack had been made on their band, Geronimo had ridden ahead with the women and children. He did not stay with the warriors to help and encourage them. The women began to speak of Geronimo as a coward" (Deming 1938, 76). As the pursuit continues, Cosel overhears his father tell his mother, "If we had only listened to Chatto instead of Geronimo.

Geronimo is not a brave warrior. When we attack or are attacked, he is always far away. We should have remembered that he is not a chief among us. He is a medicine-man. He does not help us, but he always tries to save himself" (79). Doubts about Geronimo's leadership permeated the Chiricahuas' camp. When it seemed as if Mexicans and U.S. forces had united to surround them, concerns about Geronimo surfaced:

> It would not be half so discouraging if the red men could trust Geronimo. They feared that he would not be faithful to them if they should be captured. During the last attack he had again gone ahead to be with the women and children while the fight was going on. He had not even stayed with the warriors to encourage them when they were fighting to save the body of their fallen comrade. (Deming 1938, 91)

Cosel is unclear about what caused Geronimo to surrender. He suggests that Geronimo was on the verge of giving up to Captain Emmet Crawford, who was accompanied by his aides Lawton, Wood, and Gatewood, when Crawford was killed. Afterward the Apaches did not trust Crawford's successor, Maus, enough to surrender to him, so they waited for General Crook. Cosel apparently was among those who accompanied Crook back to Fort Bowie following the negotiations at Cañon de los Embudos. He then claims that he was sent directly to Carlisle, where he was visited by his mother sometime after the surrender to Miles. He went from there back to the Southwestern homeland, according to the book's final chapter.

Several points suggest that this work may be more fiction than memoir. Even though Geronimo's purported cowardice has been suggested by other sources, even his most adamant detractors tend to fault his poor judgment and his elevation of selfish concerns over those of his community rather than lapses in courage. Moreover, some features of Cosel's story seem particularly improbable, for example, his immediate removal to Carlisle rather than to Fort Marion in Florida and his being allowed to return to the Southwest after his schooling instead of being sent to wherever the other Chiricahuas were living in Florida, Alabama, or Indian Territory. Moreover, Deming is not forthcoming about the circumstances of her relationship to Cosel. Born in 1878, she would have been a child when Cosel was attending school. Her book was published a half century afterward, and she does not specify if she and Cosel had interacted during that time period. Finally, no biographer of Geronimo or historian of the conquest of Apacheria cites the work or mentions anyone named Cosel, even though commentators wishing to undercut the positive image of Geronimo that began to emerge as time and space provided distance from the events in the Southwest of the 1880s could find support in Cosel's debunking of the strategic abilities and battlefield prowess of the famous Chiricahua. Discretion may suggest that the book be considered a novel rather than a source of historical Native American opinions of Geronimo, but it does reinforce the belief that many Apaches held him in low regard. As Thomas Cruse, who served in Arizona Territory throughout the first half of the 1880s, claimed, "Even the Apaches thoroughly distrusted and disliked Geronimo—a fact apparently unknown to thousands who have heard or read of him." Though Cruse admitted that Geronimo was "brave and shrewd" enough to "stir up a handful of wild followers," the Chiricahuas and other Apaches "knew him for the liar and assassin that he was" (1941, 207–8).

Because of her mastery of the Euro-American world and the temper of the times when she collaborated with Ruth Boyer in the late twentieth century, we may have a fairly uncontaminated perspective in the testimony of Narcissus Duffy Gayton. The great-great-granddaughter of Victorio, Gayton recalled family lore about Geronimo, almost all of which depicted him negatively. Her well-known ancestor, she had heard, "had never approved of Geronimo. His way of warfare cost the lives of too many of the younger, less experienced warriors. He fought for his own glory, not for the welfare of the Indeh" (Boyer and Gayton 1992, 67). Moreover, Geronimo "was interested only in his own welfare. He put others in useless danger" (184). Repeatedly, Gayton stressed Geronimo's reputation as a liar (73, 101). She reported the words of her mother, who was five years old when Geronimo died: "He's bad. He lies all the time. . . . He betrayed all of us. He deceived his own people—even after accepting our hospitality. . . . The man has a forked tongue, worse even than whites." Gayton suggested that this opinion was widespread at Fort Sill, becoming "Geronimo's general reputation until his death" (183). Furthermore, many Chiricahuas whose families had moved to the Mescalero reservation after the termination of their prisoner-of-war status continued to hold Geronimo in contempt as late as the 1960s (183).

The demonization of Geronimo continued throughout the twentieth century, when he often figured as the consummate villain in western fiction and film. In John Ford's *Stagecoach* (1939), for example, he epitomizes savagery, and in *Broken Arrow* (1950), which treats Cochise sympathetically,

Geronimo is seen as the principal obstructionist to the peace process. Near the end of the film, after Anglos have killed his daughter, the grieving Cochise states, "Geronimo broke the peace no less than these whites," thus implicating him in the murder. Ralph Moody's book for young readers, *Geronimo: Wolf of the Warparth* ([1958] 2006), continues the tradition of demonizing Geronimo. At one point, the narrator concludes that "thirst for blood and vengeance drove them [Geronimo and his band] on like a pack of rabid wolves" ([1958] 2006, 97). A series of comic books from the 1950s represents Geronimo as the consummate savage. One title cites *Geronimo and His Apache Murderers.* The cover depicts a snarling visage crowned by the distinctive Chiricahua scarf overlooking a scene of carnage. The continuing demonization of Geronimo has not been exclusively a practice of the establishment press. In a story in *Indian Country Today* (4 March 2009) Reede Upshaw, characterized as an "elder," vocally opposed erecting a monument to commemorate the centennial of Geronimo's death on the San Carlos Reservation. Reporter Mary Kim Titla indicated that Upshaw had grown up hearing "stories about how Geronimo terrorized and murdered his own people": "He compared honoring Geronimo to honoring Adolf Hitler."

Despite the overwhelming negativity that dominated Geronimo's image in the press during his lifetime, and which continues to a lesser degree into the present, other perspectives existed concurrently and began to supplant the demonization. A few of the obituaries, for instance, tried to humanize him. A writer for the *New York Times* on 19 February 1909 believed that it was appropriate to reassess Geronimo's life now that he had died and asserted that he was "not without certain attributes of greatness." The writer believed that Geronimo had responded to the invasion of his homeland with the resources and methods available to him, acting as any leader of an invaded population would:

> With only a handful of men under his command, he defied for years all the forces which a great Government found it convenient to send against him. Again and again he rose superior to crushing defeat, and had success been for him among the physical possibilities, he would have ranked in history with its greatest conquerors and patriots. Knowing of his opponents and their strength only what he saw, his expectations of ultimate victory were due to lack of information, not to sanguinary madness, and he yielded at last when somebody had the belated wisdom to show him the size of the task he had undertaken.

These notes echoed the positive assessments that emerged during and shortly after Geronimo's life: that he was only responding as was humanly appropriate to a situation that any community would find onerous. Norbert Barnard, who wrote a letter to the *Times*'s editor, which appeared on 21 February 1909, recalled how Geronimo must have felt when his family was killed at Kaskiyeh: "Returning home one day the great Apache saw with tortured eyes what the anguished ears of Macduff only heard—his castle surprised, his wife and babes savagely slaughtered. The saddest procession that warrior ever saw entered the gateways of his soul, filched the fashionings of the face, and he never once was seen to smile again." A writer for the *Olean (NY) Times* lamented that only with Geronimo's death were explanations for his motivation taken seriously. "Now," the paper's 24 February 1909 issue claimed, "he is recognized as the champion and defender of a wronged race, driven from its own fields and hunting grounds by a relentless invader who sought its extermination."

An article from the *Kansas City Star*, reprinted in the *Salt Lake (UT) Herald* for 11 April 1899, suggests a more human Geronimo than had previously appeared in most press coverage of this figure. The article implies that Geronimo's human qualities, though, emerged only under the mentoring of those who were superintending him as prisoner of war. The piece begins by defining his previous identity as "the most celebrated of the surviving Indian chiefs whose dark and bloody deeds in bygone days are predominant features of the early history of the western plains." It describes his appearance when he surrendered: he was "robed in a huge blanket made of human scalps," a garment that figured into rumors about Geronimo during the late nineteenth and early twentieth centuries (see chapter 3). However, now he is a "thrifty farmer, living peacefully on his farm on Medicine creek. . . . He has buried the past completely." In fact, Geronimo is among the most industrious of the Indians "who are given the same opportunities to emulate the white man." He has also promoted education among his fellow Apaches. The journalist who prepared the article has no fears that Geronimo, now humanized by the effects of Euro-American civilization, will revert to his former identity: "Surely it is difficult to realize how such a man as Geronimo, who is apparently forgetful of his past in his attempts to prove that there are good Indians who are not dead Indians, can be metamorphosed into a murderer and a fiend." Geronimo himself, who had begun his campaign to return to the Southwest by at least giving the appearance of eschewing his warlike identity and adopting the white man's values and norms, would have been pleased with this article. Even though its primary purpose was to reinforce the claim that the United States had successfully handled its "Indian problem"—now that the Spanish-American War had brought other "savages" under its hegemony—the piece insists that Geronimo was indeed a human.

The demonic Geronimo had ceased to dominate exclusively less than a decade after the man's death. Late in the 1910s, a firm in Enid, Oklahoma, manufactured several automobiles using the brand name "Geronimo." The Atchison, Topeka and Santa Fe Railway was sufficiently convinced that Geronimo no longer necessarily evoked diabolical images of atrocity to name one of its trains after him. The Southern Pacific Railroad advertised its Sunset Limited route from New Orleans to San Francisco by heralding its passage through territory won from "the merciless Apache." A version of the advertisement that appeared in the *Atlanta Constitution* for 8 March 1921 pictured a generic Indian peering over the edge of a cliff at some mounted horsemen below and touted the possibilities of a side trip to Roosevelt Dam, which had inundated "the windings of Geronimo's last war trail." Wanamaker's department store in New York City pushed a series of masks "to change your face and your personality, too" when attending "masked" parties. For only a dime one could purchase three masks: either generic figures such as tramps and clowns or recognizable personalities from American history, perhaps Washington, Lincoln, and Franklin or Sitting Bull, Rain-in-the-Face, and Geronimo. That partygoers might show up masked as clowns and as Geronimos suggests that the latter had lost much of his negative energy.

Some of the books about Geronimo targeting children and young adults and published in the 1950s attempted to humanize him by devoting attention to his childhood and by downplaying or ignoring the violence that had been routinely imputed to him (e.g., Wyatt 1952; Kjelgaard 1958; Symes 1975). The watershed in the movement from demonization to humanization, though, was Angie Debo's biography (1976). One evaluator of the book suggests that she presented him as "a man with a shrewd financial mind, an intellectual curiosity, deep religious faith, and holding a real affection for family and friends." While she may indeed have characterized him as a "man of integrity" (McIntosh 1988, 176), Debo did not ignore Geronimo's shortcomings, though she might have attributed some of them—for example, his unyielding hatred of Mexicans—to situational circumstances rather than to his own character weaknesses.

Although rare, some writers, even contemporaries of Geronimo, had anticipated Debo in attempting to put a human face on Geronimo and other Apaches by exploring the motivations for their dissatisfaction with reservation conditions and difficulty in reconciling themselves to Euro-American mores. A few expressed empathy and even a modicum of sympathy for Geronimo's situation. For example, in a letter published in the 11 March 1886 issue of the *Weekly New Mexican Review and Live Stock Journal*, John Ayers, who had been an agent to the Chihennes while they were confined to the Tularosa Reservation in the early 1870s, wrote, "I doubt if there is any tribe of Indians in our country who have been wronged more than they." He cited in particular the broken treaty that had effected the closing of the Chiricahua Reservation and the community's removal to San Carlos. Ayers recalled what his charges had told him at that time: "We can all die but once, and we will all die before we live on the San Carlos reservation. The great father is a liar; he has deceived us, and we shall raid over the country and kill the people who live on our lands." Ayers concluded, "Now, say what you please, for all this bloodshed the government is to blame. As it chooses to recognize them as a treaty-making power; when we broke our agreement in every way they had the right to go on the war path and [p]ush-back and fight the best they could with their means." Most such general sympathy for the conditions that precipitated unrest, though, found its way into newspapers outside Arizona and New Mexico. The *Atlanta Constitution*, while characterizing Geronimo as "bloodthirsty and crafty and cruel," could editorialize in its 2 March 1886 issue that he and his companions "all behaved well as long as they were honestly treated." But "when an Indian agent robbed them to the point of starvation they revolted, and every mile of their march was marked with murders and the destruction of property. The revolt of 1883 [sic] grew out of the transactions of a dishonest agent, and the recent revolt was due more to the depredations of cowboys than to anything else. The Indian agent did not properly protect them." The *New York Times* used the aftermath of Geronimo's surrender, a time when a decision about what to do with him had not yet been clearly articulated to the public, as an opportunity for commenting on conditions that precipitated the breakout.

On 25 October 1886, the *Times* noted that "the Indian wards of the Nation are continually subjected to grievous wrongs at the hands of those who are supposed to protect them, and that it is not surprising that they occasionally rebel and go upon the warpath." The New York paper used the surrender of Geronimo and ensuing end of hostilities in the Southwest to condemn U.S. Indian policy. In its 25 October 1886 edition under the headline "Our Defenseless Indians," the paper held that data from a report by the commissioner of Indian affairs "exhibit a condition of affairs on our Indian reservations which, while it cannot serve as an excuse for the terrible crimes of the Geronimos among the savages, certainly offers an explanation of the ease with which bloody-minded chieftains secure followers in their raids upon unprotected white settlers." The *Times* stood with the citizens of the Southwest in its condemnation of Geronimo's methods, at least as reported in the rumor-based dispatches coming out of the region, but recognized that demonic evil did not motivate his actions.

Some other contemporaries attempted to understand Geronimo's motivations in more human terms. While not necessarily endorsing his veracity, the *Atlanta Constitution* for 15 September 1886 reported that Geronimo claimed that "he was forced to go on the war path." He had been told by "a courier" that "he and his people would be murdered, and on hearing this he concluded to escape from the reservation and fight." On 3 October 1886, the *New York Times* recounted the same rationale: the Chiricahuas "claim that they were cruelly treated at the hands of an enemy and threatened with assassination if they remained on the reservation and they were compelled to flee. Once having left it they claim there was nothing for them to do but to raid upon the settlers."

Even those who made little attempt to empathize with the Apaches' rationale occasionally attributed positive qualities to them. Even the *Las Vegas Daily Optic* grudgingly praised Geronimo's band as "the most alert and cunning of all Indians" in its 13 June 1885 issue. Furthermore, the New Mexico paper noted the survival skills evinced by Apaches:

The Chiricahuas need no supply trains, and they carry no provisions nor haversacks. They can live on lizards, grasshoppers and roots, and go without water like the Arabs. They are so quick sighted and as keen of hearing as foxes. They have signal fires that read like a whole book to their tribe. They can smell a soldier five miles away. They can sleep anywhere without blankets, and can run like ostriches. From their sudden appearance one day a hundred miles from where they were the previous day, we are inclined to think they can fly. We might as well send out soldiers with heavy artillery to shoot fleas, as to send them after the Chiricahuas.

This story, which appeared on 23 June 1885, derives from the report of a "Tucson editor" and, of course, associates some of the Apaches' positive qualities with an essentially animalistic nature.

To explain Geronimo's violent response to the wrongs that he perceived to have been done to him and other Apaches does not excuse him, but it does put a human face on his deeds, those he actually performed and those attributed to him. As Louis Kraft has noted in his edition of Charles Gatewood's memoir of his role in effecting Geronimo's final surrender, "Way too often Geronimo has been crucified as the Devil Incarnate, a bloody butcher, and a blot on mankind. This is a cliché and a half-truth at best. Even though this image is still all most people know of him, it is not a fair assessment. . . . For him everything was at stake in his battle with the White Eyes: his religion, his language, his culture, his lifeway, his freedom. He fought back in the only way he knew how—with violence" (Gatewood 2005, 121–22).

Chiricahuas interviewed by Eve Ball in their community on the Mescalero Apache Reservation in New Mexico in the mid-twentieth century tended to view Geronimo in more human terms than those attributed to their forebears earlier in the century. Daklugie, the son of Geronimo's sister and consequently, according to the practices of the matrilineal Chiricahua, a close associate of the older man, was one of Ball's principal consultants. He suggested that many of the negative feelings about Geronimo and other leaders of the 1885 breakout among Apaches who blamed him for their post-surrender plight stemmed from envy: "The truth of the matter is that they envied them because he had the fighting spirit and courage to hold out longer than the rest" (Ball 1980, 39). As Daklugie put it, "There was only one leader remaining who did not give up and that was Geronimo. And now the descendants of the faint-hearted blame him for the twenty-seven years of captivity just because their fathers did not have the fighting spirit and the courage to risk death as he did" (77). During his discussions with Ball, Daklugie attributed a number of positive attributes to Geronimo: "He was by nature . . . a brave person" (14); "He was the embodiment of the Apache spirit, of the fighting Chiricahua" (134); "He had the courage, the fighting ability, the intelligence to outwit the officers from West Point, to fight against insurmountable odds, and to provide for his little band" (136); "Geronimo was shrewd and cautious" (173); Geronimo "walks through eternity garbed as a chief in his ceremonial robes and his medicine hat. He rides a fine horse. He has his best weapons" (182).

And Daklugie was not the only Chiricahua to offer positive testimony. While admitting the ruthlessness that forced Geronimo to commit acts of violence, Charlie Smith noted, "He was a great leader of men, and it ill becomes the cowardly to find fault with the man who was trying to keep them free" (Ball 1980, 104). Kanseah, who became a protégé of Geronimo at the age of eleven, stressed that he was proud "to be taught by a great warrior." He noted obstacles that Geronimo faced, which his adversaries in the military did not have to contend with: "Geronimo had to obtain food for his men, and for their women and children. When they were hungry, Geronimo got food. When they were cold Geronimo provided blankets and clothing. When they were afoot, he stole horses. When they had no bullets, he got ammunition. He was a good man. I think that you have desperados among your White Eyes that are much worse men and more cruel than Geronimo" (105). Velma Kanseah echoed her husband's assessment of Geronimo's character: "Geronimo was a good man and a very brave one. So was Yahnosa. Even some Apaches blame them for the twenty-seven years that our people were prisoners of war. But they just had the courage to keep on fighting after the others gave up" (303). The Ball interviews provide significant insight into Geronimo and his era that is not available elsewhere. She seems to have established sufficient rapport with her subjects that they were more likely to reveal their true opinions than those Apaches who had been interviewed earlier and whose opinions had been used to reinforce the negative, demonic image that the mainstream press was shaping during the late nineteenth century. Certainly, some Apaches regarded Geronimo unfavorably; many still do. But Ball's data, which remain largely unpublished, offer a perspective that seems less affected by the exigencies of colonialism that inform much Native American testimony offered to Euro-Americans.

As a corrective, revisionism may often result in as extreme a perspective as that which it challenges. Alternate perspectives on Geronimo, while often accepting positive attributes assigned to him by voices of humanization, have sometimes ignored or rejected disturbing features of his image—for example, excusing atrocities as appropriate retaliation for similar acts committed against Apaches by Mexicans and Anglos or as products of the specific situations and contexts of border warfare. The result has occasionally been a perception of Geronimo as hero, sometimes even saint. Few, if any, such depictions of this warrior-shaman can be found in printed sources of his time, though perhaps some of Geronimo's fellow Apaches would have endorsed them. Tendencies to elevate Geronimo to hero status, to canonize, even to apotheosize him, had to wait until a couple of generations after his death.

In *Smoke Signals*, screenwriter Sherman Alexie included a scene in which several youth on the Coeur d'Alene Reservation in Idaho are playing an informal basketball game. Junior Polatkin and Victor Joseph sound each other on some of the greatest Indian basketball players of all time. Victor claims that Geronimo was the greatest. When Junior demurs, "He couldn't play basketball, man. He was Apache, man. Those suckers are about three feet tall," Victor defends his choice: "It's Geronimo, man. He was lean, mean, and bloody. Would have dunked on your flat Indian ass and then cut it off" (1998, 17). They go on to discuss the merits of Sitting Bull, Chief Joseph, and even Pocahontas on the basketball court. Although Alexie's scene is comic, his inclusion of Geronimo in the forefront of those whom many have come to consider Native American heroes suggests that a transformation has occurred in Geronimo's reputation (fig. 1.2).

FIG. 1.2. Geronimo's image as a hero has inspired people to leave valuables at his grave. The pyramid of stones in the Apache Cemetery northeast of Fort Sill, Oklahoma, offers testimony to his evocative power. *Photograph by William M. Clements.*

For many commentators, Geronimo has come to represent that fundamental American value: freedom. His steadfast opposition to the U.S. military, no matter whether motivated by selfishness or by genuine concern for the sovereignty of his community, now stands for personal and community liberty. Yet his position in the history of the Arizona reservations, the communities from which he led his final breakouts, is somewhat problematic. Drawing upon his research at San Carlos in the 1990s, David W. Samuels notes the difficulties for that community in completely accepting Geronimo as their representative:

> Some people are quick to point out that although Geronimo was incarcerated at Old San Carlos for a time [after being arrested by John C. Clum in 1877], he was a Chiricahua Apache with little to tie him to the Western Apache people of the San Carlos Reservation. In fact, Geronimo's surrender [in 1886] was achieved with the aid of scouts hired from the San Carlos agency. He was, it is true, the last Native American leader to surrender to the U.S. government, but he was not from San Carlos. Nevertheless, his ability to hold out the longest against the forces of the U.S. Army makes him an important figure in San Carlos, despite the supposed tenuous connections. (2004, 51)

Moreover, the "Spirit of Geronimo," Samuels notes, at San Carlos and elsewhere is "to be *free*" (137).

That "spirit" assumed significance beyond its Apache context during the 1940s, when Geronimo's name became an exclamation uttered by U.S. paratroopers as they leaped from transport planes. This usage has been connected to the 1939 film *Geronimo!* (directed by Paul Sloane and released in New York City in 1940), which featured Victor Daniels, using the performance name Chief Thundercloud, in the title role. Supposedly, a group of paratroopers in training at Fort Benning, Georgia, in August 1940 attended a screening of the film. After the film, which provided some escape from the daily stress of jumping from an airplane while in flight, an attendee challenged Private Aubrey Eberhardt to prove that he was not afraid when he made his jump the following day. Eberhardt claimed that he would demonstrate his confidence and courage by yelling something that could be heard by everyone on the plane and the ground below immediately after he jumped. He chose the word *Geronimo*.[3] By the end of the summer of 1940, his practice had caught on sufficiently that other paratroopers were using the term as their signifier of courage. It became so much a part of paratrooper lore that several airborne regiments used an image of Geronimo on their pocket patches. Eventually, Lieutenant Colonel Byron Price wrote the song "Down from Heaven" to articulate the importance of the war cry for paratroopers. One stanza goes, "It's a gory road to glory / But we're ready; here we go. / Shout, 'GERONIMO,' 'GERONIMO'" (Howard 2004). A contributor to the 28 July 1944 issue of *Winners of the West* was especially impressed with the connection between paratroopers and Geronimo:

> As each brave parachutist jumps from his transport plane, he usually calls out the name of this famous old Indian of legend and history. Several of these hardy young men who spearheaded the recent invasion of Europe, are now even getting the Geronimo haircuts which consist of clipping the hair off each side of the head and leaving an ominous-looking hirsute streak down the center. Then a dab of "war paint" on each cheek, and we have modern soldiers more dangerous to the enemy than Geronimo ever was to our forefathers.

Despite some observers connecting "Mohawk" coiffures with an Apache, the association of crying "Geronimo!" with leaping from a height had become ingrained in popular American culture by the late 1940s, when children at play voiced it during their games and pastimes. In fact, the film *The Adventures of Tintin* (2011) has someone swinging from a rope and anachronistically shouting "Geronimo!" even though the action is set some fifteen or so years before parachutists began to invoke the famous Chiricahua. The *Chicago Daily Defender* for 25 March 1964 certainly violated the spirit of the parachutists' use of Geronimo's name and showed an unseemly lack of sympathy when it captioned a photograph of a suicidal young woman leaping from the fourth floor of a local high school "Geronimo-o-o-o-o." The paper's usage shows how firmly entrenched this example of Geronimo lore remains.

One specific form that the positive image of freedom-loving Geronimo has taken is part of a worldwide pattern in expressive culture. Some accounts of Geronimo's career or incidents from his life have been cast in the mold of the legendary or mythic social bandit. As far as can be determined from the historical record, Geronimo's life did not actually correspond to this widely known figure whose formulaic characterization has emerged from the work of Eric J. Hobsbawm (1959, 13–29; 1969) and others. But features of the cycle of stories and imagery about Geronimo that began to become part of popular consciousness even before his death do match what Richard E. Meyer (1980) describes as the narrative trajectory of the "rebel hero" or what Graham Seal (2009) calls the "Robin Hood principle."[4] As early as 10 September 1886, less than a week after he surrendered to Miles, the *Chicago Tribune* headlined the story "Heroic Daring of the Apache Chief" and quoted Bureau of Indian Affairs commissioner J. D. C. Atkins as saying, "There has not been such a warrior as Geronimo since the days of Rob Roy. . . . He has subsisted on the roots of the desert and the serpents of the mountains for nearly two years. He has worn out an army and has kept a vast region of country in terror. Part of the time he has been wounded and sick. His barbarous heroism and endurance are unsurpassed by anything in history."

Modifying the formulaic career pattern codified by Hobsbawm and Meyer, Seal has identified twelve elements that define the legendary career of the social bandit (2009, 74–75). About half of Seal's elements appear in accounts of Geronimo's life. The social bandit, Seal's formula suggests, "is forced to defy the law" because of "oppressive and unjust forces or interests." Geronimo's loss of family at the massacre near Kaskiyeh is the precipitating event in his career. He cites that loss in his autobiography as the turning point in his life (Barrett 1996, 75–78), and subsequent biographers have echoed his interpretation. Moreover, repeated injustices, including the closing of the Chiricahua Reservation and corrupt management, especially at the San Carlos Reservation, drive him to the warpath, according to popular lore. Seal indicates that the social bandit "has sympathy and support" from a community: Geronimo does not act alone but as part of a band of challengers to Mexican and U.S. authority. Moreover, Seal notes, the social bandit as hero "outwits, eludes, and escapes the authorities" with attention-getting adroitness, like Geronimo's uncanny ability to maintain his freedom despite the thousands of troops deployed against him. Often, Seal reports, social bandits employ magic to assist them, and accounts of Geronimo's invulnerability to weapons and his clairvoyance abound in expressive culture. Most Geronimo stories suggest that he is both brave and strong, another element in the formula for the stereotyped career of the social bandit hero. Geronimo can be captured only by betrayal and treachery of Chiricahua and other Apache scouts, which further corresponds to the lives of many legendary social bandits. Moreover, though not on Seal's list, Geronimo's acts of unexpected kindness manifested in his reputed love of children and, according to a biography aimed at young readers (Wyatt 1952, 182), his gifts of food to a settler's family fit the idealization of the social bandit as heroic figure.

This dimension of the positive image of Geronimo has contributed to his emergence as an exemplar of revolutionary defiance among critics of injustices in U.S. society. During a brief period in 1969 when members of the American Indian Movement were occupying Alcatraz, Geronimo's visage was part of an assemblage that adorned the eagle on the official signage, which had a placard proclaiming "This land is my land" hung from its neck. Attached to the placard was an 1884 photograph of Geronimo. Geronimo's "stern expression, his posture of resistance, [and] his refusal to be appropriated or mocked" made him an icon of Native American social consciousness (Rader 2011, 41). Elmer Pratt, who became the minister of defense of the Black Panther Party, also used the name Geronimo. Convicted in 1972 of murder charges that were vacated in 1997 because of prosecutorial impropriety, Pratt, a social activist, came to be known as Geronimo ji-Jaga.

Alexander Adams's biography (1971) relates Geronimo to what the author perceived as the struggle against American imperialism in Vietnam. Noting that opinion about Apaches in the 1880s was as contemptuous and dismissive of an alien culture as attitudes in the early 1970s, Adams wrote, "To most Americans . . . Apaches remained 'gooks'—alive but scarcely human, objects it would have been better to annihilate" (1971, 24). Geronimo's last stand against imperialism had heroic potential: he "fought, with skill and courage, as few men ever have against overwhelming odds. And he fought, not for greed or profit or empire, but only for the two causes Americans respect the most—his homeland and his freedom" (315). Similarly, former Vietnam correspondent Don Dedera noted parallels between the Apache wars—"the most remarkable guerrilla action in recorded history" (1971, 31)—and the Vietnam resistance. Dedera queried, "Could it be that Geronimo today, in a country he knows and loves, with near sanctuaries in neighboring weak states, facing opponents of shaky alliances, taking advantage of his foe's corruption, softness, extended supply line, and unfamiliarity with the native population—might not Geronimo frustrate the world's greatest military power for three, five, even ten—and who can say how many years?" (37).

Geronimo imagery was also part of the inventory of symbols used by the Provisional Irish Republican Army during the last quarter of the twentieth century. Bobby Sands, who died on a hunger strike while in Long Kesh (or Maze Prison) in 1981, sometimes signed himself as "Geronimo," and a mural featuring Geronimo appeared inside the prison (Porter 2008, 69). In 2002 the *New Internationalist* listed Geronimo among "Great American Rebels" (2002, 24–25). Others in the magazine's sample of "true originals in a country that has much to thank them for" included Daniel Shays, the farmer who led a group of dissidents protesting the Massachusetts Supreme Court in the 1780s; "anarchist" Emma Goldman; labor organizer Cesar Chavez; and actress Mae West.

That Geronimo has come to conform somewhat to the pattern associated with Robin Hood is one way in which his image has shifted toward the very positive. Another image from myth and legend that has informed depictions of Geronimo is the Chiricahua culture hero who defeated the forces of chaos at the time of creation. Russell Shorto's biography for young readers, *Geronimo and the Struggle for Apache Freedom*, published in 1989, uses this parallelism, which Geronimo may have meant to encourage by incorporating the creation myth into the autobiography he narrated to S. M. Barrett (1996, 49–53). Shorto's version of the myth relates a cosmic conflict in which the tribe of birds defeated the tribe of beasts, thus allowing humans to flourish. One of the few human women had lost all of her children to the depredations of a dragon until she hid away her last son, offspring of the rain. After he reached manhood, the son, named Apache, slew the dragon and found favor with Usen, who taught him the fundamentals of culture.[5] Shorto reports, "Goyathlay liked to imagine himself as the boy Apache, fighting the great battle with the dragon. One day, he told his family, he, too, would fight terrible opponents and win glorious victories" (1989, 9). At the book's conclusion, after Geronimo has fought and apparently been defeated by the forces of chaos represented by invading Mexicans and Anglos, Shorto notes that the myth of the culture hero endures as young Chiricahuas hear it and consequently maintain the values represented by Geronimo's selfless struggle to maintain a free Apache community (129). Although she uses a slightly different version of Apache creation mythology, Melissa Schwarz similarly casts Geronimo in the role of the culture hero by suggesting that all Apache men identified with Child of the Water, as that figure is often known, especially when conducting war (1992, 24).

Paul Chaat Smith notes that recent uses of Geronimo's image indicate his status as culture hero, not only for Apaches and other Indians but to some extent Americans in general. One is a T-shirt and poster that use one of C. S. Fly's photographs taken in 1886 when General George Crook was unsuccessfully negotiating Geronimo's surrender at Cañon de los Embudos. Four Chiricahua warriors, including Geronimo, stand with their rifles above the caption "Homeland Security: Fighting Terrorism since 1492." Though the design obviously comments on the European invasion of North America in light of the destruction of the World Trade Center and part of the Pentagon on 11 September 2001, it also establishes Geronimo as primarily a protector of his people (Smith 2009, 64). Smith also believes that the 1993 film *Geronimo: An American Legend* had the same kind of import: "Geronimo . . . becomes an American hero fighting for his people and his country. So the message of homeland security easily turns into a message of American patriotism" (65). Perhaps jokingly, Smith sees potential popularity for this image of Geronimo among right-wing militias, "given their Aryan mythification of Indians" (65). Even some of Geronimo's contemporaries recognized him as a patriotic defender of his people. A letter to the editor that appeared in the *New York Times* on 21 February 1909, a couple of days after his death, proposed the erection of a monument in Geronimo's honor. After all, the writer, Norburne Barnard, argued, "He faultlessly followed the ideals of his tribe, and created new ones in the direst straits of all emergency. With stick and spear he kept from his sky-canopied young the fanged beast of prey."

Though it does not present its biographical subject in purely heroic terms, *Geronimo and the Apache Resistance* (Goodwin, Carr, and Crichton 1988), a film released as part of the PBS series *American Experience*, served to counteract the image of Geronimo that emerged in much of the written material purporting to represent Apache opinion. Ignoring many published sources, including Geronimo's autobiography, that present a Chiricahua perspective on the Apache wars and their aftermath (e.g., Betzinez [1959] 1987; Ball 1970, 1980), series host David McCullough, who cited the Apache prohibition on mentioning the dead, introduced the film by noting that it provided a "privileged view" through its use of Chiricahua narrators. Among those who speak on camera about Geronimo and the situation in the Southwest in the late nineteenth century are individuals with surnames from that era (e.g., Kenoi, Kanseah), the famous sculptor Alan Houser, and—surprisingly, given her family's take on Geronimo as represented in the book she published only a few years after the film's release (Boyer and Gayton 1992)—Narcissus Duffy Gayton. The film's purpose is to present the "reality behind the Apache myth" that Geronimo was an "implacable savage." The film does not develop a fully realized portrait of Geronimo, glosses over some features of his life and career, and in a few places evinces some historical inaccuracies. But it does suggest that the "Apache" view of Geronimo that had been popularized in literature produced by Euro-American writers simplistically misrepresented the actual range of views. The film's Geronimo is a heroic figure whose motivations arose from his regard for the land. Its production coincided with the centennial of Geronimo's surrender to General Miles in 1886. The film ends with a ceremony at Skeleton Canyon, where many Chiricahuas converged to commemorate formally the hundred years that had passed.

Recently, another film for the *American Experience* series has presented a more balanced view of Geronimo. *We Shall Remain: Geronimo* (Craig, Colt, and Grimberg 2009), one of a several-part series presenting a Native American perspective on American history, is a fairly straightforward biographical narrative. It begins by identifying its subject with the Apache culture hero, but the narrator notes that Chiricahua opinion about him remains mixed: "courageous yet vengeful, an unyielding protector of his family's freedom yet the cause of his people's greatest suffering." While the film glosses over some of Geronimo's personal failings, such as his weakness for strong drink, and generally sees him as having important symbolic significance, it indicts some of his actions, too, particularly the kidnapping of Loco's band and their removal to the Sierra Madre in 1882. He is characterized as "too impulsive, too fretful, too vengeful" to have risen to the political position of chief, and his career has produced "complicated feelings" for the Chiricahua and other Apaches. One of the film's Native narrators says, "We don't look at him as a hero," while another muses, "Well, he killed a lot of people. Why is he remembered when he did all these bad things? It is because he put a mark on the American people. He put a scar on them." The film suggests, therefore, that the image of Geronimo in the twenty-first century accommodates a range of views and that his reputation remains complicated.

In 1995 Bruce Lixey and Robert Hercules produced a documentary film that unreservedly featured Geronimo as one of four of *America's Great Indian Leaders*. The Chiricahua joined Crazy Horse, Chief Joseph, and Quanah Parker as role models for contemporary Native Americans as well as others who value freedom. Here Geronimo's image is straightforwardly heroic. He is identified as a "bold guerrilla fighter and medicine man" who used his "mystical powers" to keep the band of resisters he was leading from falling into the hands of the U.S. Army. The segment on Geronimo draws extensively on his autobiography and presents him in an entirely positive light by stressing the treachery and evil of his adversaries. For example, the massacre of his family at Kaskiyeh is blamed on Mexican bounty hunters, and John Clum's arrest of Geronimo at Ojo Caliente in 1877 occurs because the agent from San Carlos "double-crossed" the Chiricahuas. The film's treatment of Geronimo concludes with the narrator, who has assumed an insider's perspective when dealing with each of the four "great Indian leaders," intoning, "His name and image will be forever engraved in our memories. History remembers Geronimo as a great leader and warrior. He was the heart and soul of a nation."

The identification of Geronimo as culture hero and role model for American Indian youth, especially those experiencing some sort of alienation, has been made explicit in the controversial work of Tim Barrus, who published several pseudo-memoirs of growing up as the half-Navajo child of a physically and sexually abusive migrant worker father during the 1950s and early 1960s. The last of three books he wrote under the name Nasdijj, which he asserts is an Athabascan word meaning "to become again," invokes Geronimo as a familiar spirit who sustains the narrator at times of greatest stress in his tumultuous life. That Barrus apparently invented what he recounts does not necessarily invalidate the symbolic role that he assigns to Geronimo as heroic father figure. For example, early in the "memoir" the narrator suggests the role of Geronimo in the imaginative life he creates to cope with the horrors of his quotidian existence:

> I wanted to be like Geronimo because Geronimo was brave and resolutely able to *see* into the deserts of his dreams. Geronimo was more than a childhood fixation. Speaking as he did of wisdoms and secrets, he was the only voice I knew who had the strength to chase the other voices in my head away. When Geronimo was with me, the cacophony of other voices, everyone telling me what to do, would disappear like smoke drifting out of the hogan and up through the smoke hole, where it mingles with the stars. (Nasdijj 2004, 3)

The image of Geronimo protected the narrator from his white father's abuse when the living adults in his life could not. He attributed Geronimo's guardianship to his Navajo mother's and grandmother's spiritual legacy:

"They gave me something spiritual to protect me" (28). He reported (with misplaced modifier) how Geronimo operated in his life and that of his younger brother: "As a child, Geronimo would rescue my little brother and myself from the talons of that great beast who was our migrant father" (37). Barrus gets some of the historical facts about Geronimo wrong, and he reports details of Navajo life that would make the work's authenticity suspect even if we did not already know that it was a sham. But this fabricator's use of Geronimo as heroic protector for his protagonist indicates the vitality of Geronimo's reputation in the twenty-first century and points to another of its dimensions—Geronimo as protector for those oppressed.[6]

Another approach to depicting Geronimo positively has been to cast the aged Geronimo as a wise elder statesman, an image that he may have cultivated to some extent during his years in captivity. The missionaries who established a school for Chiricahua children at Mount Vernon Barracks noted his role in keeping order and encouraging children to take advantage of the opportunity for education. Joseph Bruchac's novel for young adults, titled simply *Geronimo* (2006), portrays him in a similar role as the narrator presents the story of the Apache resistance in a series of flashbacks after surrender and captivity. This approach to revising Geronimo's image is also evident in the depiction by artist David Behrens: Geronimo is one of four "founding fathers," whose faces appear foregrounded before a representation of the four presidents carved into Mount Rushmore in South Dakota's Black Hills (*David C. Behrens Studio* 2010). The others in the group are Sitting Bull and Red Cloud (both Lakota) and Chief Joseph (Nez Perce). The image of Geronimo's face comes from the famous photograph that Frank Randall took on the San Carlos Reservation in the spring of 1884 after Geronimo had returned from the Sierra Madre in northern Mexico (fig. 1.3).

Geronimo's canonization became official on 23 February 2009 when the U.S. House of Representatives passed a resolution recognizing the hundredth anniversary of the death of Goyaałé by honoring his "extraordinary bravery, and his commitment to the defense of his homeland, his people, and Apache ways of life." Introduced by Raul Grijalva (D-AZ) and Dale Kildee (D-MI), the resolution praised its honoree as "a spiritual and intellectual leader, [who] became recognized as a great military leader by his people because of his courage, determination, and skill" as he directed his people in "a war of self-defense."[7]

A recent evocation of Geronimo suggests the continuing flexibility of his image. The Navy SEALS, whose secret mission to a Pakistani compound

FIG. 1.3. David Behrens, *Original Founding Fathers*. From left to right are Chief Joseph (Nez Perce), Sitting Bull (Lakota), Geronimo, and Red Cloud (Lakota). *Copyright David Behrens. Used by permission.*

resulted in the death of Osama bin Laden, employed the image of the famed Apache. Uncertainty emerged about whether they named their operation after him or were referring to bin Laden as "Geronimo," though *Time* magazine's report suggests the latter. As the SEALS gained access to bin Laden's compound in Abbottabad, someone announced, "Visual on Geronimo" (Von Drehle 2011, 16). Once bin Laden had been killed, a coded message declared, "Geronimo: E-KIA" (Von Drehle 2011, 21). If, as this report suggests, bin Laden himself was being identified with the Chiricahua's name (an interpretation that President Barack Obama supposedly confirmed during an interview on the CBS news program *Sixty Minutes* [Capriccioso 2011, 23; Newcomb 2011b, 7]), then Geronimo as the consummate demon who skulked through the mountains and deserts of the Southwest committing senseless acts of terrorism has survived for well over a century. If, though, his name was being used for the entire operation, then Geronimo as representative of American military valor, recalling perhaps the use of his name by paratroopers during World War II, has endured. Some commentators have suggested that either usage inappropriately associates an American Indian too closely and single-mindedly with violence and bloodshed. When the Native American news source *Indian Country Today* published materials about the usage, it included not only a news story commenting on the continued misunderstanding of Native Americana by mainstream sources (Capriccioso 2011), but also four separate opinion pieces (Hopkins 2011; Johnson 2011; King 2011; Newcomb 2011a). A subsequent issue of the magazine included two more commentaries (Loring 2011; Newcomb 2011b). While the usage itself confirms the enduring image of the "bad Geronimo," the commentary in *This Week from Indian Country* afforded opportunities to reiterate that the "good Geronimo" thrives as well as "an iconic symbol of Native American pride" and "a symbol of Native American survival in the face of racial annihilation" (King 2011, 4); a heroic figure who "was fighting against the invasion of his country and the oppression of his people" (Newcomb 2011a, 5); and a "symbol of the American Indian warrior" whose legacy might be perceived in the sacrifice of Lori Piestawa, a Hopi soldier who was among the first U.S. casualties after the United States invaded Iraq in 2003 (Hopkins 2011, 6). Geronimo was a "true freedom fighter" (Loring 2011, 6) who "tried to maintain our original indigenous liberty" (Newcomb 2011b, 7).

Even some segments of the conservative press asserted that identifying Geronimo with bin Laden was inappropriate. The *Arkansas Democrat-Gazette* of Little Rock editorialized in its 8 May 2011 edition that using "Geronimo" as a war cry had merit, having been developed when "American fighting men knew their history better," but balked at associating "so heroic a name with so low a villain" as Osama bin Laden. The editorialist—though clearly distancing him- or herself from "political correctness" in most contexts—argued that using Geronimo's name for bin Laden reflected "ignorance rather than malice." While recognizing that doing so was an insult particularly to American Indians, the writer elaborated its wider repercussions:

> Using Geronimo's good name to stand for someone as vile as Osama bin Laden insulted, intentionally or not, all Americans, for—lest we forget—Geronimo belonged to all of us. And we will not let it be said without protest that only a hyphenated kind of American need object when Geronimo's name is used so carelessly. For the Chiricahua Apache chief personified this land of the free and home of the brave. In that sense, he may have been the most American of us all.

Geronimo's quintessential Americanness is evident despite his having challenged the U.S. Army, for—as the editorial in the *Arkansas Democrat-Gazette*, a forthright supporter of Confederate heritage, noted—the same can be said for Robert E. Lee and other heroes of the Southern cause during the Civil War. A cartoon accompanying the editorial depicts Geronimo, clasping his rifle, glaring at the viewer, and asking "Operation what?"

A particularly evocative reaction, which suggests the symbolic power that Geronimo's image has for some contemporary American Indians, was offered by the 1491s, a sketch comedy ensemble. Eschewing their usual cynicism, the group reacted to the use of Geronimo's name to denominate Osama bin Laden with a video in which members reiterated the statement "I am Geronimo" and then modified it by citing a positive role that each spiritual legatee of the man, apparently still a "red devil" to some, is performing in modern Native communities: tutor, community organizer, tribal councilwoman, youth worker, nurse, history teacher, college student, and others who endure as American Indians in the twenty-first century. The performance ends with, "Geronimo's not dead. He's alive" (1491s 2011).

That Geronimo—"perhaps the most famous American Indian" (King 2011, 4)—rather than some other figure from nineteenth-century Native resistance has surfaced again reinforces his status as the Indian who comes to mind whenever "Indianness"—whether positive or negative—emerges into the popular consciousness. The incident also reinforces my contention that the evolution of his image has not been straightforward or linear. Sonnichsen's "good Geronimo" and "bad Geronimo" were alive and flourishing in the spring of 2011, when he represented both the spirit of "freedom-loving Americans" and the epitome of evil.

Though opinion remains mixed about Geronimo, his image has evolved in ways that most of his contemporaries likely would not have predicted. His detractors compared him to Satan himself and in their most positive assessments might have seen him in the way they viewed such historical figures as Tamerlane and Napoleon—able military strategists but otherwise not very admirable men. If he had any supporters who viewed him positively in ways other than militarily, they were largely silent (or without access to the press). After his surrender when he no longer posed an immediate threat, some people such as missionary-teacher Sophie Shepard, who knew him during his incarceration at Mount Vernon Barracks, began to see Geronimo in more human terms, but even they recognized that what they perceived was made all the more significant by their sense of how it differed from the expectations that his public image had created. More temporal distance and an era of revisionism regarding American Indians and the concept of Manifest Destiny were required for Geronimo to become the heroic figure who appeared in representations beginning, for the most part, in the late twentieth century. Though clearly savvy enough about his image to attempt to manipulate it, Geronimo himself could not have effected the transformations that changing tempers of the times have produced.

CHAPTER 2

GERONIMO STORIES

IN ONE OF THE INTERCHAPTERS OF *THE GRAPES OF WRATH*, JOHN STEIN-
beck describes amusements with which migrant workers newly arrived in
California entertained themselves. Storytellers emerged as primary sources
of escape for the weary, disheartened Okies: "The people gathered in the
low firelight to hear the gifted ones. And they listened while the tales were
told, and their participation made the stories great" ([1939] 2006, 325). The
first story from one of these verbal artists recounted by the novel's narrator
begins, "I was a recruit against Geronimo." The rest of the storyteller's personal narrative, which deals with his being forced to take a shot at an Indian
warrior at some distance, has nothing particularly to do with Geronimo,
yet beginning the tale of an adventure that occurred a half century before
Steinbeck's novel is set by referring to him is an important cue for the audience. The storyteller identifies himself with that last gasp of action on the
old frontier by specifically evoking the figure who has come to represent
that action.

Geronimo stories—many of which, like that related in *The Grapes of
Wrath*, use Geronimo only as a way of setting the scene—flourished in printed
sources and undoubtedly in oral tradition from the time that the famous
Apache emerged into mainstream consciousness in the 1870s until all those
who participated in the Apache wars had died.[1] Anyone who had been in the
Southwest during the 1870s and 1880s seemed to have a story that required
speaking Geronimo's name. Contemporary Native American author Leslie

Marmon Silko recognizes this phenomenon. One of her short stories is titled "A Geronimo Story," the indefinite article in its title suggesting that she is recounting one example of an established genre. Two themes dominate Geronimo stories, and Silko's tale exemplifies one of them. Her narrative describes how the Laguna Regulars, a militia consisting of men from Laguna Pueblo, were called out to investigate evidence of Geronimo's presence near Pie Town, New Mexico, some sixty-five miles across mountains and *malpaís* from their pueblo. As they all know, the supposed evidence represents the anxieties of the Euro-Americans in the community, and in particular a pompous army officer, rather than anything having to do with Geronimo himself, and the story represents the theme of the "near miss" wherein the narrator relates how he *almost* encountered the man who at the time was demonized as a "red devil." In fact, John Muthyala has suggested that Silko's story is "not really about Geronimo the man but about the emergence of various narratives of his life and deeds" (2006, 130). The other theme that has dominated Geronimo stories confirms his demonic status. Tales of atrocities attributed to Geronimo abounded in the nineteenth-century press, with some examples being retold in different settings. Virtually every crime in Arizona and New Mexico Territories was laid at Geronimo's doorstep if he happened to be off the reservation when it occurred.

Like the storyteller in *The Grapes of Wrath*, some speakers evoked Geronimo's presence to make their accounts more interesting. Drawing upon his notoriety allowed some of his fame (or infamy) to reflect upon the storyteller. If one had been involved in a fight with Indians, that fight became even more desperate and one's survival even more a product of one's daring resourcefulness if Geronimo was involved. Such may have been the case with John Bartlett. The brief story of his encounter with a party of Apaches at Oro Blanco, Arizona Territory, which resulted in the death of one Anglo, was titled "IT WAS GERONIMO" when the *Tucson Weekly Star* published it on 27 May 1886. Bartlett insisted that Geronimo led the attackers and described the lead warrior: "One of them came up quite close to the house, located himself behind a rock and exposed himself for a moment. He had on blue pantaloons with yellow stripes down the legs, and it is well known that Indians appreciate the distinction among soldiers and assume it themselves. This coupled with the daring of the fiend in question, leads to this conclusion"—that the figure was indeed Geronimo.

Immediately after Geronimo left the Turkey Creek settlement on the Fort Apache Reservation in May 1885, local and regional newspapers were filled with proto-stories about him, rumors produced by the fears and anxieties of a frightened Anglo public. Some rumors reported sightings of Geronimo (or at least of a band of Apaches) in the source's neighborhood: 150 Indians seen near Malone and heading northeastward (datelined Deming, New Mexico, 21 May 1885); "Chief Geronimo and his band" heading toward Hillsboro after having raided settlements on the Río de San Francisco (datelined Silver City, New Mexico, 23 May 1885); "uncaged Indians" who were "dashing around the vicinity" of Winslow, Arizona Territory (no dateline, 6 May 1885); "unabated excitement" in the Black Range over a sighting of thirty-five Indians (datelined Engle, New Mexico, 28 May 1885); Indians "on the upper Gila river" (no dateline, 28 May 1885) and gone to "stronghold" in the San Mateo Mountains (datelined Chloride, New Mexico, 28 May 1885). Other rumors reported body counts left by the Apaches: five ranchers near Alma, New Mexico (23 May 1885); twenty-four men "already buried in a radius of twenty-four miles" of Silver City, New Mexico (27 May 1885); more than thirty often "mangled beyond recognition" (29 May 1885). Many feared that the Apaches who had left Turkey Creek would be joined by other groups of Indians including 160 Navajos, Utes, and Paiutes (26 May 1885) and sympathetic Mescaleros who were "lurking" in the vicinity of Tijeras, east of Albuquerque (4 June 1885).[2]

Meanwhile, rumors were circulating orally, too. Wm. Walter Brady had been in El Paso shortly after Geronimo's 1885 breakout. He recalled in an interview for the Depression-era Federal Writers' Project, "I hadn't even got to Elpaso [sic] 'til I heard everybody talking about the things the Indian Geronimo had been pulling off. He just had everybody scared to death. All the Indians was on the war path" (Phipps 1936–1940). Most of these rumors did not become full-blown stories, nor did they remain in the public consciousness as new and conflicting reports replaced them. But they suggest the degree to which Geronimo was on people's minds from the time he left the reservation in May 1885 until his surrender fifteen months later. Conditions were optimum for the development of a story repertoire, and raconteurs in Arizona and New Mexico Territories took full advantage of those conditions.

Atrocities

Lieutenant Charles B. Gatewood, who was primarily responsible for persuading Geronimo to surrender to Miles in 1886, believed that Geronimo's Apaches were particularly prone to commit the atrocities often attributed to them. As he wrote in his memoir,

Stories of the most horrible torture & cruelties practiced by North American Indians on their captives are not exaggerations when applied to these [Apaches]. The reader is familiar with such & his imagination may supply the place of a description of acts so repulsive. So skillfully were their plans laid & carried out, coming & going like the whirlwind, that they terrorized a country that was afterwards populated by a number many times greater than their own, & continued to do so until our friend Geronimo made his celebrated journey to the Atlantic seaboard in 1886 & finally pitched his tent in Alabama. (Gatewood 2005, 17)

Yet Gatewood realized that atrocity stories had a rhetorical purpose. Responding to the breakout in May 1885, "some of the settlers are wild with alarm & raise all kinds of stories to induce us to camp near their places, to protect them and buy grain & hay at high prices" (2005, 173). John Gregory Bourke, adjutant to Crook, attributed motivations grounded in politics to storytellers who were recounting atrocities after the breakout: "The telegraph wires were loaded with false reports of outrages, attacks, and massacres which had never occurred; these reports were scattered broadcast with the intention and in the hope that they might do him [Crook] injury" (1891, 454).

Some atrocity stories are content with statistics, listing the number of the slain and mutilated that the Apaches had left behind in their marauding. Robert K. Evans recalled that in May 1882 he had been on the trail of an Apache "war-party" from near San Carlos, Arizona Territory, to San Simon, New Mexico Territory. He counted forty-two victims murdered "in mere savage caprice." When time had permitted, the killers had also committed "barbarities which curdle the blood and sicken the heart" (1886, 170). At the time of his surrender, the *San Francisco Chronicle* assigned over four hundred deaths to Geronimo's band (5 September 1886). Other stories focused on common techniques of torture utilized by Geronimo. One of the most frequently reported had the Apaches cutting off the soles of their victim's feet and then staking him over an anthill: "There, instead of killing him, they let the ants finish the job." The story, which appeared in the *Le Grand (IA) Reporter* for 11 August 1922, represents a familiar motif in narrative lore about Apache and other Indian atrocities.

In the weeks following Geronimo's final breakout, the local and regional press avidly reported the supposed movements of what reporters denominated "red devils" or "fiends." Often, victims' bodies marked the trail purportedly taken by Geronimo's group. The *Tucson Weekly Star*, for example, reported the deaths of Harvey and James Moreland near Grafton, New Mexico, in its 4 June issue: "The bodies were found about six miles north of Grafton, still warm. Moreland was shot several times, and when found was lying on his back with an iron rod driven through his head into the ground."

These accounts do not mention Geronimo by name. In fact, placing him at the scene of a particular atrocity was usually impossible, a point recognized by those who were arguing that he should be tried for murder in the civil courts once he was captured. But the stories implied that if he were not the physical perpetrator, he suborned and encouraged his warriors to commit the crimes. An example of such a story appeared in an interview with Harry Conver, a retired Philadelphia policeman who had served in Arizona Territory during the Apache wars. On a patrol after Geronimo's breakout, his unit heard gunfire near Fairview, New Mexico:

> We turned and raced to the spot, . . . but flames were already destroying the ranch buildings. At the door we found the rancher and his family, horribly mutilated. A half-mile away we found five cowboys. They had been digging holes for a fence and their rifles were stacked against a post. They had been shot from ambush, then hacked to pieces. A little black dog at their feet had been shot more than fifty times. And one of the men, as an artistic touch, had been pinned to the earth with his own crowbar, plunged through his abdomen. (Greene 2007, 4–5)

One of the most frequently cited atrocities that attached to the Apaches appeared in the *New York Times* for 31 May 1885 with a Silver City, New Mexico, dateline:

> The bodies of Col. Phillips and his family, who were murdered by Apaches, have been brought in, all of them in a horribly mutilated condition. A daughter had been hung alive on a meat hook stuck in the back of her head and Mrs. Phillips had had her eyes gouged out and her breasts cut off, and was otherwise brutally mangled. The citizens of this place are frantic that such outrages should be permitted without check.

Some versions of this story exacerbate the horror of the scene by reporting that the killers had murdered an infant child of the Phillipses' by smashing its head against a rock; the *Times* had reported that act of cruelty in the previous day's issue in a front page story, identifying the victim as the two-year-old child of a Mexican. The story of the Phillips atrocities appeared again in the *Times* the following day with the added detail that "father and son were terribly hacked." The *Las Vegas Daily Optic* alluded to it in a diatribe on Apache cruelty that appeared on 5 June 1885 and argued that those who had left the reservation were following the example of their "daddies" who had "tied white people to trees and toasted them to death over slow fires." One female victim of the current run of atrocities "was outraged and then suspended by the back of her head to a meat hook." By its 8 July issue the *Optic* had expanded the extent of this atrocity: several girls "had all been outraged and their breasts cut off. One had been suspended on a meat hook on the wall, and was not quite dead when found." This incident survived even into some obituaries for Geronimo. The *Nebraska State Journal* for 19 February 1909, for example, reported, "Hanging little girls by the under jaw to a great meat hook" afforded pleasure to Geronimo, whose "lust for blood was insatiable."

Other atrocity stories add a motif of foolhardy bravado to their accounts, suggesting that being heedless of threats posed by marauding Apaches would produce horrible consequences. A decade after Geronimo's surrender, Gordon Stimpson reported,

> Another man had lost his partner. They had a ranch about fifteen miles out in the country, and his partner said one day he was going out to the ranch to start his garden. He was cautioned not to go, but he said he had lived in California for twenty years and he was not afraid of Indians; so he departed and that was the last seen of him alive. He was expected back in a few days, but as he did not return five of his friends, becoming anxious about him, went out to the ranch. They found him dead in his garden, terribly mutilated. His hoe was found near him, and he had evidently been shot from behind while at work. The shot had not killed him immediately, and the Indians had ample opportunity to torture him before he died. (1896, 104)

Another widely reported atrocity story may have appeared first in the

Arizona Daily Citizen (Tucson, Arizona Territory) for 2 December 1885 as a way of providing the "general public" with a "conception of the picture of brutality and torture that marks the bloody attacks of the Apache Indians upon isolated settlers." The victim was the twelve-year-old son of Mrs. Clark, a "widow living in Wilcox." The youth supported his mother by working for a freighter whose route lay between Wilcox and Globe. On one fateful trip the freighters stopped for lunch and sent the boy to look after the live-stock that accompanied them:

> He was mounted on a little pony of which he was very proud, and was more so to think that he was earning something for his poor widowed mother. He had been gone some time and Mr. Graham [the freighter] thinking that he had been away too long went out to look for him. After a search of an hour or two, he came upon the unfortunate little fellow, who had so recently left the camp full of life and happiness. He was lying upon his back with his head so beaten to a jelly with large stones that he could scarcely be recognized. The fiends had evidently come suddenly upon the lad and wounded him, and then with a savage glee that is almost beyond the imagination of a civilized being, they beat his head with stones as one might crush a serpent.

The *Citizen* used this horrible story, which probably did not involve Geronimo, who would have been deep in the Sierra Madre at the time, as justification for the public outcry for retribution against the Apaches: "The people demand the utter extermination of every Indian known to have committed murder, and the immediate disarming of the rest of them." Meanwhile, the *Tucson Weekly Star* printed a letter on 3 December from a correspondent in Wilcox, Arizona, who revealed that the boy's head "was mashed to a jelly" and that his "mother, a widow, has been entirely bereft of reason since learning the news."

Atrocity stories were not confined to the north of the international border. A retrospective article in the *Danville (VA) Bee* for 26 February 1931 reported that the grandfather of Ygnacio Soto, president of a bank in Agua Prieta, Sonora, had been caught by Apaches during the 1880s. They "made him walk in his bare feet thru cactus, after removing all the skin from the soles of his feet, and then threw him over a cliff."

Perhaps the most widely reported atrocity attributed to Geronimo was the Peck Ranch massacre, which occurred in April 1886. Artisan L. Peck had a ranch near Calabasas, about ten miles north of the international border, where he lived with his pregnant wife, infant daughter, niece, and a cowboy named Owens. On the morning of the attack by a raiding party purportedly led by Geronimo, Peck and Owens were a mile or so away from the ranch house. The Indians shot Peck's wife and the Pecks' daughter and took the niece, a ten-year-old named Trini Verdin, captive. Upon hearing the gunfire Peck and Owens rushed toward the ranch house. Owens was killed while trying to ride for help, and Peck was taken captive. He began to stutter, and Geronimo and his cohorts apparently believed him to be mad—a condition they regarded as dangerous. They stripped him of his boots and escaped southward with their captive. Peck walked barefoot to the house, where he found a "ghastly, unbelievable scene," according to the testimony of Gilbert Sykes, a Forest Service employee who claimed to have heard it from Peck: "His wife's head was almost severed, her face beaten beyond recognition, her breasts cut off, stomach ripped open, legs hacked. She had been raped repeatedly. His 13-month daughter apparently had been grasped by the ankles and swung viciously against every wall in the room, all of which were spattered and smeared with blood and cranial matter. The child's head was demolished" (Burrows 2001). Other accounts suggest that the body of the cowboy Owens was also mutilated (Holden 2001).

These accounts represent the Peck Ranch massacre as atrocity story at its most sensationalistic. Other versions are less lurid. That which Miles included in his memoir is based on the testimony of Leonard Wood, who was involved in the pursuit of the perpetrators but did not witness any of the events he recounted:

> Their ranch was surrounded by these Apaches, the entire family was captured, and several of the farm-hands were killed. The husband was tied up and compelled to witness indescribable tortures upon his wife until she died. The terrible ordeal rendered him temporarily insane and as the Apaches stand in awe of an insane person, they set him free; but otherwise he would never have been allowed to live. He was found afterwards by his friends wandering about the place. (Miles 1896, 506–7)

In his journal entry for 12 May 1886, Wood recounted that Peck's wife had been "outraged and killed, and the father tied up to a tree, the Indians intending to torture him, but he became violently crazy and they turned him loose" (Lane 1970, 32). Though less gory in its details, this version nevertheless preserves the story's atrocity elements. Although most versions note that the murders took place and that Geronimo was leader of the raiders, some insist that Petra Peck and her child were killed immediately and did not suffer the mistreatment attributed to Geronimo's party. Geronimo himself did not mention the event in his autobiography but did insist that he had never harmed infants. On the other hand, some authorities disparage Geronimo for proposing that Apache mothers choke their own babies to facilitate their escape from Mexican soldiers who ambushed a band of reservation escapees at Alisos Creek in Sonora in 1882 (Shapard 2010, 180).

Most likely, what really happened at Peck Ranch will never be fully discovered. Press reports, though quick to cite the incident, provided no details, even though newspapers had frequently been very forthcoming when even a hint of atrocity could be attributed to Geronimo's Apaches. On 29 April, only a couple of days after the killings, the *Santa Fe Daily New Mexican* presented a dispatch from Nogales, Arizona Territory, indicating only that "the wife and child of A. L. Peck have been killed by Indians and his niece taken prisoner. Peck was crippled but escaped. Owen Bros., prominent rancheros, were killed." As far away from the action as Frederick, Maryland, the issue of the *News* for the same day noted the incident as did the *Daily Review*, published in Decatur, Illinois. The Colorado Springs *Weekly Gazette* printed the same information the next day. None of these mentioned the titillating subject of atrocities. Edwin R. Sweeney offers an even-handed account of the event that does not exonerate Geronimo completely but does suggest that he was instrumental in saving the life of Trini Verdin and that Artisan Peck was spared because Geronimo denominated him a "good man," not because of his apparent insanity, either real or feigned (2010, 537–38).

Opinion of the time did suggest that Geronimo was leading a band of marauders who had come into Arizona, and they may have committed the atrocities that Sykes recalled hearing about from Peck's own memories of the incident. That stories of horrible mutilations were in circulation contemporaneously finds support in the use that Forrestine Ernestine Hooker made of the Peck Ranch massacre in her novel *When Geronimo Rode*: "The mother had been tortured with indescribable fiendishness, while her husband, securely bound, had been forced to witness it all" (1924, 246). However, the very language in which descriptions of purported atrocities are couched, repeating what had been said about other horrors supposedly committed by Apaches, may represent a formulaic response to events, horrible enough in themselves without added details. Referring specifically to the Peck Ranch massacre, C. L. Sonnichsen has characterized the formula as "stereotyped horrors" (McCarty 1973, 152). The only witness to the killings of Peck's wife and child, Trini Verdin, did not suggest that she had witnessed any atrocities during two interviews that were conducted with her shortly after her rescue from captivity a couple of months after the massacre (McCarty 1973, 154, 157). Among latter-day treatments of the event, those who tend to regard Geronimo with complete negativity (e.g., Burrows 2001) accept the atrocity as fact, while those whose perspective on the Apache warrior is less negative (e.g., Debo 1976) or even positive (e.g., Adams 1971) are likely to dismiss this dimension of the tragic event at the Peck Ranch. Although Debo briefly deals with the raid, which occurred only a couple of weeks after Miles had replaced Crook as military commander for Arizona, she does not even mention the Peck Ranch massacre (1976, 269). Instead, she quotes Miles's official report, which boasts about how quickly the Apaches had been driven back into Mexico, and Geronimo's brief description of the raid given during an interview with S. M. Barrett years later at Fort Sill.

Another atrocity story frequently retold with some disagreement about what actually happened concerns an event that predates the Peck Ranch massacre by several years. Geronimo had left the reservation in 1881, having failed to persuade some important leaders—especially Loco—to accompany him. In April 1882 he returned to San Carlos in hope of persuading Loco to join him and, on his way, passed the ranch of George Stevens, some twenty miles north of Safford, Arizona. The Stevens family was not at home, but Victoriano Mestas, a Mexican who had known Geronimo while he was growing up among the Apaches, was ranch foreman. The Apaches demanded food, and Geronimo killed a pony belonging to Jimmie Stevens, son of the ranch owner. Geronimo also took a fancy to a shirt worn by Mestas, who was forced to remove the garment. Then, unaccountably, the Apaches began to kill all the Mexicans at the ranch, including Mestas, his wife, their children, and several sheepherders. The only survivors of the massacre were an Apache named Bylas, his wife, and Mestas's nine-year-old son Stanislaus, whom Geronimo intended to kill until he was stopped by Naiche. The boy provided an eyewitness report of the incident:

> The Indians rushed in from all sides and overpowered before a shot
> could be fired. . . . An Indian put the muzzle of his gun against

the head of one man and fired, blowing his brains against the floor and walls. I saw them kill my mother and two little brothers by beating their brains out with stones. They took my father and tortured him most dreadfully. He begged them to spare him, but they only tortured him the more. When they were tired of torturing him, one of them split his head with an axe. An Indian squaw, wife of one of the four friendly Apache herders who worked with us, saved my life by holding me behind her and begging them to spare me. . . . They were sorry that they had spared me, for they sent a party back to the house to kill me, but the squaw begged so hard for me that they said they would go back and tell the chief that they could not find me. (Thrapp 1967, 237–38)

One product of this incident was the grudge that Jimmie Stevens, who lost his pony, maintained sixteen years later. Stevens had accompanied Apaches from Arizona who attended the Trans-Mississippi and International Exposition in Omaha in 1898 and served as interpreter for all the Apaches who were at the fair, including Geronimo, who came up from Fort Sill. Stevens took particular delight in the discomfiture suffered by Geronimo when the prisoner of war tried to make a case to Miles for being returned to the Southwest while Miles was attending some of the exposition's Indian activities.

Stevens—now "Uncle Jimmie"—told his version of the incident to Ross Santee to "show you what Geronimo was like" (Santee 1947, 167). Santee consistently depicts Geronimo as a liar throughout the anecdotes he relates in *Apache Land* and has Uncle Jimmie emphasizing that character flaw in his account of the Stevens Camp massacre. Geronimo had promised not to harm anyone at the sheep camp as long as he and his party were fed. Despite misgivings from the Apache Bylas, Geronimo was allowed to enter the camp. Soon afterward the atrocities began: "The Chiricahuas killed many of my father's sheep. Some of the sheep they gouged their eyes out and did not kill. And Geronimo killed a two-year-old sorrel colt that belonged to me. Geronimo liked horse meat, he did not like mutton to eat" (168). After finishing their meal, the Chiricahuas disarmed the Mexican sheepherders, and despite pleas from members of his own party—including Naiche and Chatto—Geronimo superintended the massacre of "the herders, Mestas, his wife, and the two little children; they butchered them all" (170). Mestas's son was spared only when a Chiricahua warrior, a Mexican who had been raised by the Apaches, intervened on his behalf. Stevens claimed to have heard the story directly from Bylas, whom he described as his first cousin (167–71).

An Apache version of the Stevens Ranch massacre was recorded by Grenville Goodwin from White Mountain Apache John Rope.[3] According to his account, whose source may be Richard Bylas, son of one of the Apache sheepherders who was helping to care for the Stevens herd, Geronimo and his Chiricahuas came upon the Stevens ranch on their way to "free" the Ojo Caliente Apaches who remained at San Carlos. They killed all the lambs and placed the White Mountain Apaches under guard. According to Rope, a dispute over whiskey arose between Bylas and Geronimo. Seeing Geronimo heading toward him, Bylas had gulped down his only whiskey and could not offer any despite the Chiricahua's demands. The incensed Geronimo took out his anger on the Mexicans at the ranch, including his acquaintance Mestas (whom Rope identifies as the ranch foreman who "had married a White Mountain woman"). Geronimo supervised the killing of nine Mexican men and three Mexican women. The band of Chiricahuas left several guards behind when they departed from the ranch in order to prevent any reports of their movements. Unlike the Anglo accounts of this incident, Rope does not dwell so much on atrocity as he does on Geronimo's relations with the White Mountain Apaches whom Rope characterizes as "our people" (Basso 1971, 140–44). Poet Rawdon Tomlinson offered a response to this incident through the voice of Bylas. In "Geronimo," one of the sequence of poems in Geronimo after Kas-ki-yeh, Tomlinson has Bylas focus on the foolishness of Mestas, who believed Geronimo's protestations of friendliness, and characterizes Geronimo as well pleased with himself as he directs the slaughter of the Mexican sheepherders (2007, 19). Because so many versions of this incident are in print, Debo could not ignore it in her biography of Geronimo, and she presents it unapologetically in her account of the expedition to enlist Loco's people in the resisters' cause (1976, 140–41).

Another atrocity occasionally blamed on Geronimo, but actually committed by a group of Apaches led by Chatto, who later became one of Geronimo's nemeses after he signed on as a scout for Crook, was the murder of Judge and Mrs. H. C. McComas and the kidnapping of their son, Charlie. The victims' prominence made this front page news, and as for most of the era's brutal crimes, Geronimo was occasionally identified as the perpetrator. The manuscript of Florence Cravens's life story, collected by the Federal Writers' Project, assigned guilt to him. She erred on other details of the event. She recalled that on a trip from Lordsburg to Silver City, the route taken by the McComas family when they perished,

> We children were anxious to see the place where Geronimo had killed Judge Gomez and his wife and had taken their five year old son away with them. The soldiers from Fort Bayard New Mexico and the Scouts went after Geronimo and his band of Indians. They trailed them to the line of Old Mexico where they met a band of squaws who told the soldiers and scouts that the little boy's brains had been dashed out against a tree. Mr. Cravens, the man I afterwards married[,] was one of the Scouts who trailed Geronimo then. Mr. Cravens ran a livery stable in Silver City at that time and Judge Gomez and his wife and small son were on their way to Lordsburg, in a buggy rented from Mr. Cravens, when they were attacked by Geronimo and his band of Indians. They shot one of the horses to stop the buggy and took the other horse away with them. After I was married to Mr. Cravens we were down in Mexico in 1902 and we were told that the Gomez boy had not been killed, that he was the chief of a band of Indians. (Crawford 1936–1940)[4]

These atrocity stories served to confirm the stereotype encapsulated in the traditional simile "as cruel as an Apache" (Page 1915, 127). Writing when plans were afoot to end the Chiricahuas' prisoner-of-war status and allow them to settle on the Mescalero reservation in New Mexico if they wished, the *New York Times* opined, "Of all the American Indians it is conceded that the Apaches were the most bloodthirsty and cruel. Their outrages on the frontier shocked the whole world." This article, which appeared on 21 July 1912, more than three years after Geronimo's death, reminded his readers that his "name . . . was a byword for death on the frontier." Though the writer cites no specific examples, he or she asserts that the Chiricahuas were the cruelest of the Apaches: "They were so cruel that it is said of them that they tortured simply for the pleasure of giving pain, and young Apache boys took keen delight in tearing to pieces living birds, mice, or small game which fell into their clutches." Meanwhile, it was already a practice in the 1880s (and this continued into the twentieth century) to attribute atrocities to Geronimo simply because he was the most famous Apache warrior on whom they could be blamed. Jason Betzinez, not always sympathetic to Geronimo in the autobiography he related to Wilber S. Nye, recalled in 1959,

Some years ago the National Geographic Society published a map with some explanatory matter which purported to show the campaigns of Geronimo during the period 1879–1880. This was an error. It is true Geronimo was off the reservation part of that time, and with Juh in Mexico. But the raids referred to by the National Geographic were in fact the work of Victorio and his assistants Nanay, Kaahteny, and others. . . . Geronimo's career was sufficiently bloody but he has been credited with many outrages which he never committed. (Betzinez [1959] 1987, 49)

Near Misses and Narrow Escapes

Many people who visited the Southwest during the 1870s and 1880s claimed to have encountered Geronimo. Part of establishing one's credentials as someone who had genuine experience of the region involved having a personal "Geronimo story" to tell. Inevitably, these focused on narrow escapes from his hostility or on situations in which the storyteller had avoided coming into contact with the famous Chiricahua by serendipitous good fortune.

The *Atlanta Constitution* for 25 January 1891 reprinted an account from *Drake's Magazine* that related how the author and his party had barely escaped being massacred by a band of ninety Apaches led by Geronimo. This supposedly happened in the fall of 1882 as the author was moving press equipment to Kingston, New Mexico, where gold had recently been discovered, in order to set up a newspaper in the new boom town. Geronimo and his "gang" of Apaches ride into the author's camp and demand food, horses, and other goods. Geronimo makes their requests known in English. As the Indians are leaving with their appropriated supplies, one of the author's party takes a potshot at them. This, of course, results in a battle during which Geronimo's band charges the author's party again and again, only to be repelled by superior firepower. However, the situation seems on the verge of being reversed when the defenders of the camp run out of ammunition. With considerable ingenuity, they unpack the cases of type they were going to use for the newspaper and load it into their guns. Peppered by chunks of lead, the Apaches retreat, and the author and his party escape without fatality. The fundamental elements of this story—Geronimo's lack of respect for the property of the white men, his bullying nature, the ingenious method the Anglos find for saving themselves, and the lighthearted, rather jocular tone of the account written some twenty years after the event—

represent recurring characteristics of Geronimo stories that develop the narrow escape theme.

Henry W. Daly, who served as packmaster for several expeditions that pursued Geronimo during the 1880s and who later wrote magazine articles about his experiences, had his own narrow escape story. The incident happened shortly before Geronimo's conference with Crook at Cañon de los Embudos. The scout Dutchy, "with whom I was not on very friendly terms," had incited Geronimo's anger against Daly, and he set out to kill the packer. Daly saw Geronimo approaching him as he stood by a campfire whittling on a stick. Keeping his cool and not acknowledging his presence, Daly allowed Geronimo to approach within ten or so feet. The Apache even slammed the butt of his rifle into the ground in an attempt to elicit a response from Daly, who continued to whittle as if unaware that Geronimo was near. Finally, the latter stalked off in disgust. After the conference with Crook had effected his (temporary) surrender, Geronimo approached Daly: "Mule captain, . . . you pretty good white man. All the same Chiricahua." Daly believed that Geronimo "intended to convey . . . a compliment which I have never been ashamed of" (1926b, 85). Here the villain in the story is the rumormonger Dutchy, but Daly's self-containment allows him to emerge as the heroic figure—one who earns respect from Geronimo on Chiricahua terms.

Writing of her experiences in the Gila Wilderness in 1885, Nellie Brown Powers (1961) recalled what she assumed was a near encounter with Geronimo. Her family's ranch at Double Springs was fifteen miles from the nearest neighbor. Word reached them that Apaches, led by Geronimo, were raiding isolated outposts of "civilization" in the region, and under the protection of some thirty horsemen who had come to their rescue the family made their escape, but not without coming upon evidence of the Apaches' presence: the body of a settler whose cabin had been destroyed by the Indians. Powers's family did not actually see any Indians, but her account of their escape represents a common theme in Geronimo stories from the era.

Sometimes narrators or their ancestors avoided confrontations through clever trickery. This describes the experience of twenty-year-old Harry H. Halsell while he was guarding a herd of cattle in New Mexico Territory in the early 1880s. Having heard that Geronimo was nearby and seeing a band of shadowy figures one dark night, the lone cattle-herder initiated an attack on what he assumed were predatory Apaches, making them think that he had a host of companions to assist him. Geronimo made a quick retreat (Halsell 1998).

Sometimes narrated encounters with Geronimo led to the fulfillment of fantasies of wilderness adventures. Looking back to the 1880s, Buster Degraftenreid, interviewed in Clovis, New Mexico, in 1937, recalled an idyll spent in Geronimo's country in the mountains west of Roswell somewhere near the community of Capitan: "I was horseback and as it was getting late i [sic] had to get somewhere to stay all night." Coming upon a large circle of tepees, he recognized the Indians as those of Geronimo. But undaunted, the youthful Degraftenreid "finally screwed up enough courage to ask if I could stay all night." The "old chief" allowed him a place in his own tepee. The following morning Geronimo showed him how to hunt elk and deer. Though treated with suspicion when one of the hunters did not return with his horse, Degraftenreid managed to maintain his rapport with Geronimo and, in fact, stayed with him an extra day to hunt eagles (Kilgore 1936–1940).

In some accounts of encounters with Geronimo, the storyteller managed to inflict harm upon his adversary. Dan L. Thrapp reports a story told by Arizona character Charley Meadows, which appeared in an unidentified newspaper clipping in 1895. Nine cowboys, camping in a gorge, were beset by Indians who lowered themselves by ropes from the surrounding cliffs. "Old Geronimo, he was up on the cliff and tried to get down to the fight," Meadows averred, but he only managed to spook the horses. After rounding up their straying mounts, the cowboys pursued the Indians with Meadows in the lead. As Thrapp puts it, "With the last cartridge in his pistol, heroic Charley fired at Geronimo, breaking his thigh, then roped his horse, captured the warrior, and turned him in for trial" (1964, 315).

Present at the Surrender, Heroic Geronimo, Power, and Other Themes

A number of other emphases provided focus for Geronimo stories. Many veterans of the Apache wars, for instance, claimed to have had firsthand knowledge of the controversial circumstances that occurred in early September 1886 at Skeleton Canyon and which resulted in the deportation of the entire Chiricahua nation and, for practical purposes, the end of Indian hostilities in the Southwest. For the most part, the narrative of the Apache wars, which had begun in the early 1860s when the miscues of Lieutenant Bascom had alienated Cochise, did not enhance the reputation of the U.S. Army and other representatives of the federal government. Few real military victories could be reported, many of the breakouts occurred because of mismanagement or outright malfeasance by representatives of the Indian service, thousands of troops were deployed in the Southwest during the quarter century that the wars lasted, and millions of dollars were spent in a generally fruitless attempt to quell hostilities. Consequently, when Geronimo finally agreed to surrender in 1886 (his fourth surrender, as was often noted), considerable jockeying for credit occurred. Much of that played out in the press, as John Turcheneske has reported (1973), and much occurred more surreptitiously in reports and other official documents circulated through the military hierarchy. During the months immediately following the surrender, Miles enjoyed considerable acclaim for ending the Apache wars. Henry W. Lawton and Leonard Wood, who had led the final pursuit of Geronimo into the Sierra Madre, received their due. And though the general public did not know much about his role, many insiders recognized that much of the credit for the negotiations that led to Geronimo's appearance at Skeleton Canyon should go to Lieutenant Gatewood, whose central role in the proceedings has become more and more widely appreciated.

As time passed, memories clouded, and old soldiers retired, though, veterans of tours of duty in the Southwest, especially those of the mid-1880s, began to tell stories about Geronimo's surrender. Many such accounts had little connection with the actual events. Consider, for example, the tale of Captain W. B. Hicks, who claimed to be the "sole survivor of the historic Custer massacre." In its 20 June 1929 edition, the *Kerrville (TX) Mountain Sun* reported Hicks's Geronimo story. At the time of narration he was living near Lawton, Oklahoma, under the name W. N. McAlpine:

> It was after Hicks had been assigned to the Seventh Cavalry that he pursued and helped capture Geronimo in 1894. Geronimo's career had been one of pillage that had carried him through the Southwest and across the Mexican border. He crossed and recrossed the Rio Grande, with his pursuers doggedly on his tracks. Finally the cavalrymen surrounded him at Fort Huachucacca [*sic*] in the desert. There he was roped and tied while being handcuffed, and taken along with other prisoners of war to Fort Sill, where he spent the remainder of his life.

Hicks seems to have been a figure more from dime novels than from history. Not only did he escape the Custer debacle through having been assigned to deliver a message to Major Reno, but he survived an attack by Apaches and married an Apache girl, was "engaged by 'Wild Bill' Hickok to go with his Wild West show at a salary of $1,000 a week," married an Indian "pri[n]cess" named Anita after the death of his Apache wife, and joined the Salvation Army.

Not all storytellers who included narratives of Geronimo's surrender in their repertoires were as colorful as Hicks. For many, it was sufficient to claim they had been present when the surrender occurred. Other surrender stories stressed how the event received apparent supernatural validation. D. M. Kelsey related how on the day following Geronimo's agreement with Miles, a thunderstorm suddenly materialized: "The superstitious savages clung together, assured that this was an evidence of the wrath of Heaven aroused by their surrender." The storm, though, dissipated as quickly as it had arisen, leaving behind a rainbow and thus giving the Indians "promise of forgiveness and peace for the future." Kelsey wryly comments, "It never seems to have entered their heads that Heaven might be angry because they had put off surrendering so long" (1901, 494).

The importance of surrender stories in the repertoire of material about Geronimo is also evident in accounts of earlier situations when Geronimo came to terms with his Anglo adversaries. John P. Clum, for example, frequently retold the story of his arrest of Geronimo at Ojo Caliente in 1877. His publicizing that event—the only time, as Clum repeatedly noted, that Geronimo was ever captured—contributed to making Geronimo a public figure. Clum insisted repeatedly that if Geronimo had not been freed a few months after his arrest, the hostilities during the next decade would not have occurred, thus elevating Geronimo to a position of prominence in Apache affairs that he had not previously enjoyed. Stories about Geronimo's surrender to Crook and subsequent defection at Cañon de los Embudos in March 1886 have also been a staple in the narrative repertoire of the Apache wars.

Still another focus of these stories is Geronimo's daring, a trait that could be granted him even by those who were his unremitting enemies. Perhaps the most widely circulated of these stories concerned Geronimo's "rescue" of his wife from the Fort Apache Reservation several months after his final breakout. As the *Atlanta Constitution* for 31 October 1885 put it, "Geronimo's recent exploit at Fort Apache is on every tongue." The haste that characterized the breakout forced Geronimo to leave his two wives behind. After making his way into Mexico and establishing camp in the Sierra Madre, he made plans to return over several hundred miles across the heavily guarded border and through enemy lines to Fort Apache. Accordingly,

Geronimo exercised his knowledge of the terrain and his craftiness to elude troops protecting the border and find a place of refuge in the Mogollon Mountains to launch his surreptitious invasion of Fort Apache. Once he reached the reservation, "he had to pass the officers' quarters on his way to the place where it was agreed that the women should be waiting, but he stole by unobserved, and finding his wives, made off with them to the mountains." While next morning the reservation officials realized that two women had left Fort Apache during the night, a week passed before they understood the women's connection to Geronimo and that the "doughty brave himself had been within the enclosure." The *Constitution*'s story concluded, "His achievement is regarded as one of the smartest tricks ever played by a savage, and the skill with which it was executed shows how difficult is to be the task of subduing these raiders."

In a story published on 11 September 1886, a few days after Geronimo's surrender to Miles, the *Constitution* characterized this adventure as "one of the most daring and heroic deeds ever recorded." The *New York Times* reported the same event in its 5 October 1885 edition without commenting on the daring nature of the deed. The *Times* (26 December 1885) also reported that as a result of Geronimo's success, authorities at Fort Apache were able to foil a similar attempt at wife rescue led by Josanie (Ulzana). The story of Geronimo's daring accomplishment had enough appeal that D. M. Kelsey included it in his largely unfavorable account of Geronimo, *History of Our Wild West and Stories of Pioneer Life* (1901, 483).

Norman Wood included the wife rescue story as one of a few anecdotes in the Geronimo chapter of his survey of "famous Indian chiefs" published in 1906. He gets the details wrong by having the feat occur during the pursuit of Geronimo's band by Crawford and Crook in the fall of 1885, but the story still captures the essence of its subject's reputed daring: "He had the temerity to steal into camp with four warriors, and, seizing a white woman, told her that the only way to save her life was to point out his wife's tent. She obeyed. Geronimo set her down, caught up his squaw, and was off before the alarm could be given" (1906, 536–37).

Geronimo survived because of his daring, his shamanic power, and his geographical canniness. Rufus H. Dunnahoo, interviewed in 1937, was probably mistaken about Geronimo's participation in a cattle theft in the 1880s, but his attaching his story to that of the famous Chiricahua warrior makes for a more memorable account than if a less well-known figure had been involved. Dunnahoo told interviewer Georgia B. Redfield,

Another time Geronimo and sixteen other Indians broke out of the Mescalero Reservation one day, and the soldiers after them thought they had them safe in a cave about two and half miles east, a little north of Fort Stanton, two hundred yards from the Bonito River. The soldiers thought to starve the Indians out, but the Indians never came back, so the soldiers tracked them through the cave down a river about 14 miles. The Indians went through the cave to the south side of Capitan Mountains and stole a bunch of horses and drove them on down this far. They camped right where the New Mexico Military Institute is located now. I think Pat Garrett and a posse captured the Indians over in the Portales country. The cave those Indians and soldiers went in is not as large or as beautiful as Carlsbad Caverns. There is one big room. An underground river flows through all of the cave. (Redfield 1936–1940)

Another report of Geronimo's using the landscape to achieve his ends has him and his band effecting a daring ambush of a cavalry troop in the bleak, featureless desert. The story of this feat, reprinted from the *Chicago Mail* in the *Sandusky (OH) Daily Register* for 11 November 1892, quoted a witness: "Knowing we were on our return to the post they could easily calculate where we would pass. Then they burrowed in the sand, covering themselves entirely with the blistering particles, so that only their snakelike eyes peered forth. Thus we passed within a few rods of them without suspecting their presence." This motif of concealment appears in other lore, both fictive and reportorial, about Apache guerrilla warfare and, in fact, introduces the 1993 film *Geronimo* (Young 1993).

The Southwest abounds in stories of lost mines and treasures, to which Texas regionalist J. Frank Dobie devoted two volumes (1930, [1939] 1976). Occasionally, such stories might become attached to figures from the Apache wars. For example, accounts of gold associated with Victorio are localized in the Eagle Mountains near El Paso, Texas (Jameson 1989, 191–96), and Geronimo has sometimes been connected with tales of lost treasure. Jimmie Stevens recalled how Geronimo had bragged about the fortune in gold and silver that he had secreted in the Sierra Madre. Geronimo promised to reveal the location to Stevens if he would exert his influence to allow Geronimo's return to Arizona (Santee 1947, 171). A well-known treasure story associated with Geronimo indicates that he knew the whereabouts of a vein of gold-bearing rose quartz in the Superstition Mountains, which yielded sufficient treasure to finance his campaigns against the U.S. Army (Granger 1977, 102). The exact location of that gold has been subject to the vagaries of oral tradition, and it has occasionally been conflated with the famous Lost Dutchman Mine, one of the region's most well-known treasure troves. In fact, a story in the *Casa Grande (AZ) Dispatch* for 8 July 1981 cites treasure-seeker Howard VanDevender, who claimed to have located the treasure, as conflating a cache of Jesuit gold with the Lost Dutchman Mine and Geronimo's supply of gold. "Word of mouth tradition," however, "has placed his treasure lodes at various points in New Mexico and Arizona and perhaps rightly, but a favored theory would have an interesting source among the canyons of Yavapai County in Arizona, not far to the east of Prescott," perhaps in the Verde Valley near Jerome (Clark 1946, 61). Geronimo is supposed to have tried to bribe soldiers at Fort Sill with information about the mine's exact location if they would help him to return to Arizona (Granger 1977, 105–7). A variant holds that Geronimo attempted to use information about a rich deposit that the Spanish had seized in the eighteenth century to barter for freedom. Spanish miners smelted a number of gold bars from the rich vein of ore but were unable to remove their wealth from the mine itself, purportedly located in the Sycamore Canyon region in Yavapai County, Arizona. The location of those bars and the vein of ore from which they came was known only to Geronimo's Apaches, but he was supposedly willing to share the information with military officials at Fort Sill in order to secure his release from prisoner-of-war status and return home (Penfield 1966, 108–10; Rochette 1992, 19). The location of this mine varies markedly in redactions of the story from Texas to New Mexico to half a dozen sites in Arizona.

The few Geronimo stories from the Apache perspective that are available in print tend to focus on the shamanic abilities that Geronimo attained through his contact with spiritual power. For example, one of Morris Edward Opler's consultants in the early 1930s illustrated the generalization that those with power could control the length of day and night by citing an instance from Geronimo's career:

When he was on the warpath, Geronimo fixed it so that morning wouldn't come too soon. He did it by singing. Once we were going to a certain place, and Geronimo didn't want it to become light before he reached it. He saw the enemy while they were in a level place, and he didn't want them to spy on us. He wanted morning to break after we had climbed over a mountain, so that the enemy couldn't see us.

So Geronimo sang, and the night remained for two or three hours longer. I saw this myself. (Opler [1941] 1996, 216)

Another account of this incident survived in the family traditions of Narcissus Duffy Gayton. Most of the information that she had gleaned from family memories of Geronimo did him no credit. She cited Chatto and Jasper Kanseah as the authorities for her version of Geronimo's use of shamanic powers to control the sun:

> I remember one time Geronimo and his people were nearly where they wanted to be. It was still very dark, but it was near daybreak. The warriors needed the darkness so as to avoid being seen by the enemy. The enemy had lots of spies around.
>
> Well, that old Geronimo, he began to sing. He sang a long time. The men kept moving until they reached a mountain spot that had lots of big boulders. The men could hide safely there.
>
> Well, do you know the sun stayed down until they were safe! It did not come up at its usual time. It was two or three hours later than usual. (Boyer and Gayton 1992, 182–83)

Very rarely does Geronimo appear in comic vignettes. James Parker recalled that the "friendly and good natured" Geronimo had a sense of humor when Parker had known him at Fort Apache before the 1885 breakout:

> I particularly remember one day when we were out hunting how he laughed at Dr. Fisher, the post surgeon, when Fisher, wanting to light a cigarette, picked up two pieces of wood, and asked Geronimo how to produce a light by rubbing the pieces together. Geronimo, when he came to understand what Fisher was driving at, fell into paroxysms of laughter at the thought that a white man could hope to produce fire with two damp twigs. (Parker 1929, 152)

Another example of a story casting Geronimo as a figure of comedic potential comes from one of Opler's consultants and focuses on his absentmindedness in old age and his sense of victimization by his wives. "Geronimo was very absent-minded," the storyteller told Opler. "He would be looking for his hat and he would have it on his head." Once he thought he had lost the knife he used to carve the souvenir bows and arrows that he marketed to tourists: "All the time he had it in his hand, but we didn't let on." Geronimo asked his wife to search for it, but she refused to assist him. The resolution of the story has Geronimo drawing conclusions about wives and about himself: "Geronimo got pretty angry. 'Boys, you see how she is!' he said. 'I advise you not to get married.' Finally he saw the knife in his hand. 'Why, I'm nothing but a fool!' he said" ([1941] 1996, 402). Occasional stories in the press also characterized Geronimo as foolish. One such tale making the rounds early in the twentieth century had Geronimo, Victorio, and Nana leading a band of Apache warriors all the way north to Green River, Wyoming, where they attempted to lasso a train. The *Herald* of Delphos, Ohio, printed this story in its 19 March 1901 issue along with an account of how Victorio had his warriors ingest large quantities of salt to test their endurance before sending them off on dangerous assignments.

Captain Wirt Davis, one of the principals for the United States during the Apache wars, noted in 1885 that Mexicans had "Chiricahuas on the brain" (Sweeney 2010, 493), since they seemed able to find evidence of the Apache presence in even the most innocuous circumstance. More specifically, one might say that during the times when he was off the reservation, especially the period between May 1885 and September 1886, people in northern Mexico and the adjacent U.S. territories had "Geronimo on the brain." He came to embody the anxiety that pervaded the consciousness of many inhabitants of the region. Charles F. Lummis, who served as a correspondent for the *Los Angeles Times* in the theater of conflict, commented on ways in which Geronimo came to dominate rumors and stories circulating orally and in print. His dispatch from Fort Bowie, Arizona Territory, dated 7 April 1886, noted this situation:

As one of the results of the farcical "news" that has been furnished throughout, we have heard nothing but Geronimo, Geronimo, Geronimo. One would fancy that old Jerry was the only Apache that has been off the reservation. . . . The fact is, Geronimo is only one of seven chiefs who have been off the reservation with their families and followers. He is not even a No. 1 chief, but merely a war-chief. Nachita [Naiche] being the hereditary high muck-a-muck of the Chiricahuas. Nachita is an indecisive fellow, fonder of flirting than fighting, greatly addicted to squaws, and rather easily led by Geronimo, who is a talker from Jawville. Geronimo has not been the biggest fighter, the biggest schemer nor the bloodiest raider in the outfit at any time till now, when he has only the dude Nachita. Chihuahua is smarter, Nanay, Kutle and Ulzanna more blood-thirsty and daring. Their bands have done more raiding and more mischief than Geronimo's. The only claim Geronimo has to his unearned pre-eminence of newspaper notoriety is that he is one of the originators of the outbreak. He is NO GREATER AND NO WORSE than several of his co-renegades. (Thrapp 1979, 53–54)

Stories must have a point of focus if they are to provide ways in which tellers and their audiences make sense of the reality they have experienced or about which they have learned from others, and Geronimo afforded that focus. Frequently, the process by which stories create meaning involves the use of traditional patterns. Accounts that attribute atrocities to representatives of the "other," especially in times of military conflict, are staples in story repertoires of many societies. Those who circulated and listened to descriptions of the brutal deeds of Geronimo and his cohorts found justification for their hostility toward the Apaches. Such stories defined the adversaries as ultimate others, capable of actions that shocked civilized consciousness. Atrocity stories supported bounties placed on Geronimo's scalp, calls for his summary execution once he was captured, and the general belief that he and his band existed outside the bounds of humanity in the same way that the blood libel of the Middle Ages justified pogroms and other actions against Jewish populations in Europe. Tales of close encounters enabled storytellers to enjoy a small part of the notoriety that Geronimo had attained. Claiming that one had actually come into contact with him might strain credulity, especially if one was stressing his cunning and bloodthirsty nature that inevitably resulted in serious misfortune for those who had encountered him, but *almost* meeting up with the infamous figure ratified one's status as an experienced Southwesterner. If one had been in the Southwest during the 1870s and 1880s and had no near miss with Geronimo to recount, one's authenticity suffered. Other themes in the stories attaching to Geronimo reflected regional storytelling traditions—lost treasure, for example—or picked up on some of the traits that had come to be associated with him, such as boldness and access to shamanic power. That stories about Geronimo were part of the repertoires of many individuals should come as no surprise. He was the most famous American Indian of his era, and his career fostered the development of the many popular narratives that exploited his legacy.

CHAPTER 3

GERONIMO GOES TO THE FAIR

The subaltern cannot speak.
　　　　　　—Gayatri Spivak, "Can the Subaltern Speak?"

SCENE 5 OF *INDIANS*—ARTHUR KOPIT'S PLAY FIRST PERFORMED IN 1968, which uses Buffalo Bill's "Wild West" to indict U.S. imperialism, especially as manifested in southeast Asia—focuses on Geronimo. The stage is set with a cage of iron bars that rise from the floor and into which Geronimo crawls, prodded by two "Cowboy Roustabouts." Meanwhile, a voice offstage announces, "THE MOST FAMOUS INDIAN ALIVE! . . . THE FORMER SCOURGE OF THE SOUTHWEST! . . . The one 'n only . . . GERONIMO!" (1971, 33; ellipses in original). Once Geronimo enters the cage, he grasps its bars and paces about before boasting:

> Around my neck is a string of white men's genitals! MEN I HAVE
> KILLED! . . . Around my waist, the scalplocks of white women's
> genitals! WOMEN I RAPED AND KILLED! . . . *No Indian has ever*
> *killed or raped more than I!* Even the Great Spirits cannot count
> the number! . . . My body is painted with blood! I am red from
> white men's BLOOD! . . . NO ONE LIVES WHO HAS KILLED MORE
> WHITE MEN THAN I! (34; ellipses in original)

Then Buffalo Bill himself silently enters and surveys the caged captive. As he walks away, Geronimo is *"practically frothing"* and *"trembling with frenzy"* (35).

This is the Geronimo whom most people who attended the fairs and other venues at which he appeared during the last decade of his life undoubtedly expected to encounter. Exhibitors with commercial motives expected the "human tiger" to appear as an unregenerate savage, the "red devil" who had been a household name during the 1880s and who still hated representatives of the civilization that had, after many setbacks, ultimately triumphed over him.

Scholars who have examined how humans were displayed at the expositions that characterized American public life during the forty years beginning in 1876 have usually stressed how they became objectified victims of an ethnographic or touristic "gaze." As Barbara Kirshenblatt-Gimblett notes, "Where people are concerned, there is a fine line between attentive looking and staring" (1998, 55). The way in which Kopit's play depicts the display of Geronimo, exaggerated as it may be, shows human subjects reduced to zoological specimens who by "cognitive excision" are completely recontextualized from individual persons into "living signs of themselves" (18, 28). Meanwhile, the audience—outside the cage, sometimes in a darkened theater—has no human contact with the persons on display. The audience's perspective is panoptic, similar to that of the guards in a prison design suggested by the philosopher Jeremy Bentham in the late eighteenth century (Kirshenblatt-Gimblett 1998, 54; see also Woodsum 1993). Even in display situations where the viewing public could interact with the subjects—the Indian villages that became requisite at world's fairs held in the United States, for example—objectification and dehumanization remained paramount. Once again excised from their everyday lives and often with no "backstage" where they could escape from the performance in which they perpetually engaged, inhabitants of these villages remained victims of entrepreneurs, whether motivated by commercial concerns or ethnology, who exhibited them to a curious public. As Kirshenblatt-Gimblett concludes, "The inherently performative nature of live specimens veers exhibits of them strongly in the direction of spectacle, blurring . . . the line between morbid curiosity and scientific interest, chamber of horrors and medical exhibition, circus and zoological garden, theater and living ethnographic display, scholarly lecture and dramatic monologue, cultural performance and staged re-creation" (1998, 34). Kirshenblatt-Gimblett and others have stressed the obvious imbalance in agency between those who organized displays and those who were displayed.

Fairs and other exhibits of living "others" served as frontiers, contact zones defined by "enduring power imbalance[s]" in which those with lesser amounts of power participated in "coerced performances of identity" (Clifford 1997, 197). As James Clifford has noted, contact zones display not conditions of stasis, but rather "places of hybrid possibility and political negotiation, sites of exclusion and struggle" (212–13). Certainly, in all such situations the imbalance of power compelled the exhibited other to adhere to a script introduced from outside, but "it is also important to recognize a range of experiences and not to close off dimensions of agency (and irony) in their participation" (200). Clifford cites the example of the Kwagu'ls whom Edward S. Curtis exploited in making his film *In the Land of the Head Hunters* (1914). While they were "made to act out a stereotype of themselves for white consumption," Curtis's Kwagu'ł actors "made good money and enjoyed themselves" as they put on wigs to cover their European-style hair-cuts and shaved off their European-style mustaches (199). They were able to use the situation of contact to relive their traditions, at least as their heritage was filtered through their own nostalgia and the exigencies of appealing to a moviegoing audience (even though Curtis's film failed at the box office, most likely because it did not exploit the stereotypical warbonnet-wearing, buffalo-hunting Indian that the public expected).

Often in postcolonial situations, though, the victims of imperial hege-mony have been able to use their circumstances to promote their own agen-das or, at least, to emerge from something other than passive victimhood. Although Kopit's depiction of Geronimo encaged represents historical fact in the sense that Geronimo did appear on display at several venues begin-ning formally in 1898, at none of them did the Chiricahua leader perform as the "human tiger," even though some of the people who arranged his ap-pearances would have been delighted if he had. Instead, he attempted, albeit without complete success, to use situations of display as opportunities to project an image of his own making. In other words, the subaltern Geronimo did attempt to "speak" despite the imagistic "noise" over which he had to make himself heard.

Geronimo could do little to control his image in newspapers or in mem-oirs by participants in the Apache wars. That image emerged not just from his own reputation but from the ways in which Native North Americans had figured in European and American expressive culture since the sev-enteenth century.[1] Nor could he do much about the way in which he was portrayed in literary works such as the drama of G. D. Cummings, the dog-gerel of newspaper versifiers, or the novels of Edward S. Ellis. And once he was dead, of course, image-makers could depict Geronimo pretty much as they wanted. But he exercised (or attempted to exercise) some agency in the construction of his image during the almost twenty-three years he spent as a prisoner of war. Though largely unsuccessful in changing popular opinion about himself, he did attempt to do so when he came into contact with people whom he considered to be opinion-makers. During his two years at Fort Pickens, Florida; his six years at Mount Vernon Barracks, Alabama; and his fifteen years at Fort Sill, Oklahoma, Geronimo tried to counter the image of the recalcitrant, bloodthirsty savage that many in the popular media relished. When he appeared in public—at local events in Oklahoma, at three world's fairs, and at Theodore Roosevelt's inauguration—Geronimo tried to project an image of himself as someone who had accepted his situation and was assimilating to Euro-American ways. Those who promoted his public appearances usually wanted something much different from him, and often audiences came with expectations that matched those of the promoters. But Geronimo realized that the only way that he could achieve the goals that he had set for the rest of his life—primarily returning to his home in the Southwest—was by rejecting those expectations and trying as far as possible to reverse them. Historian Odie B. Faulk, whose chronology of Geronimo's life in captivity is somewhat shaky, held that Geronimo "apparently made a decision late in life not to follow the 'white man's road'" (1969, 209–10). The evidence seems to suggest, though, that his decision was much more complicated. Although we cannot be sure about his motivations and although the record is inconsistent in depicting him, Geronimo does seem to have been interested in following a "road" to freedom and repatriation that involved some acceptance of the ways of the "white man."

During the forty years beginning in 1876, cities in the United States hosted a dozen world's fairs. The first, held in Philadelphia, celebrated the centennial of the colonists' declaration of independence from Britain. Seventeen years later, the World's Columbian Exposition took place in Chicago, to be followed by fairs in Atlanta, Nashville, New Orleans, Omaha, Buffalo, Saint Louis, Portland, Seattle, San Francisco, and San Diego. Though to some degree each had a distinctive focus, occasioned especially by the state of the nation's economy when it was held, the expositions shared a common goal of providing for people in the United States "an opportunity to reaffirm their collective national identity in an updated synthesis of progress and white supremacy," as Robert Rydell, their principal historian, has noted (1984, 4). All celebrated the emergence of the United States as a nation-state founded on Eurocentric principles and grounded in the theory of unilinear cultural evolution that colored nineteenth- and early twentieth-century thinking about the rise of mankind from savagery through barbarism to civilization.

American Indians figured in each of these fairs through both museum displays of material culture arranged in developmental sequences and their actual presence. The Centennial Exhibition set a precedent for the latter with a small encampment supervised by George Anderson, a "famous Texas scout and Indian fighter," while the museum displays were organized by Otis T. Mason (Rydell 1984, 27). At the World's Columbian Exposition in Chicago in 1893, Frederick Ward Putnam relied on Indian agents and on Harvard-educated Antonio Apache, purportedly a Chiricahua, to gather participants to live in an encampment located near the Midway Plaisance, thus establishing a pattern followed by organizers at later fairs of allying entertainment with anthropology (Rydell 1984, 62–63). C. P. Jordan of the Rosebud Agency set up some of the Lakotas in his charge in an Indian Village at the Cotton States and International Exposition in Atlanta in 1895. They lived in lodges that had allegedly been removed from Wounded Knee, and the fair's director of publicity, Walter G. Cooper, noted that a couple of the Indian participants, one of them a child, had been injured during the 1890 massacre (Rydell 1984, 95).

An American Indian presence potentially contributed to two agendas that fair organizers might be promoting. On one hand, since Indian exhibits usually required the involvement of the federal government, especially its funding, displays of artifacts and appearances by individuals representing contemporary Native communities could promote federal Indian policy. Exhibits in ethnological museums on fairgrounds usually displayed sequences of material culture that reinforced the theory of unilinear cultural evolution that informed the research of such agencies as the Bureau of American Ethnology. In fact, persons associated with the BAE—including James Mooney for the Trans-Mississippi and International Exposition in Omaha in 1898 and W J McGee for the Louisiana Purchase Exposition in Saint Louis in 1904—influenced the ways in which the Indian exhibits were organized. The museum exhibits often intentionally contrasted with displays of living Indians, whose successful assimilation through programs such as boarding schools demonstrated how successful the Office of Indian Affairs had been in lifting their charges from the savagery that the artifacts might convey. Many fairs, for example, constructed model schools on their grounds, and students representing Native communities demonstrated classroom behavior for fairgoers (Trennert 1987b). Instrumental ensembles and choral groups consisting of American Indians who performed crowd-pleasing patriotic numbers also represented the successes of assimilation programs, as did athletic competitions that featured Indians vying in sports they had learned at federally supported schools (Gøksyr 1970).

Sometimes government agents brought to the fairs Indians who represented traditional lifeways to serve as a "before" in contrast with the "after" exemplified by schoolchildren and graduates. Meanwhile, unassimilated Indians who still embraced hopes of returning to their traditional way of life received reminders at expositions that their way of life was bound to disappear, and any resistance to Euro-American civilization was foolish in light of the sheer numbers of white fairgoers who came to view them as well as the technology available (or soon to be available) to those fairgoers. Fairs allowed Indians to acquaint themselves with "white men's accomplishments" (Harriman 1899, 510).

As early as the eighteenth century, some Englishmen recognized that despite their being transported across the Atlantic for political and other legitimate purposes, American Indians "are brought here . . . to be shewn like wild beasts" (Vaughan 2006, 233). Unassimilated Indians also contributed to another agenda that more commercially oriented fair promoters might have in mind for Indian exhibits. During the 1890s and into the first decade of the twentieth century, Wild West shows featuring Native participants were a staple of entertainment in the United States. Indians were also highly anticipated participants in other popular entertainments of the period (Moses 1996; Redden 1999). Fair organizers were thus simply coordinating their offerings with what the public expected. Not to have "wild" Indians on the fairgrounds invited competition from Wild West troupes, some of whom set up their own concessions as part of fairs' midways or on property near to the fairgrounds. Unreconstructed Indians, especially if they could be associated with well-known events in the history of U.S.-Indian relations such as the Battle of the Little Big Horn or the Massacre at Wounded Knee, drew crowds that might not otherwise visit the fairs' Indian exhibits. Some Indians who participated in fairs took advantage of the encouragement to reject at least temporarily the forces of assimilation and enjoyed cultural activities, especially dances, that were forbidden them in their home communities. They were also likely to receive some compensation for participation in entertainments such as the sham battles that became staples at some expositions, and thus they "reverted" (from the perspective of the Indian bureau) to savagery (Clough 2005). Consequently, individuals who were brought to fairs to demonstrate the civilizing effects of federal Indian programs might wind up reflecting the way of life that those programs were attempting to counteract.

Meanwhile, having these living dark-skinned representatives of savagery and barbarism on hand reinforced the fairs' white supremacist message by contrasting traditional Native lifeways with technological marvels that appeared elsewhere on the fairgrounds. The juxtaposition of humans still participating in primitive cultural forms with technological displays illustrating the epitome of civilized achievement afforded fairgoers stark images of the just and inevitable decline of American Indian cultures and their equally inevitable replacement, even by military force, by Euro-American culture.

The idea for a fair celebrating the American West followed the World's Columbian Exposition of 1893. People in communities on the west bank of the Mississippi, especially in Saint Louis and Omaha, believed that the Chicago event had stressed unduly industrial growth only in the East. Accordingly, boosters began meeting in 1894 to organize an exposition that would place more emphasis on their region. A conference the following year, inspired by the rhetoric of William Jennings Bryan, proposed Omaha as the site for an event that would alert the world to the promise of the trans-Mississippi region. With a site selected and funding in place, organizers began working toward an exposition that ultimately expanded its focus beyond only one region of the country to become a world's fair.

While the Omaha fair followed its predecessors by exhibiting artifacts from Native American cultures in its ethnological displays, it more fully formalized the presence of American Indians themselves on the fairgrounds. Edward Rosewater, proprietor of the *Omaha (NE) Daily Bee*, apparently first proposed that the Indian Congress bring together representatives from every Native society in the western hemisphere. Bureau of American Ethnology employee James Mooney consulted with Rosewater to suggest a less ambitious, more workable goal: using house types (e.g., tepee, hogan, wigwam) as the basis for organizing a congress representing a range of Indian cultures (Moses 1984). Rosewater agreed to the new plan and obtained the necessary funding from the federal government. William A. Mercer, the federal government's representative at the Omaha and Winnebago Agency, took charge of the congress and contacted his counterparts at other agencies to invite their charges to participate. Despite Mooney's suggestion, which would have brought together a sampling of various cultures, Plains societies dominated the congress. On 4 August 1898, the congress opened with an "Indian Day" at the exposition and a parade. The Indians set up camp on the northern edge of the exposition grounds not far from the midway. The number of individuals encamped there, Mooney estimated, varied between 400 and 550 (1899, 129). These Indians, according to Dr. Albert Shaw, who was quoted in *American Monthly Review of Reviews*, offered the "last opportunity . . . to see the red man in his primitive glory and in his various tribal divisions." It was consequently incumbent upon congress organizers that the "greatest care . . . be taken that every tribe should be costumed, not after the later manner in government blankets, blue calico, and the supplies furnished by the Indian Bureau, but in the fashion of the tribe in its previous state of independence" ("Glimpses of Indian Life" 1898, 443).

Mooney and other professional ethnologists had endorsed the Indian Congress partially because of the research opportunities it could potentially afford someone who might be interested in handily comparing and contrasting the customs of representative societies from various North American culture areas. Mooney himself made such comparisons in an essay he published in *American Anthropologist* (1899), which presented capsule portrayals of the groups in the encampment. Ethnologists were disappointed, though, when Mercer diverted the focus of the congress from ethnological comparison to daily "sham battles" that opposed warriors from various northern Plains communities in formalized theatrical displays, making the Indian Congress "in actuality . . . a Wild West show" (Moses 1996, 144).[2] Such battles had a long precedent, the first having occurred perhaps in 1550 when Tupinumbas and Tobajaras from Brazil squared off against one another in a staged conflict to entertain passersby on the banks of the Seine in Rouen (Vaughan 2006, 16). As Jess R. Peterson, a historian of the photography that emerged from the Trans-Mississippi and International Exposition, has noted, "A plan to present a more studied exhibit on Native American life was, in many ways, discarded for showmanship, featuring sham battles, dances, and other events that added to the spectacle of the Indian Congress" (2003, 101). Native participants themselves may have had a role in redirecting the exhibit toward activities such as sham battles. Instead of bowing to the government's desire for them to demonstrate the beneficial effects of assimilation, they used their presence in Omaha to stress the resilience of their cultures, not only through participation in the sham battles but through intertribal contacts and dances that turned their stay at the exposition into a forerunner of modern intertribal powwows (Clough 2005, 78). Even if it conflicted with what Rosewater and others had intended and, in fact, clouded the message about American imperialism that the exposition was designed to promulgate (Miller 2008, 41), this development was apparently fine with fair organizers in general. Placement of the encampment near the midway, only a few yards from such attractions as the ice cream offered at the Schlitz Building, the Cyclorama, and the Giant See-Saw, suggests how the event's organizers were thinking. As the *Omaha World-Herald*, perhaps inspired by rival Edward Rosewater's role in the Indian Congress, noted in its 5 August issue, "The exposition management is disposed to circus the feature as extensively as possible." Four days later, the *World-Herald* noted approvingly that Mercer had "upset the plans of the exposition management" by not charging an extra fee to allow visitors to enter the Indian encampment, which "was not to be run as an exposition side show any more than the government building on the Grand Court or the Marine band on the Grand Plaza."

Geronimo was part of a delegation of some 125 Indians and a hundred ponies from Fort Sill who arrived at the Trans-Mississippi and International Exposition about a month after the Indian Congress began. His presence may have seemed unusual to a few in Indian Country who had only recently been spreading rumors that he and his Chiricahuas were bent upon taking advantage of the military commitment to the Spanish-American War, which diverted attention from the prisoners of war at Fort Sill. In April, just after the removal of most of the post's garrison, rumors spread that Chiricahuas were "making medicine and holding war dances." The relatively low strength of the troops who remained at Fort Sill "looked to wily old Geronimo as a heaven-sent opportunity to make one last stand for freedom" (Turcheneske 1997, 69). Although no uprising was planned, the rumor suggested the distrust with which many still viewed Geronimo.

But undoubtedly, fair organizers wanted the famous Chiricahua there because he was the country's most well-known Indian and because his image from the era when stories about him appeared almost daily in newspapers throughout the nation had endured. Consequently, his presence on the fairgrounds would, organizers assumed, contribute to the popular sense of what it meant to be Indian, a sense that was reinforced by the Grass Dances and sham battles that occurred daily and which was antithetical to the intentions of the Indian Bureau and progressive "friends of the Indian." Ironically, perhaps, Geronimo preferred the bureau perspective and attempted to suggest that he was indeed bound for assimilation. However, his attempts to manipulate his image largely failed, and visitors to the fair saw in him what they expected to see. For them, he remained the "human tiger" and "red devil" of popular lore, not the wise, dignified elder who was trying to adopt the white man's ways and thus escape the burdens of being a prisoner of war. Nevertheless, Geronimo did try to assume some responsibility for the image he was conveying.

Geronimo did not arrive in Omaha until 14 September. The status of Geronimo and several other Chiricahuas (including Naiche, as well as others from the Fort Sill Military Reservation who joined the Indian Congress) as prisoners of war created special issues regarding their appearance. The *Omaha Daily Bee* for 15 September described the arriving Geronimo as the "Famous Apache Terror" and was bent on characterizing him in terms that reinforced his image of unreconstructed savagery. He was "the grizzled old terror of the whole southwest, garbed in beaded buckskin, grotesque blankets, feathers and warpaint." The *Bee* extended its negative portrait of Geronimo to his behavior:

> Geronimo is 63 years of age [actually probably 70 or more] and as straight as an arrow. He is of medium height and quite heavy. He does not speak English, though he understands considerable of the language. He is a chronic grumbler, and this was decidedly noticeable yesterday. Immediately after arriving in camp, he commenced finding fault because tents had not been erected before he and his party came. Then he grumbled because dinner had not been prepared and was awaiting his arrival.[3]

However, the Omaha newspaper's attempt to cast Geronimo and his companions (collectively called the "Geronimo Indians") as unrehabilitated savages was undercut by their living in government-issue tents rather than wickiups, as they should have if Mooney's architecturally focused scheme was to be followed. The *Bee*, though, did refer to these canvas structures as "tepees." Despite the paper's reporting, Geronimo did not wear traditional dress during his arrival and stay at the exposition but adopted a variation of the uniform of a U.S. Army scout. In fact, the rival *World-Herald* reported Geronimo's arrival more accurately in its 15 September issue. Noting that he "will be a great card at the Indian congress," the newspaper added, "At present Geronimo is engaged in agricultural pursuits and stock raising. He wears Indian scout uniform." His prisoner-of-war status may have dictated some details of his attendance at the exposition (Kosmider 2001, 324), but Geronimo's own agenda also affected those details.

Unlike other participants in the Indian Congress, Geronimo seems to have been content with the intentions of the Indian Bureau to use the occasion to bolster their claim that assimilation was effective. He was also happy to be in Omaha for the experience itself. As he did at subsequent fairs, Geronimo took advantage of opportunities for new experiences that his stay in Omaha offered. For example, he toured the Armour slaughterhouse, where after seeing "the rapidity with which hogs were killed he remarked to Interpreter [Jimmie] Stevens that there was no danger of the white people running short of lard" (*Bee* for 29 September). He also attended a production of the play *The Woman Hater* at the special invitation of actor Roland Reed. Geronimo—variously described by the *World-Herald* for 28 October in the story reporting the experience as "the old hater of all mankind" and "a heap big notable"—fell asleep before the first act of the play had ended.

More importantly, from the outset of his involvement at the Omaha fair Geronimo probably had two of his own goals in mind, and neither of them coincided with his image as the epitome of savagery that the popular press was still purveying twelve years after his surrender. On one hand, he had an eye on commercial opportunities offered by the fair similar to those from which he had benefitted ever since his surrender. One reason he wore an army jacket was so that he could cut off its buttons, sell them to souvenir hunters, and then sew on a new batch to sell the next day. His entrepreneurship also found expression in his marketing of handicrafts, especially bows and arrows, some of which he may have made himself. Moreover, he sold items manufactured by others, affixing his printed signature to increase their value. Geronimo also sold photographs of himself, perhaps— at least toward the end of his Omaha sojourn—copies of the one taken by Frank W. Rinehart (or his associate Adolph Muhr), the exposition's official photographer who set up a studio on the grounds (Bolz 1994, 35). At the end of October, as other Indians were hurrying back to their homes, Geronimo was content to remain in Omaha. Despite cold weather for which his tent was not adequately suited, he was turning "several honest pennies," as the *Omaha Daily Bee* for 27 October 1898 put it, "by selling his autograph and pictures, charging from 50 cents to $1 for each, and he found plenty of purchasers too."

Geronimo's other goal was more long range, for he wanted to convince the American public in general and those in the War Department and Indian service particularly that he was no longer the man he once was. He made a determined effort to show that he had accepted Euro-American ways and consequently should no longer be held as a prisoner of war. Though that status did not involve actual incarceration, it did mean that he could not return to his home in Arizona. He had understood that the conditions of his surrender in 1886 included his exile in Florida for only two years. It was now twelve years later, and though he was closer to home than he had been in Florida and Alabama, Fort Sill was hundreds of miles from the mountains with which he was familiar. Throughout the rest of his life, Geronimo's most pressing concern was getting home, and he manipulated his image to attain that goal.

Geronimo's first public appearance at the exposition may have been at the sham battle scheduled for 17 September. The issue of the *Omaha Daily Bee* for that day noted, "Old Geronimo will be a guest of honor and will occupy a seat on the raised platform in front of Captain Mercer's quarters. Just before the fight he will be introduced and may possibly deliver a short speech in the Apache language." The following day's issue of the *New York Times* reported that Geronimo received a standing ovation on the occasion. The *Bee* noted that in contrast to the gaudily painted Plains warriors who would carry out the sham battle, Geronimo's "little band moved up in good order and looked as fine as silk, clad in their blue blouses and black slouch hats." The *World-Herald* for 19 September noted that he wore "a neat-fitting dark blue cavalry jacket, trousers and boots, such as are worn by Indian police, the only remnant of savage garb he donned was a skull cap, woven in yellow and adorned with two short horns." After Geronimo was introduced to the spectators, "he bowed in a graceful manner, stuck the spurs into the flanks of his horse and rode rapidly away. Cheer after cheer followed the old man, furnishing conclusive evidence that he is the most popular Indian on the grounds" (*Omaha Daily Bee*). Geronimo received the ovation "in dignified and solitary state" (*Omaha World-Herald*).

The *Times* also noted that Geronimo would take command of one of the forces in the next day's sham battle. Denver's *Rocky Mountain News* confirmed that plan, holding that the "Blood Stained Chief" would command five hundred warriors in the day's mock contest. That probably did not happen, though Geronimo's attendance at these sham battles became a regular feature of the Indian Congress. But as a prisoner of war, Geronimo enjoyed less latitude than other Indians who attended the congress. The federal government would not have wanted to encourage whatever warlike tendencies were believed to have survived his captivity, and Geronimo wanted to distance himself from his bellicose past. The *World-Herald* for 17 September noted that Geronimo "has announced that his fighting days are over" and that "he will become a grand stand spectator" at the sham battles. The *Bee* for 21 September described the extent to which Geronimo assumed the role of courtly (assimilated) gentleman: "Old Geronimo appeared to be the lion of the occasion and was cheered from the time he started until he halted his animal in front of the stand. The old man rode like a general and evidently appreciated the ovation, as he doffed his hat and bowed as gracefully as a Chesterfield."

Actually, the scenario for the sham battles had already been formulated and would not have accommodated Geronimo's participation in the staged action even if the Department of War and his own inclinations had tended in that direction. When Geronimo arrived in Omaha in the middle of September, by which time the sham battles had been going on for more than a month, a narrative trajectory for the event was being replayed daily. The battle pitted the "Sioux" and their allies against the "Blackfeet" and their allies. According to the plot for the pretend conflict, a Sioux had been captured while trapping beaver in Blackfeet territory. Doomed to die at the stake, he was already feeling the heat from a fire that had been lit for that purpose when two fellow tribesmen witnessed the proceedings and returned after skirmishing with the Blackfeet, accompanied by a Sioux war party that swept down upon the Blackfeet camp. Several Blackfeet, captured during this encounter, were then doomed to the stake, but their fellows returned to rescue them. Advantage in the "battle" shifted between sides, usually ending in a draw when all blank cartridges issued to the participants had been expended. Introducing Geronimo into this scenario would have upset the pattern of action that had already been established. Better to have him on hand to attract a crowd, which sometimes numbered as many as ten thousand according to local press reports, as part of the preliminaries. Note also that the sham battles at the Trans-Mississippi and International Exposition did not follow the pattern established by Buffalo Bill's "Wild West," which presented re-enactments of actual battles as well as conflicts that pitted "the dynamic, violent action of frontiersmen, scouts, and Cavalry as they subordinated hostile landscapes and 'villainous' native populations to American civilization" (Whissel 2002, 227). The sham battles in Omaha had Indians fighting against Indians. They took viewers to an era before the Euro-American invasion, a timeless, static, ahistorical past when Indians were living (and fighting) as they had supposedly done for centuries. Geronimo, though, had turned his back on his own past. He could allow himself to be transported into precontact times along with other spectators, but distancing himself from those times served his assimilationist ends.

The most important sham battle that Geronimo attended occurred on 13 October, when General Nelson A. Miles—the military leader to whom he had surrendered in 1886 and who, according to Geronimo's understanding, had indicated that he and the other Chiricahuas would return to Arizona two years after that surrender—was present. Miles was already seated in the stands when Geronimo appeared on the grounds. When he located Miles among the spectators, "he looked steadily at the general for perhaps a couple of minutes, and then dismounting from his horse, he started toward the seats. He brushed aside the crowd with his hands and was soon at the side of General Miles." When Miles tried to shake his outstretched hand, Geronimo "clasped the white warrior in his embrace and hugged him as affectionately as would a father who had not seen his son for years." Miles returned the embrace, "and for several minutes the great chiefs stood there, neither saying a word." Then, in a gesture clearly designed to signal that the Chiricahua bore no hard feelings, "the head of Geronimo dropped over on General Miles' shoulder and the old man appeared as contented as a babe laying its head upon the breast of its mother." The *Omaha Daily Bee* reported that Miles pinned his Peace Jubilee badge from the exposition's celebration of the successful conclusion of the Spanish-American War on Geronimo's blue uniform and that then the two men sat near each other absorbed in the staged battle enacted before them. "After it was all over," the reporter concluded, "Geronimo and General Miles, through the Apache interpreter, held a long conference, but what it referred to neither cared to say."

The tête-à-tête between Geronimo and Miles was potentially crucial to Geronimo's case for being allowed to return to the Southwest. One observer noted that Geronimo's attempt at rapprochement with his old adversary was particularly apt for the Peace Jubilee celebrating the U.S. victory in the Spanish-American War, which had brought Miles to the exposition. The meeting between "the once fanatical foe to civilization and the commanding general of a victorious army that had so recently defeated the descendants of the crafty Spaniards, who centuries ago changed the innocent natives of the New World into beings as cruel and fiendish as themselves," offered "a new realization of what 'peace' means" (Harriman 1899, 510). Yet the only account of what actually occurred when Geronimo and Miles conferred comes from a somewhat questionable source. John P. Clum, notably a Geronimo hater, drew upon the testimony of interpreter Jimmie Stevens, who had a long-standing grudge against Geronimo, to describe a meeting in which Miles completely rebuffed—in fact, mocked—Geronimo for his pleas to return to Arizona.[4] Extremely ill at ease when the interview with Miles began, Geronimo could not speak to his old adversary until Naiche had paved the way. Then when Geronimo accused Miles of having reneged on his promise given at Skeleton Canyon, the general replied—in Clum's words—"I lied to you, Geronimo. But I learned to lie from the great nantan of all liars—from you, Geronimo. You lied to Mexicans, Americans, and to your own Apaches, for thirty years. White men only lied to you once, and I did it." Geronimo then purportedly tried a different approach. Relying on the figurative language supposedly characteristic of American Indian "eloquence," he told Miles, "I have been away from Arizona now twelve years. The acorns and piñon nuts, the quail and the wild turkey, the giant cactus and the palo verdes—they all miss me. They wonder where I've gone. They want me to come back. I miss them, too." Again, Miles responded dismissively:

"A very beautiful thought, Geronimo. . . . Quite poetic. But the men and women who live in Arizona, they do not miss you. They do not wonder where you have gone; they know. They do not want you to come back. . . . The acorns and piñon nuts, the quail and the wild turkey, the giant cactus and the palo verde trees—they will have to get along as best they can—without you." (Clum [1936] 1978, 289–90)

The discussion ended abruptly with this exchange, and Geronimo left "in high dudgeon" (Clum [1936] 1978, 289–90). Geronimo's nephew Daklugie told Eve Ball that he believed that the encounter with Miles was set up by promoters "in their desire to create publicity" (Ball 1980, 174). The account of the meeting, which Ball seems to attribute to Daklugie (her text is unclear), presents the dialogue almost verbatim like it occurs in Clum's narrative.

A day before the meeting with Miles when the president himself had attended the sham battle, the "once-dreaded chief of the Apaches" made appropriate obeisance to the chief executive. The 12 October issue of the *Bee*, which recounted William McKinley's extended visit to the exposition, noted, "There was less of show and more of dignity in the old warrior's mien, for of all the chiefs he was the only one that had discarded the dress of savagery and he appeared in a scout's uniform with but a few brilliant adornments."[5] Geronimo also joined the other Indians at the sham battle attended by General William Shafter, which took place a couple of days after the visits by McKinley and Miles. Once again the Apache appeared in the forefront of those who gave "three rousing cheers" for this hero of the recently concluded Spanish-American War and was first to be introduced and shake the general's hand when Shafter descended from the reviewing stands. Geronimo was clearly playing the role of the assimilated Indian by showing deference to those to whom it was due according to the Eurocentric order of things.

That Geronimo assumed the role of spectator at the sham battles, except for his performances in the preliminary parades, served his purposes and to some extent those of the establishment. The old warrior, converted from his militant savagery, viewed the spectacle beside the representatives of Euro-American civilization, who filled the grandstand to overflowing on many occasions. Many in the audiences for the sham battles came at least partially because Geronimo was there. Geronimo also appeared as spectator rather than participant at other Indian performances, including dances—many of which enjoyed more sanction from professional ethnologists such as Mooney than did the sham battles. At a dance program staged by Indians from the northern Plains, "one of the most interested spectators was Chief Geronimo of the Apaches," noted the *Omaha Daily Bee* for 16 September:

> Having lived in the south during the whole of his life, Geronimo had never seen anything of the kind before and the sight of a couple of hundred half naked Indians, painted and decorated with feathers, was something of a revelation to the old man, who had discarded the blanket and has put on the uniform of a cavalry scout. As the Indians danced and kept time to the music pounded out of a drum, the old man smiled and whispered to his lieutenant, Natches, that it must be great fun. He even intimated that if he was not wearing heavy cavalry boots, he might try the step himself.

Here Geronimo assumes, at least from the perspective of the *Bee*'s correspondent, the role of tourist, positioning himself more with Euro-American civilization than with Native American savagery. The *Bee* for 23 September noted the "highly amusing" performance of a fire dance by the Apaches, "one of the most interesting terpsichorean novelties that has yet been pulled off by the aborigines." The reporter does not mention Geronimo at all. The dance probably was staged by Arizona Apaches rather than Chiricahuas from Fort Sill, but perhaps he (or his establishment handlers, who wanted to isolate him from influences that might cause him to backslide into his old Apache ways) ensured that he kept his distance from the proceedings.

During the six weeks that Geronimo spent in Omaha, his assimilationist image also received a boost from his adopting the role of sage counselor, regarded by his fellow Indians as "a great man" whose opinion "carries a good deal of weight." For example, he spoke with an *Omaha Daily Bee* reporter about strife involving the Pillager band of Ojibwe near Leech Lake, Minnesota. Geronimo labeled the rebellious Indians as "red fools" and spoke from experience about the impossibility of their carrying the day against the U.S. military. Reflecting on his own foolhardy attempts to do so a dozen years earlier, Geronimo stated that his subsequent captivity, though galling when it began, "was the best thing that ever happened to me." He unequivocally declared where his loyalties now lay: "My days of fighting are over, except to fight for the stars and stripes, which I would be glad [to do] if I had a chance. Of course if I should be called to go to fight Indians, I would do so, but I am through shooting at white men." When the *Waterloo (IA) Daily Reporter* ran Geronimo's comments in its 11 October issue, the story paid particular attention to the disparity between the number of Pillagers and the number of Euro-Americans. Geronimo asserted that though he had never been in Minnesota, "I hear that up there and for hundreds of miles beyond, the white men are as many as the blades of grass." Based on his own experience of trying to defeat Euro-Americans in Arizona, he added, "I knew that the race of the Indian was run." Becoming philosophical, Geronimo stated,

> The sun rises and shines for a time, and then it goes down, sinking out of sight, and is lost. So it will be with the Indians. . . . It will be only a few years until the Indians will be heard of no more, except in the books that the white man has written. They are not the people that the Great Father loved, for if they were he would protect them. They have tried to please Him, but they do not know how.

Accepting the image of the Indian as vanishing American—or seeming to do so—allied Geronimo with popular sentiment among the general Euro-American public. While his response to the Pillager affair allowed him to exploit his "symbolic capital" in stressing the futility of armed response by American Indians to the government's military and political superiority, it also furthered his campaign to appear to be fully assimilated. As Bonnie

Miller has noted, "Geronimo may have hoped that a public display of deference would bring about his release" (2008, 43). He certainly seems to have learned an important lesson, one that he hoped would raise doubts about his continuing prisoner-of-war status.

Moreover, Geronimo endorsed the white man's education for Indians. In the same interview in which he criticized the Pillagers, he asserted that schools "are good things for Indians." But he noted that returning educated Indians to their home communities often resulted in their resorting to traditional ways. He called for the federal government to "give them something to do, not turn them loose to run wild on the agency." "What could an educated Indian do," he wondered, "out in the sage brush and cactus?" Geronimo also spoke on Indian education to a reporter for the *Chicago Times-Herald*, whose account was reprinted in the *Omaha Daily Bee* for 13 October. Long a supporter of education for Apache children, he had been characterized as "the friend of the school" by Sophie Shepard, who had taught the Chiricahua children imprisoned at Mount Vernon Barracks (1890b, 164). Shepard had depended on Geronimo to enforce discipline at the school, where a special chair had been placed for him to oversee the proceedings (1890a, 37). Even a decade before he visited Omaha and talked with the Chicago journalist, Geronimo had shown himself conscious of the need to project an image that contrasted with his savage reputation. During the Alabama confinement Shepard reported: he and Naiche "are both sober, and have great influence. They have behaved well during their captivity, and have done much to put down drunkenness" (1890b, 166). In his talk with the reporter for the *Times-Herald*, Geronimo once again acknowledged in "sentences worthy of an Osceola or a Red Jacket" the demographic disparity between Indians and Euro-Americans, who are "as many as the blades of grass." But again he criticized the current educational program afforded Indians, which he considered a "waste of money." Taking a child from his or her community, teaching him or her the ways of the white man, and then returning the newly assimilated Indian to the original community, Geronimo believed, had little positive impact. While supporters of the system hoped that the educated youth would have a civilizing influence back home, Geronimo believed that "instead of the educated youth becoming a missionary of civilization he discards its habiliments, puts on a blanket, and becomes an Indian again." Geronimo's criticism elicited a response from Commissioner of Indian Affairs William Jones, who insisted in an article that appeared in the *Bee* on 18 October that Indians "speaking the English language, weaned from tribal customs and iron hands of tradition" did contribute to the process of assimilation when they returned home. That the commissioner felt it necessary to rebut Geronimo's comments lent stature to what the Apache had to say. Moreover, Geronimo's criticism was addressed to what he perceived as the educational system's failure to contribute effectively to the assimilation that he wanted to appear to have achieved himself.

Though he would have realized its many inaccuracies, Geronimo might not have totally rejected a brief depiction of him that appeared in the *Indian Helper*, the house organ of the Carlisle Indian School, for 14 October 1898. Drawing upon a clipping from the *Indian Journal* that reported on his exhibition appearance, the Carlisle publication suggested that "some of us may gain a lesson in the life of the famous chief" who is now "stationed" at Fort Sill: "He is 90 years old, but straight and active with an eye like a Rocky Mountain eagle. . . . He has been fighting the whites during most of the time since the war of 1812, but is now reconciled to them and lives peacefully on their bounty, toothless, propitiatory, and composed. He has been a total abstinence Indian all his life and his age and state of preservation show that it has been a good thing for him" (Stockel 2004, 63). For the approximately seventy-year-old Geronimo, whose last breakout had involved the illicit manufacture of tiswin and who would die (indirectly) from the effects of excessive drinking a decade after the Carlisle piece appeared, projecting the image of a toothless, peaceful teetotaler would well serve his hopes for repatriation as a free man.

Geronimo's presence at the Trans-Mississippi and International Exposition may not have accomplished what its organizers hoped. In fact, it may have contributed to complicating the "portrait of empire" that the fair, which was organized at the very time that the United States was acquiring its first overseas territories, had intended to communicate (Miller 2008, 43). But Geronimo's attendance served his purposes and established him as a "fixture at expositions" (Trennert 1987a, 146). Moreover, by the time the next world's fairs took place—in Buffalo in 1901 and especially in Saint Louis in 1904—the reality of an American empire abroad had materialized. Anticipation during the weeks leading up to the Omaha fair had seemed to suffer when the United States declared war on Spain in April 1898 shortly before the scheduled opening. The national preoccupation with war could have derailed that opening, but in fact fair officials were able to capitalize on the surge of patriotism that accompanied the hostilities, which concluded in time for a Peace Jubilee Week as part of the exposition's activities (Alfers 1972).

The Spanish-American War also created an overseas empire for the United States and provided another reason to include Indians among the fair exhibits. Although this purpose was not fully realized until the Louisiana Purchase Exposition in 1904, the Trans-Mississippi and International Exposition was the first to use its Indian exhibits to show how the United States would handle its overseas colonies, especially the Philippines. Buffalo Bill Cody had early recognized parallels between the newly conquered Filipinos and American Indians when he began to incorporate the former into his Wild West show. For Cody, "non-whites everywhere resembled Native Americans," and when he brought them into the performance arena, he mounted them on horses like Indians "even though they had never ridden these animals" (Redden 1999, 132). The federal government also stressed the similarities of the savages for which they had newly become responsible and those with whom they were already successfully dealing. An assimilated Geronimo demonstrated the United States' successful handling of its "Indian problem" and implied that success with the most savage representative of the Chiricahuas, the most savage tribe of the Apaches, the most savage of North American societies, could be translated into dealing with Ilongots, Negritos, and other savage Filipinos now under U.S. hegemony.

However, on 24 October Denver's *Rocky Mountain News* issued a disturbing report. According to their account, Geronimo had been treated so well while in Omaha that he could not stand the idea of returning to incarceration at Fort Sill. Consequently, on 23 October as he and the other Chiricahuas were on their way back to southwestern Oklahoma, he escaped from custody. The savage who had spread a "campaign of blood all over the West where at different times he scalped nearly a hundred white men and women" had slipped into the woods some twelve miles from El Reno in Indian Territory. The Indian delegation from Fort Sill had arrived there by train via Wichita, Kansas, and were completing the last leg of their return on horseback. Riding at the rear of the line of march, Geronimo made his escape, having several years previously told a "sub-chief" that he had a route in mind by which he could return to the Southwest where "his band . . . would certainly protect their old chief from capture even at death."

One wonders why Geronimo, who had been projecting an image of assimilation and acceptance to persuade the government to allow him to return home, would jeopardize his hopes with such a foolhardy move. The answer is that the newspaper account is in all likelihood incorrect. It is full of errors: Geronimo had not been at Fort Sill for ten years, as the paper suggests;

he did not scalp a hundred people, since scalping was practiced rarely if at all by Apaches; he had no band waiting for him in New Mexico and Arizona, since the other Chiricahuas were also at Fort Sill; and his confinement at Fort Sill was really imprisonment in only a spiritual sense. His problem with Fort Sill was that it was not his homeland. Moreover, although the Indian Congress had begun to break up a week or so prior to the report in the *Rocky Mountain News*—the Absarokes were the first to leave on 16 October—Geronimo probably stayed in Omaha until 27 October and was among the last of the Indians to leave the exposition. In fact, a report in the *Bee* on 21 October noted,

> Geronimo says he is in no hurry to go home. He says he is being treated well and that in addition to this he is making a few dollars by selling his autographs and pictures and so long as the supply holds out and the white people want to pay for these things there is no particular hurry for going back into the seclusion of the Fort Sill reservation, where his family and the balance of his people are located.

The *Bee* indicated that he was on hand for a banquet on 20 October, which Mercer held for the Indian Congress, and feasted on beef tongue and potatoes. The Omaha paper also noted his continued presence and sale of souvenirs in articles that appeared in the 25 October and 27 October issues. The *World-Herald* reported that the delegation of Indians from Fort Sill left Omaha on 27 October.

The account in the *Rocky Mountain News* was undoubtedly a "Geronimo story" similar to those that had been appearing in the press for the last twenty or so years and suggests that Geronimo still had work to do in developing his image as an assimilated Indian. Another story, perhaps equally spurious, suggested that not everyone in Euro-America had become reconciled to Geronimo's image of himself as an assimilated savage. John Clum's memoir—the only source, through Jimmie Stevens, of the details of Geronimo's frustrating personal interview with Miles—also tells of how near the end of the exposition, Stevens, Geronimo, and Naiche became lost while driving around the countryside near Omaha. By the time they found their way back to the outskirts of the city several hours later than expected, one of the local newspapers had issued an extra edition with the headline "GERONIMO AND NACHEE ESCAPE. APACHE MURDERERS THOUGHT TO BE ON THEIR WAY BACK TO ARIZONA" (Clum [1936] 1978, 290). However, my examination of both the *Omaha Bee* and *Omaha World-Herald* has not uncovered this headline.

Other evidence that Geronimo's self-projection as an assimilated Indian had not impressed itself upon everyone comes from Mary Alice Harriman, who attended the exposition and summarized her impressions of the Indian Congress:

> Never before has there been such a gathering of men known to have been at some time inimical to the interests of the American nation. Geronimo, the "terrible Apache," was the most noted. Looking at his deeply wrinkled face, scarred and seamed with seventy years of treachery and cunning, watching his small, shifty eyes, one could well understand how even brave men had dreaded to encounter him in the days gone by. (Harriman 1899, 510)

Harriman endorsed Geronimo's status as "a paroled prisoner" and dismissed the idea of letting "him have another chance to plan and execute more of his famous raids" (510). The *Omaha World-Herald* seconded the belief that Geronimo was still not to be trusted. In its 27 October issue, the paper noted, "The character which made him famous as a wholesale murderer and a heartless and treacherous wretch is still in him, and no kindness or favor extended him is apt to be remembered over night by the old chief. Although his conduct has been that of a model Indian, so far as outside appearances go, he has needed more secret watching than ever."

Despite his efforts to appear otherwise, Geronimo remained a savage in the public eye. He may have enjoyed commercial success during his time at the Trans-Mississippi and International Exposition, but he had not convinced enough people that he was assimilated sufficiently to terminate his prisoner-of-war status. His lack of success, though, did not dissuade him from continuing to try to improve his image in the Euro-American consciousness. The lure of additional commercial opportunities and new experiences to be had also encouraged his participation in other world's fairs and celebratory occasions during the next few years.

The first of these opportunities to reappear on the national stage occurred three years later, when Geronimo was part of the Indian Congress at the Pan-American Exposition in Buffalo, New York. Planning for the Buffalo fair had begun in 1895, when promoters argued that an event designed to promote interrelationships between the United States and countries in Central and South America could succeed in a city that already could lure tourists from both the United States and Canada to nearby Niagara Falls.

Like other fairs held during the era, the Pan-American Exposition was based on the evolutionary assumption that the United States represented the apex of cultural development and should provide a model for other nations in the hemisphere while taking advantage of markets they afforded for U.S. business. Meanwhile, the exposition helped to celebrate the country's acquisition of an overseas colonial empire. As Sarah J. Moore has noted, the Omaha event "articulated an internal colonial model in its emphasis on westward territorial expansion," while the fair in Buffalo "defined empire within an international context" (2000, 112). Still celebrated for its architecture (Bewley 2003), the fairgrounds reflected the evolutionary agenda through the arrangement of its buildings and through the color scheme that gave it the name "Rainbow City." Ethnological exhibits reinforced the underlying thesis of cultural evolution. Those exhibits were organized by A. L. Benedict, a faculty member in the dental school at the University of Buffalo who had an avocational interest in anthropology. Benedict hoped to have living representatives of Indian groups from the Americas on hand, but an alternate plan for an Indian Congress as part of the fair's midway—called the Pan—ultimately reduced his exhibit of living Indians to a stockade housing several Iroquois dwellings. With input from anthropologists at the Smithsonian Institution, Benedict did create a successful ethnological museum that displayed artifacts organized geographically and in supposedly evolutionary sequences (Rydell 1984, 126–53).

The success of Omaha's Trans-Mississippi and International Exposition inspired boosters in the Nebraska city to re-open their fair as the Greater American Exposition in the summer of 1899. The manager of that event's Indian Congress, of which Geronimo was not a part, was Frederick Cummins. His experience and financial backing from the Citizens Bank of Buffalo afforded Cummins the concession for the Indian Congress at the Pan-American Exposition. One of several "ethnological villages"—including, most prominently, a Filipino community—the Indian Congress had a more clearly defined commercial agenda than did its predecessor in Omaha. Though ostensibly oriented toward presenting a "lesson in history" that could not "be gleaned from books" but only embodied in "long haired painted savages in all their barbaric splendor," according to an exposition guidebook (Rydell 1984, 149), the Indian Congress advertised regularly alongside other midway exhibits in the *Buffalo (NY) Evening News*. In those advertisements, the management of the Indian Congress highlighted particular attractions that might lure visitors away from other offerings on the Pan: Bonner the

"Horse with a Human Brain," the National Glass Company's Pan-American Plant, the Aero-Cycle, the Temple of Palmistry, and Bostock's Great Animal Arena. The Indian Congress billed itself as the "Government's Contribution," since its participants were present with permission from the Office of Indian Affairs and—in one case, at least—the War Department, and "Right on the Sunday Question," since it tried to buck the city's blue law, which prohibited it from being open on the Sabbath. Its advertisement in the 27 June edition of the *Buffalo Evening News* heralded a new attraction just arrived at the Pan-American Exposition: "GERONIMO Arrives Under Guard of U.S. Regulars at 7:30 This Evening." Geronimo would remain in Buffalo until the exposition closed in early November, and for a month or so after his arrival, he remained the principal lure at the Indian Congress. Once the novelty had dissipated somewhat, he was replaced in advertising by Peta, who walked across a live wire charged with two thousand volts of electricity; occasional dog feasts; Princess Loronette, an alleged heroine of the Apache wars who had, according to a wire service story that appeared in the *Titusville (PA) Herald* on 2 October 1901, made a daring ride through the deserts and mountains of the Southwest to warn the renegades led by Geronimo that the U.S. Army was pursuing them; and finally, as the exposition closed, a reenactment of "CUSTER'S LAST CHARGE," which involved seven hundred Indians in a sham battle with U.S. troops.

The *Buffalo Evening News* (1 September 1901) asserted that the Indian Congress was "historical, ethnological, industrial, interesting and instructive" and noted its special appeal for children. As at Omaha, the principal event each day was a sham battle with Geronimo taking a role similar to that which he had assumed at the Trans-Mississippi and International Exposition. The "premier feature of the entire exposition," as the *News* noted in its 7 July edition, he "is introduced at every performance and he rides a magnificent horse across the arena with the skill and dexterity of the celebrated jockeys of the world." The village also provided plenty of opportunities for entrepreneurship, of which Geronimo took advantage to market craft goods, signed photographs, and articles of his own clothing. His hat, apparently traditional headgear rather than army issue, went for sixteen dollars. The *News* for 6 September noted that he kept "the Apache princesses and squaws busy making hats." He also sold his own artwork and reportedly designed beadwork for others, including his daughter "Bright Eyes" (probably Eva), who remained at Fort Sill, to manufacture. His most accomplished bead design, according to a wire service story printed in the *Piqua (OH) Daily Call* for

15 October, represented the sequence of events that led to the assassination of President William McKinley in the exposition's Temple of Music. The story estimated that it would take Bright Eyes three million beads and two years of effort to finish "the beautiful and difficult piece." Thus, Geronimo was able to advance the entrepreneurial agenda that he had begun to establish for himself as early as 1886 and that had been central to his participation at the Omaha fair. Furthermore, this element of his persona also contributed to his attempt to convince the public that he was no longer a savage, and his minimal involvement in sham battles at the Pan-American Exposition again reinforced that image.

Though consistently referred to as "the human tiger"—a sobriquet attributed to Miles—Geronimo was also portrayed as the elder statesman of the Indian Congress, a role that he filled with apparent dignity and that fit the image of the assimilated Indian he was cultivating. The local press in Buffalo seems to have assumed that Geronimo had taken on a leadership role among the seven hundred Indians representing forty-two communities that formed the Indian Congress. He was their leader, the *Evening News* suggested, in matters recreational and ceremonial. For example, on 8 July the International Navigation Company took a delegation of 150 Indians for a ride on Lake Erie. Led by Geronimo, "the famous Apache chief," the group had mixed reactions to the excursion. "A few got seasick," the *Evening News* for 9 July reported, and the story singled out the experience of "Chief Spotted Tail, who had never rode the water before. . . . He became very sick and took relief by getting down on his hands and knees and burying his face in the carpet of the cabin." The trip marked the "first big water ride" for Geronimo, the *News* noted, "and it did not phase him a little bit." As a leader, he "is always a diplomat and is looking out for the best of it for all the Indians about him." Geronimo did try, according to the Buffalo newspaper, to take advantage of the boat's crossing into Canadian waters to purchase some "fire water" at the bar, but he "acquiesced" when told that although his argument about legal jurisdiction was valid, the Indians' obtaining liquor "would work harm."

Geronimo also demonstrated leadership skills, according to the newspaper, when he provided ceremonial responses to a couple of tragic events that occurred while he was in Buffalo. On 13 July, an infant whom the *News* referred to as Little Johnnie Ghost-Dog, but whose specific ethnic identity was not indicated, died at the congress. The story about his death and the subsequent mourning described how under such circumstances a "warrior is always selected . . . to hold communication with the spirit that comes for the soul of the departed." Geronimo, whose traditional mourning customs certainly did not adhere to those described by the *Evening News*, was chosen to preside over ceremonies for the infant. "The death dance is celebrated for four days," according to the news account, "and the crumbs thrown on the blanket spread over the corpse are carefully buried with the body for the use of the guide on the journey to the spirit land." Moreover, a tube was inserted into the grave so that "the medium [presumably Geronimo] may communicate with the escorting spirit." If Geronimo did indeed participate in this ceremony, he may have done so to suggest that he had severed his commitment to Chiricahua tradition, whose mortuary customs would conflict with much of what was described (Opler [1941] 1996, 472–78), and was amenable to other ritual systems, including Christianity, which he would ostensibly adopt several times during his years as prisoner of war.

Much more dramatic was the Indian Congress's response to the shooting and subsequent death of President McKinley, who had been gunned down by an "anarchist," Leon Czolgosz, while shaking hands with the public in the exposition's Temple of Music, located at some distance from the Indian Congress encampment. Czolgosz shot McKinley on 6 September, and the president died from gangrene on 13 September. The "chiefs" of the Indian Congress held a "powwow" on the morning following the shooting. Geronimo presided, according to the report in the *News* on 8 September, and each of the "chiefs" in attendance rose to condemn the act of the anarchist whom they denominated "The Rat-That-Lurks-in-the Cellar." When word of McKinley's death reached them, all of the Indians involved in the exposition remained in their tepees to lament the event. The next morning, as the *Evening News* for 14 September indicated, Geronimo convened the entire seven hundred participants in the Indian Congress to offer an address. The *News* quoted his words: "The rainbow of hope is out of the sky. Tears wet the ground of the tepees. Palefaces, too, are in sorrow. The Great Chief of the nation is dead. Farewell! Farewell! Farewell!" Historian Margaret Leech also suggests that some Indians went to see the president lying in state at the Buffalo City Hall, but she does not indicate whether Geronimo led that delegation (1959, 603).

Geronimo's years in captivity—now totaling fifteen—and his increasing understanding of the tourist impulse encouraged him to be affable and accommodating to the curiosity of those who made their way past the other enticements of the Pan to see him at the Indian Congress. He posed for a number of photographs, including one attributed to Frances Benjamin Johnston, a pioneering photojournalist who took the final photograph of President McKinley before his assassination (fig. 3.1). Geronimo participated in the "ceremony" of adoption for political dignitaries who enjoyed the publicity of having become a member of an Indian tribe. Among those whom Geronimo recognized as honorary Indians were Governor W. A. Stone of Pennsylvania, to whom he assigned the name "Chief Having-Great-Weight" because of his splendid physique; Pennsylvania congressman John P. Elkin; Governor George K. Nash of Ohio, who became "Big Buckeye"; and the sheriff of Scioto County, Ohio, to whom Geronimo gave the Indian name "Big Catch Bad Men."[6] Geronimo also allowed himself to be feted at the Buffalo Press Club, where he was honored at a "Night in Bohemia" event. After an introduction by Doc Waddell, who related the "capture" of Geronimo, which had ended the Apache wars, Geronimo "admonished his listeners to be 'strong and brave,'" according to the *Buffalo News* report for 1 July. Geronimo also permitted his palm to be read by the palmist at the Pan. The palmist's concluded that Geronimo's hand revealed that he was "of a very daring, courageous nature, a great fighter, but in danger cool and brave." Moreover, "for firmness, perseverance and determination his hand should be compared to none but Napoleon's, as he has that great Napoleonic love of bravery and sticktuitiveness."[7] While characterized by "a very obstinate disposition," Geronimo was "to a certain extent, a great diplomat." Reinforcing the image that Geronimo was trying to project, the palmist also noted in the story that appeared in the *Buffalo (NY) Sunday Morning News* for 7 July, "His love of children is very beautiful—in fact, remarkable. Knowing he would never injure a woman or child as his respect and esteem for them is very great."

Geronimo was willing to play along with the preconceptions of tourists, even when those preconceptions made him more the savage than he actually was. For instance, a story about his favorite foods had him rejecting ice cream and sweetmeats and liking peaches and apples. He liked his steak broiled rare, but his "favorite dish is rattlesnakes." With tongue in cheek, the *Buffalo Daily News* for 6 September reported, "He gets one rattlesnake cooked and served like quail on toast each week." Given the Chiricahua antipathy to scaly creatures, Geronimo—if it was he rather than the *News* reporter—was clearly playing along with touristic stereotyping to the fullest degree.

Despite his continued attempts to project an assimilated image and to accommodate himself to the demands of being a tourist attraction without compromising that image, Geronimo did not make much progress toward

FIG. 3.1. Geronimo posed at the Pan-American Exposition in Buffalo, New York, in
1901 with two men, one of whom has sometimes been erroneously identified as General Nelson A. Miles (to whom Geronimo had surrendered some
fifteen years earlier). Photograph by Frances Benjamin Johnston. The photograph was published in the *Buffalo Sunday Morning News* for 25 August 1901.
Library of Congress Lot 2967, LC-USZ62-97682.

achieving his goal of freedom and return to the Southwest during his participation in the Pan-American Exposition. A wire service story that appeared in several newspapers of the time still characterized Geronimo in terms of his earlier persona as consummately opposed to white civilization: "So great is his influence over his race, his subtlety, his hostility to the whites and his powers of leadership that the government is afraid to give him his freedom, although he is about 90 years old." The article concluded that many of the "chiefs" gathered for the Indian Congress still represented a threat to the civilization of the United States: "And yet to-day the visitor to the Pan-American exposition catches an expression on the faces of many old chieftains which makes him feel that if these former lords of the soil had the slightest hope of success they would to-day put on war paint and feathers for a more congenial occasion than to give variety to the programme of an exposition" (Lloyd 1901). Moreover, when the exposition closed in early November the Buffalo press, forgetful of his publicized leadership role on such occasions as the Indian Congress's response to McKinley's death, was still referring to Geronimo as the "human tiger."

On one hand, the congress did not provide a congenial venue for Geronimo's attempt to project an assimilated image. The most high-minded of the congress's purposes was to suggest how contemporary Indian life was largely unchanged. Geronimo was said to be "just as wild in spirit" as when he was leading "warriors in battle years ago." The same wire service story, which appeared in the *North Adams (MA) Transcript* for 17 June 1901 as well as other newspapers, declared that the goal of the congress was to stress that "the old chiefs [including Geronimo] who are survivors of an earlier era of warfare are still unreconciled to civilisation and its ways, and were they not held in check by the strong arm of the government the chances are they would be just as wild as in the days when the great Tecumseh and his brother planned to drive the whites from the continent." Meanwhile, the commercial focus of the congress, much more central than that of its Omaha predecessor because of its consignment to the midway, stressed the Indians' old-time, "savage" ways—especially in the sham battles and dog feasts. The latter received considerable media attention, were particularly advertised by the congress, and confirmed one of the period's prevailing stereotypes, thereby eclipsing any ethnological purpose the gathering of American Indians in Buffalo might have had.

Yet depicting Geronimo as a successfully assimilated savage would have contributed to the imperialist focus that colored the Pan-American

Exposition's agenda: both the general evolutionary scheme that dominated the exposition's ideology and the particular highlighting of specific alien cultures. The Indian Congress was not the only exhibit on the Pan that purportedly provided intercultural experiences. It was joined by the Esquimaux ("Cool / Clean / Artistic, Ethnographic, Entertaining"), the Moorish Palace and Panopticon ("The Artistic and Education Feature of the Midway / Everybody Says So"), M'Garvie's Streets of Mexico (which featured daily bullfights), Darkest Africa ("Dwarfs / Cannibals"), Fair Japan of the Midway ("The beautiful village where people of culture and refinement delight to linger"), and Akoun's Streets of Cairo and Beautiful Orient ("Congress of Dancing Girls"). Most important from the perspective of recent U.S. history was the Filipino village, which had opened somewhat later than the other midway attractions but which was luring considerable crowds at a time when resistance to the U.S. presence in the Philippines was making front-page news; some accounts even stressed that one leader of the Filipino resistance was named Geronimo. An assimilated Chiricahua Geronimo would have been convincing evidence that the United States was up to handling the Filipinos as well as other savages with which it might come into contact now that the Spanish-American War had made it a worldwide imperialist power. But the Pan-American Exposition, perhaps because Geronimo was a midway performer rather than a participant in the exposition itself, advanced the Chiricahua's campaign to project a new image and win freedom not at all. The next world's fair, however, would provide him another opportunity.

A *New York Times* editorial opined that the selection of Geronimo to attend the Louisiana Purchase Exposition, the world's fair held in Saint Louis in 1904, was an excellent idea. "The assembled tribes now subsisting but in remnants could not out of their roster of living heroes have sent to the front a more striking figure," wrote the editorialist. The "sunset of his life" had afforded him Cassandra-like "mystical lore" that clearly revealed that "in the competition with the white man they [Indians] have failed and gone to the wall, and that no reach of time or visitation of fortune can restore their glories or give them a new basis of action." As the defeated leader in the final days of the Apache wars of the 1870s and 1880s, Geronimo, now in his old age, was attuned to the inevitability of his people's destiny. The organizers at Saint Louis could exhibit "a particularly imposing array of chieftains," yet "among them all there will hardly be found a more imposing figure than that of old Geronimo" (4 July 1904).

Geronimo was at least seventy-five years old when he attended the Saint Louis event, where he continued to pursue his desire to change his image into that of an assimilated former savage who could be trusted to live out his days peacefully in Arizona. He accepted the prevailing view of the Indian as a "vanishing American" that had shaped relations between the American colonies, and then the United States, and the indigenous peoples of North America for at least two centuries previously. The Louisiana Purchase Exposition was his third world's fair, so he knew what was expected of him. He also knew how to exploit his situation as far as he possibly could. During the six months he spent in Saint Louis, he carried out his now familiar commercial activities of selling miniature bows and arrows, allegedly of his own manufacture, as well as photographs on which he had printed his name in block letters. The Saint Louis event, though, had a couple of dimensions that, while present in Omaha and Buffalo, now became central to the role that fair organizers expected of him. More directly than at previous expositions, Geronimo and other older Indians were to serve as a counterpoint to the exhibition of Indian schoolchildren who were learning to be the civilized mainstream Americans that in the eyes of the general public Geronimo never had been and never would be. Furthermore, he was to remind fairgoers that the United States had been able effectively to handle savages whose progress on the scale of cultural evolution paralleled that of the Filipinos, now the responsibility of American imperialists, who were exhibited elsewhere on the fairgrounds. In fact, the largest government-sponsored exhibit at the Louisiana Purchase Exposition was the Filipino village.

Like its predecessors as far back as the Centennial Exhibition in 1876, the purpose of the Anthropology Department at the Louisiana Purchase Exposition was to showcase the theory of unilinear cultural evolution—then in its last gasp among most professional anthropologists but still at the center of thought about human development among others. WJ McGee, recently removed from his position as director of the Smithsonian Institution's Bureau of American Ethnology and successor to John Wesley Powell, had assumed the task of overseeing the anthropology exhibits. Still an ardent cultural evolutionist—in fact, an adherent of "a well-defined theory of racial hierarchy based on what he claimed were differences in cranial capacity and manual dexterity" (Rydell, Findling, and Pelle 2000, 564)—McGee intended tribal peoples whom he brought to the fair, especially the Filipinos, to reveal the process that had culminated in European and Euro-American civilization.

As David R. Francis wrote in his celebratory volume *The Universal Exposition of 1904*, published almost a decade after the fair closed,

> At the Exposition were assembled numerous types of many of the primitive races of the earth. How the American Indian had begun by the exercise of his intelligence and the skill and strength of his body to make the raw materials and the animals of the earth serve his need, convenience and comfort was shown by actual examples. Groups of various tribes from different parts of the earth and of varying degrees of development were presented as in actual life. Some of the tribes were of the lowest existing types, others were fairly advanced in more primitive arts of civilization. Proficiency in the mechanical and even in many of the finer industrial arts was demonstrated by the actual achievements of hundreds of full-blood Indians, students of the Indian colleges and schools. (Francis 1913, 522)

Congress appropriated forty thousand dollars (later raised to sixty-five thousand) for the Indian exhibit primarily to show off how schools had hastened assimilation. But traditional craftspeople ("old Indians") were needed to contrast with the schoolchildren in attendance.

Ostensibly, then, Geronimo represented the "old Indians," what the schoolchildren would have become had they not enjoyed the benefits of education at such institutions as Chilocco Academy in Indian Territory. Actually, though, his role at the exposition was more complex. One proponent of his participation in the exposition—N. F. Shabert of the U.S. Fidelity and Guaranty Company of Lawton, Oklahoma, near Fort Sill—had encouraged Samuel M. McCowan, chief administrator at Chilocco Academy, who was charged with arranging the attendance of the Indians, to include Geronimo. One of the qualities that recommended the "old chief" to McCowan's attention was that he "had between eighty-five and one hundred white scalps to the credit of his savagery; also a vest made of the hair of the whites whom he has killed" (Debo 1976, 410). Rumors of Geronimo's "scalp coat" had been circulating before Shabert's claim. A fairly detailed account of the coat's acquisition by Fred Harvey appeared in several newspapers in 1901. The issue of the *New Oxford (PA) Item* for 1 March of that year reprinted an account from the *Kansas City Journal* that Harvey's son-in-law John F. Huckel had purchased the coat from "a collector of Indian curios" in San Francisco. The *Item* described Geronimo's "dress coat":

It is of buckskin, and is decorated with beaded figures of Indians and wild animals and with beaded embroidery. This alone would make it of value, for the demand for beaded embroidery is, in these times, much greater than the supply. Perhaps the most interesting feature in connection with garment, however, is that dangling from the shoulders are more than forty scalps. Some of the hair can be recognized as that of women victims, although most of the scalps evidently belonged to men.

Meanwhile, another story from the *Kansas City Journal*—this one appearing in the *Times Democrat* of Lima, Ohio, for 28 February 1901—reported grand jury proceedings against Abraham Jefferson, "a negro" who had stolen the coat from Harvey. Again, considerable detail about the coat itself appears:

It is festooned with forty or fifty long tufts of hair, which are believed to have been taken from the heads of the many white women whom the old chief had killed. Geronimo must have had a particular dislike for women with dark brown hair, or a penchant for that kind of decoration for his coat, for, with one exception, all the hair is of that color. The exception is a very light brown, which might at one time have been red. All the hair is long. It is attached in hit-or-miss fashion to all parts of the coat's exterior, and hangs down the back so thick as to almost conceal the highly colored painted figures which constitute the rest of its ornamentation. As a curio the coat was worth about $500.

According to some sources, including the *Davenport (IA) Daily Republican* for 31 March 1901, the scalps adorned not a coat but a mat on which Geronimo "plant[ed] his feet" upon arising every morning. Though we can be sure that Shabert's claim about scalps in Geronimo's possession was inaccurate, even in old age and after appearing at two world's fairs where he had attempted to project an assimilated image he still had a reputation that attracted fair-goers who expected to encounter displays of savagery at the anthropology exhibits, whether or not they were interested in cultural issues raised by the exhibits. In fact, Angie Debo, who would later write what remains the definitive biography of Geronimo, recalls hearing about the scalp coat while she was growing up in northern Kansas during the 1890s and 1910s (1976, ix). As David Francis noted in 1913, "The aged warrior Geronimo . . . illustrated at once a native type and an aboriginal personage of interest alike to special students and passing throngs of visitors" (1913, 529). Robert Trennert, a more recent student of the Louisiana Purchase Exposition, has noted that "the presence of the famed Apache warrior assured that the exhibit would attract a large crowd" (1993, 286).

Realizing the potential that his presence at the fair would have for organizers, Geronimo tried to negotiate special treatment. Indians who lived on the fairgrounds—some for as long as six months—received no salary, though travel and living expenses were covered. They could expect to profit materially by marketing crafts they produced. Geronimo insisted that he be paid a hundred dollars per month for his participation—a demand that caused organizer McGowan to dismiss him as "no more than a blatant blackguard, living on a false reputation" (Debo 1976, 410). Though Geronimo ultimately accepted the same deal offered to other Native American attendees, he was savvy enough to attempt to exploit his notoriety. He was correct in his assessment of his own value to the Anthropology Department exhibitions. In their recent book on those exhibitions in Saint Louis, Nancy Parezo and Dan Fowler have referred to Geronimo and other Apaches as "The Stars of the Fair" (2007, 109–15). People came to see him not because he represented the savage stage of the theory of unilinear cultural evolution but because he had once been a household name throughout the country and even abroad: the "red devil" who was the last "real" Indian warrior they were likely to see (fig. 3.2).

Geronimo was housed in a specially painted tent near the other Apaches, all of whom refused to live in the canvas wickiups that fair authorities wished them to inhabit. He arrived on the premises on 6 June 1904 with a thorough knowledge of how to manipulate crowds that wanted to see him and an agenda that involved immediate pecuniary gain and the long-range goal of refurbishing his image. He refused to wear traditional garb, for instance, preferring jackets with buttons that he could cut off to sell as souvenirs. He worked in the Indian School building, beginning at nine o'clock each morning, to produce his bows and arrows in a booth located between Acoma corn grinders and Laguna potters. A character in LeAnne Howe's novel *Miko Kings: An Indian Baseball Story* reports that her favorite exhibit at the exposition

FIG. 3.2. Geronimo (center) was part of a contingent of Apaches from Fort Sill who were deemed "stars" of the Louisiana Purchase Exposition. *Library of Congress Lot 12980, LC-USZ62-124430.*

was "the Apache Geronimo" from whom she had purchased a photograph and "a small arrowhead that he had fashioned" (2007, 115).[8]

As the *St. Louis (MO) Post-Dispatch* for 8 June 1904 put it, he had become "an artist and a financier" who spent his time at the fair "painting his name on cards and selling the cards to admiring visitors." The *Atlanta Constitution* ran an advertisement in its 6 August 1904 issue wherein it offered souvenir portfolios of the exposition for the cost of ten cents. A photograph of Geronimo dominates the advertisement:

> The once mighty and greatly feared Indian Chief, who, when in the zenith of his power, was King of the Plains, now deems it a pleasure to write his autograph for visitors to the Indian School at the World's Fair. The old Chieftain has provided himself with cards and several indelible pencils, and for ten cents slowly prints "Geronimo" on the card, which he hands to the visitor with stately grace.

Readers of the *Constitution* could obtain Geronimo's image along with those of other "famous Indian Chiefs" by purchasing the appropriate portfolio. The *St. Louis Post-Dispatch*, though, treated Geronimo dismissively. "The old Medicine Man does not look nearly so warlike as many other Indians about the reservation [on the fairgrounds]. There is little of the heroic about him. He dresses not only very plainly, but, to quote a visitor, 'rather sloppily,'" the paper complained in its 8 June 1904 issue. Geronimo also played the fiddle, a traditional Apache musical instrument, and sang songs that were billed as "war chants" to the enraptured throngs. When he dictated his autobiography to S. M. Barrett, Geronimo boasted of the financial benefits afforded him by his six months in Saint Louis: "I sold my photographs for twenty-five cents, and was allowed to keep ten cents of this for myself. I also wrote my name for ten, fifteen, or twenty-five cents, as the case might be, and kept all of that money. I often made as much as two dollars a day, and when I returned I had plenty of money—more than I had ever owned before" (Barrett 1996, 155). Perhaps this admission reinforces what a recent commentator has suggested was one message that Geronimo's entrepreneurship conveyed: "By selling autographed portraits and souvenir bows and arrows, Geronimo brought home one of the fair's important lessons— that everything had a price" (Breitbart 1997, 15–16). While he apparently was not allowed to leave the fairgrounds (given his continuing status as a prisoner of war), Geronimo did enjoy some of the sights at the fair, particularly trained animal performances and exhibits of sleight of hand. He also rode the Ferris wheel.

Geronimo's humanity also came to public attention in press accounts of his reunion at the Louisiana Purchase Exposition with his daughter Lenna, whom he had not seen in some fifteen years. The description of their meeting reinforced Geronimo's attempts to distance himself from the image of savage "red devil" that had played a role in the eighteen years of exile from his homeland. The *Arizona Republican* for 29 July 1904 ran the story, though with plenty of reminders of Geronimo's past reputation:

> When Chief Geronimo, the Apache warrior, who is said to be one of the most cruel and heartless of the chiefs who fought the whites, met his daughter yesterday tears coursed down his wrinkled cheeks, and the broken old warrior seemed entirely overcome with the joy of the meeting. The long record of his prowess in many wars and the story of his cruelty were all forgotten by those who saw the

old soldier weep with joy at the sight of the daughter he had not seen since she was a baby.

Despite Geronimo's record for savagery, he was "also a father and the father-heart knows neither race, color nor nationality; it is a common heritage." Geronimo also worked to ingratiate himself with mainstream American society by joining in the morning and evening salutes to the U.S. flag that began and ended the daily schedule of the Indian school on the fairgrounds, according to a story datelined Saint Louis and published in the Decatur, Illinois, *Daily Review* for 28 July 1904.

Native Americans were not the only people on display at the Louisiana Purchase Exposition. People from various parts of the world, especially the Philippines and other places where societies were still living in the evolutionary stage of "savagery," were exhibited. Geronimo seems to have been particularly interested in Pygmies from central Africa. He mentioned them in his conversations with Barrett and reportedly met Ota Benga, who later gained notoriety by being housed in the Bronx Zoo, where he died. The Pygmy's biographers described how Geronimo visited the Pygmy exhibit and presented Ota Benga with a stone arrowhead: "Rarely did the Human Tyger part with such an item free of charge" (Bradford and Blume 1992, 16). Bradford and Blume provide further details about this ceremonial gifting: "With his marvelous feather headdress on, Geronimo faced the pygmy and chanted solemn sounds at him for some time after he dropped the arrowhead into his hands, raising dust with his buckskin boots and turning in a circle" (121). This gifting, if it occurred, suggests a special connection between the savage Pygmy and the savage Apache.

Though her initial published response to the Apaches dismissed Geronimo's people as a "warlike race . . . still in the same stage of development as were our own ancient forefathers" to whom human life "is no more than the life of an animal or insect" (Patterson 2010, 87), the exposition provided the setting for Geronimo's encounter with Natalie Curtis, pioneer ethnomusicologist and collector and translator of Native American verbal art. In terms of his image, that encounter had mixed results for Geronimo. Curtis portrayed him as benign and avuncular, but he remained for her a traditionalist whose worldview did not necessarily reflect assimilation. Born into an upper-class family in New York City, Curtis had been trained in the United States and in Europe as a classical pianist. Though gender undoubtedly imposed some restrictions on her professional opportunities, she seems to have been enjoying a satisfactory career and had published several original compositions during the 1890s. She was bound for a competent, but probably undistinguished, career as performer, composer, and teacher when Native American music came to her attention. The circumstances of her encounter with that music remain somewhat unclear, but she apparently heard the music of some Southwestern groups, probably the Hopi and possibly the Laguna, while visiting her brother who had been living in Arizona. While spending what may have been an entire year there, Curtis performed the obligatory tourist duty of visiting some Indian ceremonies. She also became aware of federal policies regarding the education of Indian children, which discouraged and in many cases forbade their learning and performing indigenous music. She feared that this artistic heritage would be lost and set herself the task of saving from oblivion "the remarkable music and poetry that is gradually being lost to the world through the decadence of Indian songs" (1904, 327). In 1903 she wrote in *Harper's*, "I sought the Indian songs solely that I might reverently record and preserve what I could of an art that is now fast passing away beneath the influence of the Moody and Sankey hymn tunes and patriotic songs taught the Indians in the government schools" (1903, 626). Though Curtis did not oppose government educational programs and endorsed the theory of unilinear cultural evolution, she nevertheless recognized the value of Native American arts, including verbal and musical.

Armed with a letter to Secretary of the Interior Ethan Allan Hitchcock from family friend Theodore Roosevelt (1951, 3:523), Curtis gained ingress to reservation communities where she recorded songs. She did fieldwork on the Hopi mesas and at the more accessible Laguna Pueblo, where she made some cylinder recordings. She also decided to prepare an anthology of the material she was recording, a project that eventuated in *The Indians' Book*, published in 1907, a volume that featured lyric poetry (i.e., song texts), music transcriptions, and visual designs from eighteen Indian communities. The first successful cross-cultural anthology of Native American verbal and musical art, the volume profoundly influenced the general public as well as poets who found in the texts she translated the foundation for a truly American literary tradition upon which they could build (Patterson 2010, esp. 81–117).

Despite her fieldwork, which occurred during the summer of 1903 and during a several-month trip following her visit to the fair, much of the material that appeared in *The Indians' Book* was recorded from participants in the

Indian exhibits at the Louisiana Purchase Exposition. There, Curtis encountered representatives from Indian communities of the Plains (e.g., Pawnee, Cheyenne, and Kiowa), the Great Lakes region (Ho-Chunk), the Northwest Coast (Kwagu'ł), Pueblo communities she had not visited (San Juan, Zuni), and other Southwestern traditions (Pima, Yuma, Navajo, and Apache). Her principal source for the Apache chapter of *The Indians' Book* was Geronimo.

Specific information about Curtis's contact with Geronimo is not available.[9] Undoubtedly, she sought him out if she had heard that he habitually performed songs while making his bows and arrows. Her characterization of the source for what she has entitled "Medicine-Song Sung by Geronimo" identifies him as "perhaps the most famous of Apache war-leaders." She notes that Geronimo "is now between seventy and eighty years of age, but bears himself with the erectness of the Indian warrior, and in his eye is still the tiger-flash" (1923, 323–24). In *The Indians' Book*, she lets Geronimo provide some information about his song:

The song that I will sing is an old song, so old that none knows who made it.

It has been handed down through generations and was taught to me when I was but a little lad. It is now my own song. It belongs to me.

This is a holy song (medicine-song), and great is its power. The song tells how, as I sing, I go through the air to a holy place where Yusun will give me power to do wonderful things. I am surrounded by little clouds, and as I go through the air I change, becoming spirit only. (Curtis 1923, 324)

Geronimo also illustrated the song with a drawing that showed him passing through the sky to the holy place: "His changed form is symbolized by a circle, and this is surrounded by a 'kind of air'—a mystic aureole. The holy place is symbolized by the sun, which is decorated with a horned head-dress emblematic of divine power. Such head-dress is the insignia of the Holy Man" (324; fig. 3.3).

The text is translated as this eleven-line poem:

O, ha le
O, ha le!
Through the air
I fly upon a cloud

Towards the sky, far, far, far,
O, ha le
O, ha le!
There to find the holy place,
Ah, now the change comes o'er me!
O, ha le
O, ha le! (Curtis 1923, 324)[10]

Curtis also included a musical transcription to be sung "with spirit" (325–26), and an interlinear translation of the song appears in the appendix to *The Indians' Book* (551). She also transcribes the music for another performance by Geronimo—called simply "Song"—which appears to be completely in vocables (327).

The image of Geronimo that emerges from Curtis's portrayal of him certainly contrasts with the "human tiger" who had a coat covered with human scalps. Geronimo is an almost saintly holy man rather than an unreconstructed warrior, a spiritual pilgrim rather than a bloodthirsty hostile. His benignity suggests that his remaining a prisoner of war is unnecessary and

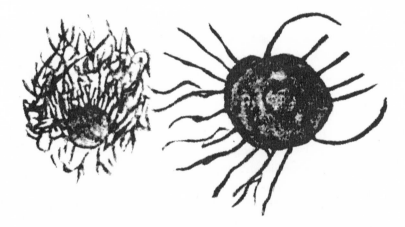

FIG. 3.3. When pioneering ethnomusicologist Natalie Curtis interviewed Geronimo at the Louisiana Purchase Exposition in Saint Louis in 1904, he made this drawing to accompany the song that she transcribed from him. *From Natalie Curtis*, The Indian's Book: An Offering by the American Indians of Indian Lore, Musical and Narrative, to Form a Record of the Songs and Legends of Their Race. *2nd ed. (New York: Harper and Brothers, 1923).*

injudicious. But aside from including the Rinehart/Muhr photograph taken at the Trans-Mississippi and International Exposition at Omaha, which shows him in Euro-American garb, Curtis does nothing to suggest that Geronimo has adopted the "white man's road" at all. It is difficult to believe that given his entrepreneurial spirit, Geronimo would have worked with Curtis without some form of monetary compensation, but she ignores this dimension of the image that he was certainly displaying at Saint Louis. Her Geronimo may no longer threaten, but he demonstrates resignation more than assimilation. Like the Indian holy men and women who continue to figure in popular lore, Geronimo, who seems to have little control of his image as shaped by Curtis, comes across as a dignified anachronism. By the time *The Indians' Book* was published in 1907, Geronimo may have realized that his case for repatriation to Arizona was hopeless, but at the time he encountered Curtis, he was still working to achieve that goal.

At least four agendas influenced Geronimo's appearance at the Louisiana Purchase Exposition in 1904: W J McGee's interest in representing the savage stage of unilinear cultural evolution with the presence of a celebrity; other fair organizers' recognition of the sensation that Geronimo's attendance at the fair would create for audiences; Natalie Curtis's assumption that Geronimo could contribute to her plans for reviving the indigenous American arts that she feared were disappearing; and Geronimo's own desires to exploit the situation for financial gain, for the experiences that attending his third world's fair would afford, and for the possibilities of manipulating his image. All of these agendas except for the last, Geronimo's own goals, were to some degree realized. One source claims that "Chief Geronimo" received a silver medal for his participation in the Louisiana Purchase Exposition (Bradford and Blume 1992, 126).

The next major stop on Geronimo's grand tour of important public venues where he could rehabilitate his image was Theodore Roosevelt's inauguration on 5 March 1905. On 2 March, the *New York Times* reported that the Inaugural Committee had appropriated up to two thousand dollars to pay the expenses of "six noted Indians" who would participate in the ceremony: Geronimo ("the old Apache chief") Quanah Parker (Comanche), Buck Skin Charlie (Ute), Little Plume (Blackfeet), American Horse (Oglala), and Hollowhorn Bear ("Sioux"). The plan at the time was for the six to appear on horseback in the inaugural parade in the company of students and a marching band from the Carlisle Institute. An earlier report (30 December 1904 in the *Sandusky [OH] Star-Journal*), probably spurious, held that Geronimo had refused to join the group "because too many curious people will stare," but given his experience at exhibitions, it is unlikely that he would shrink from such exposure. Moreover, he recognized the opportunity that the proceedings would afford him to make his case again for being returned to the Southwest.

The selection of the particular Indians who would appear officially at the inauguration may have been the responsibility of Francis E. Leupp, whom Roosevelt had appointed commissioner of Indian affairs during the term he was completing for the assassinated McKinley. In a story that appeared in the *Washington Post* on inauguration day itself, Leupp justified his choices in some detail:

> "Each of these men at one time or another, fought against the United States government; each is a thoroughly typical specimen of the old-time hostile Indian, whom civilization can never reach—whose very being seems opposed to its influence. But on the other hand, each recognizes that the only chance of the survival of the red race lies in the adoption by the younger generation of the ways of the white man. It is this latter phase in their character—their recognition of the inevitable, and their expressed willingness and anxiety to see the young men and women of their respective tribes become civilized and educated–that induced me to believe that their accompanying the 'Great Father' would be appreciated as a signal mark of favor from him, and give them prestige in their altered views with their own people."

Following the same principles that had informed the Indian exhibits at the Louisiana Purchase Exposition, Leupp reported that the six famous Indians "will march with the cadets of the Carlisle Indian school, so that the old and new Indian may be seen and contrasted by the spectator." These would be the only Native Americans allowed to participate in the parade, Leupp had told the *New York Times* on 2 March. A delegation of more than twenty had come to Washington from the Standing Rock and Rosebud Reservations at their own expense intending to march in full regalia in the parade, but Leupp forbade their involvement for fear that their appearance would turn the inauguration into a "Wild West show."

Not everyone approved of Leupp's choices, especially Geronimo. The *Post* article claimed that he still represented "the concentrated bitterness inspired by the extraordinary disasters and humiliations that have befallen his band." The paper suggested that while Geronimo commanded some respect from his community for his shamanistic powers, he was largely a laughingstock, especially for exploiting the notoriety that had recently come to him. Geronimo himself had averred, "White man damn fool on Geronimo. Geronimo no chief, no leader, no lead band on warpath—medicine man. Natchie chief; Natchie's fathers chiefs long time. Geronimo work white man." Instances of the ways in which Geronimo had been "working" the white man included his selling articles of clothing and photographs to souvenir hunters and his "Yankee graft" of a portrait painter, reportedly from New York City but more likely E. A. Burbank, a Midwesterner:

> The painter, having a fine eye for commercial advantages, learned that there was a mania in the metropolis for Geronimo souvenirs, so he went out to Fort Sill and asked the famous medicine man to sit for him, offering $2 per day. Now $2 was more money than Geronimo had received for all the sitting he had done for fifteen years, and his sittings had been long and steady, for Geronimo is a good sitter and holds that same attitude for a good sixteen hours every day, but in an unguarded moment, the artist communicated to his warlike model the profit he expected to reap in the East from the likenesses. Geronimo immediately rose and refused to pose again for less than $15 per sitting of two hours each.[11]

Meanwhile, some Chiricahuas at Fort Sill expressed concerns about Geronimo's entrepreneurship. Gossip held that the "old rascal is up to his old tricks. He's such a tourist attraction, it is disgusting. That old liar. He sells his picture, his buttons, anything—even a feather—and he lies about every item." Some also took issue with his selling crafts manufactured by others as if he had made them (Boyer and Gayton 1992, 118). His eager exploitation of the tourist meant he "had no dignity, no pride" (182). Perhaps some of the local opprobrium directed at Geronimo resulted from envy. Narcissus Duffy Gayton, who recalled family traditions relating to Geronimo from the perspective of the late twentieth century, reported the opinion of her grandmother: "He goes on all those trips to expositions where the white people think he is wonderful, and he can show off. He betrayed all of us" (Boyer and Gayton 1992, 183). A press report datelined Wichita, Kansas, which appeared in the *New York Times* for 1 January 1902, even held that Geronimo had refused to accept freedom offered by the War Department because he would lose the fifteen-dollar monthly stipend he received for services as a scout. In an article contrasting him with Naiche, the hereditary Chiricahua chief, the *Des Moines (IA) Weekly Leader* for 20 July 1901 reiterated that "Geronimo's avarice has no limitations."

Moreover, Geronimo remained devoted to vices that some believed made him an unsuitable participant in the inaugural festivities. The *Washington Post* story noted that he "is said to like whisky better than gambling when he has the whisky, and gambling better than whisky when he has the cards." His passion for gambling sometimes went to extremes. Several years prior to Geronimo's selection for the inauguration, William R. Draper reported to the *Atlanta Constitution*, "In the Indian vernacular gladness is synonymous with gambling and a great deal of the old man's money goes into the game and never comes out again." The journalist characterized Geronimo as a poor but enthusiastic card player whose favorite games were poker and monte. His "tepee" provided a frequent venue for games of chance involving not only other Indians, but soldiers from Fort Sill and Anglos from nearby ranches (1901, A3).

Another set of accusations that suggested Geronimo did not merit the public attention he had been receiving and that would be revived by his participation in the inauguration targeted his mental condition. Rumors circulated that he had become, in the words of the *Atlanta Constitution* for 27 July 1900, a "raving maniac." After rehearsing his blood-soaked career, the newspaper noted, "Geronimo was a man of brains and could plan a battle with the precision of a Napoleon. The bars of the military prison will doubtless be replaced by those of the madhouse." The *Salt Lake Herald* for the following day held, "After a long period of imprisonment, which he endured more like a ferocious wild beast than a human being, Geronimo, one of the most bloodthirsty Indians that ever figured in history, has gone stark mad." Reports of Geronimo's insanity had already been strongly denied in the *Herald* for 14 July 1900, but then that paper quoted an officer from Fort Sill who averred, "Whenever you hear rumors that Geronimo is crazy it may be set down that he is planning to fool his guards and escape. We expect him to attempt to get away at any time." Although the *New York Times* had also already printed a denial that Geronimo's mental state had deteriorated in its 25 July 1900 issue, the rumor did not immediately disappear. The *Salt Lake Herald* published an editorial on the subject in its 2 August 1900 issue, which argued that instead of trying to assimilate, Geronimo had refused to capitulate at all during the years away from Arizona: "Moody, defiant and unyielding, even with age and helplessness weighing upon him, the old savage had grown more savage until it has taken the ferocious form of madness." The editorial incidentally noted Geronimo's attendance at the Trans-Mississippi and International Exposition, "whence he escaped, wild and shrewd as ever." It concluded by noting, "There was always so much of the fiend about Geronimo that his insane ferocity may seem a second child-hood—a return to the mental state of his youth." The issue of Geronimo's mental state resurfaced in 1904, a year before he rode in the inaugural pa-rade. Then he was rumored to have lapsed into a senility that resulted in his no longer being taken seriously by other Apaches. A wire service story that appeared in various newspapers (e.g., the *Semi-Weekly Robesonian* of Lumberton, North Carolina, for 15 July 1904) reported, "The tribal relations of the Apaches have been dissolved, and they no longer look upon Geronimo as their chief. They consider him a childish old man, who is too senile to advise them."

Still another basis for excluding Geronimo from the inauguration was his reported opposition to federal Indian policy. He had, according to the *Washington Post* story for inauguration day (5 March 1905) and in contrast to what Francis Leupp had claimed for his six choices, opposed "progressive" measures, especially education—though the paper noted that his negativity might arise from the high mortality rate of Chiricahuas who had attended Carlisle.

Two years after the inauguration (24 August 1907), the *Post* reprinted a story from the *Spokane (WA) Spokesman-Review* headlined "A BAD INDIAN— Many Men in the West Would Like to Have a Shot at Geronimo," which complained about his participation in honoring Roosevelt. The *Spokesman-Review* held that vigorous objections had been made prior to the inaugura-tion but that Leupp had "pooh-poohed" them and argued that Geronimo had successfully demonstrated during incarceration his acceptance of his situa-tion. The story cataloged the body count that Geronimo had amassed dur-ing twenty-five years of hostilities in the Southwest and noted that since his surrender he had been treated more as a "pensioner" than a prisoner.

Nevertheless, Geronimo and his five counterparts did indeed lead the inaugural parade (fig. 3.4). But the persistence of the negative imagery that had dominated the press since the early 1880s and which he had not been able to overcome may explain why he failed to achieve a principal goal of his trip to Washington. Following the inauguration, Geronimo had an audience with

Roosevelt, probably along with the other five famous Indians. Geronimo made his plea to be returned to Arizona directly to the president, and interpreter George Wratten conveyed a text of that plea to journalist Norman Wood, who visited Geronimo in Fort Sill a month after he had returned from Washington. Geronimo characterized his former self as a "fool," though perhaps in a just cause: The "Great White Chief" was "my enemy and the enemy of my people. His people desired the country of my people. My heart was strong against him. I said that he should never have my country." Now, though, he claimed to have changed his attitudes and to have accepted the authority of the president: "My heart is no longer bad. I will tell my people to obey no chief but the Great White Chief. I pray you to cut the ropes and make me free. Let me die in my own country, an old man who has been punished enough and is free" (Wood 1906, 557–58). Roosevelt turned him down, citing the dangers posed to Geronimo by white people in Arizona who had "bad hearts" toward the Apaches (Wood 1906, 558). He also gave the Indians "some wholesome advice," as the *Times* put it in their 10 March issue. Although Roosevelt denied his request, Geronimo continued to sue for repatriation to Arizona. For example, when General Jesse M. Lee, commander of the Department of Texas, conducted his yearly inspection of Fort Sill only a couple of months after Geronimo's return from the inauguration festivities, the Chiricahua warrior "did not hesitate to express his discontent with Fort Sill" and requested the general influence the president on his people's behalf, adding that conditions at Fort Sill made it unhealthy (Turcheneske 1997, 93).[12]

The inauguration was apparently Geronimo's last appearance on the national stage. He continued to participate in local events, such as the intertribal "powwow" held at Comanche Quanah Parker's ranch near Fort Sill in 1904, according to the *Oakland (CA) Tribune* for 25 January of that year. Most famously, he attended a conference of the National Editorial Association held at the Miller Brothers' 101 Ranch near Ponca City, Oklahoma, in June 1905. Whether Geronimo had previously appeared in Wild West shows remains a matter of uncertainty. As L. G. Moses has argued, his prisoner-of-war status would preclude his participation in these entertainments without special arrangements such as those made for his participation at the world's fairs (1996, 158). Moses notes that when Sitting Bull joined Buffalo Bill's "Wild West" in 1885, the Oglala leader was released from being a prisoner of war. No such accommodations were apparently made for Geronimo. Yet press reports (most written before the show had occurred) and advertising by show organizers indicated Geronimo's involvement. The first show in which he may

FIG. 3.4. Geronimo, third from right, was among six "old-time" Indians who led Theodore Roosevelt's inaugural parade in 1905. To Geronimo's right are Little Plume (Blackfeet) and Buck Skin Charley (Ute). To his left are Quanah Parker (Comanche), Hollowhorn Bear (Brulé), and American Horse (Oglala). They preceded cadets and a band from the Carlisle Indian School who represented "modern" Indians. This photograph may have been taken at Carlisle on the eve of the inauguration itself. *Library of Congress Lot 12331, box 3, LC-USZ62-106790.*

have participated was organized by Frederick T. Cummins, who had supervised the Indian exhibit at the Buffalo exposition. On 19 May 1903, the *Atlanta Constitution* reported that five hundred Indians were gathering in Chicago, among them Geronimo, "the chief attraction at the Pan-American Indian congress." They were moving on to New York City, where they would be appearing in Cummins's "Indian Congress and Life on the Plains" all summer. On 18 September of that year, the *New York Times* ran a report of the program, drawing largely from a press release that held that the "famous" Geronimo was involved in the proceedings. Many years later, Frank Tripp wrote a column for the *Fresno (CA) Bee* entitled "The Old Press Agent." His installment for 8 March 1948 recalled Geronimo's involvement with Cummins at the Pan-American Exposition and apparently with the Wild West show that Cummins developed from the exposition's Indian Congress. However, historian W. S. Nye indicates that Cummins's request for Geronimo's participation in his show was denied (1942, 300).

The affair at the 101 Ranch occurred on 11 June 1905. Geronimo arrived "under guard from Fort Sill," and members of the local Ponca community appeared in ceremonial regalia. Perhaps as many as a dozen Indian ethnicities were represented at the event. A crowd of sixty-five thousand people, the largest ever to assemble up to that time in Oklahoma, observed demonstrations of horsemanship and roping skills (Collings and England [1937] 1971, 142–43). A couple of rumors fueled pre-event enthusiasm. One held that the Miller brothers were offering a thousand-dollar prize to anyone who would allow Geronimo to scalp him, and the other claimed that a herd of thirty-five animals would be slaughtered in a re-enactment of an old-time buffalo hunt. The former was easily discounted, not primarily because Chiricahuas seldom engaged in scalping, but the latter generated a public outcry. As the *New York Times* reported on 11 June 1905, environmentalist Dan Beard heard of the proposed slaughter and complained to President Roosevelt, who threatened to send troops to the 101 Ranch to prevent the killing. The threat had two effects. It limited the killing to only one buffalo and caused the Miller brothers to stage that killing a day earlier than planned. Consequently, on 10 June Geronimo led a company of twenty-five cowboys and "a band of Indians" in pursuit of an aging beast. Dr. H. F. Thomas of Chicago, who had been convalescing at the 101 Ranch following an automobile accident, fired the shot that brought the buffalo down. Geronimo, "despite his eighty years," fired twice into the prostrate beast and delivered the death blow by slitting its throat (fig. 3.5). The story of Geronimo's last buffalo hunt varied somewhat in later published versions. For example, Fred Gipson's biography of Zack Miller holds that Geronimo pursued the buffalo in an automobile. He and others believe (correctly, I think) that the famous photograph of Geronimo in a top hat behind the wheel of an automobile was taken before the hunt.[13] As Gipson described it, Geronimo took the first shot at the buffalo and failed to make a kill:

Maybe the eyes of the old Apache warrior had grown dim with age or maybe he was bothered by the plug hat that Lute Stover put on his head for a picture he took and labeled "East Meets West." It might even have been the sun glitter on the hundred or so pounds of brass the White Steamer sported along with its monstrous carriage lamps. Anyway, when they drove the old Apache out into the pasture where the buffalo grazed, he botched a standing shot. His bullet took the bull too high in the neck and a cowhand by the name of Stack Lee had to finish the job. (Gipson 1946, 230)

Norman Wood, who had visited Geronimo at Fort Sill a couple of months before his appearance at the Miller Ranch, paraphrased a letter that Lieutenant George Purington had received concerning Geronimo's participation in the event. Purington was using the letter to show the relative freedom of Geronimo's situation as prisoner of war since he was "continually going somewhere." The Miller brothers, according to Purington's letter, "propose to pay Geronimo his own price, and I am perfectly willing he should

FIG. 3.5. In 1905, a couple of months after he rode in Roosevelt's inauguration parade, Geronimo administered the death blow to a buffalo at a convention of the National Editorial Association held at the Miller Brothers' 101 Ranch near Ponca City, Oklahoma. Despite the copyright claim written on this print, the photograph may have been taken by Walter Ferguson. *Courtesy of Oklahoma Historical Society.*

go and earn something for himself. Out of the fifty or sixty thousand people expected on the ground that day, it is thought that at least ten thousand will come purposely to see Geronimo, as he is the best advertised Indian in America" (Wood 1906, 553). Wood did not indicate if he had himself witnessed Geronimo's last buffalo hunt, but he reported that Geronimo was the "most conspicuous figure" at the event and had "rushed forward and finished the animal with neatness and dispatch" after Dr. Thomas had wounded it (559).

Geronimo probably did his image more harm than good by his participation in this killing. For one thing, he embodied the stereotype of the "Indian" that predominated for the general public: a buffalo-chasing horseman. The press billed the event as Geronimo's final buffalo hunt, but very likely it was also his first buffalo hunt, since his hunting experiences in southern New Mexico and Arizona and northern Mexico would have been unlikely to bring him into contact with buffalo. Moreover, his involvement encouraged the sort of rumors about his lack of assimilation and continuance of traditional ways that those opposed to his release from captivity cherished. From the perspective of entrepreneurship, it may have contributed to the termination of his public appearances except locally.

In April 1906, a press report datelined Lawton related, "Old Geronimo, the Apache warrior and scout, today made a contract with Oscar J. Krause of Canton, Ohio, to join Major Gordon W. Lillie, or better known as Pawnee Bill's Wild West show, and become a member of that organization during the coming season." The story reported that Geronimo had received permission from the War Department to enter into the agreement and was leaving shortly to join the show accompanied by his wife, daughter, niece, and an interpreter. A story headlined "Geronimo the Grasping," which appeared in several papers (e.g., the *Anaconda [MT] Standard* for 4 April), confirmed that a deal had been struck, while also suggesting that an appearance on the Wild West circuit might be beneath Geronimo's dignity: "Once he battled with the pale faces for the land of his fathers, and was defeated with great slaughter on both sides. Now he whoops in a wild west show at so much per whoop, and sits his rearing cayuse a triumph of thrilling tragedy and transcendent thrift." Three days later the same paper reported that the Apache community at Fort Sill was unhappy that Geronimo was being allowed to assume the showman's life, while other Chiricahuas were forbidden to do so. Later that summer a couple of newspapers from eastern cities noted that Geronimo would appear as part of Pawnee Bill's "Historic Wild West and Great Far East Show." In its 10 June 1906 issue, the *New York Times* reported the imminent opening of the Pawnee Bill show at Brighton Beach. Its information about Geronimo's involvement most likely came from a press kit that was none too accurate about Geronimo's history:

> Geronimo, the Indian chief, who is said to be "very much opposed to appearing with any show," has concented [sic] nevertheless to come to Brighton Beach with Pawnee Bill. Only once before, in the Buffalo Exposition, has he been on public exhibition. This warrior is said to be over 100 years old, but he retains almost youthful vigor and activity. He was made a prisoner by Capt. Lawton, and is still technically a prisoner of war. His capture cost the United States some $2,000,000. The press agent has figured it all out.

More than two months later on 23 August, the *Washington Post* noted in advance the arrival of Pawnee Bill's show in Washington and anticipated Geronimo's participation:

> The murderous old Sioux chief, Geronimo, whose capture cost the United States more than $2,000,000, and who was chased more than 3,000 miles by nearly 2,000 government troops, under Capt. Lawton, is with the Pawnee Bill show. While Geronimo is still a prisoner of war, and will be until he is called to the happy hunting ground, Maj. Lillie succeeded in securing the permission of the government officials to take the old chief on a trip over the country with his exhibition this year.

A widely circulated poster advertised Geronimo's part in Pawnee Bill's program.

Considerable evidence suggests that Geronimo did not actually participate in the Wild West show that Lillie put together for the summer of 1906. While he might have been able to use his participation as a way to demonstrate his assimilation, most likely involvement in the Pawnee Bill spectacle would have required him to assume the guise of savagery that he needed to eschew if he ever hoped to return to the Southwest. W. S. Nye reports that the Pawnee Bill organization had been refused a request for Geronimo's participation in their exhibition as early as 1902 "on the grounds that show life was not good for the Indian because he was getting old and was bothered with rheumatism" (1942, 300), though Wild West show historian Paul Reddin indicates that Geronimo joined Pawnee Bill's show in 1904 and was billed as "The Worst Indian That Ever Lived" (1999, 153). Glenn Shirley, Lillie's biographer, stated that the request in 1906 was, in fact, turned down (1958, 165). Angie Debo categorically declares that the War Department turned down Pawnee Bill's request in 1902 for Geronimo and his company to appear in his show and notes, "The request made more publicity than the refusal, hence the frequent statement that Geronimo traveled with the show" (1976, 408). When the Pawnee Bill organization made a similar request in 1905 following Geronimo's appearance at the National Editorial Association's convention, it was also turned down, according to Debo (1976, 425). Geronimo did continue to participate in local events and made other less sensational appearances at the Miller Brothers' 101 Ranch. Debo reports on one such appearance, which she dated to 1906:

"He was sitting there. . . . They had a table with a lot of pictures of him and postcards. . . . And they had a ball and chain on him down around the ankle. . . . But then there's guards behind him with guns, too. He was sitting there and people come by. . . . He don't say a word. Just look right at them. Don't smile. Don't laugh or nothing. Somebody will come along, look at his picture, and throw down a dollar bill, maybe a five dollar bill, and he grabbed that and stick it in a pocket. Won't even give them any change back. Then the man says. Ladies and gentlemen go on by, don't bother him none." (Debo 1976, 424–25)

Blaine Kent, an "aged Iowa Indian," provided this testimony, though the reference to shackles and guards seems unlikely.

In addition to his public appearances, Geronimo was able to make a case for his successful assimilation through the series of interviews conducted by Lawton educator S. M. Barrett that resulted in the volume generally referred to as his "autobiography." Barrett had attained rapport with Geronimo by helping him to market some Indian souvenirs and through their shared enmity toward Mexicans. While the work does reveal the "progress" he had made, the circumstances of its production gave Geronimo only minimal control of how it presented his image. One of many "collaborative" autobiographies produced from interviews with Native Americans by anthropologists or journalists in the late nineteenth and early twentieth centuries, Geronimo's life story ultimately reflects choices made by the interviewer more than what the Chiricahua himself might have selected to emphasize. Not only did

Barrett have final editorial control, but he worked with Geronimo through an interpreter. In this case, the interpreter was someone who undoubtedly foregrounded Geronimo's best interests: Daklugie, the son of Geronimo's comrade-in-arms Juh. Geronimo was also Daklugie's maternal uncle, and this relationship continues to have special significance in Chiricahua culture. Moreover, Geronimo and Daklugie did control somewhat the interview agenda by limiting the focus for particular sessions to preapproved topics. Daklugie also read back to Geronimo translations of Barrett's notes and perhaps of the completed manuscript itself. Nevertheless, the final product, which reached the public in 1906, reflected mainly what Barrett (upon the approval of federal censors, purportedly including President Roosevelt) believed to be important.

The four-part autobiography begins with a version of the myth of the Chiricahua culture hero and then proceeds through other largely ethnographic topics. Geronimo dates his birth to 1829 and the massacre at Kaskiyeh to 1858. The text then focuses on hostilities between Apaches and Mexicans, particularly raids made under the leadership of Geronimo or Mangas Coloradas. Geronimo does not hesitate to note when his leadership failed and he suffered loss of face therefrom. The book's third section treats the conflict engendered by the growing presence of the United States in the Southwest and ends with Geronimo's surrender and captivity in 1886. The final portion of the volume provides overviews of such topics as Chiricahua mores and religious practices. The book devotes an entire chapter to Geronimo's attendance at the Saint Louis fair—more space than is allowed for any other event in his life. Modern historians (e.g., Debo 1976, 4–5; Sweeney 1998, 374) have generally regarded the material in Geronimo's book as reliable, though he undoubtedly mistakes most of the important dates from early in his life (probably even that of his own birth). Some other aspects of the volume, particularly the references to scalping (e.g., Barrett 1996, 82, 83, 87), which Apaches rarely did, do not ring true. The scalping references may have been added by Barrett based on his stereotypical notions of Indian behavior on the battlefield, or Geronimo and Daklugie may have been attempting to stress just how far out of savagery the assimilated Geronimo had emerged. "Conversion" narratives often stress the profundity of the transformation that an individual has undergone by exaggerating what the subject had been like before the experience (Clements 1982).

The book received widespread attention. An advertisement by its publisher in the 10 November 1906 issue of the *New York Times* billed it as one of the fall catalog's "Three Big Books—True Stories," the other two touted volumes being a biography of Molière ("a great playwright") and a memoir by George Brandes ("a great critic"). The Geronimo volume, dealing with "a great fighter," had been published under some duress according to a blurb quoted from a review in the *New York Evening World*: "About a dozen army officers and War Department men declared that these reminiscences of old Geronimo must never be printed. But Theodore Roosevelt said they should be printed, and they have been. They make a book worthy of all praise." A review appeared in the *Times* itself on 17 November 1906 and also stressed the reluctance of the military establishment to allow the volume's publication, which Barrett emphasizes probably in order to lend authenticity to what appears in the book and perhaps to create some buzz about it. The review emphasizes the "sangfroid" with which Geronimo relates military engagements, his enthusiasm for the Louisiana Purchase Exposition, and his current status as a Christian. It concludes, "His story is simple, straightforward, and interesting, and should find a large number of readers."

In his analysis of the volume, literary scholar Arnold Krupat has emphasized Barrett's "ironic" plotting of Geronimo's life history, a perspective that paralleled the "scientific" and "objective" focus of Boasian anthropology. In adopting what for him was a "sociological" perspective, Barrett did not shape Geronimo's narrative—refracted as it already was through the translation of Daklugie—to the contour of tragedy, comedy, or melodrama, argues Krupat. Instead, he used what Geronimo told him to "give the reading public an authentic reading of the private life of the Apache Indians." Krupat notes that *private* refers not so much to personal and intimate details but instead corresponds with the anthropological term *emic*, the insider's view whose representation is the goal of Boasian cultural relativism (1985, 67). Moreover, despite Geronimo's notoriety, he becomes, Krupat argues, "representative of his culture and thus more valuable for the purposes of science than he would be as an extraordinary or distinctive Apache" (64). Barrett's ethnographic (anthropological and sociological) focus accounts for the quadripartite structure of the work, in which sections that synchronically treat Chiricahua Apache culture in precontact times and in the first decade of the twentieth century frame sections that diachronically relate conflicts with Mexicans and with "White Men" (Krupat 1985, 70). Even in the historical chapters, Geronimo appears more as Apache Everyman than as a distinctive agent in the battles he recounts: "Geronimo is no more than an Indian who happened to be present at certain events, not an author of history" (70). The image of Geronimo that emerges in Krupat's estimation is neither demon nor saint, but a human (of the Apache variety) not too different from other humans. And this portrayal may have been exactly what Geronimo wanted. The book's final chapter, "Hopes for the Future"—positioned immediately after the chapter in which Geronimo praises Christianity—focuses on the narrator's desire to return with his people to their homeland: "We would . . . like to have the liberty to return to that land which is ours by divine right" (Barrett 1996, 167). And the volume poignantly ends with Geronimo's desire that his people make their way home, even if not during his lifetime (Barrett 1996, 170).

That Geronimo believed that the "autobiography" would have an impact on his chances of being returned to the Southwest finds support in his reported reaction to receiving a copy of the book after it was published. Otis Notman noted that Geronimo regarded the volume he received from Barrett to be such an accurate record of his life that he thought it could be used as evidence should someone attempt later to emend other copies of the book to impugn his reputation. In fact, he intended to ensure that his son Robert, who had grown up with his mother on the Mescalero reservation in New Mexico, received this very copy in order to guarantee that his father's image would not be undermined. Moreover, Notman indicated, "Geronimo thinks that as soon as the white men have read his book they will call him to the White House so that his story will be verified, and the white people will be obliged at last through shame to let his people return to their native land" (1907, BR62).

Despite these efforts at appearing to be assimilated, Geronimo did not return to his homeland in the Southwest, and his nostalgia for the deserts and mountains has become part of his image. In 1996 David W. Samuels heard a tape recording of a piece titled "Geronimo's Song," which had purportedly been composed by the old warrior as he pined at Fort Sill. Set off by vocables were such lines as "I'm lonely for White Mountain," "I'm lonely for the roads to Mexico," and "As water flows down from my eyes / I'm lonely for it" (2004, 92). Whether Geronimo actually created the piece is probably impossible to determine, but, as Samuels notes, it reinforces the image that he sought to cultivate during the last decade or so of his life: someone whose principal aim was to return to a homeland from which he felt an overwhelming sense of separation (93).

One fears, though, that by 1906 Geronimo realized that his attempts at projecting an image other than that of the "human tiger" were doomed to fail. His role as public performer—which began on the national level with the Trans-Mississippi and International Exposition in 1898 but which started locally soon after he surrendered in 1886 and continued through the Pan-American Exposition in 1901, the Louisiana Purchase Exposition in 1904, and the Roosevelt inauguration in 1905—had not produced a change in his status. Geronimo's autobiography ends with his assertion that Arizona was the only place on earth suited to him and his fellow Chiricahuas: "It is my land, my home, my father's land, to which I now ask to be allowed to return. I want to spend my last days there, and be buried among those mountains" (Barrett 1996, 169). An obituary for Geronimo that appeared in the 18 February 1909 edition of the Memphis *Commercial Appeal* quoted the old man as he was "near to death": "I am praying to the white man's god, who has made me a man fit for heaven, to spare my life for a few years longer—to spare it until I am freed from custody and see my people in free homes." The deity to whom Geronimo addressed this last prayer did not answer them as the old man wished, for he remained a prisoner of war until the end. Although the Chiricahua Apaches as a group also were considered prisoners of war in Oklahoma until Congress legislated their release in 1912, Geronimo's death removed a major impediment to their repatriation. However, they were not allowed to return to Arizona. Instead, those who remained—numbering 261—could either stay in Oklahoma or receive a place on the Mescalero Apache Reservation in New Mexico. Seventy-eight chose to continue to live near Fort Sill, where they received farmsteads and have endured as the Fort Sill Apache Tribe. Those who selected the New Mexico option, 183 members of the surviving community, received compensation for the property they were leaving behind and settled in mountains west of Ruidoso, New Mexico. Both groups have acknowledged a connection with Geronimo. A town near Fort Sill bears his name, and in New Mexico his descendants have actively involved themselves in concerns about the disposition of his final physical remains. One of the young women, whose coming-of-age ceremony provided the data for anthropologist Claire Farrer's study of that *rite de passage* among Chiricahuas in New Mexico, received special media attention because she was among Geronimo's descendants (2011, 11).

For Geronimo, the Chiricahuas, and many other Native peoples who had been removed from their traditional homelands, the desire to return amounted to the need to reclaim their identity. As Carter Revard has noted, Geronimo defines himself in his "autobiography" in terms of a hierarchical ranking: "cosmic through geologic to tribal, subtribal, family, and then only . . . the 'individual' self that was Geronimo" (1998, 127). As he narrated his life history to Barrett, he clearly saw that separation from his homeland meant "a change in, perhaps a loss of" his essence (Revard 1998, 128). Peoples from many Indian nations, Revard argues, shared this sense of place that was much stronger than their perception of themselves as individuals independent of social and geographical ties. A person's identity—according to what Revard calls a "wild" Indian, in contrast to "tame" Indians who defined themselves in terms of how well they had adapted to the white man's ways—was "carefully, explicitly, unmistakably linked with that of his people, with the symbolic arrangement of his village, with the marriage arrangements and hunting encampments and choosing of chiefs and war and peace ceremonies, with the animals whom he could hunt or whose feathers he could wear, the plants he would eat, the earth and sky he dwelt within" (141). Viewed in this light, Geronimo's postsurrender mission to return to the Southwest emerges as more than simply a desire to be free of the shackles (even if not really physical restraints) of prisoner-of-war status. It meant regaining the opportunity to be Goyaałé, a Bedonkohe who had been born near the headwaters of the Gila River and whose sense of self depended upon connecting with that territory. Geronimo's petitions for repatriation should not have been dismissed as peevish nostalgia on the part of an old man, but should have been regarded as his attempt to realize his true self.

As an exhibit in various venues during the last decade of his life, Geronimo the subaltern had plenty of opportunities to speak, but those to whom he addressed his message did not hear or believe it. Considerable background "noise" from the reputation that had emerged while he was leading the Apache resistance in the 1880s, from the envy and hostility of some of his own people, and from the rumors that floated out of Fort Sill drowned him out. Yet Geronimo was not merely a passive object under the touristic "gaze" of those who came to see him at fairs and exhibitions. Just as he had exercised agency by not accepting the inhospitable conditions at the San Carlos Agency, which he left in 1881, and by actively responding to implied threats at Turkey Creek on the Fort Apache Reservation, which he left in 1885, Geronimo in his last decade did not simply allow things to happen to him. He asserted himself and, though unsuccessful in achieving his ultimate goals, tried to use the system that had been imposed on him as effectively as he could.

CHAPTER 4

GERONIMO'S SPIRITUAL PILGRIMAGE

WHAT A COUP FOR THE MISSIONARIES IT WOULD HAVE BEEN! FOR THE basest of sinners—a veritable "red devil" who had raped, tortured, murdered, stolen, and generally forged a trail of terror for thirty years from the 1850s through the 1880s in Sonora and Chihuahua in northern Mexico and the U.S. territories of Arizona and New Mexico—to come to Jesus, to convert from the savage religion of his ancestors to civilized Christianity, would have redounded not only to the glory of the Christian deity but to the inspired, persuasive powers of missionaries who brought him that message. If only it was so. But not everyone was convinced that Geronimo had become a Christian, even though his conversion would benefit his post-surrender quest to adapt to Euro-American ways sufficiently to end his prisoner-of-war status and be allowed to return to his beloved homeland before he died. And if he had sincerely converted, his new identity would contribute to the Christian missionizing impulse on several levels: by showing that even the most diabolical of sinners could be saved by the grace of God, by convincing supporters of the mission effort that their contributions had yielded the richest possible results, and by proving that God had anointed the individuals who had engineered Geronimo's conversion in an especially powerful way.

Indeed, when Geronimo and his small band of warriors, women, and children surrendered to General Miles at Skeleton Canyon, few (at least of those who had access to a printing press) doubted that he was about as degenerate a human being as could be found anywhere or anytime. A drunkard who could not keep from using the mild intoxicant tiswin to excess and an inveterate gambler, he had most recently led the U.S. Army on a chase for some fifteen months during which he had committed or suborned atrocities beyond the ken of normal humanity. As noted in chapter 2, these atrocities formed a primary theme in stories about Geronimo that circulated in print and orally. A story from soon after his "breakout" from the Fort Apache Reservation in Arizona Territory on 15 May 1885, in an apparent protest of Euro-American civilization's scruples about such obvious peccadilloes as drinking, gambling, and wife-beating, had Geronimo (or perhaps some band of savages under his sway) committing acts of brutality that challenged even the lurid imaginations of the reporters who conveyed them to various news media outlets. In successive editions (30 May and 31 May 1885) the *New York Times*, for example, dwelt on atrocities committed by the Apaches who had left the reservation with Geronimo. One account held that after shooting a Mexican, the "Marauding Indians" had taken his two-year-old child by the feet and struck its head against the wall of a house. Even more shocking was their treatment of the Phillips family, whose bodies had been mutilated in particularly horrifying ways. Could a person such as Geronimo, who had committed or at least encouraged such acts, actually transform himself sufficiently to become a Christian?

Yet Geronimo was undoubtedly a man of faith. In addition to the force of his personality and his daring on the battlefield, he commanded respect from fellow Chiricahuas because of his shamanistic powers, including invulnerability to weapons, clairvoyance, and ability to heal. Geronimo's first experience with spiritual power occurred soon after the massacre of his mother, wife, and children at Kaskiyeh. Devastated by these losses, which would influence his unyielding hatred of Mexicans, Geronimo experienced his epiphany in the traditional Chiricahua manner, not by actively seeking contact with the most fundamental force in the cosmos through a vision quest but suddenly and without conscious involvement. As Sam Haozous told Angie Debo, Geronimo encountered power when he heard his name, "Goyaałé," repeated four times, the pattern number in Apache culture. Then he heard, "No gun can ever kill you. I will take the bullets from the guns of the Mexicans, so they will have nothing but powder. And I will guide your arrows" (Debo 1976, 38).[1] Other ways in which shamanic power manifested itself for Geronimo came later. Throughout his life, his contact with that power was reaffirmed, and many of his contemporaries recalled instances when he had been able to use spiritual power to his and his community's advantage (37–38). Geronimo believed in the invulnerability granted to him by this power and could cite many instances when he had escaped death in tense and seemingly hopeless situations.

The earliest recorded use that Geronimo made of sacred power occurred when his sister, married to the Nednhi chief Juh, gave birth to Daklugie. Labor was not going well, and the mother was on the verge of death. Daklugie, who had remained a close associate of his maternal uncle until his death, told oral historian Eve Ball what he had heard of the situation:

> Geronimo thought that she was going to die; he had done all he could for her, and was so distressed that he climbed high up the mountain behind Fort Bowie to plead with Ussen for his sister's life. As Geronimo stood with arms and eyes upraised, as our people do, Ussen spoke. Geronimo heard His voice clearly, as distinctly as if on a telephone. Ussen told Geronimo that his sister was to live, and he promised my uncle that he would never be killed but would live to a ripe old age and would die a natural death. (Ball 1980, 13)

One of Morris Edward Opler's Chiricahua consultants, interviewed in the early 1930s and looking back on his community's precontact culture, recalled witnessing a healing ceremony conducted by Geronimo. The patient was an elderly man suffering from coyote sickness, for which Geronimo knew the healing protocol. The ceremony lasted four nights, during which Opler's consultant was allowed to observe as long as he made no noise and did not scratch himself. Geronimo was also able to cure ghost sickness (Opler 1996, 40–41).[2]

Moreover, Geronimo had what Angie Debo calls a "mysterious ability" to determine what was occurring somewhere else (Debo 1976, 170–71). Jason Betzinez recalled an example of his use of this ability: "We were sitting there eating. Geronimo was sitting next to me with a knife in one hand and a chunk of beef which I had cooked for him in the other. All at once he dropped the knife, saying, 'Men, our people whom we left at our base camp are now in the hands of the U.S. troops! What shall we do?'" ([1959] 1987, 113). His clairvoyance also included the ability to foresee the future, at least to some degree. Daklugie, who translated for Geronimo when S. M. Barrett was conducting the interviews that became Geronimo's autobiography, told Ball that his knowledge of Geronimo's having this ability helped "keep us out of trouble" during the interview sessions (1980, 173). According to one of Opler's consultants, Geronimo's clairvoyance brought him political status in the community: "He foresaw the results of the fighting, and they used him so much in the campaigns that he came to be depended upon" (1996, 200). Geronimo was convinced that shamanic power ensured his own invulnerability in battle and told George Wratten, "Ussen has said that I am not to be killed in battle, but am to live to be old. Long ago He told the Medicine Man so. Many times I have been wounded but I live. I am not to be killed. You will see" (Ball 1970, 199). Recently, two historians have asserted, without documentation, that Apaches believe that Geronimo was able to use spiritual power to cause a devastating rainstorm on 11 July 1878, which took the lives of two U.S. Army officers at Fort Supply: "The heavens responded to his wish for the destruction of Camp Supply with a devastating rain meant to do away with this encampment, which was blocking Geronimo's pathway between Mexico and his tribal homeland" (Hudson and Wood 2005, 7). One of Opler's consultants as well as other sources reported probably the most dramatic manifestation of Geronimo's access to sacred power: his postponing sunrise so that he and his band might reach safety from pursuit while nocturnal darkness cloaked their whereabouts ([1941] 1996, 216; see chapter 2).

Geronimo remained a healer even throughout his prisoner-of-war days. A frequently reprinted report (e.g., Draper 1901) recounted how at Fort Sill he had countermanded the government physician's recommendations for treating a boil on the neck of his daughter Eva by arguing that it should be opened. "While the doctors were not watching," the report stated, "the old warrior took out his jackknife and opened the sore." The results of his applying his medical knowledge were Geronimo's confinement in the guardhouse for three days and Eva's recovery. "Among the Apaches Geronimo is called an excellent doctor and they will have no other," the reporter concluded.

Geronimo was thus already interested in and committed to spirituality when he was first exposed to the white man's religion. The earliest inklings of Geronimo's interest in Christianity appeared during the seven years he spent as a prisoner of war at Mount Vernon Barracks, Alabama. Immediately after his surrender to Miles in September 1886, Geronimo and his band had been shipped out of Arizona Territory by train. After a layover of several weeks at Fort Sam Houston in San Antonio, Texas, while federal authorities all the way up to President Cleveland were deciding what to with them, the

Chiricahua warriors boarded a train that took their families to Fort Marion in Saint Augustine, Florida, and the men themselves to Fort Pickens on Santa Rosa Island off the coast of Pensacola. Here Geronimo remained until May 1888, when the Chiricahuas were reunited at Mount Vernon Barracks, some thirty miles north of Mobile and seventy-five or so miles from Pensacola. For the next several years, the Chiricahuas lived as a community, albeit one beset by mosquitoes, unaccustomed humidity, diseases of development such as tuberculosis, and perpetual yearning to return to the Southwest.

In 1888 the Massachusetts Indian Association and the Boston Indian Citizenship Committee, both local branches of the Women's National Indian Association (WNIA), established a mission school at Mount Vernon Barracks. The original teachers were Marion E. Stephens for people over twenty years of age and Vincentine Tilyon Booth for children. Sophie Shepard replaced Booth the following year (Davis 1999, 257–58). Geronimo availed himself of the instruction offered for adults. In a letter to the *Southern Workman*, the magazine published by the Hampton Institute, founded to educate freedmen after the Civil War and also one of the boarding schools to which Indians (though apparently none of the Chiricahuas) were sent, Stephens described Geronimo's involvement in her missionizing work. Upon her return for a second year in the autumn of 1889, "Geronimo was the first to come and see me," she wrote. His purpose, she ascertained, was to introduce "his latest squaw and princess, nine days old, with a blooming ring-worm on her right cheek. He wanted some of my 'good medicine' for it." These were apparently Geronimo's sixth wife, Zi-yeh, and their daughter Eva. Stephens reported that Geronimo was present when she opened school for the first time that season and attended the services with four other "chiefs": "Chatto, K-i-a-te-na, Nai-che, Zie-le" (Folsom 1889).

Moreover, Geronimo took an active interest in the instructional program for Apache children, and one chronicler cast him as "head usher" on the occasion of the school's opening ceremony (Wood 1906, 550). Sophie Shepard, the second teacher for that segment of the population, reported that she depended upon him to ensure attendance and enforce discipline. The schoolroom was outfitted with several chairs, "one of them . . . especially set aside for Jeronimo." She noted,

There he sat in savage majesty and scowled at all bad boys and girls. I think seriously of rewarding his services after the old Greek fashion—not by a laurel wreath exactly, but by a red sash to be tied over one shoulder and under the opposite arm. If the [Boston Indian

Citizenship] committee would add some sort of a medal containing thanks for his efforts in behalf of the children, I believe we should have him for life. (Shepard 1890a, 37)

Shepard hoped she would ultimately be able to have her charges march around a Christmas tree singing "Onward Christian Soldiers" and mused, "Would it not be an idea to let Jeronimo lead them with the banner?" (38). Neither she nor Marion Stephens, though, reported anything concrete regarding Geronimo's interest in Christianity, which they were teaching along with reading and writing.

In its 12 November 1889 issue, the *New York Times* reported on the seventh annual meeting of the New-York Indian Association, another local branch of the WNIA that was "interested in the work of bringing the red men to a higher state of civilization and advancing the cause of Christianity among them." As part of the evidence that the $1,135.91 they had raised during the previous year was being put to good use, the meeting, "largely attended by ladies," learned that "the old Apache chief Geronimo, one of the most bloodthirsty and treacherous Indians of the present age, had embraced Christianity, had thrown aside the scalping knife, and was actively engaged in Sunday school work among his fellow red men." While these claims were considerably more extravagant than what Stephens or Shepard had described, they demonstrate Geronimo's exposure to Christian teachings. A couple of months later (28 January 1890) the same newspaper quoted General George Crook, Geronimo's most relentless adversary in the Southwest who was still unfavorably disposed toward him, as indicating that the Apache was now a "heap good Injun": "He is teaching a Sunday school class and, as I understand, has lost all hatred of the white people." Crook had visited Mount Vernon Barracks in January 1890. The *Pensacola (FL) Daily News* for 27 July 1890 reported that Geronimo's wife and daughter had been baptized at Saint Thomas Church by Father Henry O'Grady, while Geronimo "knelt and watched attentively." An informant noted, "He seemed to appreciate every word that was uttered" (Skinner 1987, 295; see also Stockel 2004, 76). In its edition for 4 April 1891, the *Mobile (AL) Register* confirmed that Geronimo had become a Sunday School teacher but retracted the story on 19 April, holding that "Geronimo indignantly denies that he is such a milk and water warrior as to sing psalms for a living" (Skinner 1987, 310). The retraction was too late for the *Atlanta Constitution*, which reported in its 13 April edition that Geronimo was teaching Sunday School. Major William H. Eckels, citing

Crook as his authority, reported how Geronimo had connected the story of Samson and the Philistines to his audience's experience. Using a blackboard, Geronimo had drawn the Philistines as U.S. soldiers, "a badly frightened and panic-stricken crowd" who "were fleeing for their lives." Samson appeared as an Apache warrior "with his war-paint on, his hair stuck full of eagle feathers, his belt fringed with scalps, and a tomahawk brandished aloft." Eckles reported that "this was an eminently satisfactory representation, so far as that audience was concerned, and grunts of approval rewarded Geronimo for his work." The inaccuracy in Geronimo's alleged depiction of an Apache warrior, who would not have adorned his person with eagle feathers and certainly not with scalps, suggests that his Sunday School teaching may have been more a product of wishful thinking than of anything actually observed by Crook. Undoubtedly in jest, the Prescott, Arizona, *Hoof and Horn* for 11 July 1889 even reported that Geronimo had applied his musical talents to Christian worship exercises: "Geronimo, the Apache raider, bobs up as a leader in the Sunday school of the post where he is imprisoned in Florida [*sic*]. Not only that, but he has learned to play the organ, and those who have heard him declare that he makes it an instrument of torture not inferior to the scalping knife."

Certainly Geronimo's opportunities for exposure to Christianity at Mount Vernon Barracks were extensive. In addition to Mass at Saint Thomas Church (which had been built in 1890), the weekly lessons provided by Marion Stephens, and Sophie Shepard's classroom, he could have gone to Protestant services offered by the post chaplain, W. H. Pearson, who reported that the Sabbath school was "largely attended" (Stockel 2004, 75). However, Pearson could not report a single conversion, a lacuna that—given the tendency of many who missionized to Indians to overstate their successes—seems to contradict reports of Geronimo's adopting Christianity at this point in his life.

However, we should not be surprised at Geronimo's interest in Christianity and, in fact, his integration of some of its teachings into his own system of belief and ritual. But reports in the late 1880s and 1890s, even from such an authority as Crook, of his conversion were probably exaggerations influenced by a desire to show that missionary activities among the Chiricahuas had enough successes to demonstrate their worth. For the next few years of his life, during which he and his people were moved to Fort Sill, little or nothing about Geronimo's religious convictions made its way into the popular consciousness. But as he began to re-emerge into the public eye following his appearance at the Trans-Mississippi and International Exposition in Omaha during the summer of 1898, and as he began to shape a public persona that he hoped would eventuate in his being released from prisoner-of-war status and allowed to return to the Southwest, interest in Geronimo's religious situation blossomed.

Missionary work at Fort Sill had begun in 1895, when the Dutch Reformed Church sent Frank Hall Wright, a Choctaw, to the installation. Though forbidden at the outset to interact with the newly arrived Apaches, eventually Wright, assisted by Dr. Walter C. Roe, established a school on site. In 1899 Maud Adkisson took over duties as teacher in charge of instructing some sixty Chiricahua children, who would no longer have to attend the boarding school at Chilocco in northern Oklahoma. Worship services drew both children and adults, and several of the latter—including Naiche, son of Cochise and now the Chiricahua chief, and Chatto, who had joined Crook's scouts in 1885 to assist in pursuing Geronimo and his band into Mexico's Sierra Madre—converted to Christianity (Debo 1976, 428–31). However, Geronimo himself, while endorsing the missionaries' efforts in general, reportedly expressed a lack of interest in becoming involved in Christianity: "I, Geronimo, and these others are too old to travel your Jesus road. But our children are young and I and my brothers will be glad to have the children taught about the white man's God" (Debo 1976, 428). Shortly thereafter he apparently changed his mind.

Though some press reports had him a Christian as early as 1901 (see, for instance, the *Indiana [PA] Democrat* for 14 August of that year), Geronimo's own "conversion" apparently occurred in July 1903, when, after suffering serious injuries in a riding accident, he attended a camp meeting and professed his acceptance of the Christian faith. He was baptized in Medicine Bluff Creek by Roe and clearly identified himself as a Christian when S. M. Barrett interviewed him in 1905–1906 (Barrett 1996, 166). According to Narcissus Duffy Gayton, whose family traditions generally denigrated Geronimo, "In July 1903 the meeting was held in an oak grove on Medicine Bluff Creek. It was then that an injured and contrite-appearing Geronimo, who had recently fallen from a horse, declared himself willing to find Jesus. Within a week he was baptized" (Boyer and Gayton 1992, 122). His conversion generated considerable interest in the press, which began eagerly to report news of the event, though details were often inconsistent. A wire service story that appeared in newspapers throughout the nation, including the Perry, Iowa, *Daily Chief*, which ran it several months after the event on 10 January 1904, recounted,

Bent by the trials of many a chase, cowed into submission by the strong arm of the United States government, Geronimo, chief of the Apaches, has at last yielded himself to a better life and has embraced Christianity. A few weeks ago, says a Fort Sill (I. T.) report of recent date, the old warrior, whose name 25 years ago sent a chill through the veins of almost every white person inhabiting the southwestern part of the United States, acknowledged publicly his faith in Jesus Christ, and the afternoon of the same day in the quiet waters of Medicine creek, near where his conversion occurred, he was baptized by sprinkling and received into the Reformed church. Several of his tribesmen followed his example, and the same day became members of the church with their former chieftain.

The *New York Times* for 22 July 1903 cited Deputy Sheriff F. C. Carter of Lawton, the city nearest Fort Sill, as its authority for reporting that Geronimo had become a Methodist instead of a communicant of the Dutch Reformed Church. The cause of "a sensation" among other Indians in Indian Territory, Geronimo's devotion to Christianity was evident in his being an "enthusiastic worshipper" who was "said to have made a public confession of his many bloody deeds," the *Times* averred. The *Atlanta Constitution* at first accepted Geronimo's conversion as a legitimate religious experience. In its 27 July 1903 edition it reported his joining the Methodist Church and suggested that he might get "'the power' at a love-feast." The paper speculated in its 22 August 1903 issue, "If, in his new-found religious zeal, Convert Geronimo should forget and give a full-lunged Apache war-whoop for an 'amen,' such vigorous punctuation would but add to the enthusiasm of a good old-fashioned protracted meeting." Moreover, Geronimo "has issued a proclamation to his people urging them to give up dancing and other worldly amusements and repent of their sins." Three years later, the *Times* (13 May 1906) cast Geronimo in a homilist's role. Using Psalm 23 as his text, "the old warrior spoke from a stump in a cluster of elm trees on the bank of the Medicine River. . . . When he had finished, tears dropped from his old face, and half his congregation gave evidence of a penitent mood." Geronimo concluded his sermon with a prayer for President Roosevelt.

The most authoritative source regarding Geronimo's acceptance of Christianity is the report filed by the Reverend J. T. Bergen, who visited Fort Sill sometime in late 1902 and identified the Reverend Frank H. Wright of the Fort Sill Mission of the Reformed Church of America as Geronimo's spiritual mentor. Bergen himself witnessed the warrior's epiphanic experience, which occurred after Wright had spent a Sunday afternoon consulting with him. At evening services Wright issued a special appeal to his listeners that convinced several to come forward and reconfirm their faith or make a commitment to Christianity. While the congregation was singing the invitation hymn "Jesus Is Tenderly Calling," Geronimo "came out": "Leaping to his feet, he fairly rushed to where we stood, clasped us by the hands, then turned to his people and held his finger up toward heaven, striking his breast with the other hand" (Stockel 2004, 123). Thus began the process of Geronimo's acceptance of Christianity as a way of making sense of the world where he now found himself. Bergen reported how he had counseled the old man following this public demonstration of interest in the "Jesus road." Geronimo requested "that the Christian people of America might pray for him": "He says that his heart is good toward the white people. Many of them who are in the Jesus road have told him that they love him, and he loves them. He says that his heart is good toward Jesus, that he wants to be in the Jesus road" (Stockel 2004, 123). However, Bergen noted, Geronimo required the ministrations of both Wright and other Apache converts if he was to make a final commitment to Christianity: "He is a weak character because of his sinful life, and since that meeting has given evidence that the power of sin over him is not yet broken" (Stockel 2004, 123). The efforts of the Christians apparently bore fruit at the camp meeting in October 1903 when Geronimo was baptized. He was suffering pain from injuries incurred from his riding accident, but Wright did not doubt the sincerity of his commitment. Geronimo "made a most impressive statement of his earnestness in the step which he took. He professed his faith in Christ and determination to follow Him." He asked for the prayers of his fellow Christians: "You must help me. Pray for me. You may hear of my doing wrong, but my heart is right" (Stockel 2004, 124). Drawing upon the recollections of Maud Adkisson, who had been teaching Apache children at Fort Sill since 1899 and who witnessed the event, Elizabeth M. Page confirms this account (1915, 142–47), adding her belief that Geronimo was sincere in making his commitment to the Jesus road. She recognized that he faced many temptations thereafter due to habits developed over a long life: "It is small wonder that his progress was that of a man who continually falls yet continually rises and struggles on." Acknowledging that Geronimo died several years later from the effects of a drunken spree, Page asserted, "Yet he tried, he honestly tried, and who are we to judge him" (147).

Many contemporaries, though, believed that Geronimo's acceptance of Christianity was opportunistic, and doubts about the legitimacy of his conversion figured in press reports for the rest of his life. On 10 July 1907 the *Atlanta Constitution*, which four years earlier reported that he had experienced a true epiphany, asserted that Geronimo had recently joined the Dutch Reformed Church (not the Methodists as earlier claimed) "in hopes, it is believed, of obtaining a pardon" from Roosevelt, himself a Dutch Reformed communicant. The same day's edition of the *New York Times* explicitly stated that Geronimo "had joined the Dutch Reformed Church, because the great pale face father in Washington belongs to that persuasion." The *Constitution* dismissively noted in its 12 July 1907 edition, "Geronimo 'got religion' to please Roosevelt. The old faith-fakir!" Actually Geronimo's affiliation with the Dutch Reformed communion depended in large part on the denominational choices available to him at Fort Sill. That he became a coreligionist with the president was a serendipitous outcome of who happened to be missionizing there.

Meanwhile, the press reported that the temptations of Geronimo's old way of life, particularly drinking and gambling, eroded whatever genuine commitment to Christianity he might have had. A story in the *New York Times* for 9 July 1907 has him escaping from a gathering at Cache, a small community west of Fort Sill. This was supposedly the latest in a series of infractions against the terms of his confinement and the strictures of his new religion: "Geronimo recently joined the Dutch Reformed Church, to which President Roosevelt belongs, in the hope of obtaining a pardon. Family troubles, however, interfered. His eighth wife left him and he drank liquor to excess and lay out on the reservation all night. This incensed the church-going people." Perhaps his failure to conform to the behavioral code prescribed by the Reformed Church or the Methodists explained why some believed he still needed Christianizing even to the end of his life. Father Isador Ricklin claimed to have baptized Geronimo into Roman Catholicism shortly before his death. Father Albert Braun, who missionized on the Mescalero Apache Reservation in New Mexico in 1916, a couple of years after some Chiricahuas had moved there from Oklahoma, reported Ricklin's story: "He had heard that his old friend was failing, so he went to visit him. In Geronimo's own language Father Ricklin asked, 'Have all the horses been branded?' Geronimo told him they had. Father Ricklin then asked Geronimo if he wanted to be branded a child of Jesus. Geronimo said that he did, and Father Ricklin baptized him then" (Emerson 1973, 28).[3] Another account, which seems based more on the author's fancy than on research into the matter, has Geronimo offered a final chance at Christian salvation as he lies dying: "Two young Apaches appeared to him in a vision, asking him to once and for all break with the past and accept Christianity. Geronimo had struggled for years with the ways of the missionaries. He answered it was too late for him, and that he could not abandon the old ways" (Bradford and Blume 1992, 227).

Still more evidence against his having converted to Christianity earlier included reports of his continuing to use the power he had received from Usen during the last decade of his life—and in ways other than for healing. A story from Fort Sill, published in the *Des Moines Weekly Leader* for 20 June 1901, reported that though his fellow prisoners of war no longer held him in high regard, they feared his divinely granted power: "If he doesn't like one and wants to do him an injury Geronimo can cause one of his mules to die or may be [*sic*] a member of his family. Geronimo can make it rain and do other wonderful things." Moreover, rumors persisted at Fort Sill that Geronimo's long life was partially attributable to his use of spiritual power to deflect fatal forces from himself and onto family members, most of whom—even his grandchildren—he outlived (Debo 1976, 435, 437). Narcissus Duffy Gayton reported having heard that as Geronimo aged, he used his shamanic power to divert death to others: "Not just infants were dying in his family, not just the infirm, but strong adults, young people in their prime!" Geronimo, according to Gayton, even organized a ceremony to exonerate himself from accusations that he was witching other people, but that ritual concluded with a clear articulation of his guilt: "It was you, Geronimo. *You* did it! You did it to save your own life!" (Boyer and Gayton 1992, 183).

The trajectory of Geronimo's spiritual development was clearly not a smoothly linear progression from savage heathenism to enlightened Christianity. In fact, his biographer Angie Debo suggests that his last years were marked with spiritual conflict and that he was plagued by a "collision between his two life philosophies" (1976, 438). But Geronimo's own testimony does not necessarily suggest such conflict. In the interviews with Barrett, Geronimo pointed out congruences between Christianity and Apache spirituality, especially regarding life after death, which he admitted was difficult to understand (1996, 163). He also pointed out that even though he recognized the superiority of the "white man's religion" to "the religion of my fathers," he had always been prayerful and believed that "the Almighty" had protected him even during his days in the Southwest (165). He told Barrett that he had converted to Christianity and was "not ashamed to be a Christian." He derived particular pleasure from sharing President Roosevelt's religious views and urged his fellow Apaches to consider Christianity for themselves (166). This testimony does not necessarily mean that Geronimo assumed that the Jesus road was the only route to finding meaning for one's life—especially since he claimed divine protection throughout his own life—but it does suggest that Christianity might have been the most appropriate spiritual alternative given the situation in which he and his fellow Chiricahuas found themselves. A perspective that allowed one to accept Christianity without necessarily refuting traditional religion was not unusual among Native Americans from many societies who became Christians, nor was the issue of whether Geronimo's acceptance of the Euro-American religion genuine and sincere one that would have necessarily occurred to him. Most likely, Geronimo's perception of the meaning of religious commitment did not include the exclusivity that characterizes mainstream Christianity. Instead, we might think of his view of religion in the terms or the philosophy of pragmatism: if a religion had "cash value"—that is, if it provided a meaningful and productive plan for life—then it was worth considering. Note that William James's use of "cash value" did not simply refer to the expediency of an idea, but to whether it afforded a meaningful view of existence for an individual (2000, 87–104). Geronimo may have assumed that his mission to project an image of assimilation would benefit from his becoming Christian, but he probably also realized that given his current situation, Christianity was the most reasonable strategy for making sense out of his universe. Yet accepting its teachings did not necessarily mean that one had to reject other religions. The Christian deity and Usen both offered valid solutions to the problems that life might present. If those problems occurred within the context of living as a prisoner of war on a reservation dominated by Christians, then it made sense to accept the truth of those teachings—a truth that might not have as much to offer if one were living the traditional way of life in the Sierra Madre. Hence, the question of the "sincerity" of Geronimo's conversion has little relevance.

In this respect, Geronimo's spirituality resembles that of many other Native Americans who encountered Christianity throughout the continent, including his own Southwestern homeland. One case that has received considerable attention from scholars of religion has been that of the Oglala Lakota shaman Nicholas Black Elk, who became a leading Catholic on the Pine Ridge Reservation during the first third of the twentieth century. Black Elk, though removed from Geronimo in cultural background and theological sophistication, nevertheless affords a good illustration of how an American

Indian person of faith might accept seemingly competing worldviews without necessarily being insincere in his or her commitment to either. A catechist whose picture with rosary in hand appeared on the cover of Catholic publications, Black Elk also became the authoritative source for information on several traditional Lakota rituals. Neither John G. Neihardt, who introduced Black Elk to the world in general through the interviews that form the basis of *Black Elk Speaks*, nor Joseph E. Brown, who recorded Black Elk's description of Lakota ceremonialism, suggested that he had abandoned his faith in the old-time religion. Nor is there any reason that they should have, for Black Elk may very well have had no problem in accepting both the teachings of Christianity and the spirituality he had learned and experienced within the traditional Lakota context. But considerable discussion of Black Elk's religious perspective in terms of a choice between traditional Lakota practice and Christianity emerged during the last quarter of the twentieth century. However, Clyde Holler suggests that thinking of Black Elk's religion as involving a choice represents ethnocentric compartmentalization: "The real Black Elk was not either a traditionalist or a Catholic; he was both at the same time." In terms that might be applied to Geronimo's acceptance of Christianity in 1903, Holler continues, "His conversion was not conversion as understood by the Jesuits . . . [,] the substitution of one religion for another" (1995, 22). Black Elk regarded traditional Lakota belief, Christianity, and the Ghost Dance religion that he had advocated in his youth as "expressions of the same sacred reality" (36). That perception—at least regarding the first two religious systems—provides the argument, according to Holler, behind the book that Joseph E. Brown produced from his interviews with Black Elk. *The Sacred Pipe* suggests that "traditional religion and Catholicism are both valid expressions of ultimate truth" (140). To understand Black Elk's complex religious thought, one must go beyond the assumption of an "either/or" perspective on religious commitment to one that recognizes the potentials of a "both/and" vision (182). Black Elk even moved beyond "dual participation" and syncretism to define a spiritual journey that involved recognition of consistencies in two, supposedly opposed, belief systems.

To attribute Black Elk's theological sophistication to Geronimo credits the latter with a philosophical bent that he does not appear to have developed. But if Black Elk (and, in fact, many other American Indians) could genuinely commit to two religious traditions simultaneously, Geronimo could also have done so. The concept of "dual participation" may actually be more workable in his case, for he seems to have chosen Christianity, possibly viewed as the white man's "tribal religion," when he needed sacred power to deal with modern life and to have turned to Usen for healing and for conducting rituals such as the girls' puberty ceremony, the most important corporate worship activity in Chiricahua life, as well as for other traditional concerns. If the ultimate purpose of religion is to provide some sort of cosmic meaning for existence, both Christianity and traditional religion seem to have worked for Geronimo, though—unlike for Black Elk—in different situations. We cannot know the "sincerity" of Geronimo's turn to Christianity; perhaps he did not know it himself. But the pragmatic results (in the Jamesian sense) that such a turn might have in helping him fit more suitably into the white man's world does not necessarily negate his sincerity. Nor does his inability to forego life-long behaviors that Christianity regarded as sinful.

Geronimo most likely believed that the Jesus road was grounded in a spiritual reality that was just as valid as the spirituality associated with Usen. Moreover, it had the advantage of offering an approach to existence and a way of viewing the world that would accomplish what became the goal of his life: convincing military and civilian establishments that he had abandoned his old way of thinking and behaving and could be safely repatriated to Arizona for the remainder of his life. On 13 October 1907 the *Daily Oklahoman* in Oklahoma City ran a story that purportedly quoted Geronimo's perception of the transformation in his worldview: "Geronimo has religion now. The blood of the men whom me, big chief, kill is before me. Geronimo is sorry. But the big God—Him who is friend of the white man and Indian—He forgive." In the "Red English" that the report attributes to him, he pleads with someone to write a letter to authorities in Washington arguing his case: "Say to him: Geronimo got religion now. Geronimo fight no more. The old times he forget. Geronimo want to be prisoner of war no more. He want free. Tell the great white father that—tell him in the paper" (Stockel 2004, 131). Rawdon Tomlinson, who has written a sequence of poems about Geronimo's career, suggests in "The Jesus Road" that Geronimo's commitment to Christianity was "more like hedging bets than conversion." In fact, the poem's speaker notes that Geronimo "needed their god more than they did" (2007, 66). Need drove Geronimo to Christianity, but not necessarily need for spiritual salvation. He needed to understand and use a worldview that would help him to make sense of and manipulate the environment into which surrender had thrust him.

Yet despite his realization that following Christianity might help him to make sense of his current situation and contribute to his goal of being repatriated, Geronimo seemed unable to follow the religion's code of conduct as strictly as was desired. When he died in February 1909, several obituaries reported that he had fallen from grace on a number of occasions due to the temptations of gambling and strong drink and had, in fact, been "excommunicated." His death was attributed to a severe case of pneumonia that he had caught while lying out all night after falling from his horse while returning home from a round of drinking. Probably even if he had rigorously adhered to the prescriptions and proscriptions of the Christian life, Geronimo would have never made it back to the Southwest. Some opponents of his repatriation feared that his presence there would serve as a rallying point for another outbreak of Apache resistance to U.S. control. And with some degree of validity, others feared that he would be a target for white vigilantes in Arizona and New Mexico who held him responsible for atrocities committed almost a quarter century earlier.

In any event, Geronimo's turn toward Christianity did not produce all the results that he might have wished, though perhaps it did help him to adapt to life at Fort Sill. He was buried under the auspices of the new religion. At his funeral, though, the speakers—both the Reverend L. L. Legbers and Naiche (the hereditary Chiricahua chief who seems to have committed himself unequivocally to Christianity)—used him as a negative example. The *New York Times* reported the mortuary ritual by noting, "Geronimo died in the old faith, the religion of his forefathers, which knew no white man's God. The sun was his conception of Deity. Four years ago, when Geronimo feared that the injuries received in a fall from his horse would prove fatal, he joined the Reformed Church. He was suspended from the Church two years later, however, because of excessive drinking, gambling, and other infractions of Church rules." Geronimo's spiritual pilgrimage was not a straight and narrow path. It began with his unsolicited reception of holy power from Usen and ended with his suspension from the Christian church whose teachings he had added to his spiritual inventory. Though his monument distinguishes his grave from others in the Apache cemetery at Fort Sill, he is buried among Christians such as Naiche as well as individuals from his old life such as Nana, who never made a profession of faith in the new religion as Geronimo had done.

Even into the twenty-first century the issue of Geronimo's religious convictions remains open. Faith-based websites endorse a variety of perspectives: that his conversion to Christianity was legitimate ("Geronimo" 2007), that he was guilty of backsliding after his conversion but reconciled with the Methodist Church before his death ("Baptism of Indian Warrior Geronimo"

2009), or that, unlike his comrade Naiche, he altogether rejected Christian teachings ("An Apache Chief" 2009). A recent article in *Wild West* magazine considers various possibilities regarding his conversion without endorsing any of them (Banks 2009), but its publication a century after his death suggests continuing interest in Geronimo's religious condition. Of course, the sincerity of his faith cannot be conclusively measured, but to suggest that his commitment to Christianity emerged purely out of his desire to be repatriated back to Arizona as a "good" Indian underestimates Geronimo's adaptability and his probable recognition that the white man's religion worked more effectively to create meaning in the white man's world than the old-time Apache system of belief.

CHAPTER 5

THE FACE OF GERONIMO

As a language, Garbo's singularity was of the order of the concept,
that of Audrey Hepburn is of the order of the substance.
                                           —Roland Barthes, *Mythologies*

IF GRETA GARBO'S FACE IS IDEA AND AUDREY HEPBURN'S IS EVENT, AS
Roland Barthes suggests, then Geronimo's is both idea and event. In the Euro-
American mind—certainly in the late nineteenth century and well into the
twentieth—that face represented the quintessence of recalcitrant savagism,
the most adamant and frustratingly final obstacle to civilization's progress.
When nightmares of the ignoble savage haunted the Euro-American coloniz-
ing unconscious and when the image of such ignobility graced the discourse of
Manifest Destiny, Geronimo gave a face to savagism, one of the most important components of the American myth. Even now, when revisionists have
thought again about who was victim and who was victimizer during the centuries when European, then Euro-American hegemony spread across North
America, Geronimo's face captures what it meant to be the antithesis of that
expansion. As Philip J. Deloria has noted, "If you had to pick a single person to stand for *Indianness*, you could do worse than Geronimo, the iconic
Apache leader who stands in American popular memory for resistant warriors
everywhere and the defeated prisoners we imagine they became" (2004, 136).

Yet concurrently, Geronimo's face is very recognizable as that of an individual. It is not the face of Metacom or Pontiac or Tecumseh, nor it is it the

face of Sitting Bull or Crazy Horse. It is not even the face of Geronimo's fellow Chiricahua Cochise, which might be Europeanized into that of Jeff Chandler (born Ira Grossel) in *Broken Arrow*.[1] It is a face that the general public first came to know through the photograph taken by Frank Randall on the San Carlos Reservation in 1884, after Geronimo had returned with some three hundred Mexican cattle following Crook's Sierra Madre campaign and about a year before his final breakout from reservation life in May 1885. Even though the Lakota Red Cloud may have been the most photographed Indian of the nineteenth century, Geronimo very probably holds the distinction of being the most photographed Indian in history, particularly if one includes the images made by fairgoers and tourists who brought their Kodaks to one of the world's fairs at which he appeared or to the site of his prisoner-of-war years at Fort Sill during the first decade of the twentieth century. What these photographs reveal is not simply the face of savagism, but a person different from other persons. And not just from Euro-American persons, but from other Indians, from other "chiefs," from other Chiricahuas.

One doubts that the writer for the *New York Times* who on 23 February 1913 hailed the generic "Indian" qualities of the face on the buffalo nickel when it appeared that year would have included Geronimo's visage among the indistinguishable savage faces that he believed could have provided the model for the coin's designer. The *Times* writer reported on the gathering of prominent American Indians who had assembled in New York City to celebrate the proposed memorial to the North American Indian, a project that never materialized. Someone was passing out newly issued buffalo nickels, which used on one side an image that "might have been a portrait of any one of the chiefs who took it into their hands . . . and stared at it curiously." Geronimo was dead by this time, but if he had been among the guests, the reporter would have had to mitigate his claims that the profile on the nickel could have been that of any Indian in attendance. Geronimo's face stands out at the fore of the band of threatening figures bent on perpetrating horrific acts upon the microcosm of Euro-America that is riding the last stage to Lordsburg in John Ford's classic film *Stagecoach*. Seeing Geronimo among the potential threats to the Ringo Kid, Dallas, Dr. Boone, and the rest of the travelers through Monument Valley increases the film's tension for the audience who identifies with them. When Victor Daniels (using the performance name Chief Thundercloud) appeared in the title role of the 1940 film *Geronimo!* the face told the whole story. Geronimo speaks less than a dozen lines in the film, but the camera repeatedly closes in on Daniels's grimly resolute face, which actually does bear some resemblance to that of the historical figure—one of the few nods to history in the film that inspired the World War II paratroopers' battle cry.

The face of Geronimo was so distinctive that many of those who encountered him and wrote about their experience commented on his appearance. Though he is looking back from the vantage of half a century, John P. Clum, who arrested Geronimo in 1877 at Ojo Caliente, New Mexico Territory, recalled his appearance: "He stood erect as a mountain pine, while every outline of his symmetrical form indicated strength and endurance. His abundant ebon locks draped his ample shoulders, his stern features, his keen piercing eye, and his proud and graceful posture combined to create in him the model of an Apache war-chief" (1926, 33). Another early physical description of Geronimo emerged from a meeting between him and two men seeking information about the fate of Charlie McComas, son of a judge from Silver City, New Mexico, who along with his wife had been killed by Chiricahuas in the spring of 1883. In September of that year, D. C. Leroy and Charles Wilson from Deming, New Mexico, described Geronimo as "well proportioned, carrying 190 pounds on a five-foot-ten-inch, broad-shouldered frame." Estimating the sixty-year-old warrior's age as thirty-seven, they noted his battle scars: "A bullet wound across his forehead, a bullet still in his left thigh, and the finger of his right hand is bent backward, also from a bullet wound" (Sweeney 2010, 333). Geronimo's face received more specific attention in a description that appeared in the *Las Vegas Daily Optic* for 28 May 1885. The paper noted that Geronimo, who was believed to be half Mexican, "has but little of the racial aspect of the genuine Apache." He has a "Malay face, broad and flat, but with fine eyes and well-shaped head." Less detailed but more indicative of Euro-American attitudes toward Geronimo was the dismissive statement in the *Army and Navy Journal*'s 17 April 1886 story treating Geronimo's apparent capitulation to Crook about two weeks earlier: the Chiricahua was "a most villainous-looking customer." Other descriptions appeared in reports filed after the September 1886 surrender. The *Atlanta Constitution* for 17 September 1886 described Geronimo as "a giant in strength": "His face is brutal in expression. Coarse, straight hair hides a high, narrow forehead; heavy brows shade small, black, cunning eyes, and the wide mouth, closed like an iron vise, runs a hardened seam between the long, drooping nose and powerful lower jaw. The skin is wrinkled like an alligator's, and weather hardened to the toughness of parchment." This description contrasts somewhat with the "rather . . . good natured face" attributed to Geronimo by a *Constitution* correspondent who had visited him in San Antonio while he was awaiting the federal government's decision about his postsurrender destiny. The report, published on 27 September 1886, suggested that Geronimo was in general good humor. Meanwhile, the *New York Times* was assuming a middle position regarding Geronimo's face. The paper's story, datelined San Antonio for 23 September 1886, reported, "His eyes are small, black, and bright, and his hair long, black, and glossy. It is carefully combed down on each side of his face and kept in place by a handkerchief bound across his forehead." The reporter added, "In spite of Geronimo's bad reputation he has not a bad face; it is rather good-natured and he smiled continually while his visitor was attempting to make himself understood."

Those who dealt with Geronimo militarily also noted his striking visage. For example, Henry W. Daly, military packmaster during the Apache wars of the 1880s, noted,

> The countenance of Geronimo was the most arresting I have ever seen on a human being. There was in it a look of unspeakable savagery, of fierceness, and yet the signs of an acute intelligence were also present. Geronimo was of a nervous type, which is, or was, rare among Indians. His countenance was mobile, rather than masklike. When he was mad he simply looked like the devil, and an intelligent devil at that. (Daly 1930, 30)

Anton Mazzanovich, who also served during the Apache wars, believed him to be "a fine specimen of the Apache Indian, with high cheekbones, a very determined face, straight mouth, thin lips." He recalled seeing Geronimo all "'dolled up' in his best, with a long war bonnet, the feathers of which trailed down on each side of his pony" (1931, 158–59). One wonders, though, why Geronimo was wearing Plains Indian garb. Perhaps the most widely reprinted description of Geronimo's face was that of General Miles, who included it in his account of the surrender at Skeleton Canyon: "He was one of the brightest, most resolute, determined looking men that I have ever encountered. He had the clearest, sharpest, dark eye I think I have ever seen, unless it was that of General Sherman when he was at the prime of life. . . . Every movement indicated power, energy and determination" (1896, 520–21). Tom Horn, who served as a scout and interpreter during the Apache wars, also commented on Geronimo's eyes: "Certainly a grand looking war chief, he was . . .

six feet high and magnificently proportioned, and his motions as easy and graceful as a panther's. He had an intelligent looking face, but when he turned and looked at a person, his eyes were so sharp and piercing that they seemed fairly to stick into him" (1904, 51).

When Norman Wood visited Fort Sill in April 1905, he was eager to meet Geronimo, and Wood included a description of Geronimo's appearance in the chapter of his survey eventually devoted to him. Even though Wood found Geronimo's visage to be "usual" in its Indianness, he nevertheless noted some distinctive characteristics:

> He is rather darker than the average of the Apaches, his skin being more of a chocolate than copper color. He has the usual Indian features with broad face and high and prominent cheek bones, each covered at the time with a vermilion spot about the size of a silver dollar. But the most remarkable of all his features are his eyes, which are keen and bright and a decided blue, something very rare among Indians. (Wood 1906, 554)

These commentators apparently believed that Geronimo's face was so distinctive that it merited more or less specific descriptions. Most recognized that it represented savagism, but they also noticed its particular features. Those features stood out in the photograph that Frank Randall took in 1884.

Conventional wisdom holds that American Indians distrusted the camera. As Lucy R. Lippard has written, "Initially, a picture being 'shot' must have resembled all too closely a rifle being 'shot' as the instrument was raised to the eyes and a 'trigger' was pulled. Soon it was recognized as the ultimate invasion of social, religious, and individual privacy" (1992, 29). But another perspective suggests that even from the earliest attempts to "capture" the Indian in photographs, the subjects may have understood what was happening and participated in the image manipulation that the art of photography involves. Probably the first photograph of an American Indian was that of the highly assimilated Peter Jones done in Britain in 1845, and, according to one historian, he "clearly understood the process of picture making; he deliberately poses in different modes of dress in order to obtain pictures that could illustrate and serve his various roles as missionary, fundraiser, and inspirational speaker" (Sandweiss 2002, 212). But even the first photographic portrait taken in an American studio, that of Keokuk in Saint Louis in 1847, reveals a subject who seemed to appreciate the possibilities of the camera:

"The studied formality of his pose suggests that he did understand the potential power of a two-dimensional image" (Sandweiss 2002, 212). That Keokuk had had his portrait painted earlier by George Catlin may have contributed to his recognition of that potential power.

Despite assumptions that photographs of American Indians represented just another way in which the dominant Eurocentric society exploited those whom they considered their inferiors, with the result that they became the "subject of judgmental images as viewed by the foreigner" (Tsinhnahjinnie 2003, 41), some commentators have noted ways in which Indian subjects (and photographers) have used the art for their own purposes. Comanche Paul Chaat Smith writes, "We have been using photography for our own ends for as long as . . . there have been cameras. . . . The question isn't whether we love photography, but instead why we love it so much. From the Curtis stills to our own Kodachrome slides and Polaroid prints and Camcorder tapes, it's obvious we are a people who adore taking pictures and having pictures taken of us." He notes the common assumption that photographed Indians were "victims, dupes, losers, and dummies": "Lo, the poor fool posting for Edward Curtis wearing the Cheyenne headdress even though he's Navajo. Lo, those pathetic Indian extras in a thousand bad movies." Describing the long-standing practice among various American Indian communities of adopting and adapting technology that became available through culture contact, Smith asserts, "The camera, however, was more than another tool we could adapt to our own ends. It helped make us what we are today" (2009, 4). Leslie Marmon Silko, whose grandfather Henry Marmon acquired a camera in the 1920s and whose father Lee Marmon has become an important photographer of the landscapes and people of the Southwest, writes about the adaptability of Pueblo cultures that were introduced to new technology: "Europeans were shocked at the speed and ease with which Native Americans synthesized, then incorporated, what was alien and new" (1996, 177). Photography was among the most readily adopted and adapted innovations. Most likely, Geronimo sensed what photography could do and attempted to have it do what he wanted when he posed for the camera.

A. Franklin Randall's photograph of Geronimo (fig. 5.1), which David Roberts calls "the most famous portrait ever made of an American Indian" (1994, plates), was one of several that the photographer made of Apaches on the San Carlos Reservation during 1883 and 1884. Randall, a correspondent for *Frank Leslie's Illustrated Weekly*, came to the Southwest to accompany Crook's Sierra Madre campaign in 1883. The purpose of that campaign was to restore to the reservation the Chiricahuas who had been living in and raiding from their stronghold in Mexico's mountains. Randall hoped to make photographs in the field, and had it not been for an unfortunate accident, he would have joined C. S. Fly in holding the distinction of having made the only such photographs during the various Indian wars in which the United States had engaged. However, as Crook's aide, John Gregory Bourke, recorded in his diary for 9 May 1883: "Five of our pack mules, in advancing along the trail this morning, fell over the precipice and killed themselves, three breaking their necks and two having to be shot. One of them was laden with Mr. Randall's photographic apparatus, which was crushed to smithereens" (Radbourne 2004). Undaunted by the destruction of his equipment, Randall decided upon a new project: photographing Apaches after they returned to the reservation. Operating from a base in Willcox, Arizona, he set up a studio near the San Carlos Agency and began to photograph his subjects in a setting of indigenous plants and Native artifacts.

FIG. 5.1. Frank Randall took the first and most well-known photograph of Geronimo in the spring of 1884 after Geronimo had returned from Mexico and his meeting with General Crook in the Sierra Madre. *National Archives and Records Administration, Native American Heritage Collection, American Indian Select List 101.*

Among the early subjects whom Randall photographed was Tzoe (the scout known as "Peaches," who had assisted Crook during the Sierra Madre campaign), but he did not initiate his project to make portraits of the leaders of the breakout until October 1883, when they began to return to the reservation. He subsequently produced images of most of those leaders, including Naiche, Loco, Nana, Mangus, and Chihuahua. Geronimo himself did not return to the San Carlos Agency until 16 March 1884. At some point thereafter, Randall made at least two likenesses of him, including "the portrait that would become his most famous and familiar picture, destined to be reproduced again and again" (Radbourne 2004). Geronimo is posed kneeling on his right knee with a rifle gripped tightly in both hands. He is surrounded by local flora: a barrel cactus to his right and what appears to be a yucca to his left. He is clad in a long shirt and breechclout, with a scarf around his neck and knee-high boots. His hair, parted in the middle, is shoulder length. Geronimo's mouth is curved downward, his lips firmly clamped together. His eyes, perhaps looking slightly to the left, are piercing.[2] It is in the eyes, according to the late Michael Dorris, that the viewer of photographs of American Indians can perceive an essence that transcends whatever manipulations the photographer might impose on his or her subjects (1994, 24). Especially given the notice accorded to Geronimo's eyes in verbal descriptions of him, one should pay particular attention to what seems to be communicated through them in photographs, no matter what the particulars of the picture-taking situation.

It is hard to believe that Randall's portrait represents Geronimo's first experience before the camera. He seems totally in control of the situation. Rather than conveying "colonization through photography," as Susan Sontag puts it (1977, 64), Geronimo's demeanor, like that of many other Indians who sat for their photographs, "seem[s] grimly defiant of the photographer himself" (Mitchell 1994, xvii). Sontag notes that photographic portraits that present the subject facing the camera suggest "solemnity, frankness, the disclosure of the subject's essence" (1977, 37–38). If so, Geronimo's essence is both particular and general.

Randall's image has come to stand for Geronimo both as a generic representative of savagism and as an individual. It serves as the cover design or frontispiece for almost every volume produced about Geronimo and the Apache wars. Andy Warhol used it as the source for a painting of Geronimo that he included in his Cowboys and Indians series in 1986. It provided the inspiration for the U.S. postage stamp honoring Geronimo that was issued in 1994 as part of the four-stamp series Legends of the West. Certainly by the time it had gone through its many uses and reuses, the picture could be clearly identified as representing the individual Geronimo, but it had also moved beyond its specific associations to signify something more. It has "slip[ped] the bonds of biographical explicitness and . . . assume[d] more metaphorical meaning in the eyes of the beholder." This image captured in the spring of 1884, which "once memorialized a personal, private moment," has now been "easily reimagined as a public commodity" (Sandweiss 2002, 215). Geronimo's face, as it appears in Randall's photograph, also figures into one of the most frequently reproduced images of Native Americana in the twenty-first century. In two paintings David C. Behrens has juxtaposed the four presidential faces sculpted into the rock at Mount Rushmore with images of four notable American Indians: Chief Joseph, Sitting Bull, Red Cloud, and Geronimo. In *Original Founding Fathers*, the Native figures are foregrounded with Mount Rushmore in the wispy background (see fig. 1.3). In *Founding Fathers*, the positions are reversed. Behrens's website explains that the paintings are meant to correct lessons communicated by "social studies" teachers who used the term *founding fathers* to characterize the Europeans who established the United States without acknowledging that "there was already a system and order decreed by renown[ed] Native American elders and chieftains" (*David C. Behrens Studio* 2010). The site explains the significance of Geronimo:

> Geronimo, a Chiricahua Apache, was as famous a figure as they come in the history of the West. Elusive and crafty, he was feared by all those who pursued him. Cynical of the corrupt Indian agents he dealt with, he determined in his heart not to surrender[, the] inevitable fruit of warfare being loss of loved ones and family. Geronimo seemed to have an inexhaustible appetite for vengeance. Eventually after many failed attempts Geronimo and his "renegade" band were finally captured and he was sent to a Florida jail as prisoner of war. (*David C. Behrens Studio* 2010)

In addition to framed or matted prints in various sizes, Behrens's paintings are available on refrigerator magnets, postcards, coffee mugs, and shot glasses. One can also obtain a jigsaw puzzle that uses the image.[3]

The other photograph of Geronimo that Randall took at the same sitting has not become as iconic (fig. 5.2). It shows its subject on a chair that has been draped with a geometrically decorated blanket. Surrounded by yuccas, Geronimo is clothed much as he is in the more famous photograph: Chiricahua-style moccasins and leggings, a breechcloth, and a long shirt that is open at the neck to reveal an undershirt. Perched atop his head is what appears to be a woman's straw hat. It has a wide band with a flower to the side. Geronimo looks off slightly to his left instead of at the camera, and his expression evinces more discomfort than defiance. This is not the archetype of savagery that Randall's other photograph shows. No wonder it has not survived in the American consciousness (even though it seems to have been the original for a line drawing of Geronimo that appeared in the *Tucson Daily Citizen* in 1886). This photograph serves neither the reputation of Randall nor the image of Geronimo.

FIG. 5.2. Geronimo was not so well served by a second photograph taken by Frank Randall in 1884 as he was by the more famous image. This portrait, though, provided a source for line drawings that began to appear in some newspapers during and after Geronimo's final breakout. *National Anthropological Archives, Smithsonian Institution (BAE GN 2507).*

Randall, though, took advantage of the notoriety that attached to Geronimo during his final breakout. An advertisement in the 27 May 1886 issue of the *Tucson Weekly Star* offered "cabinet sized photos for sale of these two Apache chiefs [i.e., Geronimo and Nana], taken by F. Randall." The images could be purchased for fifty cents each at the newspaper office.

Randall had another opportunity to photograph Geronimo. After shifting his base of operations to southern New Mexico (Las Cruces and Deming), he began to photograph on the Mescalero reservation. In September 1886, after Geronimo had surrendered to Miles following his final breakout from the reservation, Randall hurriedly made his way to Fort Bowie, Arizona Territory, the point of departure from which Geronimo and the others who had been involved in the breakout would take leave of the Southwest forever. There he caught Geronimo, Naiche, and other Chiricahuas on film in Arizona for the last time (fig. 5.3). Soon thereafter Randall moved to California, where he lived the rest of his life (Radbourne 2004; Rudisill 1973, 48–49; Fleming and Luskey 1986, 242).

Fig. 5.3. At the time that Geronimo surrendered in September 1886, Frank Randall had set up a photographic studio in Deming, New Mexico. When he learned that the Chiricahuas would soon be at Fort Bowie, Arizona, he caught the train there and took several pictures. Here Geronimo (on right) and Naiche sit with the fort in the background. *National Anthropological Archives, Smithsonian Institution (NAA INV02057800).*

The next photographic images of Geronimo, subsequent to Randall's original, were taken about two years later. "The only known photographs of American Indians as enemy in the field" (Van Orden 1991, 1), these images represent the work of Camillus S. Fly, who had established a photographic business in Tombstone in 1879. Much of his work was done during trips to military posts where he took advantage of soldiers' paydays to capture images of them in uniform. Fly himself persistently tried his luck as a miner and served as sheriff of Cochise County. His studio was located near the OK Corral and provided an egress from the famous gunfight for Ike Clanton, one of the principals in that notorious event. He later set up studios in Bisbee and Phoenix (Current and Current 1978, 206–8; Rudisill 1973, 27).

Fly's most important contribution to the photographic record of his times came in March 1886 when he attached himself to the party of General Crook, who had an appointment to meet with Geronimo's band to negotiate a surrender at Cañon de los Embudos, just south of the international border. Charles D. Roberts, who was part of Crook's delegation, wrote of Fly's attaching himself to the expedition: "It happened that a photographer from Tombstone named Fly was at Silver Creek when we passed through. Sensing that something interesting was in the wind, Fly asked Crook if he could follow him" (1959–1960, 213). The *Daily Tombstone* for 20 March reported, "C. S. Fly, the photographer, started for Guadalupe Canon today, with his photographic apparatus. This would seem to indicate that C. S. had received news that Geronimo and his band were likely to be in that vicinity in the near future" (Vaughan 1989, 308). During the conference between Crook and the Apaches, Fly, with the assistance of a helper recalled only as Mr. Chase, produced nineteen photographs of seventeen different views. On 25 March 1886 he took pictures of a meeting between the two parties, including the only candid shot in the series. Packmaster Henry W. Daly claimed that he had "cleared away some brush for that view with [his] pack train knife" (1926a). On the following day he visited the Apache camp, where he photographed the Indians as well as their establishment. Crook's adjutant, John Gregory Bourke, described Fly's procedure:

> Mr. Fly, the photographer, saw his opportunity, and improved it fully: he took "shots" at "Geronimo" and the rest of the group, and with a "nerve" that would have reflected undying glory on a Chicago drummer, coolly asked "Geronimo" and the warriors with him to change positions, and turn their heads or faces, to improve the negative.

None of them seemed to mind him in the least except "Chihuahua," who kept dodging behind a tree, but was at last caught by the dropping of a slide. (Bourke 1891, 476)

Off the record, Bourke apparently had not been so sanguine about the success of Fly's photographic endeavors. He told George Whitwell Parsons that the photographer was "a d——d fool for going into the camp and that he'd never come out" (Chaffin 1997, 339). But Fly seems to have had no difficulties in getting Geronimo and his band or Crook and company to cooperate— a circumstance that reinforces the argument that at least these American Indians were savvy regarding photography. The *Tucson Daily Citizen* for 2 April speculated that "even in the midst of the most serious interviews with the Indians, he would step up to an officer and say 'just put your hat a little more on this side, General. No Geronimo, your right foot must rest on that stone'" (Vaughan 1989, 310).

Fly was disappointed when the conference failed to bring an end to hostilities, for he had hoped that his shots of the conclusion of the Indian wars would be "the coup that would bring him national recognition and considerable wealth" (Van Orden 1991, 324). He did offer the series of photographs for sale, and *Harper's Weekly* published six of them in its 24 April 1886 edition. Local press reaction to the photographs was positive. The *Daily Citizen* in Tucson, for example, acknowledged receiving a set in its 3 May 1886 issue: "The pictures are excellent ones and the intrepid artist accomplished a rare feat of daring as well as a stroke of enterprise in his venture among the hostile[s] to photograph them." George Whitwell Parsons of Tombstone noted that Fly had shown him pictures of "Geronimo and his cutthroats" in early April 1886: "He'll make good money. Wish now I'd got a horse and gone with him. I might have collected some curios and made money" (Chaffin 1997, 338). Parsons purchased seven photographs from Fly, who "favored me greatly in price" (Chaffin 1997, 339). Fly apparently had to hire extra help at his Tombstone studio, so great was the demand for copies of his images. The going rate for prints was fifty cents apiece or four dollars per dozen. As Thomas Vaughan has reported, "Sales were brisk" (1989, 310). Fly apparently realized that his combination of photography and journalism was potentially profitable, and throughout the fifteen or so years that remained of his career, he took advantage of opportunities to pioneer in the field of photojournalism (Vaughan 1989, 317). After his death in 1901, Fly's widow, Mary Goodrich Fly, published a book of his photographs. But *Scenes in Geronimo's Camp* contained material that had nothing to do with its title subject and failed to include all of the images taken at Cañon de los Embudos. The complete series did not see print until 1989, when it appeared in the *Journal of Arizona History* (Van Orden 1989, 1991).[4]

Geronimo appears in at least eight of the photographs taken by Fly. (In the candid shot taken of the peace conference, the first picture in the series, his presence cannot be clearly discerned.) He appears seated to the right of General Crook in the posed version of the first peace conference (fig. 5.4). That frequently reprinted photograph was reproduced on Crook's tombstone at Arlington National Cemetery. In the other seven depictions that feature Geronimo, the warrior appears in his own camp mounted or holding a rifle, a pose that led Jimmie Durham to comment, "Geronimo is so beautifully and belligerently at home in the chaparral, and he almost always has his rifle ready" (1992, 57).

FIG. 5.4. C. S. Fly took this photograph of the peace conference between Geronimo and General George C. Crook at Cañon de los Embudos, just below the international border, on 25 March 1886. Geronimo appears seated to the right of Crook, who is wearing his characteristic pith helmet. *Courtesy of Arizona Historical Society/Tucson (PC19_78153).*

The best known of Fly's photographs, aside from the picture of the entire conference that he made on 25 March, depicts four Chiricahua warriors, each holding a rifle, standing in front of a stand of ocotillos (fig. 5.5). Fly numbered the image 174 and provided this caption: "Geronimo, Son and two picked Braves. Man with long rifle Geronimo" (Van Orden 1991, 13). Packmaster Henry W. Day added "Cossacks of the Sierra Madres" to the title. Moving from the viewer's left, the men depicted are Yanozha, Chappo (a son of Geronimo who was later to die from an illness he had contracted at Carlisle Indian School), Fun (who committed suicide at Mount Vernon Barracks), and Geronimo, who appears to be taller than the others at least partially because he is standing somewhat uphill from them. Their expressions are grim but not necessarily hostile, and they may in fact be squinting into the sun. Each holds his rifle in readiness with right hand near or on the trigger. These do not appear to be individuals on the verge of surrendering but competent, confident defenders of their way of life. This image has gained considerable currency in the post-9/11 era from its use on posters, postcards, and T-shirts with the caption "Homeland Security: Fighting Terrorism Since 1492," a use that not only challenges the defensiveness that has characterized American society since that era but also suggests how the image of Geronimo, who was regarded as an incendiary and insurgent—a "red devil" and terrorist—by many at the time the photograph was taken, has undergone a reversal in many quarters.

Another of Fly's photographs merits special attention because it has been the subject of an ekphrastic poem, one that responds to a work of visual art. Fly titled number 180 in his series *Geronimo and His Warriors* (fig. 5.6). By my count it depicts twenty-seven individuals, most of them warriors and most armed with rifles. They are posed at the top of a rise behind a couple of bunches of yucca with an empty sky behind them. Geronimo stands in the center and slightly to the front of the group. Instead of a rifle, he is holding a dance drum and drumstick. Other identifiable members of the group include Naiche, Perico, and Fun. This photograph resembles very closely numbers 178 and 179, both of which were taken in the same setting and depict a group of Chiricahua warriors with Geronimo as central focus. One of the poems in Rawdon Tomlinson's collection *Geronimo after Kas-ki-yeh* responds to this photo. Using Fly's title for the photograph as the title of his poem, Tomlinson writes in the voice of the photographer, who speaks of preparing his subjects for his "soul-catching lens." He takes particular note of how the empty expanse of sky overwhelms the scene as the Apache warriors

FIG. 5.5.   C. S. Fly posed this image on 26 March 1886. From left to right, it depicts
Yanozha, Chappo (Geronimo's son), Fun, and Geronimo. The photograph
has garnered some attention from its recent use on T-shirts and posters
with the caption "Homeland Security: Fighting Terrorism Since 1492."
Courtesy of Arizona Historical Society/Tucson (PC19_78165).

pose "as though for a wedding or an execution." Their resigned patience as
he gets ready to "draw their shadows on glass" creates a sense of permanence
even before the photographer's click of the shutter literally makes this scene
timeless (2007, 36).

After his surrender to Miles in September 1886, Geronimo continued
to elicit photographic interest. The images taken by Randall immediately
after the surrender at Fort Bowie have not received much attention, but photographs of the entire band of "Geronimo Apaches" disembarked from the
train that was taking them eastward (see fig. 6.1) and of Geronimo himself at Fort Sam Houston in San Antonio, Texas, as he awaited President
Cleveland's decision about the disposition of the prisoners of war have frequently been reprinted. Geronimo continued to be photographed occasionally during his time at Fort Pickens, Mount Vernon Barracks, and Fort Sill,
but he did not regain his status as an important subject of image-making
until late in the 1890s, when he was beginning to make public appearances
at events like the Trans-Mississippi and International Exposition in Omaha
in 1898.

FIG. 5.6. C. S. Fly titled this photograph, taken on 26 March 1886, *Geronimo and His Warriors*. It probably represents most of the contingent that Geronimo had at his disposal at the time he was treating with Crook at Cañon de los Embudos. *Courtesy of Arizona Historical Society/Tucson (PC19_78169).*

Although drawings of Geronimo appeared in the press as early as 1886, the first major artist to paint a portrait of him was probably Elbridge Ayer Burbank, who initially visited Fort Sill in 1897. Burbank had been commissioned by his uncle, wealthy Chicago businessman Edward Everett Ayer, to prepare portraits of famous American Indians for his private collection of Native Americana. Eventually Burbank painted some 150 portraits of such notables as Chief Joseph, Red Cloud, and American Horse, as well as Geronimo. Burbank's first trip into the field brought him into contact with the "wily, daring old Apache" of "fearsome reputation" (Burbank 1944, 17). Expecting to find Geronimo behind bars, the artist was surprised to discover him taking a nap in his own house. He was immediately impressed by Geronimo's appearance: "He was short, but well built and muscular. His keen, shrewd face was deeply furrowed with strong lines. His small black eyes were watery, but in them there burned a fierce light. It was a wonderful study—that face, so gnarled and furrowed" (1944, 18–19). Burbank was eventually to paint seven portraits of Geronimo, and in each of them— both profiles and frontal views—that face provides the focus. A frontal view painted in 1898 may be the most well known of these portraits (fig. 5.7). Wrapped in a robe and with a turban atop his head, Geronimo seems impassive, his downturned mouth clamped shut (as it is in almost all visual

FIG. 5.7. Edward Ayer Burbank's portrait, perhaps the first done from a sitting by the Chiricahua, was the most famous nonphotographic representation produced during Geronimo's lifetime. Burbank painted the work in 1898 at Fort Sill. *Library of Congress Lot 12976, LC-USZ62-1437.*

representations of him). He looks directly at the viewer, and Burbank has managed to capture his eyes' "fierce light." Heavily seamed, the face is that immediately recognizable visage that represents individualized savagism. Martin Padget finds a profile of Geronimo painted in 1899 as the most striking of Burbank's images: "The painstaking detail in Geronimo's craggy face contrasts with the broad brushstrokes in the lightly colored neutral background and the bright red blanket wrapped around Geronimo's upper body" (2004, 142–43).

Two aspects of their series of encounters, which lasted a couple of years, impressed Burbank. One was Geronimo's entrepreneurial spirit. He was, according to Burbank, "something of a Scotsman" (1944, 21). Within a few minutes of their first meeting, the Apache had sold Burbank a photograph for a dollar, and the primary issue in their negotiations about Geronimo's sitting for his painted portrait involved how much he would be paid. They agreed on five dollars for two portraits, but Geronimo was able to persuade the artist to buy him a chair and tried to arrange a contest in marksmanship with a grand prize of ten dollars. As he noted, "Geronimo's money-making schemes were many and varied" (22). Burbank was especially impressed by the way in which Geronimo used his trip to the Trans-Mississippi and International Exposition, which occurred during the couple of years that the pair were acquainted, to his financial advantage by selling buttons from his coat and his hat (23). Burbank estimated that upon Geronimo's death about a decade later, the Apache had more than ten thousand dollars in the bank (24).

Burbank also noted Geronimo's able participation in the process of portraiture: "I never had a finer sitter than Geronimo" (1944, 21). He valued Geronimo's critique of his work, noting that he "had a fine eye for line and color" (25). That Geronimo assumed some agency in the work produced by Burbank supports the contention that he was concerned with image management and that this concern figured into visual representations of him produced by photographers and other artists and documentarians.

Burbank finished his work at Fort Sill in 1899, but he may have crossed paths with Geronimo at the Pan-American Exposition in Buffalo in 1901 and at the Louisiana Purchase Exposition in Saint Louis in 1904. Geronimo appeared at both events, and Burbank exhibited his artwork there as well. Writing in the 1940s, Burbank evinced considerable sympathy for Geronimo, whom he believed to have been misunderstood: "To me he was a kind old man. To be sure, he had his peculiarities, and his outlook on life was not the same as the white man's, but he was certainly not as cruel as he had been pictured" (1944, 31). Burbank's memories, colored by almost a half century of elapsed time, painted Geronimo as a grandfatherly figure who doted on children and never left home without ensuring that his pet house cat had a saucer of milk. But even at the time of their encounter, Burbank was convinced that Geronimo was not what his reputation seemed to suggest. In an article in *Carter's Monthly* in 1899, he concluded, "He is very domestic in his habits, and takes very kindly to civilization" (Padget 2004, 164). Not always accurate in his account of Geronimo's history, Burbank had Geronimo's father among the massacred at Kaskiyeh in 1851. He probably borrowed from Natalie Curtis's *The Indians' Book* for the text of a song that Geronimo purportedly sang when they took breaks from their portrait work. But his recollections of Geronimo are among the most vivid of anyone from the last decade of the nineteenth century, and while his portraits maintain the image of savagism that also characterized the photographs of Randall and Fly, that savagism had become muted by an avuncularity that Geronimo himself seemed to cultivate as he mounted his campaign to be released from prisoner-of-war status and returned to the Southwest.[5]

A nineteenth-century assessment of Burbank's painted portraits of Geronimo contrasts them with available photographic images, probably those of Randall and Fly, by showing "none of the cruelty seen in earlier photographs." The critic attributes the difference not only to Geronimo's becoming reconciled to his situation ("He has undoubtedly changed, and for the better"), which may very well be the interpretation that Geronimo himself would have advanced, but the vision of the artist is also credited with the changes: "The personal bias may make a good deal of difference in our judgment as to the merits of Indians, and where the friend of the red man sees dignity, repose, often gentleness, the Indian hater sees only cruelty and wickedness" (Browne 1898, 26).

Historian Brian W. Dippie has argued that photography helped to perpetuate the image of the "vanishing American" that colored thinking about the Native inhabitants of North America from the time of colonial contact at least through the 1930s. In fact, he cites the photographic representations of Geronimo as illustrating how exposure to civilization could replace evidences of savagism with those of civility. While the earliest photographs of Geronimo depict him in warlike defiance in the field, the most well-known representations from the first decade of the 1900s—after he had been a prisoner of war for almost twenty years—show the effects of civilizing influences: he poses with his family holding a watermelon apparently grown in the patch behind him; he sits behind the wheel of a motorcar with a top hat replacing the headband he had worn as a warrior. In these photographs, Dippie suggests, one can glimpse a microcosm of the cultural evolutionary agenda: Geronimo has moved from savagery to the verge of civilization (1992, 132). Dippie exempts the most famous photograph taken of Geronimo at the Trans-Mississippi and International Exposition in Omaha in 1898 (fig. 5.8). Presumably the photograph that Geronimo sold, for which he charged extra if he affixed his hand-printed signature, it shows him "nondescript in appearance, transformed by age and circumstance." His expression is "pensive, almost wistful" (132). The photograph is usually attributed to Frank A. Rinehart, who had been contracted by the Bureau of American Ethnology as "official photographer" for the American Indian exhibitions at the exposition. Rinehart, who had worked in Denver before setting up a photography studio in Omaha in the mid-1880s, had his own studio with a "soft, ideal north light from skylights" (Sutton 1972, n.p.) on the fairgrounds and, influenced by anthropologist James Mooney, who represented the BAE's interests in Omaha, sought to make a photographic record of a people "who with their savage finery are rapidly passing away" (Fleming and Luskey 1993, 82). Undoubtedly, he was responsible for many photographs that depicted the Indian presence at the exposition. Mooney, though, wanted formal portraits of all those who participated in the exposition's Indian Congress, which he and Omaha newspaperman Eliot Rosewater had organized. That assignment largely fell to Rinehart's associate, Adolph F. Muhr, who took some two hundred carefully posed portraits of the delegates. Apparently he used a "huge studio camera capable of producing 8 × 10" glass plate negatives, equipped with a German lens" (Sutton 1972, n.p.). Geronimo's image may have been one of those captured by Muhr, who took an approach to his subjects more artistic than Rinehart's documentary emphasis (Fleming and Luskey 1993, 85). In fact, Muhr went on to work with the famous photographer Edward S. Curtis, whose pictorialist approach to photographing Indian subjects is well known.

Geronimo appears to be seated in the photograph, and he gazes directly at the camera. He wears a jacket and European-style shirt (both of whose buttons might be for sale to souvenir hunters) with a kerchief knotted under the shirt's collar. His hair is cut short, reaching just below his ears. He tilts his head to one side, and his tightly closed mouth maintains the downturned contour that marks virtually all his photographic representations. This portrait of Geronimo is one of the few in the series taken by Rinehart

FIG. 5.8. Frank A. Rinehart—or perhaps his associate Adolph F. Muhr—took this
photograph of Geronimo at the Trans-Mississippi and International
Exposition in Omaha, Nebraska, in 1898. It may have been the photograph
that Geronimo autographed as a souvenir for attendees at the fair and some
subsequent public appearances. *Haskell Archives, Haskell Cultural Center
and Museum, Haskell Indian Nations University, Lawrence, Kansas.*

or Muhr that does not pose its subject in traditional dress. That fact can be
explained in several ways. First, Geronimo himself was using the exposition
as an opportunity to demonstrate that he had assimilated sufficiently to be
returned to Arizona, and wearing Euro-American-style clothing for his portrait reinforced the imagery he was trying to project. Moreover, the soldiers
who accompanied him—still a prisoner of war—to Omaha may have wanted
to diminish any accoutrements of the savagery that they believed would be a
constant temptation for Geronimo. Also, Geronimo was such a well-known

figure that he did not need to assume a particularly Indian "look." As Geary Hobson has noted in a critique of the Rinehart portraits (2004, 111–12), the general public in 1898 had some clear preconceptions of what an Indian should look like. Lesser-known figures needed to be presented in traditional garb to meet those preconceptions. The infamous Geronimo was Indian enough without having to dress for the part. Margaret B. Blackman notes, "As far as many early photographers were concerned, the costume made the Indian" (1980, 70). But in Geronimo's case, viewer expectations of what an authentic Indian should wear could be disregarded.

Dippie concludes that the photograph transformed the figure once known as the "tiger in human form" into "the representative of a race, colourful, sad and doomed to disappear" (1992, 132). Another commentator, who sees the Rinehart/Muhr photograph of Geronimo as the product of a gender-based photographic aesthetic, also perceives Geronimo as "belittled, lost in the space around the figure." The photographer has supposedly placed him in a "feminine pose . . . which has the effect of making him look less threatening and more defeated." His expression is "deadpan like . . . ID photos." The photographer has obscured part of Geronimo's expression by allowing shadows to fall across his face, and the apparent crossed eyes give him a "derelict look" (Rahder 1996, 93). But another way of looking at the photograph suggests more involvement by Geronimo in the process. Twelve years into his life as a prisoner of war, during which he had experienced Euro-American civilization in Texas, Florida, Alabama, Oklahoma, and now Nebraska, Geronimo had come to know what was expected of him if he were ever to be released from imprisonment and returned to the Southwest. He had to play the white man's game in a way that would convince authorities that he had assimilated sufficiently that he no longer offered a threat. Just as he had not participated as more than a spectator at the sham battles fought by Indian exhibitors at the Trans-Mississippi and International Exposition, he knew that posing as a defiant savage was counterproductive. Undoubtedly, he realized that his way of life had vanished and that he could not recapture it even if he did return home to the mountains and deserts, but perhaps he thought that something did remain for him there and that the surest way for him to find out was to adopt the garb and demeanor that suggested that he had learned how to be a civilized Euro-American.

Rinehart issued the portrait of Geronimo along with some fifty or so other formal images of Indians who attended the Omaha exposition in a book that the *Omaha Daily Bee* heralded in its 23 December 1899 edition for sustaining the "widespread fame" that the city had enjoyed because of the world's fair's success. The glass plate negatives for the Rinehart/Muhr photographs are now part of the collections of Haskell Indian Nations University. In 2004 poet Simon Ortiz edited a volume that presented a generous sampling of the photographs with commentary by Native American writers, artists, historians, and photographers. Though only one of the commentators deals specifically with the portrait of Geronimo, they generally assume that the subjects whom Rinehart or Muhr photographed should be regarded as victims of Euro-American cultural imperialism. The photographs are a "manifestation of an oppressive colonial process that included the use of images to define the moral worth and character of the Indians as inferior, and also to rationalize abusive U. S. treatment of Indians" (Riding In 2004, 52). Laura Tohe vehemently insists that the Rinehart photographs represent a "construct of the colonizer. They are images that portray Native people within the framework of what the colonizer understands and believes. They are an invention of the colonizer, and they are images that are not us" (2004, 163). That perspective must be taken into account, since most photographers were indeed influenced by the cultural imperialism that their later critics so justly challenge. Moreover, since they controlled the photographic process following the sitting, their perspective shaped the final product of the process that began with the sitting itself. But it might also be useful to recall that production of a posed portrait is a collaborative endeavor that involves agency exercised by Indian subjects as well as Euro-American photographers. Contemporary viewers "must not assume that the people who sat for the camera were themselves simply passive vessels for the imperial gaze. Indeed, Aboriginal peoples brought their own forms of agency to the experience of being photographed—often with a demanding will to be recognized" (Francis 2002, 6). The stances that photographic subjects assumed, perhaps the particular pieces of clothing they wore and the expressions they adopted, were among the aspects of the photographic moment over which Indian subjects exercised some control. While the photographer had input into these matters, he or she had to rely upon the perceptions of the person being photographed. Particularly for Indians who had considerable experience with photography (and that would include Geronimo), the portrait session offered an opportunity not just to be victimized but to assert identity. Though within a few years Muhr would be working with Edward S. Curtis, who famously used light and shadow and other artistic techniques in his portraits of Indians, here the approach was more straightforwardly documentary with little post-session manipulation of the images in the process of developing them. Geronimo was not in control of the situation, but he was not totally passive either. The image imparted by the Rinehart/Muhr photograph may very well represent to a degree what Geronimo wanted to convey. As Carole Nez, a contributor to Ortiz's volume, suggests, "Geronimo's image, along with those of other Indian ancestors, is still on a mission to tell his side of the story. . . . In visual immortality, Geronimo's squinting eyes follow the viewer's every movement" (2004, 127).

Three photographs of Geronimo from the Louisiana Purchase Exposition held in Saint Louis in 1904 merit some attention. One was taken by Mamie and Emma Gerhard, the first women to have a photographic studio in Saint Louis. Their studio work focused primarily on portraits, and their studio shot of Geronimo suggests their skill at that art (fig. 5.9). Their bust-length portrait shows Geronimo in European-style coat and vest worn over a striped shirt. He wears a knotted bandana around his neck. His hair is cut short and parted in the middle. He looks directly at the camera with dignity and evinces no trace of discomfort or lack of control of the situation. This seems to be Geronimo at his most confident. As Bobbi Rahder, contrasting this image with that of Rinehart/Muhr, notes, the effect is "more intimate." Geronimo looks "muscular and alive, vibrant, and fierce." Moreover, his eyes "are directly engaging the eyes of the viewer, with no flinching, no lowering of eyes in defeat" (1996, 94). Rahder attributes the success of this photograph directly to the gender of the photographers, who were more apt, she argues, to form personal relationships with their photographic subjects than were male photographers whose work was informed by the ideology of the "vanishing American." Perhaps Geronimo himself had something to do with the product as well, since he was a seasoned (and successful) photographic subject. Another portrait from the Louisiana Purchase Exposition, the one attributed to H. W. Wyman, also seems to convey the image that Geronimo wished to project.

Less successful in conveying a Geronimo in charge of the situation is a photograph by Charles H. Carpenter that poses him before a curtain with a painting of the pedestals of classical columns (fig. 5.10). A full-length likeness, the photograph has Geronimo seated and at work on bows and arrows that he was manufacturing for sale from a booth at the fair. Evidences of his industry and craftsmanship lie scattered about him. He is dressed largely in European clothing except for his footwear, Chiricahua-style moccasins with upturned toe guards. He holds a small knife in one hand as he whittles at a stick that is

FIG. 5.9. Mamie and Emma Gerhard, the first women to open a photographic studio in Saint Louis, took this photograph of Geronimo while he was attending the Louisiana Purchase Exposition in their city in 1904. *Library of Congress Lot 4863, no. 14, LC-USZ62-17723.*

likely to become an arrow. The expression on his face and his posture, though, render the photograph less successful than that of the Gerhard sisters at conveying an air of confident assimilation. Geronimo is looking to the left with what appears to be suspicion, certainly wariness. His shoulders slump in a way that suggests perhaps fatigue, perhaps disillusionment, perhaps disgust. The viewer gets the sense of someone who is unhappy with his situation and may be feeling put upon as he poses for the camera. Randal Rogers has suggested that two types of photographs emerged from the Louisiana Purchase Exposition: "anthropological photography" eliminated contextual detail and focused on its subject with "scientific objectivity," while "touristic photography" positioned its subject within a contextualized frame (2008, 358). The photographs by the Gerhards and by Wyman could exemplify the former, and that by Carpenter represents the latter category. But, as Rogers notes, touristic-type photographs were not candid and unposed. They were often staged representations of the "reality" that the photographer might be trying to create with the cooperation of the subject or in spite of his or her "insubordination" (to use Rogers's term). Thus, Geronimo in Carpenter's photograph is presented in the context of a staged craft endeavor that he undermines by his facial expression and posture. Maybe he is suspicious, or maybe he is taking a cue from someone standing to the photographer's right. Certainly the setting before a generic backdrop also undermines any notion that this image represents him in the midst of unstaged action.

The most well-known photographer to capture Geronimo's visage on film was Edward S. Curtis, who photographed him as part of his North American Indian project, which lasted throughout the first couple of decades of the twentieth century and resulted in a publication of that name. Curtis took advantage of Geronimo's attendance at Roosevelt's inauguration and encountered him en route to that festivity at the Carlisle Indian School. There he took two photographs, the more famous of which made it into the twenty-volume overview of the "vanishing" populations that was the final result of the project. Geronimo's portrait is the second image in the first volume of the twenty-volume series (fig. 5.11). It follows one of Curtis's most famous and evocative photographs, *The Vanishing Race—Navaho*, in which a line of mounted Indians seems to fade into the darkened background. In his treatment of Geronimo, Curtis posed his subject in profile facing left. His heavily seamed face fills the print, which is lit from the left to highlight those seams. Geronimo wears a headband, and what appears to be a heavy blanket swallows him up. The clothing worn beneath the blanket

Fig. 5.10. In another image from the Louisiana Purchase Exposition, Geronimo adopted the pose of a craftsman for Charles H. Carpenter. Geronimo sold not only signed photographs but also objects supposedly of his own manufacture at a booth near the Indian school on the fairgrounds. *National Anthropological Archives, Smithsonian Institution (OPPS NEG TI5792).*

is obscured. Geronimo's expression is grim and meditative, perhaps occasioned, as Curtis would probably have the viewer believe, by his recognition of the inevitable passing of the way of life that he and his ancestors had enjoyed, which is symbolically represented in the image that precedes this portrait in the volume. Of course, by this time in his own life Geronimo had been prisoner of war for almost twenty years and was enjoying both public attention and some financial success as a result of his celebrity. He was on the verge, many observers believed, of stealing the inauguration show from Roosevelt.

FIG. 5.11. Edward Curtis took this photograph of Geronimo when he stopped over at Carlisle Indian School in Pennsylvania on his way to participate in Theodore Roosevelt's inauguration parade in 1905. Curtis included this as the second image in his twenty-volume collection of portraits of "vanishing Americans." *National Portrait Gallery, Smithsonian Institution, gift of Katie Louchheim.*

Curtis provided this caption for the photograph: "The picture was taken at Carlisle, Pennsylvania, the day before the inauguration of President Roosevelt, Geronimo being one of the warriors who took part in the inaugural parade at Washington. He appreciated the honor of being one of those chosen for this occasion, and the catching of his features while the old warrior was in a retrospective mood was most fortunate" (Lyman 1982, 80). However, that retrospective mood may have been as much a product of Curtis's manipulations as of fortunate accident. Curtis and his darkroom assistants, especially Adolph Muhr, employed a number of techniques to create the "rather mythical imagery of 'the Indian'" that they were seeking (Lyman 1982, 21). When taking a photograph, Curtis might pose his subject before a plain backdrop, perhaps in the studio tent that he took with him on his field trips. He carefully arranged his subject's posture and chose lighting and camera angles that would emphasize what Curtis wanted to convey. He eliminated what he regarded as the clutter of background detail from his images and replaced it with fog and shadow. For any material objects that might indicate contact with Euro-American civilization, he substituted props that would help to convey his own sense of what it meant to be Indian. Prints were often cropped to highlight what Curtis wanted to suggest, and negatives were frequently retouched. Moreover, Curtis used photogravure and platinum printing techniques to create a soft, faded quality that suggested that his subjects were vanishing into an unrecoverable past. The results were images that reflected the pictorialist aesthetic that informed Curtis's photography but which usually misrepresented contemporary realities of Native American life (Lyman 1982, 62–78). Following practices that he had used to become a successful portrait photographer in Seattle and following the pictorialist aesthetic that characterized the work of many of his contemporaries, Curtis manipulated "light, line, and composition in ways which frame the image being photographed in a romanticized form" (Francis 2002, 11).

Perceiving his photography as a high art that rejected "faithful depiction" for "more evocative and expressive photographs" (Marien 2002, 173), Curtis, the pictorialist, accepted the widely held belief that Indians were "vanishing Americans." Most of his photographs portrayed his subjects as they were imagined to have been before the forces of U.S. imperialism had impacted their lives. He believed that "Indians were only real Indians when they behaved as they were imagined to have behaved prior to contact with Whites" (Lyman 1982, 19–20). As the *Seattle Times* for 15 November 1903 noted, Curtis "took the present lowness of today and enshrined it in the romance of the past. . . . he changed the degenerated Indian of today into the fancy-free king of a yesterday that has long since been forgotten in the calendar of time" (Lyman 1982, 53; ellipses in original). Hence, Geronimo cannot be shown wearing European-style garb as he appears in the photographs by Rinehart/Muhr, the Gerhard Sisters, Wyman, and Carpenter.

The portrait of Geronimo has no context except as a picture. Curtis did not place him against a background of desert flora as did Randall. Nor is he holding the craft objects that appear in Carpenter's photograph from the Louisiana Purchase Exposition. Nothing, in fact, distracts the reader from his face. He becomes the generic savage, contemplative now that his way of life has vanished. As scholar Mick Gidley has noted about Curtis's Indian portraits in general, "The faces of Curtis's Indians were often 'carried in one great mass of shadow,' and certainly—especially in the cases of older figures whose facial lines were sometimes accentuated by a slightly downward camera angle—'character' rather than 'likeness' (in the sense of 'accuracy') was stressed" (1998, 67). As Gidley suggests, Curtis's photographs do not so much preserve individualized identity as they represent a sense of "Indianness" (102). Certainly, this approach informs the portrait of Geronimo. Nevertheless, its subject's face is so distinctive that it becomes more than simply idea even in Curtis's rendering. In one of his letters to solicit subscribers for his project, Curtis disingenuously claimed that subject matter took precedence over artistry in his work: "Being photographs from life and nature, they show what exists, not what one from the artist's studio presumes might exist" (Gidley 1998, 130). This claim becomes true in the Geronimo portrait in spite of Curtis, but only because the distinctiveness of the subject's physiognomy overwhelms the move toward generalizing that informed the actual aesthetic of Curtis's work. However, Geronimo's involvement in the process of producing the final photographic image seems to have been much less than his role in other portraits of him.

Geronimo at the Wheel, certainly one of the most well-known photographs of Geronimo (fig. 5.12), is also one of the most misunderstood.[6] It shows the famous Apache in the driver's seat of a vehicle. Except for his footwear, he is wearing Western clothing: long pants, a long-sleeved white shirt, a vest, and a top hat perched on his head. Seated beside him is a man wearing a full Plains headdress. He has been identified as Edward Le Clair Sr., a Ponca, while two Indians in the back seat, both wearing traditional garb, remain unidentified. The photograph is usually attributed to Walter Ferguson and

Fig. 5.12. Probably taken on 11 June 1905 at the National Editorial Association meeting near Ponca City, Oklahoma, this image of Geronimo has inspired several responses in popular culture. He is seated behind the wheel of what appears to be a 1904 or 1905 Locomobile. Beside him is Edward Le Clair Sr., a Ponca. *Courtesy of Oklahoma Historical Society.*

dated either 1904 or 1905. If the latter date is correct—which seems to be the case—it may have been taken on 11 June when Geronimo appeared at the convention of the National Editorial Association held at the Miller brothers' ranch near Ponca City, Oklahoma. This was the event that featured what was billed as "Geronimo's Last Buffalo Hunt." The featured target was pursued by automobile, perhaps the one in which Geronimo and his colleagues posed, and though Geronimo apparently did not fire the shot that brought the animal down, some commentators credit him with jumping from the car to wield the fatal blow with his knife. A photograph of Geronimo apparently knifing the buffalo shows him bent over the carcass wearing what seem to be the same clothes he has on while seated in the automobile, with a traditional Chiricahua shaman's hat replacing the top hat (see fig. 3.5). That *Geronimo at the Wheel* was taken on this occasion finds support in the crowd observing the proceedings. The Indians seated in the passengers' seats are members of the group and are wearing the same clothing.

Though the vehicle in which Geronimo is pictured seems to be a 1904 or 1905 Locomobile, it has been variously identified in popular culture as a White Steamer or most often as a Cadillac, thus spawning at least two popular songs titled "Geronimo's Cadillac." The earlier, written by progressive country-and-western performer Michael Martin Murphey, a member of the so-called outlaw movement of the early 1970s, appeared as the title track on his first album, released in 1972. It casts Geronimo as the stereotyped "vanishing American" who has been given the trappings of Euro-American civilization in return for his freedom and the accoutrements of his traditional way of life. The other song entitled "Geronimo's Cadillac" was released by the German dance music duet Modern Talking in 1986.

The photograph has also produced the phrase "Geronimo's Cadillac," which is used in contemporary high-tech jargon to refer to technology made available to people who are not equipped fully to make use of its potential. As contemporary British techies explain,

> Geronimo, last free leader of the Apache nation[,] agreed to a peace treaty and was sent to live on a reservation. As a peace offering the US government made a gift to Geronimo of what was at that time one of the most advanced items of technology they had—a new Cadillac motor car. The trouble was that on the reservation there was no one who could drive, no mechanics, no oil, no petrol and no roads. Geronimo was forced to pose in it for photographs but after this car was used as a chicken coop. (Casey, Proven, and Dripps 2006)

They attribute the phrase "Geronimo's Cadillac" to "Irish American songwriter" Michael Martin Murphey. Although their history is seriously flawed, they are probably correct that Geronimo was not a driver. Henrietta Stockel, though, boosts Anadarko, Oklahoma, as having a "historic downtown where Geronimo, wearing a top hat, once drove an old car in the exposition parade" (1991, 103). Paul Chaat Smith also suggests that Geronimo knew how to drive a car: "Geronimo really did have a Cadillac and used to drive it to church, where he'd sign autographs" (2009, 21).

Jimmie Durham has suggested that "Indian people are ashamed, or at least embarrassed" by this photograph since it apparently depicts Geronimo as "a foolish old man." "We do not want," he writes, "to see the valiant and 'savage' old warrior in a top hat, as though he had given up and accepted 'civilization'" (1992, 57). Certainly, one way of looking at this photograph is to see it as Geronimo's capitulation to forces that removed the threat of savagery by domesticating it to the point of absurdity. That may very well have been Ferguson's intention; he is exploiting a familiar pose used by photographers of American Indians during the first couple of decades of the twentieth century. As Christopher Lyman notes, "Costumed Indians were often photographed with symbols of White culture. The 'humor' of such images traded on racist stereotypes of Indians as primitively inferior" (1982, 56). Very frequently the symbol of "White culture" is an automobile with a group of Indians, dressed in war bonnets or other stereotypical garb, poised as if about to go for a drive. Lyman reproduces a photograph entitled *Chief Wildshoe and Family* (1982, 57), which represents this genre of Indian photography.[7] Philip Deloria suggests that the well-publicized relationship between Indians and automobiles in the early twentieth century, often manifested in photographs such as that of Chief Wildshoe, has been exploited for two meanings. On one hand, American Indians shown at ease with automobiles and other manifestations of Euro-American technology suggested that the civilizing process was working. On the other hand, when an Indian "squandered" his money (from the sale of his land allotment perhaps) on an automobile, he was seen to be essentially childish in nature (2004, 139–47).

But one can also perceive Geronimo using the occasion to emphasize that he has assimilated more than those Indians who are merely actors in the charade of automobiling and who are continuing to wear traditional costume while he has adopted formal white man's fashion. Reconstructed and ready to be repatriated, he regards the camera calmly and with dignity. June 1905 was only three months after Theodore Roosevelt had rejected Geronimo's direct plea to be allowed to return to his home in the Southwest. He may have attempted to use this photograph to prove that he had accepted Euro-American civilization sufficiently to take up residence as a member of that civilization in his beloved homeland. Even in this staged photograph, which could be dismissed as a stunt meant to demean him, Geronimo may have exerted some agency. The relationship between Geronimo and automobiles continued after his death. Between 1917 and 1920 some ten cars per month were assembled by the Geronimo Company in Enid, Oklahoma, a short-lived enterprise that was founded by one Merle Allen (*Daily Record*, Oklahoma City, 1 April 2002).

While Geronimo usually assumed some control of his photographic image when professional photographers solicited his cooperation either at exhibitions or at his home at Fort Sill, he was not as successful at managing the picture taking of the general public. William R. Draper, who wrote a rather inaccurate account of Geronimo's situation at Fort Sill, noted his interest in cameras and reported that he charged five dollars for a photograph, a price that seems unlikely. But, Draper noted, "there are those that can fool the old man." The journalist believed that Geronimo had not kept abreast of new developments in photographic technology: "He has not yet awakened to the ways of kodaking. He thinks all pictures are taken by looking under the cloth which covers a large camera." However, people visiting Fort Sill "frequently get him in range and take snap shots without his knowing what they are up to" (1901, A5). A news story that made the rounds of several papers in 1901, including the *Rocky Mountain News* for 3 June of that year, suggested that when Geronimo knew that his picture was being taken, he played the part of the savage warrior, increasingly so as he got older. The reporter noted, "He always looks his toughest in his pictures. He likes to strike an attitude of devilish ferocity when being photographed":

Five years ago, when he first came to Fort Sill, he was content to wear white men's clothes and consented to have himself photographed wearing them. Now when he poses he looks like the old-time redskin of the Apache tribe. This is because he sees that his war clothes attract more attention from white visitors. He does his best to give them their money's worth and to live up to their expectations.

Another writer, whose note appeared in the *Anaconda (MT) Standard* for 23 May 1901, indicated that "the old sinner before facing the camera always gets himself into war paint, strikes a ferocious attitude and looks as fiendish as possible." These characterizations of Geronimo's pictorial persona were published before production of some of the photographs that suggest, in fact, the opposite: that Geronimo was posing in a way to suggest that he had assimilated enough to have put his warlike past behind him. However, the reporter may have been accurate, for Geronimo was a conscious enough manager of his image to be willing to manipulate it to please a paying public.

The history of the representation of Geronimo's face generally follows the trajectory of the development of American Indian photography. One commentator has outlined that development:

The early expeditionary photographers saw the indigenous people as part of the natural scene and as curiosities whose images could be sold at a profit to incredulous easterners. After the Western conquest was completed live examples of the Native personage were displayed and endlessly photographed in a series of expositions and world fairs. Then, as the influence of the Romantic Movement permeated photography, the Pictorialist photographers saw in the indigenous people a vision of a noble but doomed race. For these Romantics, the Native Americans were essentially the New World equivalent of the ancient Greeks, whose more noble civilization inevitably fell before the crass but more powerful imperial order of the Romans. The emotional piquancy of Pictorialist imagery was based on the assumption that their idealized Native subjects would soon be extinct. (Brumbaugh 1999, 223)

Generally Geronimo fares pretty well in the photographic record. Despite a few unfortunate shots that depict him as somewhat decrepit and a few that suggest that he was not able to control his image as effectively as he might have wanted, he seems to have understood the power of the medium as early as 1884. He also seemed to understand what he needed to do to exploit photography to his own ends. He eschewed the potential for appearing as the "human tiger," an image that might very well have been more marketable than the more assimilated version of himself that he projected. He also understood that people were eager to own his image, especially if they could prove through his autograph that the physical photograph that they held had once been held by the famous Chiricahua. He also seems to have been able to translate his skill at sitting for photographs to other artistic media. Though E. A. Burbank was one of the few artists actually to paint Geronimo from life, his testimony suggests that Geronimo understood what he should do to help Burbank produce images that satisfied both their agendas. In Geronimo's case, at least, the analysis of photography as one more imperialistic usurpation of Indian identity is, at best, oversimplified. Even if such usurpation was on the mind of the photographers, Geronimo seems to have had other ideas about how his image should be realized on the photographic negative and painter's canvas. While, from the alien observer's perspective, Geronimo's visage can carry a double message as both abstract idea and concrete event, as a subject Geronimo seems to have used the medium to project at least to some degree what he wanted his audience to see, from the dignified defiance caught by Frank Randall's camera to the dignified acceptance captured through the lenses of Frank Rinehart/Adolph Muhr and the Gerhard sisters. He even made the best of situations that might reduce less resourceful individuals to buffoonery. His photographic likenesses suggest that Geronimo was able to draw upon the spirit of what Gerald Vizenor calls "tricksterism": the purported victim may not be in total control of the situation, but he is nevertheless not totally devoid of power to shape his own image.

CHAPTER 6

LITERARY GERONIMO

WHILE GERONIMO HAS APPEARED IN AMERICAN LITERATURE WITH some regularity since as early as the 1880s, he has seldom emerged from the background in many of the works in which he is a character. In fact, some novels and short stories have involved him only in their titles—drawing upon his notoriety without troubling to present him at all. When he has appeared in fiction (the genre most likely to invoke him), his role may be no more than that of nebulous representative of savagery against which Euro-American characters find themselves pitted. Even when his image has improved (a process that began by the late 1920s), Geronimo's fictional role has usually been subsidiary, perhaps as a catalyst for the maturation of a young protagonist or as someone with whom an adult protagonist has developed a relationship that redounds well on that character. Whether foil to the positive forces in fictional works or a more positive presence himself, Geronimo has remained, for the most part, flat and undeveloped. Only in poetry has he taken a lead part, and usually he functions to represent values for or against which the poet is versifying.

Verse

Political partisans relied upon Geronimo as a device to advance their views in the earliest literature treating him. What may be the earliest example was reprinted from an Oakland, California, newspaper in the *Las Vegas Daily Optic* for 20 June 1885, a month after Geronimo's final breakout. The *Optic* attributed "The Flight of Geronimo" to "General Crook" and dated it 1 June 1885 from San Carlos. The editorial commentary accompanying the poem implies that the principal army officer in Arizona Territory is writing poetry instead of doing his military duty in pursuit of the Chiricahuas, who, it was believed, were threatening the tranquility of the Southwest. The poem, if it really were his work, affords a rare, perhaps unique, example of Crook's versification:

> Now the wild Apache takes the trail,
> And blood is on the moon.
> Call forth the girded warrior bold,
> And call him very soon,
> For Geronimo, pampered ward,
> Has blanketed his band,
> And full five hundred nimble bucks
> Are flitting o'er the sand[.]
> Full many a scalp is dangling free
> From painted chieftain's side;
> The tomahawk and rifle too
> The agent has applied.
> Then turn our little army loose,
> And chase the fleeing band,
> Across the southern boundary,
> Far down the tropic land.
> And if we fail to catch them,
> And fail, perhaps, we may,
> Then Mexico's sons must do the work
> And we will watch and pray.

These lines articulate some common criticisms of Crook's handling of the Apache community, epitomized by public opinion about a single personage, Geronimo. As a resident of the Turkey Creek community on the Fort Apache Reservation, Geronimo had often been characterized as a "pampered ward" by the local, generally anti-Crook press, who believed that when the Chiricahua returned from his previous flight from the reservation in 1884, Crook had treated him with too much leniency. But the verse gives its provenance away by misrepresenting many specifics of Chiricahua culture to rely poetically on stereotypical signals of Indianness: scalping and tomahawks. Also, having pursued Geronimo into Mexico a couple of years earlier, Crook would have had little compunction about his troops crossing the border again. While his many critics might believe that he had not handled the Apache campaigns in which he participated effectively, Crook was already in the summer of 1885 doing more than offering prayers in support of the Mexican military's pursuit of Geronimo. Whoever actually authored the poem, its publication clearly contributed to the anti-Crook campaign that was particularly active during the summer of 1885. Other poetic productions of the period used Geronimo similarly.

The following summer a parody of Alexander Pope's *An Essay on Man* appeared in newspapers throughout the country. The version that appeared in the *Tucson Weekly Star* for 15 July 1886 does not break the piece into lines:

> Lo, the poor Indian whose untutored mind, to deeds of blood and rapine inclined. He roams the trackless country o'er and o'er, in search of plunder and of paleface gore; on every hand we hear his wringing whoops, and while his trusty scouts mislead the troops, he fears not danger from the blue-coat hosts, of whose wild ardor Uncle Samuel boasts. His well-trained eye the looked for signals catch; his trusted spies are ever on the watch; and when the troops think to him they are near, he's at his bloody work back in the rear. Just as the cat with captive mouse doth play, so does Geronimo day after day; in wild hilarious glee play 'round the troops, and fills the air with loud, disdainful whoops. The poor commanders, blinded by the scouts, march painfully o'er wild tortuous routes, and when the insolent foe they'd pounce upon, they charge in bold array and find him—gone. The smoke yet rises from the smouldering coal where last he made his fire near water hole; here did he rest but one short hour ago—but now, oh! where is Geronimo? Go ask the wind which round the forest play, and bear the chieftain's sneers from far away. Go ask the scouts, whose ready native wit, by signals told him to git up and git; and knowing well the signals, like a shot, the painted warriors got up and got; and while the troops still round the fire did stay, they murdered settlers five short miles away. The officers deceived by Indian trick, retrace their steps—oh God! it makes us sick!

The lines focus on one of the principal criticisms of Crook's methods: his use of Chiricahua (and other Apache) scouts in pursuit of Geronimo. Despite considerable evidence to the contrary, including the Sierra Madre campaign, popular belief held that the scouts were in league with the Indians they were supposed to be pursuing. This resulted, so public opinion held, in the Chiricahuas being forewarned of troop movements, as the verse suggests, and consequently able to maneuver around their adversaries. Moreover, some held that the scouts were likely to mutiny should actual conflict arise, as had happened when U.S. forces broke up the religious exercises led by Nock-ay-del-klinne in 1881. That outbreak of hostilities had resulted in the prophet's death but was the only instance of mutiny by Chiricahuas in the employ of the U.S. government. Some people also feared that the scouts as well as people who remained on reservations were funneling supplies, including armaments, to the Chiricahuas. Although this poem appeared in the *Tucson Weekly Star* several months after Crook had left Arizona Territory and his replacement, Nelson A. Miles, had largely terminated the use of scouts, it may have been written sometime earlier. Its sentiment helped to justify the imprisonment of the entire Chiricahua people, including the very scouts who had helped to convince Geronimo to surrender, in Florida, Alabama, and Oklahoma, until 1913.

On 7 September 1886, the *Kansas City Evening Star* published the poem "Geronimo's Plea," which had previously appeared in the *Washington Critic*. No attribution or commentary appears with the verses, which use the *Kalevala* meter associated with Henry Wadsworth Longfellow's epic poem *The Song of Hiawatha*:

Listen, children of the sunrise!
Soldiers from the distant Eastward!
I am but a poor Apache;
You are wise and strong and mighty,
And I come now to surrender,
Inasmuch as I am weary
Of the raw life in the mountains,
And the unremitting worry
Which I seem to throw you into
By my most unkind refusal
To submit myself to capture.
Having come, then, to surrender
Let me name first one condition:
Do not kill the poor Apache!
Time, I've killed a hundred people,

Shot your soldiers, scalped your women;
Burned your houses, stole your cattle,
Run off horses, caught your children.
Ravaged fields and swept through ranches;
Fire and knife and spear and rifle
I have ever used as playthings.
Yet, oh children of the sunrise!
I have grounds to claim your mercy
Hear me, paleface, as I swear it!
Yesterday I scalped an umpire
Fleeing from an outraged ball game!
I have finished. Who among you
Has done more to win a people's
Everlasting recognition,
And to come in for a pension!

This poem appeared in the *Star* on the day following a story entitled "A Wise Indian," in which Geronimo is reported to be "developing enough military genius to know the meaning of 'unconditional surrender,' and his rooted antipathy to that sort of business reflects credit on his head." The parody's dismissive treatment of the conditions associated with Geronimo's surrender would probably have found a less appreciative audience closer to the scene of the conflict. There those conditions were and would remain the subject of heated discussion. Some favored turning Geronimo and other Apaches over to civil courts to face charges of capital murder, of which they would inevitably be convicted. Virtually everyone favored at least a lifetime exile at a site far away from southeastern Arizona. In fact, the conditions that Miles made with Geronimo are still not fully clear and were ignored by higher authorities, including President Grover Cleveland, who did not make a final decision about the disposition of Geronimo's band until six weeks after the surrender.

Using Geronimo to advance political and social agendas, these poems intended to be no more than clever commentaries on the events of the day. Verse with significant literary aspirations waited until those events had disappeared from the immediate consciousness of potential readers. For example, Charles F. Lummis, who had been a correspondent for the *Los Angeles Times* at Fort Bowie during the Geronimo campaign in the summer of 1886, included an attempt at serious poetic treatment of Geronimo in his collection of poems *A Bronco Pegasus*, which appeared in 1928. Lummis begins "Man

Who Yawns" with an account of Geronimo's mistreatment by the agent at San Carlos and ends with his surrender to General Miles—an event engineered in Lummis's opinion primarily by his friend Leonard Wood. In contrast to the tone of his dispatches in 1886, the poem treats Geronimo positively. Though he does not gloss over his violence, Lummis suggests that the killings and tortures attributed to Geronimo were rooted in justifiable grievances and, in fact, paled when compared with atrocities perpetrated on Native Americans by Euro-Americans, noting that in all his years of violence he had killed "half the toll" that the U.S. Army had slain in only one day at Wounded Knee (1928, 41). Lummis also portrays Geronimo as a master tactician and in a prose commentary on the poem gives him credit for an Apache battle strategy that, in fact, had long been part of the community's raiding and warring traditions (44). Geronimo's successes, Lummis stresses, were especially remarkable because of the paucity of warriors as compared to dependent women and children who were part of the band that baffled the U.S. Army (except for Leonard Wood) as well as their Mexican counterparts during some fifteen months in 1885 and 1886. The commentary ("The Prose of It," as Lummis characterizes his contextualization of the poem) emphasizes that Geronimo was not a "Chief" but a "Prophet" who was "outranked by several men," including Cochise. But "Geronimo became an eikon and a proverb for the whole Apache outfit, among the newspapers, and the Army and the world" (44). Lummis's poem is also an elegy for the "vanished American" and for the vanished way of life that the poet had been a part of for much of the late nineteenth century. The last stanza, which he labels "envoy," suggests this theme: "The Primitive must go!" (43). Almost half a century would separate Lummis's ballad from the next flowering of Geronimo poetry.

Perhaps a product of the elevation of Geronimo and other Native American resisters to the invasion of North America to near-canonical status, Geronimo poems began to appear with some frequency in the 1970s. Examples from the last third of the twentieth century include George Cuomo's "Geronimo and the Girl Next Door" in 1973, David Huddle's "Bill Spraker's Store, or the Day Geronimo Couldn't Find the Scoop" in 1979, Ted Kooser's "Geronimo's Mirror" in 1985, Jimmie Durham's "Geronimo Loved Children" in 1998, and an untitled haiku by Linda Jeannette Ward in 2000 (Moses 2004, 103).

Meanwhile, Geronimo was appearing in popular songs.[1] The earliest English-language song mentioning Geronimo that I have encountered comes from 1885. During their tour of duty in the Southwest that year, Company E,

8th U.S. Infantry, were singing about the obstacles to their well-being encountered in the field: uncomfortable sleeping arrangements; poor diet; the ravages of sun and heat; and Geronimo, the "dirty, pesky skate" (Greene 2007, 353). Some ninety years later, country-and-western performer Michael Martin Murphey released "Geronimo's Cadillac" (1972). Inspired by Walter Ferguson's 1905 photograph of Geronimo behind the wheel of a Locomobile, Murphey's song casts Geronimo as heading for the "sunset." The authorities have "ripped off the feathers from his uniform." In return for the loss of the accoutrements of his traditional way of life, he has received the trappings of Euro-American civilization represented by an automobile he cannot drive. To make up for land stolen and not returned, authorities "sent Geronimo a Cadillac." Murphey comments on a system that buys off the freedom-loving Geronimo with a useless gift of modern technology. A decade or so later, in 1986, the German dance duet Modern Talking released a song of the same title. It does not effectively connect its title phrase to the famous Chiricahua but associates the automobile with the speaker's desire to express his emotions freely without fear of rejection by others.

Another song that comments on the contrast between modern technology and Geronimo's idyllic way of life in the wilderness of the Southwest is Sid Hausman's "Geronimo's Land" (1994). This piece focuses on the disparity between the stark austerity of the desert as Geronimo once knew it and modern-day Tucson, Arizona, where "twisted steel and concrete" have replaced indigenous vegetation. Hausman's final image has Geronimo riding alone into the sunset, thus employing the trope of the "vanishing American," which has informed the imagery that shaped policy regarding American Indians since the beginnings of European contact. The same year that Hausman's song came out, country-and-western performer Billy Ray Cyrus included a similarly themed piece titled simply "Geronimo" on his album *Storm in the Heartland* (1994). Written by Cyrus in collaboration with Keith Hinton and Don Von Tress, the song casts Geronimo as a spokesperson for ecological responsibility. He appears to the song's narrator in a vision and suggests his kinship with earth and sky. Geronimo then notes the degradation of the environment caused by Euro-American civilization racing a "steel horse" to the end of rainbow while natural waterways "run black." Planet Earth is suffering from the same lack of respect as Geronimo's way of life on the part of the European invaders.

Perhaps inspired by the advance press for the film *Geronimo: An American Legend*, which opened late in the year, German-born keyboardist and vocalist Mars Lasar included a cut titled "Geronimo" on his CD *The Eleventh Hour* (1993). Heavy chords and crashing percussion set against a background of hoofbeats, whinnying horses, and vocables give way to a vocalist articulating at little more than a whisper in lilting "rez" speech patterns. The listener learns that Geronimo was born in late June 1829 to a father from the Sierra Madre and a mother from the headwaters of the Gila River. Despite his being a "peaceful man," Geronimo suffers the loss of wife and children. Then, "like any man," he vows pitiless revenge for his loss. This sympathetic commentary, set in a "New Age" musical context, reflects the role that Native American imagery was playing in alternative spiritualities in the late twentieth century.

Arigon Starr's "About Geronimo" (1997) takes its inspiration from the characterization of its subject in Leslie Marmon Silko's novel *Almanac of the Dead* (treated later in this chapter). Though not an actual character in Silko's work, Geronimo figures significantly in one of the novel's two major plotlines: preparations for a revolution in which tribal peoples in the Americas will re-possess the land that has been stolen by corrupt Europeans. Geronimo's enduring archetypal significance, developed by Silko, receives allusive treatment in Starr's song: those who believe that Geronimo abandoned his values and is now dead "don't know jack" about him. For Starr (and Silko), Geronimo's significance as a historical individual must bow to a symbolic import that transcends the details of his life.

Like the newspaper doggerel of the 1880s, twentieth-century songs use Geronimo as vehicle for sociopolitical positions. Several extended projects in poetry also use Geronimo's career and image to address the poets' personal concerns as well as their responses to contemporary social issues. One of the most idiosyncratic poetic uses of Geronimo occurs in August Plinth's collection of twenty-five octets titled *Geronimo's Cadillac*, published in 1973. The title, according to a note the poet appends to the collection, comes not from the photograph that suggested Michael Martin Murphey's song but from a folk etymology. Plinth tells the story, which I have encountered nowhere else, that Geronimo was a sickly child excessively attached to his mother. His father tossed him into a river so that its spirit could decide the child's fate. That spirit carried Geronimo back to the spot where his father had placed him in the water, thus forecasting that he had an important destiny to fulfill. The site on the riverbank became known as "Geronimo-Carried-Back," but "later settlers were to change it to Geronimo's Cadillac" (1973, n.p.). References to "Geronimo-Carried-Back" or "Geronimo's Cadillac" appear only a few times in Plinth's twenty-five octets, but he uses those references to denote a condition of tranquility where one is immune to the invasions of the outside world. This usage is evident, for example, in the fourteenth octet in which a father "brought [his offspring] back to life again" by casting him into the waters "the natives call Geronimo Carried Back" (1973, n. p.).

The theme of invasion recurs throughout the octets, which are introduced by a poem titled "The Landlord," which depicts a property owner entering and despoiling the home of one of his tenants. The octet that follows this introductory verse begins, "Take me back, take me back, Geronimo's Cadillac"—a refrain that recurs in the final poem in the series. The twentieth octet most forcefully characterizes "Geronimo's Cadillac" as a place of refuge. There, the speaker, "riding homeward in the dome car of the A.T.S. & F. [*sic*; i.e., Atchison, Topeka, and Santa Fe Railway]," tells a fellow traveler, "'I won't be myself till I get back to Geronimo's Cadillac'" (1973, n.p.). The speaker's interlocutor responds by pointing out a constellation that he names Geronimo's Chariot (which Plinth glosses as the legendary "place in the heavens where Geronimo's [Cadillac?] in climbing up the Tree of Life, crawled through the crack in the heavens to go to his final home" [1973, n.p.]) and that supposedly provides a gateway into a more congenial environment for "misfits" like these two train riders.

Often defined in terms of his critique of postmodern, consumer-oriented, late-capitalist American society, Edward Dorn used the conflict between Apaches and the United States in the 1880s as the basis for a series of poems that pit the "otherness" of the Apaches against contemporary values the poet finds hollow. *Recollections of Gran Apachería* (1974)—which came out a year before what many regard as his masterwork of socially conscious poetry, *Slinger*—utilizes Geronimo and other figures from the Apache wars and their aftermath as celebrations of "difference from European tradition particularly in terms of the ideas the two cultures have of private property and the role of the individual in a post-tribal world" (Dresman 1985, 88). The structure of *Recollections* rests upon "a dialectic between the Apaches and the whites" (107). That dialectic replaces the binary opposition between East Coast and Far West that informs Dorn's poetry in general (Beach 1991, 212). The climax of the epic poem *Slinger*, for example, casts the opposing factions in a war produced by an oil crisis as the "Single-Spacers" and the "Mogollones"—the latter term derived from the landscape of Apachería (Foster 1997, 92).

In *Recollections*, Victorio rather than Geronimo seems to epitomize the "internal resistance" to established authority that the Apaches represent, but the poem "Geronimo" stresses that its title character remains "notorious" because of his stance against "alien authority" (1974, n.p.). Dorn foregrounds Geronimo's otherness by noting that the "invaders" consider his "pleasures" to be "depredations" (1974, n.p.). "Juh & Geronimo" contrasts the Apaches' "obsessive democracy" with the "Military Republicanism" of Euroamerica (1974, n.p.). Throughout *Recollections* Dorn makes use of his characteristic devices such as puns and wordplay, ironic humor, and the debunking of clichés. Though it conflates the separate exile of Geronimo's band with that of the rest of the Chiricahuas, the book's concluding poem, "La Máquina a Houston," encapsulates the theme of cultural chasm developed throughout the work. Inspired by the well-known photograph of Geronimo's band sitting beside the train that is taking them eastward after their surrender to Miles in September 1886 (fig. 6.1), the poem adopts the point of view of the photographer, who recognizes the vast differences between his own and the Apaches' view of the world. The train from which they have exited to have their picture taken is a "máquina," an "agent of frag mentation [*sic*]." The poem ends with this manifestation of the Euro-American rejection of "natural Apache philosophy" ("One cannot have a piece of what is indivisible") being pursued by the Apaches' dogs who howled and moaned as they "saw the smoking creature" carry their masters away. Geronimo, whom Dorn implicates somewhat in his mediation of oppositions by noting that Geronimo's notoriety has endured because of "sensational advertising," nevertheless joins the other indigenes of Apachería to embody the antithesis of the cultural values that "the Clint Eastwood of American poetry" (Wesling 1985, 4) has consistently challenged in his work.

In 2001 Armand Garnet Ruffo, a Canadian Ojibwe, published *At Geronimo's Grave*. A dozen or so of the pieces in the collection respond specifically to Geronimo, and he is a presence in many of the others. Ruffo has strategically placed the Geronimo poems among poems dealing with more personal concerns with family and other issues, perhaps to suggest parallels with what Geronimo experienced and what the oppressed peoples who populate his other poems face. Geronimo emerges as a figure who is both victim of circumstance and, to some degree, molder of his own destiny. For example, in "Power," the first Geronimo poem in the collection, Ruffo writes of the responsibilities that reception of spiritual power places on the recipient: "This beast, this stallion / is not for the weak willed / who bloat like a frog / for personal gain / and turn themselves to dust" (2001, 3). Power is not something that a person should seek; instead it comes to those who have suffered as Geronimo suffered after the massacre at Kaskiyeh, the watershed event in his life.

Fig. 6.1. Somewhere probably in Texas, the Apaches who surrendered with Geronimo (seated in the front row, third from right) disembarked from the train that was taking them to Fort Sam Houston. This photograph was taken in September 1886. *National Archives and Records Administration, Native American Heritage Collection, American Indian Select List 148.*

As the speaker pauses at Geronimo's grave in Oklahoma in the poem that provides the title for the collection, he is impressed by the ambiguity of Geronimo's image: on one hand he was "caught, / they say herded," but on the other the speaker is "reminded / that it took five thousand troops" to effect the surrender of the small band he led (Ruffo 2001, 6). Thinking of the jail at Fort Sill where Geronimo was occasionally incarcerated, usually for drunkenness, the speaker carries flowers to put on the grave located a few miles northeast of that site, where the landscape is filled with "oilfields and prairie flowers, barbed wire and distant mesas," and he wonders "about who [Geronimo] really was." We see that images of Geronimo have become famous worldwide as the speaker relates his purchase of a postcard version of the photograph of Geronimo in the Locomobile at a gift shop in Brighton on the English Channel (7).

"In the Sierra Blanca" has Geronimo remembering an attempt to poison his people with strychnine-laced piñon nuts and reacting to a more egregious outrage: the contamination of the earth by nuclear dump sites. Geronimo has learned much about his materialistic white adversaries, but he is still taken aback by their willingness to destroy the earth (Ruffo 2001, 33). In "Dance to Hold On" the poet references the many appearances by the once feared and respected warrior at national and local venues during the last decade of his life and his status as the principal tourist attraction in southwestern Oklahoma during his confinement at Fort Sill (89).

The penultimate piece in the collection, a prose poem, begins with the expectations that S. M. Barrett, the interviewer who produced Geronimo's autobiography, brought to his encounter with Geronimo. Barrett was anticipating the stereotypical savage warrior but instead encountered a grandfatherly figure dandling a child on his knee. The story that Barrett "extracts" from Geronimo is a litany of deaths: those of his original family at Kaskiyeh as well as the many that occurred during the nineteen years that the Chiricahuas had been prisoners of war. These included other wives, his children, even his grandchildren. Geronimo is left with recourse to shamanic power that he must now incorporate into the new religion that the missionaries have brought to his people (Ruffo 2001, 104).

Ruffo illustrates his collection with well-known photographs of Geronimo in various poses: manufacturing bows and arrows in his booth at the Louisiana Purchase Exposition in 1904 in the photo taken by Charles H. Carpenter, gazing steadfastly at the camera in the famous portrait taken by Frank Randall in 1884, lounging with other Chiricahua prisoners of war outside the train that is taking them eastward into what will be for most of them permanent exile from the their homeland in 1886, and standing with his family holding a watermelon that he has apparently grown in the field behind them sometime in the 1900s. The last two photographs provide references for Ruffo's postscript to the collection, in which he imagines himself aboard the trains that are taking Geronimo to Florida, then Alabama, then Oklahoma, and speaking to the prisoner of war. On one hand, the images evoked by that train ride are tragic or perhaps pathetic: "I see you chained, wrists and ankles, sweating in dismay, swallowed by the beast of progress winding its way toward doom" (2001, 107). But the speaker also prophesies a future in which Geronimo "will swallow them [the forces of Euro-American progress] in the power of myth and the beauty of a galloping horse" (107). There is much to lament in Geronimo's situation, which reflects that of other Native North Americans, including Canada's Ojibwe, and, in fact, oppressed peoples everywhere: violence and imprisonment, adoption of unfamiliar lifeways such as watermelon farming, loss of language, trivialization at fairs and expositions. But the tone of the postscript is not despairing, for the speaker sees in Geronimo's "spirit," his defiance in defending the values that contrast with what is going on around him, a hope that manifests itself in something as simple, contemporary, and seemingly ineffectual as a "Free Leonard Peltier" rally (111).

The most ambitious poetry project involving Geronimo is Rawdon Tomlinson's book-length sequence *Geronimo after Kas-ki-yeh*. Therein, Tomlinson provides a multiple-perspective portrait of Geronimo from the life-changing massacre of his family near Janos, Chihuahua, in 1851 through his death at Fort Sill in 1909. Prefacing his Geronimo poems with a rendering of an etiological myth collected by Morris Edward Opler that attributes the origin of death to Coyote, Tomlinson organizes his sequence of poems into four sections. The first, titled "Year One," treats the massacre at Kaskiyeh and its immediate effects on Geronimo. The seven poems in this section, all voiced by Geronimo, move from a sense of overwhelming grief to hatred for the perpetrators and those like them to self-recrimination. Responding to his mother's death, Geronimo torches the earth at No-Doyohn, the site at the headwaters of the Gila River where she gave birth to him. He burns everything associated with Alope, his wife, even "the words with which you charmed / sickness from my wounds" and the imaginative hopes of his children (2007, 7). Geronimo moves into a frenzy of hatred for all Mexicans: "I sweat everything / but hate" (9). That hatred and the vengeance it inspires will be endless:

> For all of the day I will live,
> and for all of the children
> and wives I will cherish—never enough blood
> for my first,
> perfectly loved. (Tomlinson 2007, 12)

But he also wonders if he shares blame for what has happened. The poem "Only Son" lists prophylactic measures that he had taken to ensure the well-being of those for whom he was responsible but concludes, "What did I forget? / How could I have caught your breath?" (16).

The second section of Tomlinson's book, "After the Crows, Before the

Owls," consists of seven poems mostly reflecting on events that affected Geronimo during the early 1880s, the period when he emerged as the face of savagism on the southwestern frontier. Several speakers voice their responses to that emergence: Bylas, who witnessed the Stevens Camp massacre in 1882; John Clum, who had "captured" Geronimo in 1877 and regretted that he had not been able to have him executed then; an unidentified third-person narrator; and Geronimo himself. Among the incidents about which Tomlinson writes are the massacre of several Mexican sheepherders at the Stevens sheep camp, the deaths of Judge and Mrs. H. C. McComas and the abduction of their son Charlie (which Chatto, not Geronimo, perpetrated), and the futile efforts of a posse led by Clum and Wyatt Earp in pursuit of Geronimo and his band. Geronimo learns something of the ways of the "white eyes" by watching Apache boys kill frogs for Lieutenant Britton Davis and by comparing wounds with scout Al Sieber. This section ends with Geronimo's reactions to the teachings of Nock-ay-del-klinne, the prophet whose death had precipitated the 1881 breakout from San Carlos and the mutiny of the Apache scouts. Drawing upon Geronimo's comments to S. M. Barrett as he narrated his autobiography in 1905, Tomlinson suggests that Geronimo did not take seriously otherworldly visions of the prophet who had "never held / a dead son, felt the body's / stone doll, its eyes opening / a cave in the chest that won't / close with age or steps" (2007, 27). Thirty years after Kaskiyeh, Geronimo remains overwhelmed by the tragedy that befell his family.

Eleven poems make up "A Brief History of the Geronimo Campaign, 1885–1886," the book's third section. The initial poem, "Wire, 1885," evokes the provocation that led to Geronimo's last breakout, which occurred in May 1885 and spawned the fifteen-month campaign that led to his final surrender and deportation. Drinking the proscribed "gray water" does not provide escape from the image of "wall-eye Mickey Free [who] draws his hand / across his throat" while the decapitated head of "Roan Sleeves [as Tomlinson translates the name Mangas Coloradas] floats by" (2007, 31). The bleak tone of this section reflects the perspective of Geronimo and his Chiricahuas, and "Guadalupe Canyon," voiced by William B. Jett, presents the perspective of four troopers ambushed fatally by the Apaches (33). Meanwhile, "They Are Killed" catalogs from the Apache perspective the roster of those who perished during the campaign: named individuals on both sides as well as those who remain unnamed but are identified by their ethnicity ("too many Mexicans to count" in retribution for the loss that initiated Geronimo's enmity and "anonymous black pelts with killed ears / cured of noise" turned in for the bounty paid for Apache scalps [34]). The Apaches who surrender become like a wood ibis shot by General Crook and eviscerated to become a museum cabinet specimen (39–40). They are already dead ("*indeh*").

Tomlinson shows particular interest in the postsurrender condition of the Chiricahuas and devotes the longest and most complex section of his book, "The Tiger of the Human Race," to poems in which several speakers address their situation in Florida, Alabama, and Oklahoma. On one hand, the reader encounters a range of responses to the Chiricahuas' imprisonment. That of the Indians themselves collectively blends confusion and despair with a sense of alienation in an environment populated by rats, hogfish, alligators, and tourists. John Gregory Bourke, who served as General Crook's aide during the Apache wars and gained a reputation as a pioneering ethnologist, assumes a clinical, detached perspective. Tomlinson uses letters from Geronimo's son Chappo, who was sent to the Carlisle Indian School after the surrender and contracted fatal tuberculosis there, and from Geronimo himself to reveal tentative movement toward assimilation. The toll taken on the prisoners distills in the experience of Fun, who joined the U.S. Army but committed suicide at Mount Vernon Barracks ostensibly due to sexual jealousy. When the suicide occurs, "it looks more like defense" (2007, 53).

Other poems in the section focus on Geronimo's situation and reactions to it. The transfer of the community to Fort Sill from Mount Vernon Barracks in 1894 brought them into contact with much that was familiar: distant mountains, deer, quail, sage, mesquite beans, and coyotes (Tomlinson 2007, 54). But it is still not home. Geronimo's entrepreneurship allows him to profit from his image as "The Tiger of the Human Race" since he provides people with souvenirs, "something to prove you've seen / whatever it was you thought you saw" (55). Three Euro-American speakers, who had known Geronimo during the 1880s, react to Geronimo's celebrity and to what life has brought to them: Bourke notes his lack of fulfillment as he lies dying in an army hospital (58); Tom Horn, scout and interpreter, expresses envy, frustration, and a sense of irony as he contrasts Geronimo's fame with his situation as he awaits the gallows in Wyoming (59–60); and Jimmie Stevens, whose pony Geronimo had killed and eaten during the Stevens Camp massacre in 1882 and who later became an interpreter for the non-Chiricahua Apaches who remained at San Carlos, expresses bitterness at the attention Geronimo receives at the Trans-Mississippi and International Exposition in Omaha, where he was translator for his enemy (61–62). Geronimo emerges as trickster, repository of oral tradition, witch, and convert to Christianity in other poems in this section of Tomlinson's work.

This is a complex portrait of an individual whom Tomlinson perceives as exemplifying a response to grief. Geronimo's reaction to the death of his family at Kaskiyeh spawned a career that brought him notoriety and projected his image into the mainstream of American popular culture. Unlike many other writers who have used Geronimo to represent an abstraction, such as savagism or, more recently, resistance to colonial hegemony, Tomlinson has focused on the more human aspects of this figure and produced not only an image but a multifaceted character.

Tomlinson has distinguished himself in the genre of Geronimo poetry. In other works the Chiricahua is merely a vehicle for editorializing on how the "Apache problem" was being handled in the 1880s. Or he represents an enduring spirit of freedom and commitment to tradition as well as an older, idealized lifeway: literally one lost to the encroachments of Euro-American civilization, symbolically one degraded by the undermining of the natural environment. Only Tomlinson sees him as a whole person. In fact, *Geronimo after Kas-ki-yeh* represents the only full realization of Geronimo as a human being not only in poetry but in drama and fiction as well.

Drama

The only nineteenth-century dramatic depiction of Geronimo that I have found assumes the anti-Crook theme of the era's newspaper verse. The five acts of *The History of Geronimo's Summer Campaign in 1885*, written by George Duncan Cummings and copyrighted in 1890, four years after Geronimo's final surrender, received a scathing review in *Overland Monthly* for October 1893, which dismissed it as "easily the worst" historically oriented publication of the year. Cummings's work was a "mere pamphlet slip, without a publisher or address; a scurrilous attack, ignorantly written and full of misspellings, upon General Crook and the army" ("Verse of the Year" 1893, 442). More than a century later one finds little to challenge in this assessment. It is unlikely that the play enjoyed much success when it was published, since issues regarding Crook's alleged mishandling of affairs in Arizona Territory were definitely old news by that time. But the real focus of the play is not so much Crook as the depiction of Geronimo as savage and lustful. In fact, the play—as carelessly written as it is—represents the fullest literary development of Geronimo's image from the nineteenth century and does so in terms that advance a prevailing stereotype of American

Indians, like other dark-skinned males, as sexual predators. Cummings's play is one of the few literary treatments of Geronimo that subject him to that stereotype.

Written in either blank verse or heroic couplets with no apparent rationale for using one rather than the other, the play focuses on the reactions of several groups of Anglos to the murder by Geronimo and his band (including such figures as Tarantula-Hawk, Cactus-Worm-Sucker, and Chipmonk [sic]) of a wealthy Arizona rancher named Parolenus and the capture of his wife, Lauruna (whose name Cummings spells variously in the play).

The play's Geronimo has legitimate grievances about the treatment of his people. In his first speech, he complains to Tarantula-Hawk:

> Our people have humiliation long
> Withstood from this intruding foreign throng;
> Who come with rifles shooting down our deer,
> And herding us on Reservation here;
> They first compell'd us move our rancherias,
> Then trampled down our crops of corn and maize. (Cummings 1890, 6)

But his principal motivation for violence is sexual predation. He tells Tarantula-Hawk that after attacking the ranch maintained by Anglo interloper Parolenus, "I'll feast my fancy on his pretty spouse," while the other Apaches can have his livestock (6). When he captures Lauruna, he recalls for her how his ancestors had, after conquering the Zunis,

> seized their maturing squaws, who followed our
> Victorious, young voluptuous chiefs
> To shady nooks to share the sweetness of
> Enamor'd bliss without a murmur. (14)

He exclaims to her, "White squaw, you look upon your paramour" (14). Tarantula-Hawk carries her off with the words, "I'll guide you where / You may our gallant chief's affection share" (15). Later her guard urges her to keep up her strength and health: "I want to keep you fat for our big chief; / He likes fat squaws to love with all" (28). Moreover,

> He likes you more
> Than any squaw he ever met before;

And he will use you in so fine a way
That every buck would long to have the play. (30)

The play, though, does not depict Lauruna as naive ingenue. She appears, in fact, to have had premarital relations with Norrian, leader of a band of rustlers; with Carl Manden, a prospector who comes as close as any character to being the play's protagonist; and with "heaven knows how many other men and wild rape-roving Indians" (43), as Manden's sidekick McSweedom suggests. In the scene leading up to her husband's death and her capture, she appears to be somewhat shrewish, not "this fairy goddess of the Gila plain" (62), as she is later referred to. Her sexual experience does not diminish the image of Geronimo as lustful predator, but it tended to make Lauruna's being targeted by that lust less shocking than if she had been sexually innocent. The play concludes with Geronimo returning to the reservation and Lauruna rescued, apparently untainted, and returned to Carl Manden. He is hailed by General Juárez, whom he encounters during a scout into Sonora, as

the only man
. . . in the history of the West,
[who] Rescued a woman from the Chiricahuas
Unmarr'd. (72)

The play does have a strong anti-Crook bias, though that is not as central to its development as the critic in *Overland Monthly* implied. Geronimo believes that Crook's experiences during the Sierra Madre campaign a few years earlier had made the general hesitant about taking decisive action against the Apaches: "He was so worried on that rugged brow / That he won't venture on the warpath now" (Cummings 1890, 7). Just moments before his death at the hands of Geronimo's band, Parolenus is complaining about the ineffectiveness of the army as compared with his own efforts to thwart them:

I filled a thieving Ing [Indian]
So full of lead, that neither Satan or
His other black companions recognized
His hide. That was the only Indian killed
For many years, though army men boast of
Their fine exploits and many conquests won

While hunting desperate, bold Apaches down;
Though I believe they seized upon an old lame squaw,
In one campaign, and made her prisoner of war. (14)

When he brings the news of Parolenus's death and Lauruna's capture to Crook, the courier asserts that the rancher is "deader than / The government's late Indian policy" (18). Crook's response to this news and to entreaties that he take action to prevent other atrocities, which the characters enumerate in titillating detail, suggests that he is in denial: "For goodness sake you harping fiends let up, / 'Tis Injin, Injin, Injin that you roar" (20–21). He does, though, send Captain Crawford (the only historical figure besides Geronimo and Crook to appear in the play) to bring Geronimo's band "as prisoners of war, / Surrendered unconditionally to us" (21).

The play's anti-Crook message is strengthened by the introduction of Dubrans, an "Indian lover" from back East who has come to Arizona Territory on an investigative mission for the organization he has formed to "protect / the noble redman from being pilfer'd by / The wicked element who settles here" (31). With the apparent sympathy of Crook, who admiringly refers to Geronimo as "Caesar of the plains" (36), Dubrans announces his intentions "to see that you adventurers do not / Corrupt the morals of the Indian" (33). In what amounts to poetic justice from the playwright's perspective, Dubrans is captured by the Apaches and tortured by Geronimo's band, who use him for target practice. As the prospector McSweedom, who represents the voice of reason in the play when it comes to Indian policy, reports with apparent satisfaction, they then "cut his head off with the scalp, / And hanged it from the dangling branches of / a greenwood tree" (61).

Eighty years after Cummings's play was published, Geronimo again appeared as a dramatic character in a scene in Arthur Kopit's *Indians* (1971), which uses Buffalo Bill's Wild West show to criticize U.S. imperialistic ventures, including the Vietnam War. Shown encaged, raging, and boasting of his history of sexual violence, Kopit's Geronimo suggests the effects not only of the "touristic gaze" (see chapter 3) and nineteenth-century Indian policy but also of continuing attempts to establish Euro-American hegemony over non-Western peoples. When Robert Altman turned Kopit's play into the film *Buffalo Bill and the Indians, or Sitting Bull's History Lesson* in 1976, he omitted Geronimo from the dramatis personae.

Fiction

While fiction has offered the most fertile literary soil for developing Geronimo's image, few authors have taken the opportunity to do so. Geronimo's fictional appearances have almost always been in subsidiary roles even when his name stands prominently in the title of a short story or novel. Usually Geronimo only lurks in the background as a menace to the sympathetic Euro-American characters and possibly as worthy adversary to enhance a protagonist's stature. This describes Geronimo's role in five fictional works by Edward S. Ellis. In its column Literary News of Philadelphia for 11 April 1908, the *New York Times* announced that this "veteran writer of stories for boys" and pioneer dime novelist had turned over to his publisher the manuscripts of three books comprising the Arizona Series: "The scene of these stories is in Arizona, about 1885, when Geronimo and the Apaches were on the warpath. The last volume is said to bring the young hero's adventures to a triumphant end in the style which Mr. Ellis's thousands of readers have long loved." These volumes were not the prolific Ellis's first attempt at Geronimo fiction. He had published a novel, *On the Trail of Geronimo, or In the Apache Country*, in 1889 (republished in 1901) and a novella, "A Campaign of Strategy," in *The Argosy* in 1897. The latter foregrounds Geronimo as an actual character more than Ellis's other four works, though the real narrative focus is the plight of the Euro-American characters, including the requisite gallant hero and endangered female.

In *On the Trail of Geronimo*, perhaps the first novel to be written about Geronimo, a recent graduate of West Point comes to Arizona on his maiden assignment shortly after Geronimo's departure from Fort Apache in 1885. The protagonist's initial misadventure puts him in the clutches of a war party of Apaches, "the most venomous red men that ever lived" (Ellis [1889] 1901, 59), led by Geronimo, from whom he escapes when a troop of soldiers handily appears. Much of the novel's plot focuses on the plight of a family group whose ranch is burned by the Apaches, who carry off the womenfolk. An exchange is effected when soldiers capture Geronimo's son.

Geronimo, "one of the mightiest scoundrels since the time of Victorio and the old leaders of the Apaches" (Ellis [1889] 1901, 79), actually plays a larger role in this novel than in the three books that make up Ellis's Arizona Series. The narrator describes the leader of the "dusky fiends of the Southwest" (137) in terms that suggest a familiarity with Frank Randall's 1884 photograph: "He was a heavy set man in middle life, his long, wiry black hair straggling about his shoulders, with a broad mouth, teeth stained by tobacco smoke, twinkling lead-like eyes, square massive jaws, and a villainous expression, in which it would have been hard to find a trace of kindness or magnanimity" (75). Much of the novel's characterization of Geronimo and his band, though, focuses on their subhuman savageness. Each individual sleeps "as lightly as a panther" (141); they evince a "frightful ferocity" (181); fighting is "the work for which they seem to believe they are born" (241); they are the last people in the world "to be accused of mercy" (242); they exhibit mastery of "every bit of low cunning of which the human race is capable" (263); and they speak a "mongrel tongue" (326). Ellis probably had no special complaint against Apaches or Geronimo, but his fiction required a clear demarcation between heroic Euro-Americans and savage adversaries. Using the names Apache and Geronimo would evoke that demarcation for most readers, and Ellis relies on the images, fostered by most of the press accounts during the Apache wars, that these appellations and epithets would elicit. At one point, the novel's protagonist has the opportunity to shoot Geronimo from a hidden position but gallantly declines to do so. The narrator laments that the protagonist's code of honor has prevented him from killing the Chiricahua leader: "Such an act, though seemingly cruel in itself, would have been the best possible service he could render to the frontier, for with Geronimo slain, the revolt of the Apaches could be put down with little difficulty and many innocent lives saved" (278).

In 1897 the prolific Ellis, writing under his occasional pseudonym Latham C. Carleton, published a twelve-chapter short novel titled "A Campaign of Strategy," which features Geronimo as leader of a band "of the unspeakable Apache, the most terrible red men that ever spread death among the settlements" (1897, 579). Geronimo and his fellow "imps"—a term used without the semi-positive connotations it has in contemporary discourse— have broken away from the reservation and are threatening communities in southwestern Arizona, not far from the Colorado River. The plot follows a couple of women left alone at a cattle ranch who manage to escape into nearby foothills before the Apaches burn down the ranch house. After several wrong turns and red herrings, the hero finds them wandering about the wilderness. The three are confronted, though, by three Apaches, among them Geronimo himself. The standoff, which seems to be leading to the deaths of everyone there, resolves itself when the Indians realize that the hero's sidekick, an amateur photographer, has come upon the scene. They rush off in terror, for "the aboriginal American has a mortal antipathy to having his picture taken" (578).

Like Ellis's other fictions in which Geronimo figures, the famous Apache appears sparingly in "A Campaign of Strategy," but Ellis goes beyond simply using his name and image to cue the reader that the setting for the story will involve consummate savagery. Early in his narrative—on the third page of the published text (579)—Ellis identifies that what follows is a Geronimo story. But here the Apache warrior is more than a menacing off-stage presence. The physical description of Geronimo when he believes that he has his prey—particularly the two women—in his power again recalls the image from the Randall photograph: "His seamed and hard countenance[,] one of the most forbidding that can be imagined, was without a smile, but there was something in the twinkle of the little black eyes and in the twitching lines at the corners of the mouth that told of his enjoyment of the scene" (619). Geronimo's face is "hideous"; he has "no paint on his features, and he could scarcely have made them more terrifying had he daubed his face like most of his fellows. His eyes [suggest] those of a rattlesnake." Geronimo's "gruff, grating" voice completes the image of consummate savagery that Ellis conveys (620). Readers are prepared long before Geronimo makes this climactic appearance to expect an utter villain, one beyond the margins of humanity. Some of that preparation stems from Geronimo's iconic power, but Ellis does not run the risk that his readers might not have known the imagery, that they might be among those people, easterners for the most part, for whom Geronimo had come to have some claim to human identity in the eight years since Ellis's earlier Geronimo novel had appeared. Throughout the story Geronimo and Apaches in general become not only "imps" (583, 597, 605, 612) but also "devils" (581, 609), "miscreants" (586, 591, 619), "murderous wretches" (586), "demons" (597, 598), "fiends" (610), and "the embodiment of inextinguishable hate and ferocity" (613). Ellis also repeatedly, though obliquely, reminds readers of the fate that will befall the women if they are captured by the Apaches: "You know what it means, sister, to fall into their hands! Better that we should let them set fire to the house and burn us to death" (591). Each carries a pistol with which to kill herself should she face dishonor from Geronimo. The younger of the pair "had lived but a short time in the Southwest, but long enough to know that every white woman exposed to capture by the demons carried a revolver with which to blow out her brains, on the instant that all hope of escape was gone" (598). When the climactic confrontation occurs, the two resolve to shoot each other should their heroic male protector fail them.

Ellis thus presents nothing really new in the narrative, and over a decade after the Apache wars had ended at Skeleton Canyon he is still drawing upon the hysterical rhetoric of territorial newspapers. His only innovation is having Geronimo and his bloodthirsty band cross miles of desert as they make their way from San Carlos or Fort Apache all the way to the banks of the Colorado in their desire to provoke terror, for he suggests no other motive for the Apaches' actions.

Ellis's principal contribution to expressive culture about Geronimo was his trilogy of novels featuring young Bob Goodale and his sister Minnie, who venture from their uncle's farm in Pennsylvania to Arizona Territory for adventures with another uncle, a rancher. *Off the Reservation, or Caught in An Apache Raid, Trailing Geronimo, or Campaigning with Crook*, and *The Round-Up, or Geronimo's Last Raid*, all published in 1908, formed the Arizona Series, one of several sets of connected novels that Ellis published. The first of the Arizona novels has Bob Goodale visiting his uncle and then joined later by his sister, Minnie. Back East they had already met Cochita, an educated Apache. While Bob is in Arizona, he learns that Geronimo has left the reservation at the very time when Minnie is to arrive. She and their aunt fall into the hands of Cochita, who has gone "back to the blanket" and become a political rival of the much older Geronimo. Cochita tries to extract an acceptance of his marriage proposal from Minnie in return for restoring the women to their family. A night in the foothills of the Santa Catalina Mountains involves a microcosm of the southern Arizona population: two bands of Apaches (one led by Cochita, one led by Geronimo); Bob, his uncle, and two Arizona scouts; and some U.S. Cavalry officers. Geronimo kills rival Cochita, and the women return safely to their friends. Geronimo remains a secondary character throughout the novel but is consistently characterized as the worst of a very bad lot of Indians.

In *Trailing Geronimo* (fig. 6.2), Bob and Maris Royden, whom he and Minnie have met on the train while returning from the Arizona adventures of the first novel and who is a distant relative of General Crook, go back to the Southwest and join Crawford's expedition into the Sierra Madre. The novel describes Crawford's death and continues through Geronimo's surrender to Crook and subsequent escape, thus setting up the final installment in the series. Set in the summer of 1886, *The Round-Up* focuses again on Bob Goodale and Maris Royden, who, along with the colorful Corporal Billy Bidewill, join the final pursuit of Geronimo, who does not figure personally

FIG. 6.2. Edwin J. Prittie provided illustrations for the three volumes that comprised Edward S. Ellis's Arizona Series. The caption for the frontispiece of the second volume reads, "They picked up the trail." *From Edward S. Ellis,* Trailing Geronimo or Campaigning with Crook *(Chicago: John C. Winston, 1908).*

in the novel until the end when Ellis presents fictionalized accounts of his encounters with Gatewood, Lawton, and Miles.

Geronimo remains a background figure throughout the three books. Ellis does not provide enough information about him for the reader to see beyond the stock figure of the "red devil," and what information he does provide is not always accurate. For example, in *Off the Reservation*, the Goodales' uncle says of Geronimo:

> He is the leader of the Warm Springs Indians. He inherits his ferocious nature from his father Mangus Colorado, who was never ill-treated by the whites, but who raged like a tiger up and down the southwestern frontier. I am glad to say that I helped to hoist that demon over the Great Divide without giving him time to take off his "boots." (Ellis 1908a, 52–53)

The trilogy does little beyond demonizing Geronimo as well as Apaches in general: "the most terrible Indians that ever scourged our continent" (1908a, 12); "the worst body of wretches on the American continent" (1908a, 131); "the worst tribe of American Indians" (1908a, 144); "abominable red men, the most repellent and terrible beings that imagination can picture" (1908a, 180); "wily imps of the Southwest" (1908c, 185); "scourges of the Southwest" (1908c, 342); "fitted by nature and training to be the most fearful desperadoes that ever ravaged a country's frontiers" (1908b, 86); "merciless demons" (1908b, 156). Chapter 27 of *Off the Reservation*, titled "An Interruption," summarizes the narrator's perception of Apaches, especially Geronimo. Therein Ellis jumps ahead more than twenty years to report on Geronimo's appearance at Theodore Roosevelt's inauguration in 1905. There Roosevelt demonstrated his insight into the situation—confronting the "whining old scamp," who begs "with tears in his eyes" to be allowed to return to his Arizona home—by noting that many people in the Southwest were still interested in vengeance for Apache depredations during the 1880s. Ellis's narrator also recalls that twenty years previously Geronimo had been unmatched in his "hatred of the white people." Moreover, he was noted for his ability to dissemble: "When he played the good Indian he did it with perfect skill." Geronimo could be "docile even to the point of humility" and would genially chat with military officials on the reservation about their conflicts. He would vow to have given up his former life for the contentment of the reservation. However, "if the officers who thus chatted with the scourge of the Southwest inquired for him the next day, they were probably told that he and a party of turbulent bucks were skurrying for Mexico, leaving a trail of blood and fire and death behind them" (1908a, 277–78). For Ellis, Geronimo and Apaches in general are consummate villains, figures who provide the context of conflict against which the novels' protagonists act out the roles with which his young readers can identify. His only departure from the imagery that had been coloring most accounts of the Geronimo campaign in the press and other literature is his positive comment about General Crook: "not only a brilliant plainsman, but also a humane one" (1908c, 90).

Among the earliest novels for adults set against the backdrop of the Apache wars, Gwendolen Overton's *The Heritage of Unrest*, published in 1901, also treats Geronimo only sparingly. The novel only touches on conflicts between soldiers and Apaches during the 1870s and 1880s and instead focuses on life on military posts in the Southwest. Geronimo and his companions receive the customary epithets of "devils" (1901, 102, 296) or "fiends" (131). The narrator also recounts an atrocity story whose motifs resemble those that had been circulating in the press and probably by word of mouth in the 1880s:

> A raiding party of hostiles had passed near the fort, and had killed, with particular atrocity, a family of settlers. The man and his wife had been tortured to death, the baby had had its brains beaten out against the trunk of a tree, a very young child had been hung by the wrist tendons to two meat hooks on the walls of the ranch-house, and left there to die. One big boy had had his eyelids and lips and nose cut off, and had been staked down to the ground with his remains of a face lying over a red-ant hole. (Overton 1901, 195)

Such stories, the reader learns, had affected Geronimo's morale in particular, and one of his Apache cohorts claims that the war shaman had been praying "to the Dawn and the Darkness and the Sun and the Sky to help him put a stop to those bad stories that people put in the papers about him." Geronimo feared that the frequent recommendation in the press that he should be hanged would be realized (270). The only appearance by Geronimo in the novel occurs at the re-creation of negotiations with General Crook at Cañon de los Embudos. There the narrator supplies one of those physical descriptions of Geronimo that had been a staple of press accounts some fifteen years before the novel's publication:

The character of Geronimo, as already manifested, was not one to inspire much confidence, nor was his appearance one to command respect. The supposititious dignity of the savage was lacking entirely. The great chief wore a filthy shirt and a disreputable coat, a loin-cloth, and a dirty kerchief wound around his head. His legs were bare from the hips, save for a pair of low moccasins. His whole appearance was grotesque and evil. (Overton 1901, 297)

Geronimo then presents his "usual tale of woe," focusing on the threat of hanging. The narrator makes much of Crook's lack of cordiality (297–98), and after Geronimo makes his plea he disappears from the novel except for an appended note of his final surrender and deportation to Florida. Novelist Overton evinces little interest in her setting except as context for the romantic triangle that is central to the story between a soldier, an English expatriate who sometimes serves the army as a scout, and the soldier's wife, whose mother was an Apache. Overton does little with the wife's Apache heritage in terms of the specifics of the Apache wars but stresses instead the role of "biracial" identity in shaping her character.

Following the lead of Edward S. Ellis, Everett T. Tomlinson used the Geronimo campaign of the summer of 1886 as a backdrop for an adventure novel for young adults. *The Pursuit of the Apache Chief*, published in 1920, places Jack Mcbrier, an engineer who has spent two years in Arizona, and his younger brother Alfred, who is spending time there during his summer vacation, in a Southwest filled with elements of fantastic adventure reminiscent more of the late nineteenth-century dime novel tradition than of other fictions in which Geronimo appears: a reclusive giant, underground passages through mountains that emit mysterious sounds, caverns filled with glittering stalagmites and stalactites, and a "Great Medicine Stone" sacred to the Apaches. The Indians led by Naiche and Geronimo are on the warpath because of a dispute over water rights, and the novel's heroes face the constant threat of capture and subsequent torture. The novel repeatedly stresses that Geronimo, though not the hereditary chief, is the real leader of the insurrection. A seasoned prospector tells the Mcbrier brothers, "He's a dangerous man. I never saw such bright eyes in any human face as he has got, and when you look at his jaw you know he wouldn't give up until he's dead and even then you'll have your work cut out to prove that he is dead" (5).

Despite repeated references to the threat posed by Geronimo, especially due to his wiliness and the devotion he inspired in his followers, he does not actually appear as a character in the novel. In fact, the only historical figures who do so are Henry W. Lawton and Naiche (as "Natchez"). After a series of improbable adventures, Jack and Alfred find themselves in charge of one of the heliostats that Nelson Miles had introduced to the Southwest to facilitate communications among his troops. The novel then rushes to a conclusion, tying up few of the loose ends in the affairs of the two brothers, by summarizing the events surrounding Geronimo's surrender to Miles, whose laudatory biography consumes the entire penultimate chapter of Tomlinson's book. Though not vilified as in many other pro-Miles pieces, George Crook receives somewhat dismissive treatment. Clearly, Tomlinson, though relatively accurate when he treats Geronimo's surrender, was using the Chiricahua primarily as a way of grounding his narrative in the familiar and the sensational. A notice of the book in the *Atlanta Constitution* for 12 December 1920 characterizes it as "a story . . . full of thrillers, made up of dangers and hard fighting backed by the best brand of courage."

Because of its overt polemics regarding how the Geronimo campaign should be remembered, *When Geronimo Rode,* a romance novel published by Forrestine C. Hooker in 1924, warrants a more significant place than these other novels in my examination of Geronimo in fiction. Hooker was the daughter of Charles L. Cooper, who is credited with organizing the Rough Riders during the Spanish-American War and, more importantly for the purposes of this novel, the captor of Mangus, who had not surrendered with Geronimo at Skeleton Canyon. This novel sets its love story against the background of the final Geronimo campaign, which allows the author to promote three agendas: that Geronimo was a consummate villain, certainly not worthy of any of the celebrity that he attained during the last couple of decades of his life; that the Apache wars did not end with Geronimo's surrender at Skeleton Canyon but with her father's apprehension of Mangus some six weeks after that surrender; and that the policies of General George Crook, especially his use of Indian scouts against Geronimo, were wrongheaded.

The romantic plot is conventional and formulaic. Bonita, a military child who had been orphaned, arrives at Fort Grant after having finished schooling back East to take up residence with the foster family that had adopted her at just about the time of Geronimo's 1885 breakout. Among the largely African American troops there, she finds love with one of the white officers. Misunderstandings that create distance between them ensue, but eventually they reunite despite these and other obstacles, most of which have nothing to do with Geronimo.

In her foreword, Hooker claims that in order to write the novel "it was not necessary for me to read what other authors had already written" (1924, x). Instead, she relies upon her own memories from when she "lived in the heart of the Geronimo campaign" (x). In fact, she seems to have been roughly a contemporary of her protagonist and was at Fort Grant, where her father was stationed, during the mid-1880s. She also notes that after her marriage to a rancher in 1886 she remained in the region through the first decade of the twentieth century. Moreover, conversations with many participants in the campaign, including General Miles, contributed to her view of the circumstances that provide the setting for her love story.

Geronimo himself, a minor figure in the story, is always characterized negatively. His appearance repels the viewer: "Those who saw Geronimo for the first time shrank at his cruel mouth" (Hooker 1924, 1). The real cause of the breakout in May 1885 is his desire to exercise "absolute dictatorship over Natchez, Mangus, and the entire tribe" (5). He aspires to unite not only the Chiricahuas at Fort Apache, but the "San Carlos, the Yuma, and the Mohave Apaches . . . into one immense band that should drive every white person out of Arizona Territory and leave it to his despotic rule" (6). Hooker, though, portrays Geronimo as the intellectual inferior to "Natchez," who is manipulating him so that when the U.S. Army eventually and inevitably triumphs, Geronimo, "the puppet of Natchez, would be held responsible for the atrocities committed during the outbreak" (7). Geronimo has a reputation for "craftiness and unreliability" (52), and he can attract followers among the Chiricahuas only by reminding them of their common legacy from Cochise and of some of the more notable instances of U.S. perfidy against the Apaches.

None of the novel's principal characters even meet Geronimo, though a band led by him does entrap the protagonist, her foster mother, their African American cook, and a gallant African American soldier who protects them in a cave until the fortuitous arrival of troops who drive the Indians away. Shortly afterward that band perpetrates the Peck Ranch massacre, which Hooker describes only indirectly: "The mother had been tortured with indescribable fiendishness, while her husband, securely bound, had been forced to witness it all. Death was merciful to her. The tiny mangled form of the babe had been tossed across its mother's body" (1924, 246). Scheming, manipulative, egotistical, and remorseless, Hooker's Geronimo is an unmitigated villain, the ideal adversary in "the great game of civilization against savagery" being played out in the Southwest (269). When the end for Geronimo occurs at Skeleton Canyon, he is "a crushed and broken old man" (272). Hooker's depiction of the terms of surrender indicates that the exile of the entire Chiricahua nation is to be permanent and that Geronimo apprehends this condition: "He understood fully in that moment that his ambition and treachery had ruined his entire tribe. When he raised his head there was no defiance in his look. The Apache leader who had never granted mercy to the helpless knew that he deserved none. His shoulders sagged, the shrewd gleam faded from his eyes" (270–71). He abjectly pleads with Miles to spare his life, no matter what the cost.

Mangus appears to be Geronimo's superior in every way throughout the novel. He is particularly disdainful of Geronimo and tries to prevent depredations north of the border because he recognizes the danger of eliciting pursuit by U.S. forces. Hooker suggests a divergence of ways between Geronimo and Mangus when the spoils of Josanie's raid include thirty-eight scalps taken in Arizona despite an agreement to avoid incursions into that region: "It was a thing unprecedented in Indian history; for an Indian's pledge in those days was more rigidly kept than the average white man's oath" (1924, 54). Subsequently, Mangus, the man whom Geronimo "most feared and envied," is excluded from the renegades' leadership circle (56). Nevertheless, more than Geronimo he reflects the supposed intent of the breakout: to obtain freedom rather than to terrorize. The narrator reports, "While Mangus with his loyal followers struck trail into the heart of northern Mexico, Geronimo's band slipped from place to place, leaving in their wake mutilated bodies of those who travelled alone, or cattle slaughtered and the loin cut out while the rest of the carcass lay untouched" (64). Most likely, Mangus receives such positive treatment in order to make him a suitable adversary for Charles L. Cooper, who appears just at the end of the novel and effects the final resolution to the Apache wars by daringly capturing Mangus and affording him a dignity in defeat that Geronimo neither received nor deserved.

Hooker's broader view of the campaign decidedly undercuts the approach taken by Crook, especially his use of Indian scouts to pursue Geronimo ("an extraordinary example of misapplied strategy" [218]). Though criticism of Crook is muted, often consisting of references to how the local press is treating him, the novel's extravagant praise of the abilities of Crook's replacement, Nelson A. Miles, shows the contrast between the two generals to Crook's disadvantage. Miles is a "gallant and experienced officer, a man of heart as well as of invincible purpose and military science" (218). The protagonist's foster father recalls his previous service under Miles: "I want to tell you that the big thing about him is that the human material cooperates with him, and credit is given by him where it is deserved—not made into a halo for his own head." In what is perhaps a nod to Miles's subsequent political career, the speaker predicts, "But he will never get credit for his work while he lives. Too much politics in the army, my boy. Too much politics!" (225). The positive view of Miles extends to other figures who assumed post-Crook leadership positions in the campaign, especially Henry Lawton and Leonard Wood, whom the narrator lauds: "But not even Miles's perspicacity suggested to him then that one day the whole American nation, and even Europe, would be familiar with the name of the fair-haired, blue-eyed young doctor. A name that America has written on the pages of her history—Leonard Wood" (220). While Lawton and Wood receive the most credit for convincing Geronimo to surrender, Charles L. Gatewood does garner some attention, though significantly, the Chiricahua scouts who helped to effect his contact with Geronimo are not mentioned at all.

The novel's negative depiction of the scouts appears most strikingly in its treatment of Emmet Crawford, the only historical figure developed as a character. Crawford had known Bonita as an infant and spends an evening at Fort Grant reminiscing about old times before heading into Mexico as one of the few regular army officers amid a large company of Chiricahua scouts (71–87). Though the scouts are not blamed directly for Crawford's death, Hooker's narration of the event suggests that their presence aroused sufficient suspicion among Mexican forces that the armed conflict in which Crawford received his fatal wound was inevitable (171). Hooker implies that Crawford's death resulted from Crook's misguided approach.

While Hooker's love story meets its readers' formulaic expectations, she has taken the opportunity afforded by popular fiction to create a vehicle for her perceptions of what had happened in Arizona Territory forty years previously. Some of her facts are incorrect (for instance, she has all the Chiricahuas, including Geronimo, shipped off to Fort Marion), and racism characterizes her depictions of the Indian characters (except for one scout who had been influenced by training at Carlisle) and African Americans, who may be heroic but are inevitably childlike and obsequious. However, as a vehicle for a particular perspective on the Apache wars, the novel deserves some particular attention.

Best known for creating Tarzan, Edgar Rice Burroughs also published two novels set during the time of the Apache wars. *The War Chief* ([1927] 2009) and *Apache Devil* ([1928] 2009), both serialized in *Argosy All-Story Weekly*, feature Geronimo as an important secondary character whose image contrasts with other fictional portrayals of him at the time. Burroughs's Geronimo differs so markedly from the Geronimo of earlier fictions that his novels represent a watershed in the literary imagining of the well-known Chiricahua. But the protagonist of both novels is Andy MacDuff, a boy captured in a raid led by Geronimo, who raises the white child as his own son. In *The War Chief*, young MacDuff becomes Shoz-Dijiji, the Black Bear, under the tutelage of his foster father and does not realize that he is not a full-blood Apache. Influenced by the theory of unilinear cultural evolution, which had dropped from academic anthropology a generation earlier, Burroughs shows that the "bare, unlovely germ of savagery" ([1927] 2009, 2) resided in the essential nature of MacDuff's Scots-Cherokee parents and was paramount in the identity of "Go-yat-thlay," as he calls Geronimo: "It abode in the breast of Go-yat-thlay, an Apache[,] and identical, in the breast of Andy MacDuff, the infant white" (3). While the fundamental savagery of MacDuff's forebears had remained hidden by a patina of civilization, "back of Go-yat-thlay there was no civilization." In fact, "down through all the unthinkable ages from the beginning the savage germ that animated him had come untouched by any suggestion of refinement." Geronimo was a "stark savage" (3). Nevertheless, he saves the infant from the ambush that claims the lives of his mother and father and makes him into an Apache warrior: "From fierce and terrible Go-yat-thlay, who was never fierce or terrible to him, he learned that it was his duty to kill the enemies of his people— to hate them, to torture them, to kill them" (10). Geronimo comes across as model father, instructing MacDuff in the ways of the "Shis-Inday," praising his accomplishments, and defending him from detractors. And one of Shoz-Dijiji's principal detractors is envious and vain Juh, who had wanted to brain the white infant at the time of the deaths of his parents and tries to undermine Shoz-Dijiji's increasingly important position in the community by hinting at his non-Apache ancestry. Juh becomes Shoz-Dijiji's rival for his childhood sweetheart Ish-kay-nay, tricks her into marrying him by convincing her of Shoz-Dijiji's death, and is indirectly responsible for her death. In one of the novel's most gripping scenes, Shoz-Dijiji kills Juh in revenge.

On one hand, despite his military service in the Southwest during the 1890s, Burroughs is somewhat loose with historical and ethnographic fact. Not only does he cast Juh as the rival of his protagonist and thus hostile to Geronimo, but he errs several times in the novel about Apache culture: asserting that the traditional residences of the Bedonkohes were "hogans" (7), claiming that Geronimo was "elected" chief of the Bedonkohes (8) and later war chief of all the Apaches (37), suggesting that Apaches relished the meat of the black bear that Shoz-Dijiji killed to earn his name (13), attributing the cut-the-tent episode to Mangas Coloradas rather than Cochise (15), indicating that successful warriors returned with scalps of fallen enemies (66, 108), attributing a diet of "lizard and snakes" to warriors in the field (202), and assigning considerable age to Geronimo at the time when the novel is set (225–26). Yet he carefully dates much of the narrative: Geronimo was born in 1829; the massacre of the MacDuff family occurs in 1863; Shoz-Dijiji kills his black bear in 1873. Though Burroughs makes no attempt to relate the action of his novel to specific historical occurrences, its final events coincide with the breakout that occurred after the death of the prophet "Nakay-do-Klunni," in which the novel's Geronimo refuses to participate.

Of course, readers do not go to Edgar Rice Burroughs for anthropological or historical information about either colonial Africa or the American Southwest. His slips suggest that he was relying on a smattering of knowledge about the Apache wars, which he must have obtained from contemporary literature. The interest lies in his improving the image of Geronimo compared to how it frequently appeared in that literature. Burroughs knew that Geronimo had attained the status of "red devil" in the popular mind in the 1880s and retained it almost twenty years after his death. For example, he cites Geronimo's "cruel face" ([1927] 2009, 16), a characterization of his appearance that had been a commonplace in descriptions of the Apache since the 1880s. Geronimo is "ugly, morose, vengeful" and has "cruel, blue [!] eyes" (83–84). He is boastful, especially when under the influence of tiswin (101), and Burroughs denominates him "terrible old Geronimo" (134). When Shoz-Dijiji brings a white woman who has befriended him to Geronimo's camp for protection, her initial reaction evokes the demonic image that had often attached itself to Geronimo in press reports: "Geronimo! The fiend, the red devil, murderer, torturer, scourge of two nations!" (233). The woman "recalled every hideous atrocity that had ever been laid at the door of this terrible old man, and she shrank from the thought of permitting herself to be taken to his hidden den and delivered into his cruel and bloody hands" (234–35). Geronimo's gentle, welcoming behavior belies her prejudgments, and throughout *The War Chief* Burroughs challenges conventional wisdom to portray Geronimo as a human undeserving of the opprobrium that popular opinion had assigned to him: "A simple, kindly old soul was the old chief when compared with the diplomats of civilization who seek by insidious and false propaganda to break down the defenses of whole nations that they may fall easier prey to the attacks of their enemies. Yet ever will the name of Geronimo be held up to a horrified world as the personification of cruelty and treachery" (93). Geronimo is no noble savage in Burroughs's novel, but he is not a "red devil." Though a secondary character in the novel, he is more a presence than in previous fictional incarnations. Geronimo provides the lure to attract readers to the story of Andy MacDuff, child of civilization who reverts to the savagery of his ancestors.

Shoz-Dijiji, whose enculturation by Apache savages parallels the experience of Burroughs's more famous protagonist, Tarzan of the Apes, and who may have been inspired by the historical figure of Zebina Streeter, a "White Apache" who led his adopted community in raids against whites (Robinson 1999),[2] is the title character in *Apache Devil*, Burroughs's sequel to *The War Chief*, which begins shortly after its predecessor concludes. Here, Burroughs relates the events from May 1885 until Geronimo's surrender at Skeleton Canyon more or less accurately. Shoz-Dijiji has become the most militant of the Apaches and chides his foster father for his hesitancy in following the path of war. Geronimo, portrayed again as a judicious elder with a weakness for alcohol, recognizes the futility of continued opposition to U.S. troops. At a council immediately preceding the breakout from the reservation in May 1885, Geronimo comes across as a reluctant but resigned warrior: "He did not wish to fight the white men again, for he realized, perhaps better than any of them, the futility of continued resistance." His attempt to speak with the "conservatism of mature deliberation" ([1928] 2009, 65), though, is not persuasive. Geronimo ends up staging the final armed resistance so that until September 1886, "from one end of the country to the other Geronimo and his bloody deeds occupied more front page newspaper space than any other topic, and to the readers of the newspapers of all the civilized world his name was a household word" (153). Meanwhile, a subplot focuses on the developing romance between Shoz-Dijiji and Wichita Billings, a white woman whom he had rescued from the violence following the death of religious leader Nakay-do-Klunni in *The War Chief*. That Shoz-Dijiji himself is white, though he does not know of his biological heritage throughout most of the novel, allows Burroughs to initiate the potential relationship without facing charges of promoting miscegenation.

Burroughs, of course, had explored this fictional territory previously. In many ways the situation of Shoz-Dijiji resembles that of Tarzan of the Apes, who falls into the hands of savages at an early age and under their tutelage becomes at least their equal in survival skills while instinctively developing an incipient sense of civilized humanity. As Tarzan has his Terkhoz, the ape who carries Jane Porter into the jungle with intentions of making her his mate, so Shoz-Dijiji has Juh, who has been his enemy since he first became a part of Geronimo's band and ultimately becomes his sexual rival. Just as Tarzan slays Terkhoz, Shoz-Dijiji kills his own rival. Both characters ultimately come to love women whose position in civilization seems to make them unattainable. While Burroughs's first Tarzan novel ends with the apparent thwarting of its hero's romantic intentions, the situation for Shoz-Dijiji at the end of *Apache Devil* seems more hopeful. Though he is not yet ready to take his place beside Wichita Billings, the reader assumes that with a little more refinement he will undoubtedly do so.

The most surprising feature of Burroughs's novels is their failure to support popular imagery depicting Geronimo. They are probably the first works of fiction to portray Geronimo positively. Robert E. Morsberger's assessment of Burroughs's two Apache novels is off the mark when he praises them for being "meticulously accurate," for following "the facts of the Apaches in remarkably close detail" (1973, 280), and, especially in the account of the events leading up to Geronimo's surrender, for being "scrupulously accurate and correspond[ing] precisely" to such "authorities" as Dee Brown, author of *Bury My Heart at Wounded Knee* (286). Moreover, Morsberger overstates the literary qualities of the novels when he compares the initiation scenes in *The War Chief* to similar events described by Faulkner and Hemingway (282). But Burroughs does seem to be "one of the first white novelists to portray the Apaches in particular and Indians in general with sympathy and understanding" (281). Morsberger notes particularly his characterization of Geronimo: "Burroughs portrays him not as a monster but as a person capable of both cruelty and affection, a great military leader but one who sometimes becomes irresponsibly drunk on tizwin" (284). His depiction of Geronimo in human terms surpasses those of Indians who appear in the fictional works of James Fenimore Cooper, Mark Twain, and even Helen Hunt Jackson (281). Moreover, Geronimo and other Apaches in the two novels come across as less sentimentalized than the Navajos who populate Oliver La Farge's Pulitzer Prize–winning novel *Laughing Boy*, which appeared a couple of years after Burroughs's Apache novels had been serialized (281).

After Burroughs's work, Geronimo continued to appear as a subsidiary character in fiction that focused on other figures of the Apache wars, both characters created by the authors and historical personages. For example, Elliott Arnold's *Blood Brother*, probably best known as the source for the important film *Broken Arrow*, which came out three years after the novel, has Tom Jeffords for its protagonist and deals with his relationship with Cochise, which led to the latter's agreeing to terms of peace after a decade of active warfare against Anglo encroachers in the Southwest. The novel actually begins in the early 1850s, a decade before the Bascom Affair, which alienated Cochise from the white man. Arnold presents Cochise considering the necessity of coming to terms with the white man's presence. His most vocal adversary is Gokliya, whom the author dramatically identifies at the conclusion of the Apaches' debate on the subject as "Geronimo." He addresses Cochise "in a sly and conciliatory voice": "'For as long as the memory of our people carries we have lived by our bravery and by our wits. It is not the Apache way to live like women, to grow things from the ground, to be grandmothers to cattle. Our people would become soft and womanly in such a life. Their enemies would soon rise and kill them'" (Arnold [1947] 1979, 25). Geronimo decides to leave the community governed by Cochise instead of agreeing to accommodate the white man. He becomes leader of a band of dissidents, many having little connection with the Chiricahua community headed by Cochise: "They were for the most part men discontented with the leadership in their own tribes who had abandoned their own people and formed a new unit under Gokliya" (55). Appearing hardly again in this long novel, Geronimo is occasionally mentioned as the leader of a band of renegades (71). Arnold has Cochise explaining who Geronimo is to the army commander at Tucson: "'He was a warrior of mine. He is now called Geronimo. He has gathered renegades from several tribes'" (73). Yet the reader hardly encounters even references to Geronimo again until after the dying Cochise has agreed to the terms of peace that he negotiates with General O. O. Howard; then he is named as the leader of those who resist the terms (420). To the extent that he is characterized at all, the Geronimo of *Blood Brother* represents an obstructionism matched by the more fully realized white Indian-haters whom Jeffords encounters at Tucson. Perhaps if the novel had developed Cochise's point of view as fully as it did Jeffords's, Geronimo would have emerged from the narrative's shadows.

Geronimo also appears as a background character in fiction treating other luminaries from the Apache wars. A major character in Will Henry's *Chiricahua* is Tzoe (referred to as "Peaches" by the U.S. military because of his light complexion). Tzoe, a reluctant participant in the breakout from the San Carlos Reservation following the death of the prophet Nock-ay-del-klinne in 1881, had returned to Arizona Territory from Sonora the following year as part of Chatto's raiding party and defected to become a scout for General Crook. He was largely responsible for guiding Crook's command into the Sierra Madre, where the general contracted peace with Geronimo. Henry's novel is set during the period between Tzoe's departure from Chatto's group and his contact with Crook. During that time, he aids a band of besieged Euro-Americans in escaping from the depredations of Chatto, "next only to Geronimo in wildness and in war" (Henry 1972, 17). Geronimo himself appears a few times in the novel as an aging warrior who is grooming Chatto to succeed him. From the novel's perspective, Geronimo, the barrier to civilized progress, represents a fading way of life, while the more perspicacious Tzoe recognizes the inevitability of the incipient Euro-American hegemony. Near the end of the novel, Tzoe declares, "It is almost sad. . . . The wild ones are going away. Their kind will come no more. Chatto, Geronimo, Lucero, Juh, Nachez, Durango, Ka-ya-ten-na, Nana, Zele, Bonito, Chihuahua, Hieronymo, Loco, all will be but names soon" (221).

Geronimo does not appear at all in Lewis B. Patten's *The Hands of Geronimo* (1971). But all of the action of the novel occurs because of his attack on a stagecoach near Globe, Arizona Territory, in 1885—apparently just after he left the Fort Apache Reservation in May. While his band killed most of the people on the stage, they had taken a small boy with them and left his mother injured but still alive. The narrator, a hired hand for the mother who is now a widow, had been a special friend of the captive and takes upon himself the pursuit of Geronimo in hopes of rescuing the child. Many figures from history appear in the novel as the narrator joins the company led by Britton Davis into Mexico. Al Sieber, Mickey Free, Emmet Crawford, and Chatto get in on the action—the last taking an active role in the rescue of young Jimmy, a happy outcome that occurs shortly after Crawford's death in January 1886. But Geronimo remains elusive.

The catalyst who remains offstage throughout the novel, he is "that bloodthirsty renegade" (Patten 1971, 29) who "hates white men worsen pizen" (34). A "wily old devil" (46) and "wily old butcher" (107), Geronimo and his "hostiles" were, according to common knowledge, guilty of committing atrocities "all across Arizona Territory" (108). The novel, though, does not dwell upon demonizing Geronimo and, in fact, has its narrator express some understanding for Apaches who have left the reservation: "Freedom must be very precious to the wild Apache for him to go to such lengths to obtain and keep it. Bloodthirsty savages they might be. Beyond the understanding of the white men they might also be. But they were strong, wily, and resourceful men" (52).

The Hands of Geronimo follows most fiction focusing on the Apache wars by placing the hostile adversaries in secondary roles. Patten's model, though, may not be earlier fiction so much as the numerous memoirs produced by military personnel who had been in Arizona Territory in the 1880s. Very often—John Bigelow's series of periodical articles "After Geronimo" (retitled *On the Bloody Trail of Geronimo* when it was first published in book form in 1958) being an example—the famous war leader and shaman does not appear in the work at all. The focus, as it is in Patten's novel, is on hardships faced by those in pursuit of him across deserts and through rugged mountains.

The action in Hunter Ingram's novel *Fort Apache* (1975) occurs during Geronimo's final breakout. Several historical figures appear as characters, including Generals Crook and Miles, Captain Crawford, Tribollet the bootlegger, Chatto, and Geronimo himself. The protagonist, though, is the novelist's own creation. Though we do not learn how it happened, Lieutenant Owen Parnell has a special relationship with Geronimo and is sent to dissuade him from leaving the reservation despite the inadequate rations and the corrupt commercial alliance known as the "Tucson Ring," which aggravates problems on the reservation for its own financial gain. Parnell is present for several of the more notable events in the campaign against Geronimo in 1886: the death of Crawford in Mexico, Crook's negotiations with Geronimo at Cañon de los Embudos, and the talks with Geronimo that eventuate in his final surrender. In the last, Parnell assumes the role taken by the historical Charles B. Gatewood.

The novel's Geronimo is a reasonable elder statesman, though a pawn in the conflicts that pit Parnell, Crook, Crawford, and other sympathetic soldiers and civilians against those who are trying to prolong the conflict to add to their profits by providing supplies to the military. Geronimo's case against the Anglos is presented as justified, and his breakout occurs because conditions at San Carlos, where the novel has him living, are impossible. The novel suggests that Geronimo has real leadership qualities. Meanwhile, it does not hesitate to suggest Geronimo's capacity for violence. Yet he is a minor character in the work—the central conflict being that between Parnell, on the side of right, and, on the wrong side, Tribollet and an army officer who is not only in league with the Tucson Ring but is also Parnell's rival in romance.

Of the historical personages associated with the Apache wars who figure in novels in which Geronimo also has a role, interpreter and scout Tom Horn appears most frequently. In fact, a subgenre of Geronimo fiction focuses on his association with Horn, invariably the protagonist in these works.

In 1904 a Denver-based publisher issued *Life of Tom Horn*, allegedly written by its principal character, who had been hanged for murder in Wyoming the previous year. The book, subtitled *A Vindication*, seeks to rehabilitate the image of a marginal figure who served briefly as head of scouts during the final Geronimo campaign. Though he undoubtedly exaggerates his role therein, Horn had been present when Captain Emmet Crawford was killed and, by most accounts (including his own), had acquitted himself well, perhaps even heroically, on that sad occasion. Drawing upon Horn's continuing name recognition and basing most of his book on Horn's supposed autobiography, novelist Will Henry published *I, Tom Horn* in 1975. As the title suggests, Horn himself narrates the novel, which he presents as a corrective, particularly regarding the experiences in Wyoming that culminated in his execution. Since much of what the fictional character must do to rehabilitate his image requires developing the heroic presence he believes he projected during his time in the Southwest in the 1880s, author Henry brings Geronimo into the action as a much more important supporting player than he is in *Life of Tom Horn*.

Narrator Horn first encounters Geronimo when the Apache—"ever the one with an eye for women"—tries to seduce Horn's "Yaqui bride." He notes that Geronimo, whom he also refers to as "Gokliya," had developed a reputation as "a *macho*, even among a people notoriously callous in their handling of horses and women" (Henry 1975, 118). He is also impressed by Geronimo's imposing physical appearance. "He was something to see" and looked "like a marble statue of a Roman headman." Geronimo for Horn was the "most ominous of all" the Apache adversaries whom he faced as member of General Crook's command (171).

Henry's purpose in characterizing Geronimo is to provide his narrator with a worthy foil for his adventures in the Southwest. The fictional character Tom Horn is trying to salvage his own good name—so that he will not be remembered as an assassin who fatally ambushed someone (a boy, in fact)—by suggesting that he had been a part of the noble enterprise that led to the taming of a "six-foot devil" (171).

Other novels also presented Geronimo as a foil to Horn. Predating Henry's novel, though not based as directly on Horn's life story, Gene Caesar's *Rifle for Rent* casts Geronimo as a foil who establishes Horn's positive qualities that had emerged in the Southwest. Caesar claims that his work is "a true story. All characters and incidents are factual" (1963, n.p.), but his presentation of Horn's interactions with Geronimo does not correspond to the historical record. Of course, Caesar's central character plays a much more prominent role in negotiations with Geronimo than history suggests that he did, and Geronimo is a more formidable adversary—at one point having "1200 braves" at his command in the Sierra Madre (15). Ultimately, according to Caesar's fictional account, Horn, not Gatewood, is responsible for persuading Geronimo to surrender.

Another novel with Tom Horn as protagonist and Geronimo as stock antagonist is Andrew J. Fenady's *Claws of the Eagle: A Novel of Tom Horn and the Apache Kid*. Here the action begins when General Crook summons Horn, Al Sieber, and the Apache Kid to assist in pursuing Geronimo into Mexico, with whom the United States has just fashioned an agreement to allow its armies to cross the international border in pursuit of Apache raiders. The Geronimo action climaxes when U.S. troops surround his encampment just south of the border and Tom Horn captures him. Miles, who has replaced Crook as commander, soon banishes an enchained Geronimo to Florida. Geronimo, who is called "Goklaya" until captured (e.g., Fenady 1984, 6), is unremittingly characterized as the consummate enemy of Euro-American civilization: the "last and most cunning chief of the Chiricahua," who in turn were "the most defiant and dreaded enemy ever encountered by the United States Army" (24, 25). Aside from a passing reference to the massacre at Kaskiyeh, little in the novel offers any excuse for Geronimo's malignity. The only extended description occurs after his capture by Tom Horn, and following the customary trope, that description focuses on his physical appearance:

> Geronimo stood captured, bloodied but unbent. By sight his age was indeterminate. He might have been fifty, but actually he was more than sixty. He was tall, nearly six feet, and broad of chest. He had a terrifying countenance, with black, bullet-hole eyes that reflected cunning and hate but never fear—even now. He had a hawk nose and a thin slash of mouth that, because of an old wound, drooped to the right in a perpetual sneer. (53)

One of the most interesting scenes in the novel, one that confirms the one-dimensional depiction of Geronimo, has children at Fort Bowie playing cowboys and Indians just after Geronimo's train eastward has departed. The child chosen for the role of Geronimo is "the homeliest boy," and even he must streak mud across his face to fully achieve the baleful image of Geronimo

(126). Geronimo disappears from the novel with still a hundred pages left to go, but he has served the purpose of establishing the clearly demarcated enmity between Apache and Anglo in the Arizona Territory of the 1880s and of identifying Tom Horn as a heroic figure—in fact, as much a stock character as Geronimo himself.

Geronimo and Tom Horn make still another joint fictional appearance in *Mr. Horn*, a novelization by D. R. Bensen of a screenplay written by William Goldman for a made-for-television movie that was broadcast in 1979. The narrative traces Horn's career from his involvement in the Apache wars—greatly exaggerated in the screenplay and novel—to his hanging in Wyoming in 1902. The first two-thirds of Bensen's novelization focuses on the conflict between Horn and Geronimo, though the latter appears as a character only sporadically. However, Geronimo stands as a worthy antagonist for the novel's central character: "They didn't come any shrewder than Geronimo, nor any crueler" (Bensen 1978, 23). Geronimo's cruelty is demonstrated by his smiling with satisfaction at the killing of Emmet Crawford by Mexican troops (72) and by reports of how his Apaches treat their prisoners: "Cut-off eyelids and being staked out for the ants wasn't anywhere the worst of it" (127). When Horn, who assumes the historical role of Charles Gatewood in effecting negotiations for Geronimo's surrender, first meets Geronimo face-to-face, he notes that despite his age Geronimo exudes "an aura of power" (145). Their negotiations have Geronimo listing his grievances, including the massacre at Kaskiyeh, from which he claims to have suffered more than anyone else: "And then the whiteskins—the whiteskins in one day—they killed my mother—they killed my mother and my wife— they killed my mother and my wife *and my baby and my baby and my baby*" (147). Geronimo agrees to surrender when Horn promises that he and his band will be able to return to live in peace on the reservation. The failure of General Miles to adhere to that agreement and his decision to ship the Chiricahuas, including Horn's scouting colleague Mickey Free, to Florida confirm the cynicism that already pervades Horn's character. When Miles, who does not encounter Geronimo until Horn brings him all the way to Fort Bowie (bypassing Skeleton Canyon altogether), receives credit for the surrender, Horn seems not to care that he has been left out. But the reader gets the sense that the concluding events of the Apache wars contributed directly to the reputation that Horn developed over the next fifteen years: as a hired killer. As he awaits execution for a murder that the novel suggests he did not commit, Horn senses a kinship with Geronimo, whom Bensen has "still steaming away down in Florida" in 1901. Both of these frontier figures have outlived their times: "It don't seem as though the fancy folks can stand to have the ones like us around," Horn muses (226). So Geronimo's role in this novelization shifts from that of foil for the protagonist to a figure who serves as his double.

The end of Horn's life and career makes for a compelling narrative, and John Chandler's *Wyoming Wind* explores the subject once again. Moreover, Geronimo reprises his usual role: that of reflecting a positive image of Horn. The Chiricahua is, in fact, "one of the handful of men Horn had ever come to respect" (2002, 73). Fighting a losing battle in the Southwest against overwhelming odds, Geronimo represents what the character Horn also stands for: a way of life that has passed. Neither figure can really adjust to modern times. Chandler hyperbolizes Horn's role in effecting Geronimo's surrender, but in the few pages of flashback in which the Apache appears, he comes across as a worthy antagonist for Horn during the latter's youth in Arizona.

A fictional depiction that foregrounds Geronimo as the protagonist had to await Forrest Carter. The Geronimo who appears in Carter's *Watch for Me on the Mountain* (1983; originally published as *Cry Geronimo!* in 1978) is a patriotic servant of his people. Though driven to the extremes of violence that he perpetrates, especially against Mexicans, by the massacre of his family at Kaskiyeh, Carter's Geronimo is motivated by higher causes than vengeance. In fact, he embodies an anti-Mexican and anti-government sentiment that pervades the volume. Carter reinterprets the history of the Apache wars in striking ways, consequently focusing and simplifying his narrative.

Carter's story opens at San Carlos, which the narrator characterizes as a "Camp of Apache Concentration" (1983, 11). Geronimo has just been released from a lengthy stay in the guardhouse and is organizing what will become his final breakout. After he successfully leads a group of Apache warriors, women, and children into the Sierra Madre, the narrative arcs to the past and relates Geronimo's childhood and early adulthood. It brings matters to a climax with the transformative massacre at Kaskiyeh and then returns to the time of the breakout through a series of incidents, some having little or no basis in history, that illustrate the identity that Geronimo has assumed after the massacre. Carter's interest is not in the historical Geronimo, but in Geronimo as a vehicle for exploring an anti-authoritarian and mystical commitment to a higher law. At the center of Carter's depiction of Geronimo is a religious concept, imputed to the Apache, that the novel refers to as the "Great Wheel," a system adapted from Eastern religious philosophies that allows an individual's "spirit body" to be incarnated many times. Geronimo, according to his mentor Mangas Coloradas, incarnates the archetypal figure of the "War Shaman" (100). As such he has a formal position in Apache political organization. After the massacre at Kaskiyeh, the three principal Apache chiefs, Mangas Coloradas, Cochise, and Juh, meet to discuss what should be done to respond to the "Mexican Enemy" (115). From this meeting Geronimo emerges as battlefield commander. Mangas Coloradas makes the announcement: "Let us all go as one. Let us follow a single Leader to guide us. Let him lead us on the trail of War! Let him lead us to Kaskiyeh! *Gokhlayeh—War Leader of the Chiricahuas!*" (117). At the attack on Kaskiyeh that follows, Gokhlayeh receives the name Geronimo since the event occurs on the feast day of the town's patron, Saint Jerome. Geronimo then becomes less an individual character than a manifestation of a foundational entity in the religious system that Carter has created for the Apache. He is beyond mundane distinctions of good and evil, and Mexican and U.S. imputations of atrocities to him are meaningless.

The reader learns the fundamentals of Apache religion from Tom Horn, who, according to Carter's narrative, had lived with the Apaches though now is serving the forces of General Crook as chief of scouts. Early in the novel, as he joins in the pursuit of the Apaches escaping San Carlos for the Sierra Madre, Horn notes, "Geronimo is a hero. . . . He ain't fightin' fer no money, er glory, er promotions, not even fer land. That makes him a hero" (62–63). This encapsulates Carter's image of Geronimo: that he is the archetypal hero who lives out his role regardless of external circumstances or personal concerns. Even loss of family at Kaskiyeh plays a lesser role in the motivations of the Geronimo of *Watch for Me on the Mountain* than the philosophy of the Great Wheel.

Heroes require antagonists, and Carter provides plenty of them for Geronimo in most of the non-Apache characters in the novel. Every Mexican who appears in *Watch for Me on the Mountain*, for example, is presented negatively: as greedy, opportunistic, cowardly, and especially lascivious when it comes to Apache women. As the archetypal enemy, Mexicans represent values antithetical to those of Geronimo. Though they come off better than the Mexicans, U.S. soldiers and their colleagues, for the most part, are also villainous. The principal exception is Tom Horn, and General Crook also receives positive treatment. Both these figures as well as a couple of others whom the novel depicts somewhat favorably share an anti-authoritarian perspective. Horn disregards protocol, and Crook allows him to do so. However, both ultimately suffer at the hands of the authority: Horn is hanged for murder in Wyoming some fifteen years after the end of the Apache wars and Crook loses his command to the effete General Miles, who is dismissed by Carter's novel as a self-promoter. They reinforce what may be the basic issue that Carter's novel develops: the conflict between high laws (those adhered to by Geronimo) and low laws (those associated with the U.S. government). The war shaman as hero must follow the former and reject the latter. Carter's novel lines up the forces in a cosmic conflict. On the side of the high law are Geronimo and other Apaches; on the side of the low law are most representatives of the U.S. government. The Mexicans are beings too despicable to deserve a role in the conflict except as foils to Geronimo and as occasional catalysts for his archetypal heroism. Though Geronimo ultimately surrenders, he has ensured that the Apache way of life will endure by secreting survivors of massacres in an Edenic valley hidden deep in the Sierra Madre. There, they will be able to live and live again as the Great Wheel turns.

Knowing that novelist Forrest Carter achieved infamy during the civil rights movement (when under the name Asa Carter he was responsible for some of the segregationist and antigovernment rhetoric used by figures such as Governor George Wallace of Alabama) certainly correlates with the views on federal officials and Mexicans as a "race" that characterize his Geronimo novel. Writing of Carter's novel *Gone to Texas*, whose protagonist is an outlaw who served in the Confederate Army, Shari M. Huhndorf has suggested a "peculiar elision" with Geronimo. Josey Wales and the Geronimo of *Watch for Me on the Mountain* share a hatred for the U.S. military and other representatives of the Washington-based federal government, who are imposing upon them an unwelcome, external notion of progress and usurping their rights to land and liberty (Huhndorf 2001, 14). Carter, who tried to conceal (or at least downplay) his identity as Klansman when he turned to fiction, did not abandon the fundamentals of his philosophy even though he might celebrate a person of color such as Geronimo.

Carter's making Geronimo the central figure in his novel did not seem to have much influence on subsequent fictional treatments, and it remains the only novel in which he is the protagonist. But though he is a minor character in the novel, Geronimo makes an interesting appearance in George MacDonald Fraser's *Flashman and the Redskins* (1982). One of a series of comic historical novels about Harry Flashman, who originally appeared as a bully in the boarding-school novel *Tom Brown's School-Days* ([1857] 1911) by Thomas Hughes, this installment in the series twice brings its antihero into the Wild West: along the Santa Fe Trail in 1849 and to Dakota Territory in 1876. Geronimo appears in the 1849 section.

Having married the proprietor of a New Orleans brothel who decides to move her establishment to take advantage of trade afforded by the California gold rush, Flashman finds himself in Santa Fe. Here he decides to leave his wife (whom he is using only to get to California where he can find passage back to his native England) and head down the Rio Grande. He falls in with some scalp hunters who make the mistake of attacking a camp of Apaches affiliated with Mangas Coloradas. While his colleagues are tortured and killed, Flashman charms Mangas's daughter and escapes a similar fate. One of the Mimbreños particularly stands out. Called Yawner, he was, according to Flashman, "one of the ugliest devils I've ever seen." Flashman first meets him when Yawner kicks Flashman awake. He describes what meets his eye: "a young Apache in hide kilt and leggings, with a dirty jacket about his shoulders and a band round the lank hair that framed a face from the Chamber of Horrors. Even for an Apache it was wicked—coal-black vicious eyes, hook nose, a mouth that was just a cruel slit and wasn't improved when he laughed with a great gape that showed all his ugly teeth" (Fraser 1982, 190). Looking back over the years, Flashman, who narrates his own adventures, states, "If you'd told me then that this monster would one day be the most dreaded hostile Indian who ever was, terror of half a continent—I'd have believed you; if you'd told me he would be my closest Indian friend—I wouldn't" (190). During the six months that Flashman spends in Mangas Coloradas's camp—most of that time married to Sonsee-array, Mangas's daughter—Yawner serves as his mentor, overseeing his courtship, saving him from a jealous adversary, and introducing him to the sweat lodge. Yawner assists Flashman in preparing a flower garden for the wickiup that he and Sonsee-array will share during their honeymoon, and Flashman, looking back after almost sixty years on his adventures in the Southwest, rhapsodizes,

> That's how I remember him, not as the old man I saw last year, but as the ugly, bow-legged young brave, all Apache from boots to head-band, so serious as he arranged the blooms just so, cleaning the earth from his knife and looking sour and pleased among his flowers. A strange memory, in the light of history—but then he's still the Yawner to me, for all that the world has learned to call him Geronimo. (216)

Fraser's novel is perhaps no more than an entertainment, and Flashman is made to articulate his unmitigated dislike of Apaches in general. Yet Geronimo comes off as quite human at this time in his life, at some point before the death of Alope in Mexico. To some degree Fraser presents him as a more fully rounded figure than does almost any other writer who has used Geronimo as a fictional character. The Geronimo material in the novel provides only a single episode in this picaresque work as Flashman has a knack for meeting the famous and potentially famous in all his adventures. He is rescued from the Mimbreños by Kit Carson and Lucien Maxwell and befriends Spotted Tail and a boy named Curly (the future Crazy Horse) among the Oglala before he finally gets back to England.

Geronimo figures significantly in the ideational context for Leslie Marmon Silko's controversial novel *Almanac of the Dead*, whose title comes from a set of notebooks bequeathed to a Yaqui Indian woman in the nineteenth century. One of her granddaughters, a psychic living in Tucson, Arizona, has assumed the task of deciphering these documents, which recount Native American history and prophesy a unified millenarian movement of tribal peoples who are attempting to resume control of lands they have lost to an increasingly corrupt Eurocentric civilization. *Almanac of the Dead* manages two major plotlines—translation of the almanac and preparations for revolution—as well as dozens of characters by stressing the recurrent point that the Americas as dominated by Euro-American civilization have become a place of a deep and pervasive corruption that can be purged only when tribal peoples from whom the land has been stolen reassume control. Geronimo appears in the novel as an exemplary figure who had opposed the takeover of tribal lands, the first significant tribal leader "since Montezuma" (1991, 89). From the Euro-American perspective he was a "public enemy," and one of the novel's characters, Sterling, a Laguna Indian living in Tucson who enjoys reading the *Police Gazette*, recalls a special issue in which Geronimo had been included along with John Dillinger, Pretty Boy Floyd, Bonnie Parker and Clyde Barrow, and Billy the Kid. For this perspective on Geronimo, Silko draws upon his reputation as the "'Bad Injun,' the perfect embodiment of the evil the Native Indians were capable of, namely deceit, murder, bloodthirstiness, cunning, and savage brutality" (Muthyala 2006, 125). Geronimo had turned to "crime," though only after Mexican troops had illegally crossed the border into the United States and slaughtered his wife and children. Since the United States had taken no action against the troops, "Geronimo had been forced to seek justice on his own"

(Silko 1991, 39). Then his second wife and their children were killed at the infamous Fort Grant massacre, when a "mob of deranged white people" came from Tucson and attacked the reservation camp of the Aravaipa Apaches, killing more than a hundred, mostly women and children (39). While Sterling believes that crime has no excuse, he realizes that "for Geronimo it had been war in defense of the homelands" and notes that Geronimo's ultimate fate, imprisonment at Fort Sill, had been a "punishment worse than death" (40).

Sites in Tucson recall the role of Geronimo and the Apache wars in developing the now-dominant Euro-American culture there. Many of the city's elites owe their status to exploitive activities of their ancestors—the "Tucson Ring" that had undermined the U.S. Army by encouraging hostilities in order to maintain the profitable military presence and by cheating or colluding with Indian agents to divert to their own treasuries funds intended to support reservation Indians. Sterling comes upon an abandoned house on Main Street, which is identified as the site where Geronimo had signed the papers effecting his final surrender. That event had come about through trickery, false promises, and chicanery by the Tucson business community. They were responsible for Geronimo's bolting after his talks with General Crook at the Cañon de los Embudos when they sent a whiskey peddler to get the Apaches drunk and to convince them that, despite Crook's promises, they would be hanged by civil authorities when they returned to Arizona (79–81).

Another perspective on Geronimo emerges from the recollections of Yoeme, the Yaqui woman who has passed on the titular almanac to her granddaughter. She asserts that the person known as "Geronimo" was not the real leader of the Apache resisters during the late nineteenth century but a double who assumed the place of the actual Geronimo in public venues such as treaty negotiations with General Crook (whom Yoeme misidentifies as General Miles) (Silko 1991, 129). She asserts that this double assumed the role of prisoner of war so that the "real" Geronimo could continue his resistance:

> He [the double] is a man who always accompanied the one who performed certain feats. He is the man who agreed to play the role for the protection of the other man. The man in the photographs [by C. S. Fly] had been promised safe conduct by the man he protected. The man in the photographs was a brilliant and resourceful man. He may not have known that while he would find wealth and fame in the lifelong captivity, he would not again see the mountains during

his life. The man who fled had further work to do, work that could not be done in captivity. (129)

Still another take on Geronimo in *Almanac of the Dead* comes from the elderly Yaqui woman Mahawala, who asserts that U.S. troops misunderstand the Mexican war cry "Geronimo" as a reference to an individual Apache adversary. In fact, four different warriors became known as "Geronimo"—a case of mistaken identity reinforced by the fact that to "whites all Apache warriors looked alike" (225):

> So the Apache warrior called Geronimo had been three, even four different men. The warrior of prominence and also of controversy among other Apaches had been born in the high mountains above the river now called Gila. The man had not been a warrior but had been trained as a medicine man. As the wars with the *americanos* and Mexicans had intensified, and the ranks of the warriors wanted men, the medicine man had begun riding with them on the raids. His specialty had been silence and occasionally, invisibility. With his special skills, the raiders had been able to move so silently not even the Apache scouts who worked for the U.S. cavalry had been able to hear the warriors walk past their bedrolls. (225)

The various photographs of Geronimo that appeared in the late nineteenth century captured the images of four different individuals: Red Clay ("the final Geronimo who died in Oklahoma" [226]), Sleet ("the youngest of the Geronimos" [226]), Big Pine (who denied his identity as Geronimo after being shackled for allegedly breaking away from the reservation [226–27]), and Wide Ledge (one name for the medicine man who had been born on the Gila River [227]). When the four Geronimos met on various occasions, they compared prints of photographs that had been taken of them: "The puzzle had been to account for the Apache warrior whose broad, dark face, penetrating eyes, and powerful barrel-chested body had appeared in every photograph taken of the other Geronimos" (228). Clearly taking the physiognomy of the ideal Geronimo (of which the four men are avatars) from Randall's 1884 photograph, Silko has Mahawala create a mythic figure who embodies the spirit of resistance that is remanifesting itself in the pan-Indian movement that the novel suggests will result in the apocalyptic termination of Euro-American hegemony in the American Southwest.

The Geronimo who surrenders at Skeleton Canyon, though also referred to as Red Clay, is given the less romantic designation Old Pancakes and was "the best customer the Tucson bootleggers had ever had" (229). He assumed that he would be allowed to rest and recuperate from the rigors of the warpath and then could escape to fight again, though his fight was not for land and independence but "for his right to drink when and what he wanted to drink, and as much as he wanted to" (229). The jubilation of the U.S. military and of the press that Geronimo had finally been subdued becomes hollow when one realizes that the figure who actually surrendered was an "old Apache man more sorrowful than fierce" (231). Mahawala's "Geronimo story" deflates the results of the millions of dollars and thousands of troops that the United States had invested in pursuit of Geronimo. It also suggests the literal survival of the resistant spirit of Geronimo in Mexico and the American Southwest.

Although the Geronimo material in *Almanac of the Dead* is scanty compared with other threads in the complex novel, it epitomizes Silko's "revisionary history" (Moore 1999, 166). Of course, the novel misrepresents the "facts" about Geronimo known by Euro-American historians, but part of Silko's point is to articulate a "spirit of knowing and perceiving, an epistemology of witness, different from a European colonial fascination with names and numbers" (167). "Geronimo" becomes an idea that represents different abstractions for Indians and whites. For Native American characters such as Yoeme and Mahawala, those abstractions include the interdependence of individual, society, and land that must be preserved (or restored) if the cosmos is to endure. For Euro-Americans the abstractions include savagism manifested in acts of criminality. Rather than a historical figure who lived from the 1820s until 1909, Geronimo is a multivalent symbol capable of being interpreted according to the observer's preconceptions.

Before *Almanac of the Dead*, Silko had already used the perception of Geronimo in the Euro-American imagination in "A Geronimo Story" (1981, 212–23), a coming-of-age tale in which a boy named Andy accompanies the Laguna Regulars when they check out indications that Geronimo has camped near Pie Town, New Mexico. Geronimo himself does not appear as a character in the story, but the adventure that introduces Andy to the world beyond his pueblo occurs due to anxiety about him. As John Muthyala has noted, this short story "is not really about Geronimo the man but about the emergence of various narratives of his life and deeds" (2006, 130). The reader encounters a perspective on Geronimo that is the total antithesis of

Mahawala's in the character of Major Littlecock in "A Geronimo Story." A self-important, ethnocentric representative of the U.S. Army who has recently arrived in the Southwest, Littlecock is responsible for calling the Laguna Regulars into service. He insists that his superior communications networks have identified Geronimo as being in the area, and he has an abandoned campsite as proof. As Siteye, principal scout for the Lagunas, knows, Geronimo is nowhere nearby, but Littlecock perceives him even where he is not. Mahawala, representing an indigenous perspective, perceives that Euro-Americans such as Littlecock require tangible signs—abandoned campsites, photographs, old men who can be deported to Florida—of an entity who exists primarily in the realm of the ideal.

Like many nonfiction works with Geronimo's name in the title, Bill Dugan's 1991 novel *Geronimo (War Chiefs)* deals more with the Apache wars than with Geronimo himself. The novel progresses through a series of vignettes written from different characters' points of view and encompassing events from the death of Nock-ay-del-klinne in August 1881 through Geronimo's surrender to Crook at Cañon de los Embudos in March 1886. Besides Crook, the reader sees through the eyes of such historical figures as Thomas Cruse, Britton Davis, Emmet Crawford, and Geronimo. The perspective of the last becomes most evident in a chapter that recounts an attack on a wagon train near Apache Pass in January 1882 and a couple of chapters dealing with the massacre by Mexican soldiers of Chiricahuas who have come to trade at Casas Grandes, Chihuahua, in March 1883, an event that recalls the Kaskiyeh massacre some thirty years earlier and is loosely based on an event that occurred in May 1882.

Novelist Dugan presents a fairly rounded picture of Geronimo, especially given that we see him mostly from the viewpoint of members of the U.S. Army. Those members' consensus of opinion is that the grievances that drive Geronimo off the reservation twice during the course of the book's action are justifiable, that he and the other Apaches have indeed been cheated by nefarious Indian agents, often allied with the corrupt Tucson Ring. Volatile and consequently more unpredictable and dangerous than many other Apache leaders, Geronimo receives this characterization from the more tractable Loco: "Geronimo does not always think things through. He is too angry" (Dugan 1991, 45). He is described elsewhere in the novel as a "lit fuse" (218). Nevertheless, he demonstrates good sense in many cases in the course of the book's narrative arc. For example, he alone among the Chiricahua leaders remains sober and suspects the treachery that leads to the massacre at

Casas Grandes. His influential presence helps to avert violence directed at Britton Davis and leads to the arrest of the even more volatile Ka-ya-ten-nae. Moreover, the author presents him as particularly burdened by the plight of his people: "It seemed to him that the world had been dark for a long time. The sun might try to smother him with oppressive fire, heating the air around him until it hurt to breathe, but there were still so many things that no one saw. His power told him things that no one else wanted to hear spoken" (133). Geronimo is neither the archvillain who populates earlier fictional depictions, such as those of Edward Ellis, nor the almost saintly figure who appears in works by Forrest Carter and later Joseph Bruchac.

While trying to capture "the essence of the real events," Dugan admits that he has occasionally exercised literary license "for the sake of compression or dramatic enhancement" (308). For example, he attributes the death of Judge McComas and his wife and the capture of their son to a band led by Chihuahua rather than Chatto. And he has Emmet Crawford die after Geronimo and his band have already surrendered to him and are ambushed by Mexican forces while heading northward toward the international border. Yet the novel does present a fairly well-developed fictional portrait of its title character, and it involves some historical personages, especially Thomas Cruse, who have seldom figured in literary or cinematic treatments of the Apache wars.

While Geronimo cannot really be considered the protagonist of Dugan's novel, his role therein is larger than in most other fictional treatments, not only those written earlier but even works produced during the 1990s and later when Geronimo's image has been generally positive. Set largely in the 1850s, for instance, Frank Burleson's Apache Wars Saga uses Geronimo only sparingly. But he does figure into the six-volume story of Arizona rancher Nathaniel Barrington, former U.S. soldier and former apprentice warrior for the Apaches. His narrative plays out against the backdrop of emerging hostilities between Apaches and Anglos, when Geronimo was only beginning to make a name for himself. Nevertheless, Geronimo does appear as a minor character in some of the volumes. In *Night of the Cougar*, for instance, set in 1858, Geronimo takes form as a "warrior and medicine man" who is "thirty-two, medium height, heavily muscled, with a wide, grim mouth and oriental eyes" (Burleson 1997, 7). At some points in the novel—when he attempts to play a piano in the parlor of Barrington's house (7), for example—he comes across somewhat clownishly. At this point in his career he values the friendship of an Anglo and treasures a pistol that Barrington has given him (174), but he is aware of the threat to his way of life from Euro-American invaders and engages a captive in a debate about who has caused the interethnic violence that has begun to plague the Southwest (175). Burleson does not simplistically present Geronimo as the epitome of savagery that one encounters in earlier fiction, but Geronimo remains a minor character in this series of western novels.

Joseph Bruchac's fictional treatment of Geronimo for young adults, straightforwardly titled *Geronimo: A Novel* (2006), eschews the mystical lore that infuses Carter's novel and the abstractions of Silko to depict Geronimo from the perspective of a young man who has surrendered with him and lives through their days of captivity in Florida, Alabama, and Oklahoma. Despite its title, the novel uses Geronimo as a subsidiary character and focuses on this narrator. While most of Bruchac's characters come from history, the protagonist is a composite of several Chiricahua youths who grew up as prisoners of war after the final surrender. The narrative covers twenty-two years from September 1886, when the unnamed narrator, along with Geronimo and others who had come in at the time of the Skeleton Canyon surrender, board the train that will ultimately take them to Florida, through 1908, when the narrator revisits Fort Sill after being repatriated to Arizona because of his military service and listens to Geronimo's memories and musings about the homeland to which he will never return.

Flashbacks from the narrator's memory retell the story of the Apache wars. The novel's tone is often elegiac as the narrator and Geronimo himself stress the importance of memory as a way of sustaining a sense of personal and communal self. When the novel opens at Fort Sill in 1908, the narrator is concerned about the imminent passing of Geronimo and the memories that have sustained him and the rest of the Chiricahuas. The old man provides comfort, as he does throughout the experiences recounted in the narrative: "Your memories will keep you strong" (Bruchac 2006, 4), and "You will remember, grandson. You will remember it all" (5). The novel's early chapters especially juxtapose what is happening at the time of the narrative—that is, the exile and imprisonment of the Chiricahuas—with remembered incidents from the circumstances that have led to this situation. Among the events recounted from Geronimo's or the narrator's point of view are the massacre at Kaskiyeh, the death of Nock-ay-del-klinne in 1881, and details of the surrender itself. These conflicts anticipate the continued conflicts between Chiricahuas and their Euro-American captors that play themselves out as the narrator matures. Better than other authors who have written about Geronimo for young readers, even those whose works purport to be nonfiction, Bruchac has vividly provided historical detail. Moreover, his focus on the postsurrender years gives the reader a perspective on a less sensationalistic era in Apache–Euro-American relations than the more customary treatment of the wars themselves. Bruchac has drawn extensively on the scholarly record; he even attaches a bibliography to his work of fiction. Yet he admits that he has not always presented the conventionally agreed-upon "facts" of Geronimo's life and career, even those included in the autobiography dictated to S. M. Barrett—a work that is "not completely Geronimo's own story" (2006, n.p.).

The novel's Geronimo is an avuncular figure, one whom the orphaned narrator calls "grandfather." He is consistently characterized as devoted to the children of his community: "Geronimo truly loved children and wanted to protect them" (Bruchac 2006, 58). Particularly concerned with their education, Geronimo tells stories to teach the Chiricahua children and encourage them to confront the adversities they face (32). As the narrator notes, "Geronimo never missed a chance to give Chiricahua children the lessons they needed to survive" (41). When Geronimo recounts traditional narratives such as the myth of the Chiricahua culture hero, he identifies with the character who faces down the forces of chaos to establish an ordered cosmos for his descendants to enjoy.

His identification with the hero Child-of-the-Water casts Geronimo as a patriot whose stand against the U.S. and Mexican armies was motivated not by selfish desires for independence but by commitment to community service. Bruchac dedicates the novel "To all those who have fought for their country," thus placing Geronimo in the company of other patriots. The narrator assures us, "There are good reasons that Geronimo fought as he did" and warns the reader that those who portray him negatively are guilty of lying (122–23). He especially dismisses those Chiricahuas who blame Geronimo for their plight: "Some Apaches were angry with Geronimo, blaming him for their exile. If he had not broken out from the reservation, they thought, we would not have all been punished this way." But just as many people in the community believed that they would have suffered no matter what Geronimo had done and that, even in captivity, he "was still the one who carried our hope in his strong old hands" (187). Bruchac's Geronimo also demonstrates the importance of assimilation. He is among the first to have his hair cut in the Euro-American fashion; he strongly supports the missionary-provided formal education for Chiricahua children that began while the community was imprisoned in Alabama; he becomes a master entrepreneur; and he eventually subscribes to the Jesus road. The flaws of character that emerge in other portraits of Geronimo—his enjoyment of gambling and strong drink, for example—find little place in Bruchac's novel.

The novel approaches hagiography by portraying Geronimo through the hero-worshiping eyes of a young acolyte as an aging patriot who has become a wise elder. But in treating him in this way, Bruchac does no more than what biographers of figures such as George Washington and Abraham Lincoln have done when they have written for young readers. When we recall that this is a work of fiction designed to convey particularly the postsurrender experience of the Chiricahua people through the perspective of a maturing youth, we realize that such an exclusively positive view is appropriate. The Geronimo who lives in the memory of the narrator is not so much a historical entity as a positive role model who is able to adjust to life as a prisoner of war despite his devotion to independence and freedom. Meanwhile, the young reader gets a sense of the situation faced by American Indians from various communities who underwent the process of assimilation in the late nineteenth and early twentieth centuries.

Geronimo has also served as apparent inspiration for a number of characters whose creators have assigned them original names. The plots of some of these fictional works follow the career of Geronimo fairly explicitly, while others use Geronimo and other characters from the Apache wars more or less loosely. *Apache Dawn*, one installment in the Long Rider series by Clay Dawson, has its hero drifting through the Southwest, where he encounters the war leader Diablito, "a seething bundle of rage," as he is characterized in the blurb on the back cover of the 1989 paperback edition. Though Diablito perishes at the novel's climax, readers are likely to think of Geronimo as they read of his hostility toward the hated Euro-American invaders.

More ambitious is Paul Horgan's *A Distant Trumpet*. Presented entirely from the point of view of the U.S. military, the novel is set at the fictional Fort Delivery in the bleakest reaches of the Arizona desert during the 1880s. Much of the novel deals with the social and romantic intrigues of the main characters both at Fort Delivery and during the past experiences that have brought them to this military outpost. But they are there to end hostilities between Apaches and the white settlers who are invading their country. Though none of the characters comes directly from a single historical figure, several possess traits recognizable to a reader knowledgeable in the history of the conflict during which Horgan's novel is set. The protagonist, Matthew Hazard, resembles Lieutenant Charles Gatewood, and the general who has charge of the theater of operations, Alexander Upton Quait, reminds the reader of General George Crook. The Geronimo-inspired character is Rainbow Son, whom Hazard has to seek out in Mexico, accompanied only by the scout White Horn, to effect his surrender to Quait. Rainbow Son is less a character than a presence in the novel, but that presence has Geronimo-like attributes. When Quait gives Hazard his assignment, he describes his adversary in terms that one finds reserved for Geronimo by his actual contemporaries: "I have made enough case for good Indian people in my time to be in a position to speak honestly of the bad. Rainbow Son is one of the bad—very possibly the worst. He is clever. He is vain. He is neither a fool nor a saint. They will die for an idea, but not he. Abstractions will mean nothing to him. He is an intensely practical man" (Horgan [1960] 1991, 540).

Usually Geronimo is a meagerly realized fictional personage—part of the setting for short stories and especially novels that highlight adventure and romance involving Euro-American characters in the Southwest of the 1870s and 1880s. He sometimes serves as a foil to highlight a white protagonist's heroic qualities or epitomize the danger against which central characters must play out their roles. In only one novel, Carter's *Cry Geronimo!*, might Geronimo himself be considered the central character, and there he serves as vehicle for a semitheological ideology tinged with racism. More positively, though, Geronimo may represent an enduring spirit of independence or serve as catalyst for a young protagonist's maturation. But fictional works that are primarily Geronimo's own story remain scarce.

Comic Books and Graphic Novels

As might be expected, a figure whose eminent savagism continued to capture the public imagination long after the frontier had passed has found his place in many popular literary forms. Though he does not seem to have appeared in dime novels, which were past their heyday when he became known, Geronimo has appeared in one of their twentieth-century descendants. Long before comic books became graphic novels, Avon periodicals published four installments in a series featuring a highly fictionalized Geronimo. The first installment, *Geronimo, Indian Fighter, No. 1: The Massacre at San Pedro Pass*, came out in 1950, and the final installment appeared in 1952. Though not irredeemably sensationalistic, the four volumes unabashedly exploit the image of Geronimo as the "most feared and hated of all the bad Indians" and "the last and worst of the Chiricahua Apaches" (Cohen 1950, 3), as headings on the first page of *No. 1* exclaim.

The inaugural volume covers Geronimo's entire career in a highly condensed, error-filled format. Subsequent issues generally depict him in episodes that lack even a tenuous relationship to history. Geronimo emerges as the quintessential recalcitrant savage. Although he is not really a match for the courageous gallantry of the U.S. Army, which can thwart most of his schemes, Geronimo himself manages to survive so that the series can continue.

The first narrative in *No. 1* bears the title "Geronimo and His Horde of Redskin Devils." The opening image, which covers the upper half of the first page, shows the title character firing a pistol point-blank at a covered-wagon driver who is surrounded by other hostiles armed with rifles and bows and arrows. To the driver's left stands a distraught redhead with plunging neckline, apparently perched on thin air. Nothing related to this scene occurs in the first narrative, but it suggests a tone for the imagery that pervades all four comic books: Geronimo's targeting innocent settlers, his threat to voluptuous white womanhood, his ability to attract a band of faithful followers to participate in his devilment. The story explains Geronimo's enmity in an incident loosely based on the massacre at Kaskiyeh. A Sonoran rancher wants to water his cattle at the campsite of Geronimo's band. His henchmen launch a massacre in which Geronimo's wife and family are killed. The grieving husband vows retribution: "I swear upon the honored bones of my ancestors that all white men will feel the power of my wrath. I spend my life in vengeance" (5). His first act of revenge targets the rancher, whom Geronimo drags across the desert behind his horse. After several other raids in which taking scalps is a principal activity, Geronimo "began to forget that he raided for vengeance and slowly he began to turn into a murderous killer with an implacable hatred for the white man" (7). His successes gain him the position of chief, but he is captured by "Colonel Bridewell" during a battle in the Rincon Mountains and sent to the San Carlos Reservation. Tried for his crimes, he is acquitted because not "a shred of actual evidence" links him to specific acts (9). Thus, Geronimo is released from reservation confinement to resume his depredations. This section of the comic book ends with General Crook appointed by the president to deal expressly with Geronimo.

Of course, virtually nothing about this tale has any relationship to history. Even the acts that inspired Geronimo's hostility are misrepresented. But more important than historical and ethnographic inaccuracies in terms of the imagery of Geronimo is the comic book's focus on this figure who never left the popular imagination and was enjoying some resurgence in the public eye, perhaps because of his role as recalcitrant savage in the recently released film *Broken Arrow*. He was still undoubtedly the most recognizable Indian in American (and perhaps international) popular culture.[3]

Central to the aesthetic of comic-book creation has been the process of encapsulation (Duncan and Smith 2009, 131–41). The success of a comic-book narrative depends on its creators' ability to convey plot in a highly condensed manner, to rely on very few frames—fifty or so in most of the Geronimo comics—containing images that must convey the meaning that the sparse dialogue cannot communicate effectively. Moreover, employing a narrative pace that resembles what critics of the English and Scottish popular ballad called "leaping-and-lingering" (Hodgart 1962, 31), what Danish folk narrative theorist Axel Olrik referred to as "tableaux scenes" (1965, 138), and the montage effect pioneered by filmmaker Sergei Eisenstein (1949, 72–83), comic-book creators eschew transitional devices and focus their attention on conveying as much as possible through each frame. The effects of encapsulation are particularly evident in the second story in the book, an interesting mishmash titled "Geronimo and the Crawford Expedition," which depicts the Chiricahua leader in "an act of treacherous malevolence that reached an all time low" (Cohen 1950, 10) and juxtaposes events that the historical record indicates were separated by several years and many miles. The killings of Judge H. C. McComas and his wife are attributed to Geronimo rather than Chatto, and the judge's brother Jim, who was accompanying the couple (in young Charlie's place), manages to escape and bring word to General Crook that Geronimo is nearby. Crook sends Captain Crawford in pursuit of the murderers, but a spy overhears this plan and takes word to Geronimo, who conceives his own nefarious plan: to trick the Mexican forces, who are also pursuing Apaches, into a conflict with Crawford's expedition. In the ensuing battle between Mexican and U.S. troops, an Apache sharpshooter under Geronimo's direction kills Crawford. The troops believe that Mexicans are responsible and pursue them until the dying Crawford reveals Geronimo's guilt. The wrath of the U.S. Army over this trickery is so intense that even the wily Geronimo feels its effects, and he agrees to meet with General Crook at "Canyon des Embudos" to discuss surrender. After the surrender occurs, the Apaches renege on the deal under the influence of Tribollet's bootlegged whiskey. The section ends with General Miles replacing Crook.

The retelling of these events characterizes Geronimo as the archvillain: the murderer of a judge and his wife, a plotter who suborns the assassination of a gallant U.S. Army officer, an opportunist who wants peace only when the hostilities become too much for him to handle, and a drunkard who betrays the solemn handshake that he and Crook had used to seal their agreement. The comic book writer has exercised considerable license with the historic record but has taken advantage of the strengths and limitations of the medium, especially its need to tell a vivid, uncomplicated story in a highly condensed format.

By occasionally alluding to the historical record, albeit with considerable inaccuracy, the comic book manages to ground its narrative in an aura of authority. It effectively demonizes Geronimo by associating him with the stereotypical savagery that colored treatments of American Indians even before the captivity narrative tradition began in the eighteenth century. The comic book does this with considerable condensation, the creators having merged some episodes from Geronimo's actual career with incidents that seem to be invented out of whole cloth. Illustrations such as the one of the alluring white woman that introduces the volume but that has no bearing on the actual narrative reinforce the connection of the first volume in Avon's Geronimo series not only to captivity narratives but to dime novels, pulp western fiction, and popular film, which was continuing to portray Geronimo as the implacable opponent of civilization even while it was beginning to celebrate such figures as Cochise.

The cover illustration of the second installment in the series depicts an Indian, apparently Geronimo, in what is probably supposed to be Plains Indian garb, mounted on a rearing horse as he grasps a rifle and glares at the viewer. Behind him a battle in front of a log stockade is in progress. *Indian Chief Geronimo on the Warpath, No. 2* bears the subtitle *The Murderous Battle at Kiskayah!*, thus preparing the reader with some knowledge of Apache-Mexican relations for an account of the incident that Geronimo credited with having turned him toward a life of vengeance. The inside front cover of this 1951 publication by Avon provides an overview of Geronimo's reputation in a few lurid captions: "Cunning, bloodthirsty and cruel, the name of Geronimo brought a chill to the stoutest heart!"; "With his renegade band he swept across the plains, leaving a trail of blood behind"; "The dauntless chieftain who emerged from the rocky wastes of Arizona and became the most feared raider of the old untamed west." We are prepared to learn about this historical figure despite the copyright notice at the bottom of the page advising us, "All names in this periodical are entirely fictitious and no identification with actual persons is intended" (Cohen 1951a, 2). The next installment, *Geronimo and His Apache Murderers, No. 3*, has some of the most sensationalistic cover art in the series of four. The visage of a grimacing Geronimo looms over a scene in which he raises a hatchet above the head of a gallant soldier. Tepees and a covered wagon fill the background. Overarching the whole is Geronimo's name in garish red letters. The signature on the cover is that of Everett Raymond Kinstler, who later achieved success as portraitist of the rich and famous, including several U.S. presidents. Avon's series concludes with *The Savage Raids of Chief Geronimo, No. 4*, copyrighted in 1952. Inside the front cover, illustrator Kinstler has provided a passable drawing of Geronimo based on the now well-known photograph taken by Camillus S. Fly, which depicts Geronimo and three other Chiricahuas poised with rifles during the negotiations with General Crook at Cañon de los Embudos.

The stories that fill these volumes have less and less to do with the historical Geronimo and become more and more realizations of a narrative formula. What began as at least a desultory attempt to represent the historical Geronimo, though in a way that exaggerated his image as the quintessential "bad Indian," gave way to episodes that usually had almost no connection with history and increasingly adhered to a pattern: Geronimo succeeds or fails at a massacre or other crime; Geronimo plots another, more grandiose act of evil; the U.S. Army or its representative prevents Geronimo from accomplishing his goal and kills a number of his warriors; Geronimo escapes and boastfully reiterates his policy of vengeance. The pattern often involves historical personages from the Apache wars: Powhatan H. Clarke, Emmet Crawford, John P. Clum, Al Seiber, and Tom Horn. Perhaps the series could have continued indefinitely to create new situations and occasions for Geronimo to demonstrate his savage, evil ferocity and for the U.S. Army to thwart his machinations without ever being able to capture or kill him. But the last story in the final installment, "The Flaming Fingers of Death," does not even feature Geronimo, and no more volumes in the series came out. By the time the reader gets through the four volumes, he or she has experienced a Geronimo unwavering in his savagery, whose principal talent is treachery, who has a reputation as a threat to white womanhood, and who proves to be inept at everything except preserving his own life. The illustrations reinforce what amounts to a generic depiction of the "bad Indian." The only really visual feature that distinguishes Geronimo from other Indians is that he usually is wearing a headband rather than a warbonnet, and even that does not mark him off from the other Apaches who appear in the frames. Illustrator Kinstler could produce drawings of images from the photographs of Geronimo with some precision— as he does particularly on the inside front covers of several of the volumes— but he opted for a more generic savage when the business of storytelling began.

Geronimo comics went international with the publication of *Geronimo: Apache vuol dire nemico* in 1974. Comics artist Rino Albertarelli, who produced several volumes devoted to Wild West themes, made the Geronimo book the first in his series I protagonisti del West. Belgian-French screenwriter Jean-Michel Charlier and comics artist Jean Giraud (also known as Moebius) have included an adventure featuring Geronimo in their multiple-volume series of western-themed graphic novels about Michael Steven Donovan, a Union veteran of the Civil War who uses the nickname "Blueberry." Previous installments in the series depicted a series of adventures in the Wild West. *Geronimo l'Apache* appeared in 1999 as part of a narrative arc with a southeastern Arizona setting that encompassed at least three volumes. Its predecessor in the series was *Ombres sur Tombstone*, and it was followed by *OK Corral*. Though several volumes in the Blueberry series have been translated into English, *Geronimo l'Apache* appears only in a Spanish translation and in the original French.

Despite the novel's title, Geronimo is as subsidiary a character as he is in most fiction. He provides a subplot for hostilities between the Earps and Clantons that will erupt at the OK Corral. The nefarious Ma Clanton has staged a series of robberies, resulting in fatalities, to make it appear as if Geronimo's band of Chiricahuas are the perpetrators, and we find that corruption in Tombstone runs through the highest levels of the community's elite. The series protagonist, Blueberry, bedridden from injuries received in a previous installment, has a history with Geronimo, whose grudging admiration he had gained in the 1860s, a decade or so before the action in *Geronimo l'Apache*. The reader encounters that history through flashbacks into Blueberry's memory: Geronimo had saved Blueberry's life in defiance of others in his band. "Ma vision dit qu'il doit vivre!" Geronimo forcefully asserts (Charlier and Giraud 1999, 19). Meanwhile, in the present tense of the novel, Geronimo has taken John P. Clum, editor of the *Tombstone Epitaph*, as prisoner in hopes of getting him to expose the Chiricahuas' innocence of the crimes. Nothing much is resolved by the end of the narrative, but lines are drawn for the shootout at the OK Corral that highlights the next Blueberry volume.

Giraud's drawings of Geronimo, especially that which decorates the cover, reveal him as implacable but honorable. In the protagonist Blueberry he had found a worthy adversary who could also serve as his advocate when the Clantons attempted to tarnish his image by implicating him in the killings. Though several scenes depict Geronimo and his band panoramically, Giraud relies heavily on details of the face that stares out of many photographs and that offered perhaps the most memorable images of the Chiricahua.

Another graphic novel, *Geronimo: The Last Apache Warrior*, with story by Eric Griffin and art by Chaz Truog, may be as historically inaccurate as many other attempts to depict the famous Chiricahua in literature. But it uses his image effectively to explore the nature of Death spelled with a capital *D*. The book uses two perspectives—that of an older Geronimo reviewing his conflicts with Mexican and Anglo intruders shortly after he has surrendered to General Miles and that of an external narrator who often verbalizes in the *Kalevala* meter of *The Song of Hiawatha*. The story deals with two events in Geronimo's career. One, narrated by the older Geronimo himself, focuses on the first person he killed, a Mexican muleteer whom he encountered at age seventeen while part of a raiding party led by Mangas Coloradas. The killing itself is presented through Truog's images, but the point of the story is not so much the deed itself as Geronimo's hearing the final sound made by the dying man: "The sound of his life leaving his body. It was a single word. A quiet word. No scream of defiance. No entreaty, prayer, or stream of profanity. The word didn't even slip past his lips. . . . . . But issued from the ragged wound in his chest as I slid my knife free. It sounded like 'hush'" (Griffin and Truog 2005, n.p.; ellipses in original). This sound allows Geronimo to equate the experience of dying with that of being born. As the kicking, screaming infant is quieted with a "hush," so does the person taking leave of this life and perhaps being born into a "strange world" articulate the soothing sound. The death sound made by a human contrasts with the sound made by other animals as they die, and the seasoned warrior Geronimo has had many opportunities to hear that sound (n.p.).

The external narrator presents the other focal event in the novel: Geronimo's courtship of Alope. The courtship begins during festivities that greet the returning raiding party, for they have taken from the Mexican mule train sufficient supplies to last their community throughout the winter. The celebration involves a recitation of the great deeds done by the raiders, including Geronimo, and athletic competitions at which Geronimo excels. For him, though, the memory of the sound and an awareness of the omnipresence of Death color the celebratory atmosphere. His compatriots—the oafish Juh, the trickster Porico, even Mangas Coloradas—do not understand. They "could not follow to Death's country," but "moon-born" Alope knows "the tread of Death's returning" and feels ominous stirrings upon hearing "his stealthy step among them" (n.p.). The narrator characterizes the courtship in adversarial terms. We see Alope holding a knife at Geronimo's throat, teaching him "a hard lesson about taking kisses like scalps" (n.p.), and he must meet her father's exorbitant bridewealth demands in order to marry her. After he does so, they marry, and we see the couple embracing. However, the next scene in the novel depicts the massacre at Kaskiyeh with Alope receiving a blow to the head from the butt of a Mexican rifle. The remaining pages take us through the deaths of Mangas Coloradas and Juh, the exile of Porico to Florida, and Geronimo finding himself "trapped" in Skeleton Canyon. The last two pages return to the narration of Geronimo as he relates how he and Miles made a "stone oath" to end the Apache wars.

Geronimo: The Last Apache Warrior successfully depicts the specter of Death haunting the Southwest during Geronimo's lifetime, and its elliptical story relies as much upon the artwork as on the narrators' words. It allows those narrators, especially Geronimo, to remain laconic, thus reinforcing the stereotype of the inarticulate savage but also suggesting the grand, perhaps incommunicable, mysteries of Death that have been thrust upon Geronimo.

◇

THE LITERARY HISTORY OF GERONIMO CERTAINLY HAS NOT DEVELOPED linearly and thus reinforces the pliability of his image. In some cases (and not just in the early material), he remains the utter archvillain, and in some cases (and not just in his recent manifestations), he emerges more positively, often as a child-loving elder statesman. Most literary works, especially the fiction, trade upon his name recognition without involving him significantly as a personage in the proceedings. In others, the authors have taken features of his historical persona and created fictional characters only loosely based on that persona, often even renaming them. Into the twenty-first century he has remained a staple of pulp western fiction, while authors whose purposes go beyond entertainment, especially poets, have found in Geronimo a vehicle for their own ideas and causes. Since the late nineteenth century, Geronimo has appeared in a range of literary genres: poetry, drama, and short and long fiction. During the twentieth century, he not only continued to appear in those genres but also made his way into newly emergent forms such as comic books and graphic novels. He also seems a natural for a new medium that emerged in the early 1900s, and film has made frequent use of this iconic representative of savagism.

CHAPTER SEVEN

GERONIMO SCREENED

HIS COMPELLING STORY, HIS ENDURING REPUTATION, EVEN HIS PHYSI-
cal appearance make Geronimo ideal for film treatment. As a wire service
item that was making the rounds with the showing of the film *Geronimo!* in
1939 and 1940 noted, "There certainly was never a more appalling one [figure
from the Southwest] than Geronimo, arch fiend and war lord of the Apache
Indian tribe which fought the United States to the death for the arid waste-
land they know as home" (*Chilicothe [MO] Constitution-Tribune* for 2 March
1940). Geronimo's first cinematic appearance occurred only three years after
his death. Now lost to the disintegrating effects of time, *Geronimo's Last Raid*
came out in 1912. But Geronimo has enjoyed considerable subsequent screen
exposure, usually in secondary roles, in films made for theatrical release as
well as in those intended for television. Geronimo has also been a character
in episodes of several television series, especially those broadcast during the
heyday of the western in the late 1950s and early 1960s. He even inspired a cartoon character, Geronimoo, in an ABC-TV offering, *The C.O.W.-Boys of Moo
Mesa*. In fact, Geronimo has probably appeared in more "Hollywood oaters,"
as one historian calls them (Langellier 2011, 58), than any other American
Indian, including Crazy Horse and Sitting Bull. In many films he is the only
historical character on screen. Characters meant to recall Geronimo undoubtedly appeared in the very early days of film, but he did not fully emerge as a
recognizable cinematic figure until the late 1930s. Most always—at least early
in his cinematic career—he took the role of what Michael T. Marsden and

Jack Nachbar call the "Savage Reactionary," a stereotypical villain who is a "killer because he detests the proper and manifest advancement of a White culture clearly superior to his own and often because of his own primal impulses" (1988, 609). Of the two dimensions that the "Hollywood Indian" was capable of representing—"the old bloodthirsty savage and his alter ego, the noble savage" (Kilpatrick 1999, 15)—Geronimo usually assumed the role of the former. For example, he is the principal menace threatening the passengers bound for Lordsburg in John Ford's classic *Stagecoach* (1939). There the audience hears his name invoked as threat at the film's beginning, and Geronimo (Chief White Horse) is a clear and menacing presence among the phalanx of hostile Apaches who ominously loom over the stage's route in a series of low-angle shots that depict them stalking their quarry. While just his name is enough to induce anxiety among those who hear it (Bunscombe 2006, 95), Ford also exploited the glowering face that stared out of Frank Randall's photograph taken in 1884 and that is shown in later Geronimo films. He is the main "outside threat" to the microcosm of frontier folk, "the motley social group traveling together," who provide the film's focus (Nolley 2003, 83).

Victor Daniels (using the performance name Chief Thundercloud) took the title role in *Geronimo!* (released in New York City in 1940 after its debut in a couple of Arizona cities the previous autumn), the film that re-introduced the figure to American popular culture and is generally credited with inspiring World War II military paratroopers to yell as they leaped from airborne troop carriers (along with the many children who continue to yell "Geronimo" as they jump from lesser heights). Daniels was born in 1899 in Muskogee, Oklahoma, and may have been a member of the Cherokee Nation. His looks guaranteed him roles among the extras in many western films during the 1930s. He also originated the role of Tonto in the first Lone Ranger films.

Geronimo!, a Paramount production directed by Paul H. Sloane, premiered in Phoenix and Safford, Arizona, on 25 November 1939 and was released in New York City the following February. The film was promoted in ways that stressed its depiction of the intersection of civilization and savagery. The press kit advised exhibitors to "play an Indian sound effects record in their theater lobbies, with tom-toms and war cries" (O'Connor 2003, 34). Advertising billed the film as the story of "The Most Feared Warrior That Ever Ravaged The West!" Among the titillating scenes that the audience could expect to view were "10,000 Indians roar[ing] into battle against a whole U. S. Cavalry regiment" and "the fiendish torture den of the ruthless Geronimo."[1] In fact, the *Monthly Film Bulletin* suggested that scenes of "Indian torture" were "too horrific" for young children under ten, though "the film should appeal especially to schoolboys" (N. K. 1940, 39). However, the film reviewer for the *New York Times* on 8 February 1940 was not as impressed by the violence and action as by the taciturnity of the title character, who was characterized as "a remarkably genuine redskin with a vocabulary of one grunt and a histrionic repertoire of two expressions: grim, and very grim" (fig. 7.1). The *Times* wondered whether the part could even be considered a "speaking role." A rough count indicates that Victor Daniels had less than a dozen lines—all delivered in a taut version of what was meant to be the Apache language—in the entire film. Instead, he makes his dramatic point (that Geronimo is, as the film's opening caption states, "a great enemy") by staring balefully and menacingly into the camera. In terms of plot, the *Times* awarded the film "one faint whoop" in its 11 February 1940 issue and dismissed it as the "script of 'Lives of a Bengal Lancer' superimposed on the Apache country, with John Ford's 'Stagecoach' rolling across the background." Raymond William Stedman's dismissive treatment of the film encapsulates contemporary and later opinion:

> Paramount's *The Lives of a Bengal Lancer* (1935), with a change of continent, a selection of stock footage from various Paramount Westerns, and an Apache demon-in-chief, lived as *Geronimo* (1939), a sun-scorched garrison of men in blue, not white, braving the terrors of a frontier too large to defend. Although Geronimo's warriors seemed more thuggees than Apaches, Chief Thundercloud, in the title role, delivered a chilling performance vastly removed from his likeable Tonto of the Lone Ranger movie serials. (Stedman 1982, 162)

The film's plot indeed reworks *The Lives of a Bengal Lancer* (Hathaway 1935) with the American Southwest substituting for northern India and Apaches assuming the obstructionist roles of Muslim guerrillas. Geronimo's own fight against Manifest Destiny stems from the bloody massacre of his family by white men. The unrest in Arizona brings General Steele (Ralph Morgan) to the region, where he has command of his own son Jack (William Henry), a greenhorn fresh out of West Point whom the general has not seen since his offspring was a child. Unable to deal with his father's harsh treatment, young Steele resigns his commission and resolves to settle in California, bringing his mother and his fiancée with him. The former is killed and the latter seriously injured when Apaches attack their stagecoach, and Jack Steele vows to exact vengeance. After being captured by Geronimo, the young man is

Fig. 7.1. Geronimo, portrayed by Victor Daniels/Chief Thundercloud, had few lines in *Geronimo!*, released in New York City in 1940 after premiering in Phoenix and Safford, Arizona, the preceding November. However, Daniels uses facial expressions to convey the title character's ferocity. *Source: Photofest, Inc.*

rescued when his father realizes that his neglect of family has precipitated the crisis and leads a battalion to find him. Jack later saves his father's life when Geronimo, in soldier's disguise, is on the verge of killing the general. Clearly, *Geronimo!* focuses its attention not so much on the title character as on family conflicts among his adversaries. The Apache merely provides the catalyst that effects a reconciliation.

Like most such productions, the film departs significantly from the historical record, and, in fact, Geronimo is captured in the resolution of the main plotline. The historical novelist MacKinlay Kantor even wrote to the *New York Times* complaining about some of the inaccuracies. Most significantly, the action is set in 1877, some ten years before the end of the Apache wars, and the triumphant soldiers are congratulated by President Ulysses S. Grant, whose term had ended before the climactic action in the film, rather than his successor, Rutherford B. Hayes—a somewhat trivial complaint, given the film's neglect of virtually any contact with the historical record. In its April 1940 issue, *Winners of the West* reprinted a review of the film from the *Chicago Tribune* that held that *Geronimo!* "gives an exaggerated idea of that celebrated Indian's importance, while considerably underrating his abilities." The reviewer was especially concerned with the film's claim that the Chiricahua, who after all was not even a chief among his own people, was heading a force of five thousand Indians from various Southwestern groups. The paper's edition for July 1940 included a letter from Western writer E. A. Brininstool, who characterized the film as "absolutely the rawest and rottenest thing ever thrown on the screen." The writer claimed to have contacted Paramount Studios about historical inaccuracies but received no satisfaction from their response: "They ACKNOWLEDGE IT—and said they made it for a 'Western thriller' and KNEW it wasn't correct! Can you beat that! What are these film concerns coming to when they will bugger up our Western history and Indian Wars in the contemptible and dishonest way they do? There was not ONE SINGLE THING in that film that was right." Brininstool particularly disliked the anachronistic use of Winchester rifles that did not become available until twenty years after the film's setting and the depiction of Apache warriors on horseback instead of as the unhorsed "FOOT INDIANS" that they were as historical missteps in *Geronimo!*

Daniels portrayed Geronimo at least a couple more times following his appearance in the 1940 film. In *I Killed Geronimo* (Hoffman 1950) an army officer assigned to kill Geronimo in 1882 is ultimately successful when he stabs the Apache during an attack on a stagecoach. Like many films that exploit Geronimo's notoriety, it deals much less with him than with conflicts among the Euro-American characters. Daniels re-assumed his role as Geronimo very briefly in an episode of the television series *Buffalo Bill Jr.* in 1955, the year of the actor's death.

Another performer who portrayed Geronimo several times was the Mohawk Harold J. Smith (as Jay Silverheels), best known, of course, for his recurring role as the Lone Ranger's sidekick, Tonto. Smith first played Geronimo in *Broken Arrow* (Daves 1950), which deals with the process by which Cochise (played by Brooklyn-born actor Jeff Chandler) and General O. O. Howard (Basil Ruysdael) forged a peace agreement through the intermediation of Tom Jeffords (James Stewart). Geronimo stands as an obstacle to the peace process. At a conference among Chiricahua leaders discussing Howard's proposal for a reservation in southeastern Arizona that will restrict movements back and forth across the international border, Geronimo declares,

"I trust none of it. Four days ago we were given our own country on a piece of paper. Today we cannot go into Mexico. The American general says 'No.' Already our territory is smaller. Where will we get corn, blankets, horses if not by taking them from the Mexicans as we always have?" When Cochise replies that now the U.S. government will provide for their needs, Geronimo is scornfully dismissive: "The answer of a woman! I am not afraid. I speak from my heart. It is not the Apache way to be grandmother to cattle. Cochise has lost his taste for battle, and so he is ready to surrender. He throws away our victories." Cochise, in turn, stresses the importance of change and flexibility, breaks the symbolic arrow, and declares, "I will try this way of peace." Geronimo is having none of this peacemaking and asserts, "I will walk away," thus rejecting Cochise's authority. Cochise declares his enmity for Geronimo and those who endorse his obstructionist position. Geronimo responds, "I leave you my name also. Now I am ashamed of your Chiricahua. I will take the name Mexican enemies have given me. The whites will learn it and you will learn it. From now on I am Geronimo!"

That Geronimo represents an obstacle to progress, a theme that will persist in other films in which his character appears throughout the 1950s (Bunscombe 2006, 111), becomes particularly evident after Sonseeahray (Debra Paget), Jeffords's wife and Cochise's daughter, is killed by whites in ambush. Their action is seen as retribution for the depredations that Geronimo has been perpetrating since leaving Cochise's band; however, Cochise accepts that "Geronimo broke the peace no less than these whites." The screenplay for *Broken Arrow*, based on Elliott Arnold's novel *Blood Brother* ([1947] 1979), was the work of Albert Maltz, one of the blacklisted Hollywood Ten. Maltz, who had joined the Communist Party in the 1930s, used Michael Blankfort as his front for *Broken Arrow*, and the film's positive take on Native American issues may reflect his progressive ideals. The film is often regarded as a primary influence on the new image for Indians that post-1950 films presented (Marsden and Nachbar 1988, 613). It has been described as "the work that transformed the depiction of the Native Americans and resulted in a new cycle of 'Indian Westerns'" (Money 1997, 369). Geronimo, though, did not benefit from this improvement until a decade later.

In fact, Geronimo emerges as the principal villain in both prequel and sequel to *Broken Arrow*. The prequel, *The Battle at Apache Pass* (Sherman 1952), casts the volatile Geronimo (reprised by Jay Silverheels) in direct opposition to Cochise (reprised by Jeff Chandler). The setting is about a decade before that of *Broken Arrow* and deals with the events that led to the long conflict between Cochise's Chiricahuas and the United States. Those events include the massacre of a group of stagecoach passengers heading for Tucson by Geronimo and his minions, chicanery on the part of some evil white men, and a misguided attempt by Lieutenant George Bascom to retrieve a child kidnapped by Geronimo. The event that turns the conciliatory Cochise into a hostile is a staging of the Bascom Affair, which results in the capture of his wife and three of his warriors. The latter are executed, and these killings precipitate the battle that provides the film's title. The conflict between the recalcitrant savage Geronimo and Cochise climaxes when Geronimo tries to convince the Chiricahuas to reject Cochise as leader and challenges him to mortal combat. Though Geronimo loses the fight, Cochise decides not to kill him. Instead, he makes Geronimo an outcast. The film ends with the hope that Cochise and his Anglo counterpart will eventually be able to restore peace. As in *Broken Arrow*, Geronimo remains the principal hindrance to civilized progress, the ultimate recalcitrant savage who dares to challenge the highly respected Cochise.

Broken Arrow's sequel, *Taza, Son of Cochise* (Sirk 1954), seems ahead of its time. It ostensibly assumes a Native American perspective by focusing on the intra-Chiricahua power struggle between Cochise's sons Taza and Naiche following the chief's death. Very few scenes in the film do not have at least one American Indian character, and most present Indians exclusively. The white characters are clearly subsidiary. Moreover, a Euro-American narrator does not intrude as in *Broken Arrow* and *Geronimo: An American Legend* (Hill 1993), which appeared at a time purportedly more sensitive to Native perspectives. However, two concerns undercut the film's progressive- ness. One, the major characters are played by Euro-American actors: Jeff Chandler again appears as Cochise, who is on screen only briefly on his deathbed at the film's beginning; Rock Hudson appears as the title charac- ter; Rex Reason is Naiche; and Ian MacDonald takes the part of Geronimo. Barbara Rush, the only credited female, plays a daughter of the fictional Grey Eagle, and Taza and Naiche vie for her hand. Moreover, the film's sen- timents lie clearly with the peaceful, conciliatory Taza, the "good Indian" who must contend with the influential Geronimo, who is leading Naiche and others among the Chiricahuas astray. Geronimo's role as principal antago- nist recalls the part he plays in *Broken Arrow*, but this film shows him car- rying out threats he had made in that film after Cochise had treated with General Howard. Historically minded viewers will also recoil at the film's revision of history. Set in the 1870s, it concludes with Taza (who, according to historical records, perished from illness during a trip to Washington after a couple of years as the Chiricahua leader) and his philosophy of peace triumphant, Naiche (who lived well into the twentieth century) dead, and Geronimo (who did not surrender until 1886) on his way to exile in Florida. Nevertheless, the film continues to promote the image of Geronimo that its cinematic predecessors established: the "bad" Indian who epitomizes savage resistance to inevitable and beneficial progress.

Following *The Battle at Apache Pass*, Jay Silverheels appeared as Geronimo once more in feature films. In 1956—by which time he had firmly established himself as Tonto in the American popular imagination—he was the recalcitrant Geronimo in *Walk the Proud Land* (Hibbs 1956). This film, based on *Apache Agent*, Woodworth Clum's biography of his father, John P. Clum, allowed Audie Murphy, who had established himself as an action hero in western films, to assume a more fully rounded role as a white man somewhat sensitive to Apaches' concerns, even those of the still-resistant Geronimo.

Other actors who portrayed Geronimo in several films have included Miguel Inclan, Daniel Simmons as Chief Yowlachie, Pat Hogan, and Monte Blue. The first, a Mexican actor known for his villainous roles in Mexican films of the 1930s and 1940s, appeared in *Indian Uprising* (Nazarro 1952) and *The Great Indian Wars, 1840–1890* (Dalton 1991). Simmons, a Yakama Indian whose most famous film appearance occurred in John Ford's *Red River* (Hawks 1948), assumed the role of Geronimo in *Son of Geronimo: Apache Avenger*, a fifteen-episode serial (Bennet 1952), and in one episode of the television series *Stories of the Century* (Witney 1954). Hogan, who specialized in Indian roles during the 1950s and early 1960s, appeared as the Chiricahua in three episodes of "Texas John Slaughter," a recurring series that was part of the weekly television program *Disneyland* in 1960 and 1961. He had previously played the part of Naiche in the episode of *Stories of the Century* in which Daniel Simmons portrayed Geronimo. Blue had appeared as Geronimo's interpreter in Paul Sloane's 1940 film *Geronimo!* and had a larger speaking role than Victor Daniels. He assumed the small role of Geronimo in *Apache* (Aldrich 1954), an account of Massai, an Apache who escaped from one of the trains carrying the Chiricahuas to Florida and managed to make it back to the Southwest, where he survived for several years. The film is based on Paul I. Wellman's novel *Broncho Apache* (1936).

Meanwhile, Geronimo was appearing as a supporting character in vehicles for well-known actors. For example, Tom Tyler is Geronimo in *Valley of the Sun* (Marshall 1942), which features Lucille Ball. Although he makes only a brief appearance on screen, Geronimo (played by Lakota actor John War Eagle) is an important focus in the 1951 film *The Last Outpost* (a.k.a. *Cavalry Charge*; Foster 1951). This vehicle for Ronald Reagan, who portrays Vance Britton, a Confederate officer who is trying to ensure that the Apaches remain neutral in the Civil War, is set in the Southwest at the onset of the conflict. His brother is the Union commander at Fort Point. Disguised as a Union negotiator, Vance Britton meets with the Apache tribal council, consisting of such luminaries as Mangas Coloradas and Cochise. He learns that the only way he can secure their impartiality and prevent their supporting the Union cause and collecting bounties for Confederate scalps is to release Geronimo, "one of our young chiefs," who is awaiting trial or possibly lynching for having massacred a wagon train. Geronimo has only a few lines in the film. He justifies his killing the trader whose wagons he had destroyed to Britton: "He sold my men bad whiskey and bad guns. The whiskey poisoned them, and the guns blew the heads off many Indians. He deserved to die." Geronimo crosses his arms and turns away, disdaining further dialogue. As in many other treatments of him in popular culture, his name is enough to catch the audience's attention. Though both Mangas Coloradas and Cochise had active leadership positions in the early 1860s, many Anglos did not know of Geronimo. But in 1951 he was undoubtedly the best-known Indian to the general public—the one most likely to be recognized as a worthy adversary for the film's star. Even though Geronimo in the film is more pawn than agent of action, he offers a point of general recognition in this attempt to combine the Civil War theme of brother-against-brother conflict with a western setting. The film has the merit of providing a retributive rationale for Geronimo's actions.

Geronimo was an occasional presence in television westerns during their height of popularity in the 1950s and early 1960s. One notable instance is an episode of *Stories of the Century*, originally broadcast 14 February 1954. The Emmy-winning series, which ran for thirty-nine episodes in 1954 and 1955, featured the adventures of railroad detective Matt Clark (Jim Davis), who serendipitously encounters an infamous western badman in each episode, usually at the climactic moment in the historical figure's career. The Geronimo episode has Clark accompanying Lieutenant Charles Gatewood on the mission to convince Geronimo (Daniel Simmons/Chief Yowlachie) to surrender to General Miles. But before this action, which occupies only the last few minutes of the twenty-seven-minute program, we see Geronimo attempting to steal a shipment of guns and allowing Naiche, "one of the war chiefs," to be captured. Then Geronimo and a large band of Apache warriors attack the wagon train that is transporting Naiche to trial in Tucson and successfully liberate him. Next he leads an attack on an undermanned fort, only to be thwarted when the cavalry arrives to rescue the beleaguered defenders. So the historic encounter between Geronimo and Gatewood—Clark's presence at which is highly contrived—is an afterthought. Throughout the short film, Geronimo is almost as speechless as he is in the 1940 *Geronimo!*, but Simmons cannot project the baleful stare that Victor Daniels had used so effectively in the earlier film. In fact, his Geronimo comes across as more senescent than threatening. And the film has its share of historical, ethnographic, and geographical inaccuracies. Like other episodes of *Stories of the Century*, its main object is to place the recurring character Matt Clark in the presence of the well-known (and, in some cases, famous only to Wild West buffs) historical personages. Among other figures whom he encounters in the series's episodes are outlaws Jesse and Frank James and gunfighters Doc Holliday, John Wesley Hardin, and Tom Horn.

Among other television series that featured Geronimo as a character in at least one episode were *Annie Oakley* (1956), *Broken Arrow* (1956, 1957), *Casey Jones* (1957), *Tombstone Territory* (1958), *Death Valley Days* (1960), *Zane Grey Theater* (1960), *F Troop* (1966), and *Bret Maverick* (1982).

Called a "masterpiece of unwise casting" (Stedman 1982, 210), the selection of Chuck Connors, familiar to audiences for his role in television westerns, to portray the title character in Arnold Laven's *Geronimo* in 1962 has elicited virtually unanimous disdain (fig. 7.2). The film's cast includes other non-Indians in Indian roles: Ross Martin as Mangus, Armando Silvestre (a Mexican American actor) as Naiche, and Kamala Devi (an Asian Indian actor) as Teela, a reservation schoolteacher whom Geronimo marries. The film begins shortly after Geronimo's surrender to General Crook in the Sierra Madre in 1883. Conditions on the San Carlos Reservation, to which Geronimo's band returns, are worsened by the chicanery of the whites who oversee it and mitigated only by Teela, who tries to convince Geronimo to learn Euro-American ways, including reading and writing, so that he can share in the new way of life that is inevitably coming to his homeland. When conditions at San Carlos become unbearable, Geronimo escapes, taking Teela with him. He hopes that his actions will bring national attention and sympathy to the Apaches' plight. He is so successful in attracting attention back east that on the brink of his community's being annihilated by U.S. forces, a senator arrives to convince Geronimo to agree to surrender again.

FIG. 7.2. Though perceived by most commentators as miscast in the title role of *Geronimo* (1962), Euro-American actor Chuck Connors led the cast of a film that presented what was intended to be an Apache perspective. *Source: Photofest, Inc.*

While the film's casting deserves the aspersions cast upon it, it is also a watershed in the screen image of Geronimo, since he does not come across as the mindless force of savagism that is his role in the earlier films in which he is featured, even when other Indian characters are shown as more sensible and conciliatory. In fact, upon learning that Teela has become pregnant, Geronimo expresses the hope not only that his son will become a "fine warrior" but that he will also know how to read. Moreover, the principal negative force in the film is not Geronimo, but the disdainful Indian-hating army officer Captain Maynard (Pat Conway), who has also schemed to benefit financially from the fraud perpetrated at San Carlos. Maynard's attitudes are evident not only in his criminality but in his careless treatment of others. For example, after fruitlessly pursuing Geronimo and a small band of warriors, he fires his revolver aimlessly into the surrounding brush. One shot accidentally but fatally hits Geronimo's sidekick, Mangus. As Geronimo and his band prepare to perish under the bombardment of a cannon that Maynard has called up to rout them from their camp in Mexico, a well-placed arrow from Geronimo's bow kills Maynard and provides the Apaches enough respite so that General Crook and Senator Conrad can arrive with the promise that surrender will include respect for the "rightful heritage" of the Apaches. Moreover, the film does depict Geronimo as a human being—albeit more the laconic Euro-American hero of many western movies than a Chiricahua Apache. Though its recognition of the legitimacy of Geronimo's cause had been anticipated somewhat (though with Geronimo in a much more subordinate role) in *Indian Uprising* (1952), this 1962 film was the earliest thorough screen presentation of Geronimo as a positive figure. Characterized by critics at the time of its release as "pro-Indian in an uncontroversial way," the film was regarded at best as unexciting: "a Western suitable for those with weak hearts or high blood pressure" ("Geronimo" 1962, 80–81).

A couple of somewhat notable television movies featured Geronimo in supporting roles. *Mr. Horn* (Starrett 1989) stars David Carradine in the title role as Tom Horn, scout and interpreter in the Apache wars who was later hanged for murder in Wyoming in 1903. The historical Horn had some contact with Geronimo and had been present at some of the major turning points during the Apache wars, including the killing of Captain Emmet Crawford by Mexican soldiers early in 1886. Directed by Jack Starrett from a screenplay by William Goldman and broadcast on 1 February 1979, the film cast Mexican actor Enrique Lucero as Geronimo, who, though a thinly realized presence, must emerge as a satisfactory foil for the title character to establish his credentials as the heroic westerner who is later executed, perhaps unjustly. (D. R. Bensen's novelization of the film's script receives some attention in chapter 6.)

Another somewhat significant appearance of Geronimo in a made-for-television movie allowed James Arness, who is usually identified with the character Marshal Matt Dillon of Dodge City in *Gunsmoke*, a very successful dramatic television series, to assume the role again. In *Gunsmoke: The Last*

Apache (Correll 1990), broadcast 18 March 1990, Arness's character has retired from his official position and comes to Arizona Territory to reconnect with a woman whom he had known before his Dodge City days. He had not realized that their relationship had yielded a daughter, who has been taken captive by a hotheaded Apache named Wolf. Matt Dillon has an important bargaining chip: two sons of Geronimo who are held prisoner by the U.S. Army. Played by Joaquin Martinez, another Mexican actor, Geronimo—particularly in contrast to Wolf—appears as a peaceful, perhaps superannuated leader of his people who is willing to treat with Dillon. This is not the savagely intransigent Geronimo at all, but an old man who has accepted the inevitable disappearance of his way of life.

Another more ambitious (at least as far as Geronimo is concerned) made-for-television film, *Geronimo* (Young 1993), originally broadcast on 5 December 1993, exemplifies the biopic and is the only fictional film dealing with this historical figure that attempts to provide an overview of his life before the dramatic events of the 1880s. Like most examples of the genre, it oversimplifies both its central character and the events that it recounts, often condensing or conflating events that may have occurred over many years into a single incident. Yet it does attempt to present Geronimo's life from an insider's perspective. After an exciting opening scene in which young Geronimo escapes from Mexican troopers by burying himself in the Sonoran sand, the film jumps far into the future as the aged Geronimo reconnects with his nephew Daklugie at the 1905 Independence Day festivities in Washington, D.C., where the old man has come at President Roosevelt's request. There, an elderly Geronimo (played by Jimmy Herman, a Chipewyan actor) has arrived to ride in a parade and to meet with the president. Upon arriving at the hotel where he will stay, he meets Daklugie, whom he has not seen for twenty years. They sit up all night, and Geronimo tells the younger man, now a student at an eastern school (perhaps Carlisle), his story. That story focuses on several key events in Geronimo's life: his courtship of Alope, which is successful after he pays the bridewealth of sixteen horses; the massacre at Kaskiyeh and his subsequent reception of spiritual power; his revenge at Avispe, where he receives the name Geronimo because the battle occurs on the feast day of Saint Jerome. The revenge attack on the Mexican town features a who's who of the Chiricahuas: not only Geronimo himself (played by Pueblo Indian actor Joseph Runningfox), but also Juh, Mangas Coloradas, Cochise, Chihuahua, and Nana. While the victory suggests an Apache triumph over the Mexicans, the next segment of the film follows the Apaches' building tensions with the Anglos who are beginning to infiltrate the region. Geronimo often finds himself at odds with the more conciliatory Mangas Coloradas, and the climax of this part of the film occurs when the old Bedonkohe chief is killed on a peace mission to the military encampment at Pinos Altos, New Mexico Territory. The soldiers stage a massacre recalling the one at Kaskiyeh. Here Geronimo's second wife perishes, as do his sister and his friend Juh, father of Daklugie, whom Geronimo is able to rescue. Too dispirited to exact the sort of triumphant vengeance that he sought after Kaskiyeh, Geronimo and the other Apaches engage in a desultory conflict with representatives of the United States until Cochise effects a peace treaty, thus establishing the Chiricahua Reservation. The death of Cochise and retribution for the Battle of the Little Big Horn, according to the elderly Geronimo, terminate that reservation. The Apaches, including Geronimo, are moved to San Carlos, where taunts and threats of hanging drive him to his final breakout, which the film has lasting eight years. As he leaves San Carlos, he also leaves Daklugie, who is still a toddler.

The film returns the viewer to 1905 as Geronimo skims over those aspects of his life that have become the focus of most biographical depictions of him, fictional and nonfictional. We do not see him gallantly thwarting the might of the U.S. and Mexican militaries with a small band of warriors who are burdened by women and children. Nor do we witness his surrender to General Miles and his exile from the Southwest. Instead, we encounter an old man who accepts the necessity of assimilation and congratulates Daklugie, who is wearing a cadet's uniform, for his pursuit of a Euro-American education. When he meets with Roosevelt, he makes no abject plea to be returned to Arizona (though he does correct an introduction that designates him as "Mr. Geronimo from Oklahoma"). Instead he declares, "The Apaches will fight no more, but they will never surrender. And they will always be." While Geronimo literally walks into the sunset as he exits the front door of the White House, Roosevelt remarks to an aide in the film's final bit of dialogue, "The irony is I would have done exactly the same as he."

Despite its tendency to oversimplify the historical record, a lapse common to its genre and probably impossible to avoid, this fictionalized cinematic biography of Geronimo effectively tells its story from what seems to be a Native point of view. Not only does Geronimo serve as the occasional voice-over narrator, but all but one or two scenes in the film have him as the focus. The narrative contour, which is elegiac in its vision of the past but also forward looking in its recognition of the necessity of assimilation, moves Geronimo from triumph through despair through triumph through defeat to acceptance. The film personalizes his conflicts with Mexicans and Anglos in a way that removes them from the politics of imperialism and transforms them into a human story. The point of the film according to its director was to put a human face on Geronimo (Harrison 1993), and it sought to achieve that goal by using a Native American cast not only for the principals but for the many extras. Not only Herman and Runningfox, but Ryan Black, who plays the youthful Geronimo, as well as the actors who portrayed Alope, Cochise, Mangas Coloradas, and many others have American Indian heritage. Of all the fictional Geronimo movies to date, this one probably is the most effective in presenting an Indian perspective.

Five days after *Geronimo* (sometime later subtitled *The Untold Story*) was initially broadcast, another Geronimo film came out—this one theatrically. *Geronimo: An American Legend* (Hill 1993), which has received much more attention than the television production, reached theaters on 10 December 1993. Perhaps as a result of the "seismic shift in popular culture's depiction of Native Americans" occasioned by the release of *Dances with Wolves* in 1990 (Money 1997, 376), the most celebrated realization of Geronimo as a character in theatrical film has been his portrayal by Wes Studi in this movie. Larry Gross, who assisted in writing the final version of the film script, noted that director Walter Hill intended the film to be "implicitly critical of all previous depictions of white/Native American relations," but he also asserted that no attempt was made to whitewash Apache violence even in the response to contemporary positive attitudes toward Indians: "The Apaches are highly violent in the film and that may not be in some political interests" (1994, 24). Some critics, though, saw the film as too reverent in its depiction of Geronimo, as turning the career of the historical figure into a "patriotic scheme of things in which he represents all that is best and most enduring in the American spirit" (Tunney 1994, 47).

Thus, *Geronimo: An American Legend* is another in a series of attempts at a "revisionist" treatment of American Indians that began with *Broken Arrow* and included *Cheyenne Autumn* (1964), *Little Big Man* (1970), *Soldier Blue* (1970), and *Dances with Wolves* (1990). According to Armando José Prats, these films follow a formula: "First establish the character of the Indian as Savage Reactionary; then transform that character by ways of insights that recognize both the traditional misrepresentation of the Indian and the Indian's ideal humanity" (1996a, 18). That humanity becomes evident to the viewer through a voice-over by a white character, one who rejects the negative stereotyping of American Indians but nevertheless is defining the Indian characters in an outsider's terms. In *Geronimo: An American Legend*, the voice-over comes from Lieutenant Britton Davis (Matt Damon), who tells the story of Geronimo's final surrender "less for the Indian's sake than for the sake of dissociating himself from the shame of conquest" (Prats 1996a, 23). In fact, the film's central character is not Geronimo but Lieutenant Charles B. Gatewood (Jason Patric). It deals with his divided loyalties: as a former Confederate he seems not totally committed to the U.S. Army and even admires Chiricahua culture. Moreover, an important outcome of the film is Gatewood's relegation to obscurity while General Miles takes credit for Geronimo's surrender. Gatewood also serves as a mentor for Britton. The film begins with the latter's arrival in the Southwest fresh from West Point, and its narrative trajectory reveals his gradual acclimation to his new life in the terms exemplified by Gatewood.

Hence, even a film with Geronimo's name in the title produced at a time when the movie industry and its public were supposedly more attuned to Native concerns assigns him a supporting role. As Jacquelyn Kilpatrick has noted, "This is a film about the white man's experience of Geronimo, not about the man or his people" (1999, 144). While she admits that this Geronimo is a more complex character than in most earlier screen depictions of him, he nevertheless serves as catalyst for the heroism of the Euro-American who acted as principal agent in effecting the surrender that leads to the film's final scene: the train taking Geronimo and his band of Chiricahuas eastward and away from their homeland forever. The train vanishes in the distance in a shot recalling Edward S. Curtis's famous 1904 photograph of a line of Navajo horsemen fading into the hazy background, *The Vanishing Race*. In fact, Prats has noted that this Geronimo film, like others from the 1990s that are generally perceived as presenting a revisionist perspective on Indian-white relations, actually consigns its Indian characters to an ahistorical past. History begins with the sympathetic Euro-Americans who—in the tradition of the Adamic figures who have characterized American expressive culture—stand at "America's real beginning," which can occur only after the Indian has been removed (Prats 1996b, 199). Meanwhile, the film relies heavily on the trope of the vanishing American, but it is not just the Indian who is vanishing. The sense of honor represented by Gatewood, whom we last see riding off alone to a new assignment against a background of Southwestern mesas (actually southeastern Utah), and by Davis, who resigns his commission because of the treatment of Gatewood and the exile even of the Chiricahua scouts who had assisted in the pursuit of Geronimo, also is vanishing from the scene of action. Earlier, the death of scout Al Seiber (Robert Duvall) at the hands of a scalp hunter signals that the old way of life that had provided the context for a man like him to succeed is no longer viable. Davis's voice-over intones, "A way of life that endured a thousand years was gone. This desert, this land that we look out on would never be the same." And Geronimo himself aboard that train heading eastward forgives Chatto for assisting the army because the small Chiricahua population (one of whom has already contracted the "coughing sickness" aboard the train) requires that intracultural enmities should be forgotten. "Now," Geronimo says, "my time is over; now, maybe, the time of our people is over."

Following MacKinley Kantor, historian Gerald Thompson has devoted considerable space to noting the film's inconsistencies with the historical record. Even though he notes that the subtitle includes the word *legend* and attributes to Walter Hill the aim of developing his material from a "legendary perspective" (1994, 212), the thrust of Thompson's critique dwells upon historical inaccuracies. James Sandos and Larry Burgess have seen the film as "an improvement" in its "attempts to provide an Indian perspective" but fault it for dealing exclusively with only a brief segment of Geronimo's life and for not placing his visionary experiences into a context that allows viewers to understand their significance (2003, 119). However, its depiction of Geronimo, though seen through Euro-American eyes, does suggest a more complex person than the recalcitrant savage that marked his cinematic characterizations long after other Indian characters had emerged as more sympathetic figures.

Of special interest regarding this film and its place in the history of Geronimo on screen is director Hill's emphasis on facial close-ups. The opening credits run over a background of Studi's visage, and like Victor Daniels, Jay Silverheels, and Chuck Connors, Studi stares into the camera as he delivers his lines in both sententious Apache and English.

Although the depiction of Native Americans in films may indeed be "a sort of weathervane of social and political currents" that respond to, among other things, varying emphases in federal Indian policy regarding assimilation, sovereignty, termination, and other concerns (Kilpatrick 1999, 178), Geronimo's image was not pliable enough to be subject to the changes that have affected cinematic depictions of Indians in general. "From his first appearance in a sound film," Edward Bunscombe notes, "Geronimo more than any other historical figure came to represent the intractable, rejectionist Indian" (2006, 112). While Crazy Horse and Sitting Bull enjoyed their sympathetic though admittedly ill-conceived treatments in films from the 1950s, Geronimo had to await the Chuck Connors vehicle from 1962, and that film had to revise his story considerably to make it positive from the perspective of Hollywood. In fact, one technique of the "sympathetic" cinema that has characterized fiction films featuring Indian characters involves making a distinction between good Indians and their counterparts (for example, the Lakotas versus Pawnees in *Dances with Wolves*). Geronimo seemed to carry the burden of being the "bad" Indian even when his fellows were regarded more positively. His adversarial stance toward the wise Cochise in *Broken Arrow*, his evil and shadowy but alluring presence in *Taza, Son of Cochise*, and his recalcitrance in *Walk the Proud Land* identify him as a foil to the expectations of the "good" Indian in Hollywood's "sensitive" depictions of Indian subjects. And even when he does receive a more positive treatment— for example, in *Geronimo: An Indian Legend*—he must assume a subsidiary role to Euro-American characters with whom the intended audience can identify. Having Geronimo as a character in a film has meant that one could treat other Indians with special sympathy. Not only did Cochise and other "good" Indians have to contend with the hostile forces of invading Euro-American civilization, but they had to confront the unyielding savagery of Geronimo as well. As Ted Jojola has lamented, "Because Geronimo has been cast in so many fierce roles, everyone has genuinely forgotten how to deal with the humanization of such a legend. In spite of all their efforts, Geronimo remains, well, Geronimo" (2003, 18).

Geronimo may remain Geronimo, but exactly what that means has not been static. Coming into public consciousness at a time when the printed word could, within twenty-four hours, spread reports of his heinous misdeeds to readers throughout the continent and abroad, surviving the late nineteenth- and early twentieth-century exposition culture that exploited him for his entertainment and propaganda values, coexisting with the emergence of popular photography that perceived him as an especially appealing subject, and dying just as films that portrayed him similarly to writers of fiction were beginning to assert themselves in popular culture, Geronimo attained a celebrity status that has not vanished in the least. But it has varied in its emphasis between overly simplistic extremes of demonization and canonization as well as in more subtle characterizations. The practice of imagining Geronimo has endured beyond the centennial of his death and continues to flourish as the bicentennial of his birth approaches. While variations in the resulting images suggest that the "real" Geronimo may not ever be fully understood, the process shows us one way in which the allure of the Native American continues to affect the postcolonial imagination.

Notes

INTRODUCTION

1. An exhibit at the Fenimore Art Museum in Cooperstown, New York, titled *Geronimo: An American Indian Legend* ran through 31 December 2004. Among the items on display were posters and lobby cards for several of the films featuring Geronimo, Geronimo bubble gum and cigarette cards from the 1930s, postcards with images of Geronimo taken by various photographers, a Geronimo doll from 1974, and examples of various Apache craft objects, some allegedly manufactured by Geronimo. For a description of the exhibit, see Fenimore 2004. In 2012 the Heard Museum in Phoenix, Arizona, mounted the exhibit *Beyond Geronimo: The Apache Experience* to run from February 2012 through January 2013.

2. The following overview of Geronimo's life follows the standard narrative developed most fully by Debo (1976) but largely replicated in other treatments of his biography.

CHAPTER 1

1. On 15 October 1887 (by which time Geronimo had been incarcerated at Fort Pickens, Florida, for almost a year), the Grand Jury of the First Judicial District of the Territory of Arizona, Pima County, issued a bill of indictment for "Geronimo, an Apache Indian." The document accused Geronimo of the murder of Jesus Robles on 15 April 1877. Using "a certain gun of the value of ten dollars," Geronimo "then and there had and held, then and there feloniously, willfully and of his malice aforethought did discharge and shoot off, to, against, and upon the said Jesus Robles" with the result being "one mortal wound of the depth of six inches and of the breadth of half an inch."

2. Geronimo had no daughter named Anna. His daughter Lenna, born in 1886 at Fort Marion, Florida, was the child of Geronimo's Mescalero wife, Ih-tedda, who had taken the child with her to Mescalero shortly after the Chiricahuas were transferred to Mount Vernon Barracks, Alabama. Most likely the account of Geronimo's daughter having murdered a lover at Fort Sill is false.

3. On 1 July 1942, the *New York Times* published an article datelined Fort Bragg, North Carolina, that summarized the account of the origin of this parachutists' usage.

4. The lore of the Southwest is replete with figures whose careers have been made to conform in expressive culture to the Robin Hood principle—for example, the gunman Billy the Kid, more or less a contemporary of Geronimo. Songwriter Woody Guthrie applied the formula to the Depression-era outlaw Charles "Pretty Boy" Floyd." For another example from the Chiricahua Apaches, see the career of the Apache Kid as recounted in the novel *Niño* (Fisher 1961).

5. In the early 1930s Morris Edward Opler recorded a detailed version of the Chiricahua culture hero myth from storytellers in New Mexico (1942, 2–11).

6. Sherman Alexie (2006) has written about the real harm caused by false accounts such as those of Barrus because they may tend to raise doubts about legitimate histories of abuse and oppression.

7. House Resolution 132 easily passed after comments from a number of legislators, who used the occasion to voice their support for Native American concerns.

Chapter 2

1. Sharon S. Magee (2002) organizes her recently published popular biography of Geronimo according to "stories," a technique that creates a readable text. She does not, however, consider the narrative vignettes in terms of their status as stories, and she ignores, for example, the sources for her material and the existence of multiple versions of the same incident. These issues lie beyond the focus of her work.

2. All these stories appeared in the *Las Vegas (NM) Daily Optic*, whose pages during the early summer of 1885 were filled with reports, usually based on rumor, about the Indians who had left the reservation. In fact, the front page of the *Optic*'s 28 May issue devotes five of its thirteen articles to the Indians. The *Optic* reprinted materials from many southern New Mexico newspapers.

3. Grenville Goodwin recorded information from John Rope in 1932 near Bylas, Arizona. Rope was probably born in 1855. He seems to have used the account of the Stevens Ranch massacre as a way of distancing himself and his people from the Chiricahuas led by Geronimo and as a way of indicting Geronimo for his lack of appropriate behavior, especially his improper questioning and undue subornation of violence.

4. Marc Simmons (1997) has thoroughly treated the details of the massacre of the McComas family.

CHAPTER 3

1. That imagery has been extensively studied in works by Pearce (1988), Berkhofer (1978), Stedman (1982), and many others. Its roots probably lie in such worldview fundamentals as the concept of the "other" (Kearney 1984), and it can clearly be traced through philosophers such as Vico, literary artists such as Shakespeare, and many other European thinkers to classical antiquity.

2. The first few sham battles may have involved representatives of the Indian Congress in feigned combat with members of the Improved Order of Red Men, a fraternal organization of Euro-Americans. Mercer led the Indian contingent, while "Rattlesnake Pete" (William Liddiard) captained the latter group. See, for example, the *Omaha World-Herald* for 10 August 1898, which includes a brief article and an advertisement trumpeting, "REALISTIC SHAM BATTLE / Clash of Arms by Members of the Red Men's Order / and Capt. Mercer's Indian Warriors." Some authorities suggest that the Red Men did not actually participate even in the early sham battles, forcing Mercer to enlist the involvement of Indians from the Wild West show that was operating just outside the fairgrounds (Miller 2008, 47). Presumably as soon as the full contingent of Native Americans had arrived for the Indian Congress, the services of the Improved Order of Red Men were no longer needed.

3. This description of Geronimo as a traveler parallels William Robertson Smith's orientalist description of the Arab traveler: "The Arabian traveller is quite different from ourselves. The labour of moving from place to place is a mere nuisance to him, he has no enjoyment in effort, and grumbles at hunger or fatigue with all his might" (Said 1978, 237; I have deleted Said's interpolations).

4. Stevens, who had held a grudge against Geronimo since an incident in which the Chiricahua war leader killed a favorite horse more than a dozen years earlier, had accompanied a delegation of Apaches from the San Carlos Reservation to the Omaha fair. He claims to have served as translator during the meeting with Miles and also accompanied Geronimo on some of his off-grounds field trips in Omaha. Other depictions of this meeting between Geronimo and Miles (e.g., Ball 1980, 174–75; Debo 1976, 405–6) can be ultimately traced to the account that Stevens provided John P. Clum, whose memoir, published and reworked somewhat by his son in 1936, characterized Geronimo as "America's most audacious and persistent murderer" (Clum [1936] 1978, 280). The elder Clum claimed to have been the only person who had actually "captured" Geronimo, an incident that occurred in 1877 when he transferred Chiricahuas who were living at Ojo Caliente, New Mexico Territory, to the San Carlos Reservation. He believed that if he had hanged Geronimo at that time, ten years of bloodshed in the Southwest and Mexico would have been averted (Clum 1926; Clum [1936] 1978: 220–22). As John Clum put it, his was "the first and only *bona fide capture* of GERONIMO THE RENEGADE," whose shackles—put on him at Clum's direction—"never should have been

removed except to allow him to walk untrammeled to the scaffold" (1926, 34). The national press did not report the private meeting between Geronimo and Miles at all. For the horse-killing incident that inspired interpreter Stevens's enmity, see chapter 2.

5. Miles may have been present at the sham battle attended by McKinley. The *Arkansas Gazette* for 13 October 1898 reports that he "saw face to face his old New Mexico enemy Geronimo" then. The effusive public meeting between the two men and the private conference that followed, though, probably occurred the next day—as the *Omaha Daily Bee* indicated—when the president was not in attendance.

6. For accounts of these "adoptions," see the *Indiana (PA) Weekly Messenger* for 9 October 1901; the *Piqua (OH) Daily Call* for 18 July and 20 July 1901; and the *Portsmouth (OH) Times* for 27 July 1901.

7. In 1909 M. Salzman Jr., drawing largely from the reminiscences of General Adna R. Chaffee and of Antonio Apache, published a lengthy article about Geronimo that was subtitled "The Napoleon of Indians." Though he did not really develop a comparison between the Apache and French warriors, Salzman cited such apparently Napoleonic features of Geronimo's character as his "great military genius" (1967, 216). He sums up his subject in a quotation from an interview with Antonio Apache: "Geronimo was a crafty general, a forceful leader, though rather vain of his powers. A great talker, he had a leaning toward soothsaying, and was a representative man among our people, assuming the leadership of his clan whenever any matters arose that affected their welfare" (219). The *Journal of Arizona History* reprinted Salzman's difficult-to-find article in 1967.

8. Another character in Howe's novel—this one a Choctaw—thinks when he hears of the white woman's purchase: "The government likes to trot out Geronimo every goddamn chance they get. He's a living war trophy for the U.S. Cavalry at Fort Sill" (2007, 115).

9. Parezo and Fowler provide a roster of the Indians who attended the Louisiana Purchase Exposition, and many in the list correspond to the list of contributors that Curtis appends to *The Indians' Book* (1923, 561). However, it does not include the Apache sources besides Geronimo from whom she collected material, Fleming Lavender and Rivers Lavender. On one hand, that may simply be a lacuna in the records or the result of an inconsistency in naming Apache attendees at the exposition. On the other, it may suggest that she encountered Geronimo and the Lavenders at Fort Sill. The latter view finds support in the absence of some of her Kiowa contributors, whom she could have recorded at Fort Sill, from the exposition roster. Yet while we do know that Curtis attended the Saint Louis event, nothing of her presence at Fort Sill has turned up. Moreover, if she had done fieldwork at Fort Sill, she would undoubtedly have included Comanches among her contributors, and no Comanche material appears in *The Indians' Book*.

I am opting for her having recorded material from Geronimo at the Louisiana Purchase Exposition, and that hypothesis has been confirmed by a notation in the diary kept by Curtis's brother George, who attended the exposition with her and joined her in traveling to several American Indian communities afterward (Patterson 2010, 341n56).

10. The artist E. A. Burbank, who had visited Geronimo at Fort Sill in 1897, reported that during breaks while Geronimo was sitting for his portrait he would sing Apache songs. Burbank presents the text of one of these songs (1944, 27), which replicates verbatim that which Curtis published in *The Indians' Book*. Though Burbank had come into contact with Geronimo seven years earlier than Curtis, his memoirs did not appear in print until 1944, and one suspects that he may have reproduced Geronimo's song from Curtis's work rather than his own memory.

11. Consider also Geronimo's dealings with photographer De Lancey Gill. Never having paid an Indian for the opportunity to photograph him, Gill may have been taken aback when Geronimo charged him a fee, based on a scale that Geronimo himself had created: "A portrait made with a hand-held camera cost ten cents; if a tripod was used, the price rose to twenty-five cents; and for a studio portrait, 'the sky was the limit.'" Geronimo charged Gill two dollars and then asked for another twenty-five cents, which Gill had to borrow. The photographer may have enjoyed some satisfaction when he took two images of Geronimo rather than only the one they had contracted for (Fleming and Luskey 1986, 180).

12. Geronimo's participation in Roosevelt's inauguration is one of the case studies of American Indian visits to the seat of the federal government in Turner's *Red Men Calling on the Great White Father* (1951, 182–93). The photograph that Turner uses, the less famous of the two taken by Frank Randall in 1884, is captioned "Geronimo—'an unlovely character, a cross-grained, sour, mean, selfish old curmudgeon'" (plate), a quotation attributed to Hugh Scott, who had been commander of Fort Sill during part of Geronimo's tenure there.

13. See chapter 5 for a discussion of this and other visual images of Geronimo.

CHAPTER 4

1. Opler's ethnographic research in the early 1930s confirms that Geronimo's experience adheres to a traditional model ([1941] 1996, 204).

2. It is not clear if this healing occurred during the days of relative freedom in Mexico and Arizona or after the Chiricahua imprisonment at Fort Sill. If the former, Opler's consultant would have had to be at least in his sixties when he was interviewed.

3. I am not aware of any other sources for this occurrence, which does not correspond to other reports about Geronimo's religious situation during his last few years. Moreover, Braun was inaccurate regarding other incidents in Geronimo's life, asserting, for example, that Geronimo had come to hate Anglos when a party of

white hunters had fired a cannon into an Apache encampment and killed his sister (Emerson 1973, 28).

Chapter 5

1. Though the Mohawk Jay Silverheels played Geronimo in *Broken Arrow* (1950), some Euro-American actors, including Monte Blue (possibly part Cherokee), Ian MacDonald, and Chuck Connors, did assume the role of the Chiricahua war leader in films.
2. This and other photographs of the Chiricahuas have sometimes been attributed to the Gallup-based photographer Ben Wittick, who did encounter Randall's images shortly after he had taken them. Wittick seems to have made copies of at least some of them and subsequently issued them under his own name.
3. Behrens has another Geronimo painting, *The Three Faces of Geronimo*, that incorporates images from photographs by Edward S. Curtis and other photographers who captured the Chiricahua war leader in his old age.
4. The publication of some of Fly's photographs in *Harper's Weekly* provided the opportunity for some newspapers to mock Crook's campaign against the Apaches. On 9 May 1886 the *New York Times* quoted from a piece that appeared in the *St. Louis Globe Democrat*: "If an Eastern illustrated weekly paper affords any criterion for forming a judgment, the principal business transacted at the recent meeting of Gen. Crook and Geronimo was having their pictures taken. No doubt it is highly desirable to have photographs of the Apaches, but if such mementoes are really necessary, it would be cheaper to hire them to sit than to send a force of troops to chase them all over the country." Van Orden's presentation with commentary on the Fly photographs appeared in the *Journal of Arizona History* 30 (1989): 319–46, and was reissued two years later as a monograph (1991) by the Arizona History Society.
5. O. B. Jacobson, who became head of the art department at the University of Oklahoma, reported that Burbank believed that Geronimo grew more mellow and assimilated with the passage of time, an impression with which Jacobson, who visited the warrior at Fort Sill a couple of times, concurred (Jacobson and d'Ucel 1954, 276–77).
6. Probably inspired by the photograph, a short-lived bluegrass band from the 1980s called itself Geronimo at the Wheel. A notice of an "East Hampton Hoedown," which appeared in the *New York Times* in 1984, announced that the group would be performing at the Woodhouse Gallery in East Hampton, Long Island. I am grateful to Emily Olson for this reference. Some disagreement about the circumstances of the photograph has colored the literature on Geronimo. Fred Gipson, for example, places Lute Stover behind the lens in his history of the Miller Brothers' Wild West Show. Most authorities, though, do assign photo credit to Walter Ferguson (e.g., Lippard 1992, 54; Deloria 2004, 137). The reproduction of the famous photograph in Paul Chaat Smith's book *Everything You Know*

about Indians Is Wrong comes from the National Archives and is inscribed "To Hon. C. J. Rhoads with the compliments of J. Walter Ferguson" (2009, 21).

7. Deloria includes a mini-portfolio, including the image of the Wildshoe family, of photographs of American Indians in automobiles in his chapter "Technology: 'I Want to Ride in Geronimo's Cadillac'" (2004, 172–75).

Chapter 6

1. Instrumental music in several genres has also evoked the image of Geronimo. Examples include guitar rock ("Geronimo" by Hank Marvin and the Shadows [1963] and "Geronimo" by Tony Levin [2002]), postbop jazz ("Geronimo's Song" by Glenn Spearman's G-Force [1997] and "Geronimo's Free" by Ted Sirota's Rebel Souls [1999]), New Age music ("Geronimo's Surrender" by pianist Peter Kater and flutist N. Carlos Nakai [1993]), and bluegrass ("Geronimo Stomp" by Appalachian Grass [2003]).

2. Streeter was a figure of some mystery in the Southwest during the 1870s and 1880s. He is supposed to have married Geronimo's daughter, a circumstance that brought considerable embarrassment to the father. Robinson reports that he "stood alone as the only white man on record to conduct raids with his adopted Apache" (1999). See also Thrapp 1967, 279, and Robinson 2000, 45–48. Streeter's story was also making the rounds of the national press in the early 1880s. See, for example, the *Davenport (IA) Daily Gazette* for 30 May 1883. That Burroughs, who spent time in the military in Arizona Territory in the 1890s, had heard of Streeter is possible.

3. French author Georges Fronval, referred to in the 5 August 1972 issue of *The Stars and Stripes* as "one of the most prolific proponents of the Golden West," devoted one of his books to *Geronimo, l'Apache indomptable*. Other titles in the body of work by this "Writer of the Purple Seine" treat Sitting Bull, Buffalo Bill, and Kit Carson.

Chapter 7

1. The advertisement released by Paramount showed a pair of sinister eyes peering out from above the film title. Chief Thundercloud is not listed among the film's performers on the poster. See, for example, the *Chilicothe (MO) Constitution-Tribune* for 2 March 1940.

Works Cited

Books, Articles, Websites

1491s. 2011. "Geronimo E-KIA: A Poem." 1 June. www.youtube.com/watch?v=y7vKu7X4aNA, accessed 17 February 2012.

Adams, Alexander B. 1971. *Geronimo: A Biography*. New York: Putnam.

Albertarelli, Rino. 1974. *Geronimo: Apache vuol dire nemico*. Milano, Italy: Sergio Bonelli Editore.

Alexie, Sherman. 1998. *Smoke Signals: A Screenplay*. New York: Hyperion.

———. 2006. "When the Story Stolen Is Your Own." *Time*, 29 January. www.time.com/time;printout/0,8816,1154221,00.html, accessed 9 June 2011.

Alfers, Kenneth G. 1972. "Triumph of the West: The Trans-Mississippi Exposition." *Nebraska History* 53: 313–29.

"An Apache Chief Chooses a New Name." 2009. *Regeneration Reservation*. www.regenerationreservation.org/rgnaiche.htm, accessed 22 April 2009.

"The Apache Outbreak." 1885. *The Nation*, 2 July, 8–9.

Arnold, Elliott. (1947) 1979. *Blood Brother*. Reprint, Lincoln: University of Nebraska Press.

Ball, Eve. 1970. *In the Days of Victorio: Recollections of a Warm Springs Apache*. Tucson: University of Arizona Press.

———, with Nora Henn and Lynda Sanchez. 1980. *Indeh: An Apache Odyssey*. Provo, UT: Brigham Young University Press.

Banks, Leo W. 2009. "Longtime Prisoner Geronimo Said He Found Christianity." *Wild West*, April, 22–23.

"Baptism of Indian Warrior Geronimo." 2009. *Glimpses of Christian History*. www.christianhistorytimeline.com/DAILY/2002.07/daily-07–01–2002.shtml, accessed 22 April 2009.

Barrett, S. M., ed. 1996. *Geronimo: His Own Story*. Revised and edited by Frederick Turner. New York: Penguin.

Barthes, Roland. 1972. *Mythologies*. New York: Hill and Wang.

Basso, Keith, ed. 1971. *Western Apache Raiding and Warfare from the Notes of Grenville Goodwin*. Tucson: University of Arizona Press.

Beach, Christopher. 1991. "Migrating Voices in the Poetry of Edward Dorn." *Contemporary Literature* 32 (2): 211–28.

Bensen, D. R. 1978. *Mr. Horn*. New York: Dell.

Berkhofer, Robert F., Jr. 1978. *The White Man's Indian: Images of the American Indian from Columbus to the Present*. New York: Vintage.

Betzinez, Jason, with Wilbur Sturtevant Nye. (1959) 1987. *I Fought with Geronimo*. Reprint, Lincoln: University of Nebraska Press.

Bewley, Michele Ryan. 2003. "The New World in Unity: Pan-America Visualized at Buffalo in 1901." *New York History* 84: 179–203.

Bigelow, John. 1958. *On the Bloody Trail of Geronimo*. Los Angeles: Westernlore Press.

Blackman, Margaret B. 1980. "Posing the American Indian." *Natural History* 89 (10): 69–74.

Bolz, Peter. 1994. "More Questions than Answers: Frank A. Rinehart's Photographs of American Indians." *European Review of Native American Studies* 8: 35–42.

Bourke, John Gregory. (1886) 1958. *An Apache Campaign in the Sierra Madre: An Account of the Expedition in Pursuit of the Hostile Chiricahua Apaches in the Spring of 1883*. Reprint, New York: Scribner's.

———. 1891. *On the Border with Crook*. New York: Scribner's.

Boyer, Ruth McDonald, and Narcissus Duffy Gayton. 1992. *Apache Mothers and Daughters: Four Generations of a Family*. Norman: University of Oklahoma Press.

Bradford, Phillips Verner, and Harvey Blume. 1992. *Ota: The Pygmy in the Zoo*. New York: St. Martin's.

Breitbart, Eric. 1997. *A World on Display: Photographs from the St. Louis World's Fair, 1904*. Albuquerque: University of New Mexico Press.

Browne, Charles Francis. 1898. "Elbridge Ayer Burbank: A Painter of Indian Portraits." *Brush and Pencil* 3 (1): 16–35.

Bruchac, Joseph. 2006. *Geronimo: A Novel*. New York: Scholastic.

Brumbaugh, Lee Philip. 1999. "Shadow Catchers or Shadow Snatchers? Ethical Issues for Photographers of Contemporary Native Americans." In *Contemporary Native American Cultural Issues*, edited by Duane Champagne, 217–24. Walnut Creek, CA: AltaMira Press.

Bunscombe, Edward. 2006. *"Injuns!": Native Americans in the Movies*. London: Reaktion Books.

Burbank, E. A., with Ernest Royce. 1944. *Burbank Among the Indians*. Edited by Frank J. Taylor. Caldwell, ID: Caxton.

Burleson, Frank. 1997. *Night of the Cougar*. New York: Signet.

Burroughs, Edgar Rice. (1927) 2009. *The War Chief*. Reprint, Victorville, CA: ERBville Press.

———. (1928) 2009. *Apache Devil*. Reprint, Victorville, CA: ERBville Press.

Burrows, Jack. 2001. "Geronimo's Last Hurrah in Arizona Territory." *Wild West*, August. web.ebscohost.com, accessed 4 December 2007.

Caesar, Gene. 1963. *Rifle for Rent: The True Story of One of the Most Colorful Figures of the Untamed Southwest*. Derby, CT: Monarch Books.

Cantley, Janet. 2012. "Out of Geronimo's Shadow: The Apache Experience." *Native Peoples* 25 (1): 54–58.

Capriccioso, Rob. 2011. "He Ain't No Geronimo." *This Week from Indian Country Today*, 25 May, 20–23.

Carter, Forrest. 1983. *Watch for Me on the Mountain*. New York: Dell.

Casey, John, Jackie Proven, and David Dripps. 2006. "Geronimo's Cadillac: Lessons for Learning Object Repositories." Paper delivered at ECDL Conference, Alicante, Spain, 22 September. www.csfic.ecs.soton.ac.uk/Casey.doc, accessed 9 July 2010.

Chaffin, Carl, ed. 1997. *The Private Journal of George Whitwell Parsons: The Tombstone Years 1879–1887*. Vol. 2, *Post-Earp Era, June 28, 1882–March 31, 1887*. Tombstone, AZ: Cochise Classics.

Chandler, Jon. 2002. *Wyoming Wind: A Novel of Tom Horn*. New York: Leisure Books.

Charlier, Jean-Michel, and Jean Giraud. 1999. *Geronimo l'Apache*. Paris: Dargaud.

Clark, Howard D. 1946. *Lost Mines of the Old West*. Buena Park, CA: Ghost Town Press.

Clements, William M. 1982. "'I Once Was Lost': The Oral Narratives of Born-Again Christians." *International Folklore Review* 2: 105–11.

Clifford, James. 1997. *Routes: Travel and Translation in the Late Twentieth Century*. Cambridge, MA: Harvard University Press.

Clough, Josh. 2005. "'Vanishing' Indians: Cultural Persistence on Display at the Omaha World's Fair of 1898." *Great Plains Quarterly* 25: 67–86.

Clum, John P. 1926. "Geronimo." *New Mexico Historical Review* 3 (1): 1–40.

———. 1931. "Apaches as Thespians in 1876." *New Mexico Historical Review* 6 (1): 76–99.

Clum, Woodworth. (1936) 1978. *Apache Agent: The Story of John P. Clum*. Reprint, Lincoln: University of Nebraska Press.

Cohen, Sol, ed. 1950. *Geronimo, Indian Fighter, No. 1: The Massacre at San Pedro Pass*. New York: Avon Periodicals.

———. 1951a. *Chief Geronimo on the Warpath, No. 2: The Murderous Battle of Kiskayah!* New York: Avon Periodicals.

———. 1951b. *Geronimo and His Apache Murderers, No. 3*. New York: Avon Periodicals.

———. 1952. *The Savage Raids of Geronimo, No. 4*. New York: Avon Periodicals.

Collings, Ellsworth, and Alma Miller England. (1937) 1971. *The 101 Ranch*. Reprint, Norman: University of Oklahoma Press.

Cook-Lynn, Elizabeth. 2011. "The Lewis and Clark Story, the Captive Narrative, and the Pitfalls of Indian History." In *Native Historians Write Back: Decolonizing American*

Indian History, edited by Susan A. Miller and James Riding In, 41–51. Lubbock: Texas Tech University Press.

Crawford, [Edith] L. 1936–1940. "I was born in Austin, Texas." *American Life Histories: Manuscripts from the Federal Writers' Project*. memory.loc.gov, accessed 19 December 2008.

Cruse, Thomas. 1941. *Apache Days and After*. Edited by Eugene Cunningham. Caldwell, ID: Caxton.

Cummings, G. D. 1890. *The History of Geronimo's Summer Campaign in 1885: A Drama*. Unknown publisher.

Cuomo, George. 1973. *Geronimo and the Girl Next Door*. Shawnee Mission, KS: BkMk Press.

Current, Karen, and William R. Current. 1978. *Photography and the Old West*. Fort Worth, TX: Amon Carter Museum of Western Art.

Curtis, Natalie. 1903. "An American-Indian Composer." *Harper's* 107: 626–32.

———. 1904. "Indian Music at Hampton Anniversary." *Southern Workman* 33: 327–28.

———. 1923. *The Indians' Book: An Offering by the American Indians of Indian Lore, Musical and Narrative, to Form a Record of the Songs and Legends of Their Race*. 2nd ed. New York: Harper and Brothers.

Daly, Henry W. 1926a. Letter to Major Gatewood. 5 February. Gatewood Collection, Arizona Historical Society, Tucson.

———. 1926b. "The Powder-Stained 70's." *American Legion Monthly*, October, 18–21, 80–85.

———. 1930. "The Capture of Geronimo." *American Legion Monthly*, June, 30, 42–45.

David C. Behrens Studio. 2010. www.davidbehrens.com, accessed 17 November 2010.

Davis, Britton. 1929. *The Truth about Geronimo*. New Haven, CT: Yale University Press.

Davis, Jerry A. 1999. "Apache Prisoners of War at Alabama's Mount Vernon Barracks, 1887–1894." *Alabama Review* 52: 243–66.

Davis-Baltz, Sandy. 2005. "The Making of a Monument: Social Implications of Arkansas Case Studies." PhD diss., Arkansas State University.

Dawson, Clay. 1989. *Apache Dawn*. New York: Charter Books.

Debo, Angie. 1976. *Geronimo: The Man, His Time, His Place*. Norman: University of Oklahoma Press.

Dedera, Don. 1971. "Is Geronimo Alive and Well in the South Vietnamese Highlands? A Comparative Study in Guerrilla Tactics." *Mankind: The Magazine of Popular History* 3 (2): 24–37.

Deloria, Philip J. 2004. *Indians in Unexpected Places*. Lawrence: University Press of Kansas.

Deming, Therese O. 1938. *Cosel with Geronimo on His Last Raid: The Story of an Indian Boy*. Philadelphia, PA: F. A. Davis.

Dippie, Brian W. 1982. *The Vanishing American: White Attitudes and U. S. Indian Policy*. Middleton, CT: Wesleyan University Press.

———. 1992. "Representing the Other: The North American Indian." In *Anthropology and Photography, 1860–1920*, edited by Elizabeth Edwards, 132–34. New Haven, CT: Yale University Press.

Dobie, J. Frank. 1930. *Coronado's Children: Tales of Lost Mines and Buried Treasures of the Southwest*. Dallas, TX: Southwest Press.

———. (1939) 1976. *Apache Gold and Yaqui Silver*. Reprint, Albuquerque: University of New Mexico Press.

Dorn, Edward. 1974. *Recollections of Gran Apachería*. San Francisco: Turtle Island.

Dorris, Michael. 1994. "In the Eyes of the Beheld." *Natural History* 103 (11): 24.

Draper, William R. 1901. "Geronimo, Famous Chief, as a Prisoner." *Atlanta Constitution*, 21 April, A5.

Dresman, Paul. 1985. "Internal Resistances: Edward Dorn on the American Indian." In *Internal Resistances: The Poetry of Edward Dorn*, edited by Donald Wesling, 87–112. Berkeley: University of California Press.

Dugan, Bill. 1991. *Geronimo (War Chiefs)*. New York: HarperCollins.

Duncan, Randy, and Matthew J. Smith. 2009. *The Power of Comics: History, Form, and Culture*. New York: Continuum.

Durham, Jimmie. 1992. "Geronimo!" In *Partial Recall*, edited by Lucy R. Lippard, 55–58. New York: New Press.

———. 1998. "Geronimo Loved Children." In *Through Indian Eyes: The Native Experience in Books for Children*, edited by Beverly Slapin and Doris Seale, 52. Los Angeles: American Indian Studies Center, University of California.

Duthu, N. Bruce. 2008. *American Indians and the Law*. New York: Penguin.

Eisenstein, Sergei. 1949. *Film Form: Essays in Film Theory*. Edited and translated by Jay Leyda. Cleveland: World Publishing.

Ellis, Edward S. (1889) 1901. *On the Trail of Geronimo, or In the Apache Country*. Reprint, New York: Steet and Smith.

———. 1897. "A Campaign of Strategy." *Argosy* 24 (4): 577–602.

———. 1908a. *Off the Reservation, or Caught in An Apache Raid*. Chicago: John C. Winston.

———. 1908b. *The Round-Up, or Geronimo's Last Raid*. Chicago: John C. Winston.

———. 1908c. *Trailing Geronimo, or Campaigning with Crook*. Chicago: John C. Winston.

Emerson, Dorothy. 1973. *Among the Mescalero Apaches: The Story of Father Albert Braun, O. F. M.* Tucson: University of Arizona Press.

Evans, Robert K. 1886. "The Indian Question in Arizona." *Atlantic Monthly*, August, 167–76.

Farrer, Claire R. 2011. *Thunder Rides a Black Horse: Mescalero Apaches and the Mythic Present*. 3rd ed. Long Grove, IL: Waveland.

Faulk, Odie B. 1969. *The Geronimo Campaign*. New York: Oxford University Press.

Fenady, Andrew J. 1984. *Claws of the Eagle: A Novel of Tom Horn and the Apache Kid*. New York: Walker.

Fenimore Art Museum. 2004. "Geronimo: An American Indian Legend." www.tfaoi.com/aa/4aa/4aa494b.htm, accessed 26 February 2008.

Fisher, Clay. 1961. *Niño*. New York: William Morrow.

Fleming, Paula Richardson, and Judith Luskey. 1986. *The North American Indians in Early Photographs*. London: Phaidon.

———. 1993. *Grand Endeavors of American Indian Photography*. Washington, D.C.: Smithsonian Institution Press.

Fly, C. S. 1905. *Scenes in Geronimo's Camp: The Apache Outlaw and Murderer . . .* Tombstone, AZ: Privately published.

Folsom, Cora M. 1889. "Indian Department." *Southern Workman*, November, 115.

Foster, Thomas. 1997. "'Kick[ing] the Perpendiculars Outa Right Anglos': Edward Dorn's Multiculturalism." *Contemporary Literature* 38 (1): 78–105.

Francis, David R. 1913. *The Universal Exposition of 1904*. Saint Louis, MO: Louisiana Purchase Exposition Company.

Francis, Margot. 2002. "Reading the Autoethnographic Perspectives of Indians 'Shooting Indians.'" *Topia: A Canadian Journal of Cultural Studies* 7 (Spring): 5–26.

Fraser, George MacDonald. 1982. *Flashman and the Redskins*. New York: Penguin.

Gardner, Mark L. 2006. *Geronimo: A Biography*. Tucson, AZ: Western National Parks Association.

Gatewood, Charles B. 2005. *Lt. Charles Gatewood and His Apaches Wars Memoir*. Edited by Louis Kraft. Lincoln: University of Nebraska Press.

"Geronimo." 1962. *Monthly Film Bulletin* 29: 80–81.

"Geronimo." 2007. *Ab Initio ad Infinitum*. abinitioadinfinitum.wordpress.com/2007/09/04/geronimo, accessed 22 April 2009.

Gidley, Mick. 1998. *Edward S. Curtis and the North American Indian, Incorporated*. Cambridge: Cambridge University Press.

Gipson, Fred. 1946. *Fabulous Empire: Colonel Zack Miller's Story*. Boston: Houghton Mifflin.

"Glimpses of Indian Life at the Omaha Exposition." 1898. *American Monthly Review of Reviews* 18: 436–43.

Gøksyr, Matti. 1970. "'One Certainly Expected a Great Deal More from the Savages': The Anthropology Days in St. Louis, 1904, and Their Aftermath." *International Journal of the History of Sport* 7: 297–306.

Goodwin, Grenville. ca. 1930s. "Sherman Curley, Western Apache Scout." Grenville Goodwin Collection, Arizona State Museum, Tucson.

Granger, Byrd Howell. 1977. *A Motif Index for Lost Mines and Treasures Applied to Redaction of Arizona Legends, and to Lost Mine and Treasure Legends Exterior to Arizona*. Folklore Fellows Communications 218. Helsinki, Finland: Academia Scientiarum Fennica.

"Great American Rebels." 2002. *New Internationalist*, November, 24–25.

Greene, Jerome A., ed. 2007. *Indian War Veterans: Memories of Life and Campaigns in the West, 1864–1898*. New York: Savas Beatie.

Griffin, Eric, and Chaz Truog. 2005. *Geronimo: The Last Apache Warrior*. Edited by Joe Gentile and Garrett Anderson. Calumet City, IL: Moonstone.

Gross, Larry. 1994. "The Screenwriter and Geronimo: A Film Diary." *Sight and Sound* n.s. 4 (10): 22–25.

Halsell, Grace. 1998. "Cowboy Harry Halsell Once Dug His Spurs into Pythias and Bluffed His Way Past Geronimo." *Wild West*, August. web.ebscohost.com, accessed 5 December 2005.

Harriman, Mary Alice. 1899. "The Congress of American Aborigines at the Omaha Exposition." *Overland Monthly* 33: 505–12.

Harrison, Joanne. 1993. "Geronimo Reconsidered: TNT Movie Replaces Myth with Real Person." *Los Angeles Times*, 5 December. articles.latimes.com, accessed 12 July 2011.

Hatfield, Shelley Bowen. 1998. *Chasing Shadows: Apaches and Yaquis along the United States–Mexico Border, 1876–1911*. Albuquerque: University of New Mexico Press.

Hays, Robert. 1997. *Editorializing "the Indian Problem": The New York Times on Native Americans, 1860–1900*. Carbondale: Southern Illinois University Press.

Henry, Will. 1972. *Chiricahua*. Philadelphia, PA: Lippincott.

———. 1975. *I, Tom Horn*. Philadelphia, PA: Lippincott.

Hobsbawn, Eric. 1959. *Primitive Rebels: Studies in Archaic Forms of Social Movement in the 19th and 20th Centuries*. New York: Norton.

———. 1969. *Bandits*. New York: Delacorte.

Hobson, Geary. 2004. "The Folks Left Out." In *Beyond the Reach of Time and Change: Native American Reflections on the Frank A. Rinehart Photograph Collection*, edited by Simon Ortiz, 109–14. Tucson: University of Arizona Press.

Hodgart, M. J. C. 1962. *The Ballads*. New York: Norton.

Holden, Walter. 2001. "Geronimo's Last Captive, Trini Verdin, Has Been Draped in Discrepancies and Wrapped in Contradictions." *Wild West*, August. web.ebscohost.com, accessed 4 December 2007.

Holler, Clyde. 1995. *Black Elk's Religion: The Sun Dance and Lakota Catholicism*. Syracuse, NY: Syracuse University Press.

Hooker, Forrestine C. 1924. *When Geronimo Rode*. Garden City, NY: Doubleday, Page.

Hopkins, Ruth. 2011. "Geronimo and the Myth of the Bloodthirsty Savage." *This Week from Indian Country Today*, 25 May, 6.

———. 2012. "Where Are *Time* Magazine's Cojones?" *This Week from Indian Country Today*, 25 January, 5.

Horgan, Paul. (1960) 1991. *A Distant Trumpet*. 30th anniv. ed. Boston: David Godine.

Horn, Tom [?]. 1904. *Life of Tom Horn, Government Scout and Interpreter, Written by Himself Together with His Letters and Statements by His Friends: A Vindication*. Denver: Louthan.

Howard, Ed. 2004. "Paramount's 1939 Western GERONIMO . . . a Forgotten Movie with a Giant Legacy." *The Old Corral*. www.b-westerns.com/geronimo.htm, accessed 10 June 2011.

Howe, LeAnne. 2007. *Miko Kings: An Indian Baseball Story*. San Francisco: Aunt Lute Books.

Huddle, David. 1979. "Bill Spraker's Store, or The Day Geronimo Couldn't Find the Scoop." *Harper's*, June, 34.

Hudson, J. Lee, and Richard A. Wood. 2005. "Geronimo's Revenge." *Journal of the West* 44 (4): 3–7.

Hughes, Thomas. (1857) 1911. *Tom Brown's School-Days*. New York: Harper and Brothers.

Huhndorf, Shari M. 2001. *Going Native: Indians in the American Cultural Imagination.* Ithaca, NY: Cornell University Press.

Hutton, Paul Andrew. 2011. "Was Geronimo a Terrorist?" *True West*, August, 22–31.

Ingram, Hunter. 1975. *Fort Apache*. New York: Ballantine.

Jacobson, O. B., and Jeanne d'Ucel. 1954. "Art in Oklahoma." *Chronicles of Oklahoma* 32: 262–77.

James, William. 2000. *Pragmatism and Other Writings*. Edited by Giles B. Gunn. East Rutherford, NJ: Penguin Putnam.

Jameson, W. C. 1989. *Buried Treasures of the American Southwest: Legends of Lost Mines, Hidden Payrolls, and Spanish Gold*. Little Rock, AR: August House.

Johnson, Tim. 2011. "Time for an Editor in Chief." *This Week from Indian Country Today*, 25 May, 7.

Johnston, Charles H. L. 1909. *Famous Indian Chiefs: Their Battles, Treaties, Sieges, and Struggles with the Whites for the Possession of America*. Boston: L. C. Page.

Jojola, Ted. 2003. "Absurd Reality II: Hollywood Goes to the Indians." In *Hollywood's Indian: The Portrayal of the Native American in Film*, edited by Peter C. Rollins and John E. O'Connor, 12–26. Lexington: University Press of Kentucky.

Kearney, Michael. 1984. *World View*. Novato, CA: Chandler and Sharp.

Kelsey, D. M. 1901. *History of Our Wild West and Stories of Pioneer Life . . . Relating the Exciting Experiences, Daring Deeds and Marvelous Achievements of Men Made Famous by Their Heroic Deeds. Replete with Stories of Exciting Hunts, Indian Fights and Adventures with Wild Animals and Border Bandits*. Chicago: Charles C. Thompson.

Kilgore, Mrs. Belle. 1936–1940. "Buster Degraftenreid." *American Life Histories: Manuscripts from the Federal Writers' Project*. memory.loc.gov, accessed 30 December 2008.

Kilpatrick, Jacquelyn. 1999. *Celluloid Indians: Native Americans and Film*. Lincoln: University of Nebraska Press.

King, Lise Balk. 2011. "Bin Laden Code Name Is a Bomb in Indian Country." *This Week from Indian Country Today*, 25 May, 4.

Kirshenblatt-Gimblett, Barbara. 1998. *Destination Culture: Tourism, Museums, and Heritage*. Berkeley: University of California Press.

Kjelgaard, Jim. 1958. *The Story of Geronimo*. New York: Grosset and Dunlap.

Kooser, Ted. 1985. *Flying at Night: Poems, 1965–1985*. Pittsburgh, PA: University of Pittsburgh Press.

Kopit, Arthur. 1971. *Indians*. New York: Bantam.

Kosmider, Alexia. 2001. "Refracting the Imperial Gaze onto the Colonizers: Geronimo Poses for the Empire." *ATQ* 15 (4): 317–31.

Kraft, Louis. 2000. *Gatewood and Geronimo*. Albuquerque: University of New Mexico Press.

Krupat, Arnold. 1985. *For Those Who Come After: A Study of Native American Autobiography*. Berkeley: University of California Press.

Lalire, Gregory. 2001. "Editorial: Geronimo! Geronimo!" *Wild West* 14 (2): 6–7. web. ebscohost.com, accessed 4 December 2007.

Lane, Jack C., ed. 1970. *Chasing Geronimo: The Journal of Leonard Wood, May–September, 1886*. Albuquerque: University of New Mexico Press.

Langellier, John. 2011. "Geromino, According to Hollywood." *True West*, January/February, 58–63.

Leech, Margaret. 1959. *In the Days of McKinley*. New York: Harper and Brothers.

Lippard, Lucy R., ed. 1992. *Partial Recall*. New York: New Press, 1992.

Lloyd, Charles Edward. 1901. "The American Indian at the Pan-American Fair: Forty-Two Tribes Are Represented in a Great Congress of Red Men." *Republican News* (Hamilton, OH), 9 September, 3.

Loring, Donna. 2011. "Time to Honor Native American Veterans." *This Week from Indian Country Today*, 1 June, 6.

Lummis, Charles F. 1928. *A Bronco Pegasus*. Boston: Houghton Mifflin.

Lyman, Christopher M. 1982. *The Vanishing Race and Other Illusions: Photographs of Indians by Edward S. Curtis*. Washington, D.C.: Smithsonian Institution Press.

Magee, Sharon S. 2002. *Geronimo! Stories of an American Legend*. Phoenix: Arizona Highways Books.

Marien, Mary Warner. 2002. *Photography: A Cultural History*. New York: Henry N. Abrams.

Marsden, Michael T., and Jack Nachbar. 1988. "The Indian in the Movies." In *History of Indian-White Relations*, edited by William C. Sturtevant, 607–16. Vol. 4 of *Handbook of American Indians*. Washington, D.C.: Smithsonian Institution Press.

Mars Laser Official Web Site. 2011. www.marslaser.com, accessed 22 March 2011.

Mazzanovich, Anton. 1931. *Trailing Geronimo: Some Hitherto Unrecorded Incidents Bearing upon the Outbreak of the White Mountain Apaches and Geronimo's Band in Arizona and New Mexico. The Experiences of a Private Soldier in the Ranks; Chief of Pack-Train Service, and Scout of Fort Grant. Also with New Mexico Rangers*. 3rd ed. Hollywood, CA: Privately published by the author.

McCarty, Kieran, O. F. M. 1973. "Trini Verdin and the 'Truth' of History." Introduction by C. L. Sonnichsen. *Journal of Arizona History* 14 (2): 149–64.

McIntosh, Kenneth. 1988. "Geronimo's Friend: Angie Debo and the New History." *Chronicles of Oklahoma* 66 (2): 164–77.

Meyer, Richard. 1980. "The Outlaw: A Distinctive American Folktype." *Journal of the Folklore Institute* 17 (2–3): 94–124.

Miles, Nelson A. 1896. *Personal Recollections and Observations of General Nelson A. Miles, Embracing a Brief View of the Civil War, or From New England to the Golden Gate and the Story of His Indian Campaigns . . .* New York: Werner.

Miller, Bonnie M. 2008. "The Incoherencies of Empire: The 'Imperial' Image of the Indian at the Omaha World's Fairs in 1898–99." *American Studies* 49: 39–62.

Mitchell, Lee Clark. 1994. "The Photograph and the American Indians." In *The Photograph and the American Indian*, edited by Alfred L. Bush and Lee Clark Mitchell, xi–xxvi. Princeton, NJ: Princeton University Press.

Money, Mary Alice. 1997. "Broken Arrows: Images of Native Americans in the Popular Western." In *American Indian Studies: An Interdisciplinary Approach to Contemporary Issues*, edited by Dane Morrison, 363–84. New York: Peter Lang.

Moody, Ralph. (1958) 2006. *Geronimo: Wolf of the Warpath*. New York: Sterling.

Mooney, James. 1899. "The Indian Congress at Omaha." *American Anthropologist* n.s. 1: 126–49.

Moore, David L. 1999. "Silko's Blood Sacrifice: The Circulating Witness in *Almanac of the Dead*." In *Leslie Marmon Silko: A Collection of Critical Essays*, edited by Louise K. Barnett and Robert Franklin Gish, 149–83. Albuquerque: University of New Mexico Press.

Moore, Sarah J. 2000. "Mapping Empire in Omaha and Buffalo: World's Fairs and the Spanish-American War." *Bilingual Review* 25: 111–26.

Morsberger, Robert E. 1973. "Edgar Rice Burroughs' Apache Epic." *Journal of Popular Culture* 7 (2): 280–87.

Moses, L. G. 1984. *Indian Man: A Biography of James Mooney*. Urbana: University of Illinois Press.

——. 1991. "Indians on the Midway: Wild West Shows and the Indian Bureau at World's Fairs, 1893–1904." *South Dakota History* 21: 205–29.

——. 1996. *Wild West Shows and the Images of American Indians, 1883–1933*. Albuquerque: University of New Mexico Press.

——. 2004. "Geronimo: The 'Last Renegade.'" In *Chiefs and Generals: Nine Men Who Shaped the American West*, edited by Richard W. Etulain and Glenda Riley, 85–104. Golden, CO: Fulcrum.

Mullane, William H. 1968. *Apache Raids: News about Indian Activity in the Southwest as Reported in the* Silver City Enterprise *November 1882 through August 1886*. Unknown publisher.

Muthyala, John. 2006. *Reworlding America: Myth, History, and Narrative*. Athens: Ohio University Press.

N. K. 1940. "Geronimo." *Monthly Film Bulletin* 7: 39.

Nasdijj. 2004. *Geronimo's Bones: A Memoir of My Brother and Me*. New York: Ballantine.

Newcomb, Steven. 2006. "The Order of Skull and Bones and Geronimo." *Indian Country Today*, 7 June, A3.

——. 2011a. "Geronimo: Indian Wars Continue Ad Nauseum." *This Week from Indian Country Today*, 25 May, 5.

——. 2011b. "'Geronimo Was the Code Name for bin Laden.'" *This Week from Indian Country Today*, 1 June, 7.

Nez, Carole. 2004. "Unless You Were There." In *Beyond the Reach of Time and Change: Native American Reflections on the Frank A. Rinehart Photograph Collection*, edited by Simon Ortiz, 124–27. Tucson: University of Arizona Press.

Nolley, Ken. 2003. "The Representation of Conquest: John Ford and the Hollywood Indian (1939–1964)." In *Hollywood's Indian: The Portrayal of the Native American in Film*, edited by Peter C. Rollins and John E. O'Connor, 73–90. Lexington: University Press of Kentucky.

Notman, Otis. 1907. "Authors Talk About Their Books." *New York Times Saturday Review of Books*, 2 February, BR62.

Nye, W. S. 1942. *Carbine and Lance: The Story of Old Fort Sill*. Norman: University of Oklahoma Press.

O'Connor, John E. 2003. "The White Man's Indian: An Institutional Approach." In *Hollywood's Indian: The Portrayal of the Native American in Film*, edited by Peter C. Rollins and John E. O'Connor, 27–38. Lexington: University Press of Kentucky.

Olrik, Axel. 1965. "Epic Laws of Folk Narrative." In *The Study of Folklore*, edited by Alan Dundes, 129–41. Englewood Cliffs, NJ: Prentice-Hall.

Opler, Morris Edward. 1938. "A Chiricahua Apache's Account of the Geronimo Campaign of 1886." *New Mexico Historical Review* 40: 360–86.

———. (1941) 1996. *An Apache Life-Way: The Economic, Social, and Religious Institutions of the Chiricahua Indians*. Lincoln: University of Nebraska Press.

———. 1942. *Myths and Tales of the Chiricahua Apache Indians*. New York: American Folklore Society.

———. 1969. *Apache Odyssey: A Journey between Two Worlds*. New York: Holt, Rinehart, and Winston.

Ortiz, Simon, ed. 2004. *Beyond the Reach of Time and Change: Native American Reflections on the Frank A. Rinehart Photograph Collection*. Tucson: University of Arizona Press.

Overton, Gwendolen. 1901. *The Heritage of Unrest*. New York: Macmillan.

Padget, Martin. 2004. *Indian Country: Travels in the American Southwest, 1840–1935*. Albuquerque: University of New Mexico Press.

Page, Elizabeth M. 1915. *In Camp and Tepee: An Indian Mission Story*. New York: Fleming H. Revell.

Parezo, Nancy J., and Don D. Fowler. 2007. *Anthropology Goes to the Fair: The 1904 Louisiana Purchase Exposition*. Lincoln: University of Nebraska Press.

Parker, James. 1929. *The Old Army: Memories, 1872–1918*. Philadelphia, PA: Dorrance.

Patten, Lewis B. 1971. *The Hands of Geronimo*. New York: Ace Books.

Patterson, Michelle Wick. 2010. *Natalie Curtis Burlin: A Life in Native and African American Music*. Lincoln: University of Nebraska Press.

Pearce, Roy Harvey. 1988. *Savagism and Civilization: A Study of the Indian and the American Mind*. Berkeley: University of California Press.

Penfield, Thomas. 1966. *Dig Here!* Rev. ed. San Antonio, TX: Naylor.

Peterson, Jess R. 2003. *Images of America: Omaha's Trans-Mississippi Exposition.* Charleston, SC: Arcade.

Phipps, Woody. 1936–1940. "Wm. Walter Brady." *American Life Histories: Manuscripts from the Federal Writers' Project.* memory.loc.gov, accessed 20 December 2008.

Plinth, August. 1973. *Geronimo's Cadillac: Poems.* New York: Black Sun Press.

Porter, Joy. 2008. "'Primitive' Discourse: Aspects of Contemporary Irish Representations of North American Indians." *American Studies* 49 (3–4): 63–85.

Powers, Nellie Brown. 1961. "A Ride from Geronimo, the Apache." *New Mexico Historical Review* 36: 89–96.

Prats, Armando José. 1996a. "His Master's Voice(over): Revisionist Ethos and Narrative Dependence from *Broken Arrow* (1950) to *Geronimo: An American Legend* (1993)." *ANQ* 9: 15–29.

———. 1996b. "'Outfirsting' the First American: 'History,' the American Adam, and the New Hollywood Indian in *Dances with Wolves, The Last of the Mohicans,* and *Geronimo: An American Legend.*" In *The Image of the American West: Selected Papers—1996 Conference, Society of Interdisciplinary Study of Social Imagery,* edited by Will Wright and Steven Kaplan, 197–208. Pueblo, CO: Society for the Interdisciplinary Study of Social Imagery.

Radbourne, Allan. 2004. "Capturing the Apaches: The Photographs of A. Frank Randall." *Wild West,* February, 48–74. web.ebscohost.com/ehost/delivery?vid=16&hid=109& sid=f25b6a52–8fbe-4d73–97c, accessed 4 December 2007.

Rader, Dean. 2011. *Engaged Resistance: American Indian Art, Literature, and Film from Alcatraz to the NMAI.* Austin: University of Texas Press.

Rahder, Bobbi. 1996. "Gendered Stylistic Differences between Photographers of Native Americans at the Turn of the Century." *Journal of the West* 35 (1): 86–95.

Reddin, Paul. 1999. *Wild West Shows.* Urbana: University of Illinois Press.

Redfield, Georgia B. 1936–1940. "Rufus H. Dunnahoo." *American Life Histories: Manuscripts from the Federal Writers' Project.* memory.loc.gov, accessed 19 December 2008.

Revard, Carter. 1998. *Family Matters, Tribal Affairs.* Tucson: University of Arizona Press.

Riding In, James. 2004. "Legacy of Resistance." In *Beyond the Reach of Time and Change: Native American Reflections on the Frank A. Rinehart Photograph Collection,* edited by Simon Ortiz, 52–55. Tucson: University of Arizona Press.

Roberts, Charles D. 1959–1960. "Letter from Brigadier General Charles D. Roberts, USA. Ret." *Military Affairs* 23: 212–14.

Roberts, David. 1994. *Once They Moved Like the Wind: Cochise, Geronimo, and the Apache Wars.* New York: Simon and Schuster.

Robinson, Sherry. 1999. "A White Frontiersman, Zebina Streeter, May Have Led Apache Raids and Married Geronimo's Daughter." *Wild West,* October. ebscohost.com, accessed 4 December 2007.

———. 2000. *Apache Voices: Their Stories of Survival as Told to Eve Ball.* Albuquerque: University of New Mexico Press.

Rochette, Edward C. 1992. *Lost Mines and Buried Treasure: A Guide to Sites and Legends of the Southwest.* Phoenix, AZ: Renaissance House.

Rogers, Randal. 2008. "Colonial Imitation and Racial Insubordination: Photography at the Louisiana Purchase Exhibition of 1904." *History of Photography* 32 (4): 347–67.

Rollins, Peter C., and John E. O'Connor, eds. 2003. *Hollywood's Indian: The Portrayal of the Native American in Film.* Exp. ed. Lexington: University Press of Kentucky.

Roosevelt, Theodore. 1951. *The Letters of Theodore Roosevelt.* Edited by Elting E. Morrison. 8 vols. Cambridge, MA: Harvard University Press.

Rudisill, Richard. 1973. *Photographers of the New Mexico Territory, 1854–1912.* Santa Fe: Museum of New Mexico Press.

Ruffo, Armand Garnet. 2001. *At Geronimo's Grave.* Regina, Saskatchewan: Coteau Books.

Rydell, Robert W. 1981. "The Trans-Mississippi and International Exposition: 'To Work Out the Problem of Universal Civilization.'" *American Quarterly* 33: 587–607.

———. 1984. *All the World's a Fair: Visions of Empire at American International Expositions, 1876–1916.* Chicago: University of Chicago Press.

———, John E. Findling, and Kimberly D. Pelle. 2000. *Fair America: World's Fairs in the United States.* Washington, D.C.: Smithsonian Institution Press.

Said, Edward W. 1978. *Orientalism.* New York: Random House.

Salzman, M., Jr. 1967. "Geronimo: The Napoleon of Indians." *Journal of Arizona History* 8: 215–47.

Samuels, David W. 2004. *Putting a Song on Top of It: Expression and Identity on the San Carlos Apache Reservation.* Tucson: University of Arizona Press.

Sandos, James A., and Larry E. Burgess. 2003. "The Hollywood Indian versus Native Americans: *Tell Them Willie Boy Is Here.*" In *Hollywood's Indian: The Portrayal of the Native American in Film,* edited by Peter C. Rollins and John E. O'Connor, 107–20. Lexington: University Press of Kentucky.

Sandweiss, Martha A. 2002. *Print the Legend: Photography and the American West.* New Haven, CT: Yale University Press.

Santee, Ross. 1947. *Apache Land.* New York: Scribner's.

Schmitt, Martin F., ed. 1960. *General George Crook: His Autobiography.* Norman: University of Oklahoma Press.

Schwarz, Melissa. 1992. *Geronimo: Apache Warrior.* New York: Chelsea House.

Seal, Graham. 2009. "The Robin Hood Principle: Folklore, History, and the Social Bandit." *Journal of Folklore Research* 46: 67–89.

Shapard, Bud. 2010. *Chief Loco: Apache Peacemaker.* Norman: University of Oklahoma Press.

Shepard, Sophie. 1890a. "The Apaches at Mount Vernon." *Lend a Hand* 5: 37–42.

———. 1890b. "The Apache Captives." *Lend a Hand* 5: 163–66.

Shirley, Glenn. 1958. *Pawnee Bill: A Biography of Major Gordon W. Lillie.* Albuquerque: University of New Mexico Press.

Shorto, Russell. 1989. *Geronimo and the Struggle for Apache Freedom*. Englewood Cliffs, NJ: Silver Burdett Press.

Silko, Leslie Marmon. 1981. *Storyteller*. New York: Seaver Books.

———. 1991. *Almanac of the Dead: A Novel*. New York: Simon and Schuster.

———. 1996. *Yellow Woman and a Beauty of the Spirit: Essays on Native American Life Today*. New York: Simon and Schuster.

Simmons, Marc. 1997. *Massacre on the Lordsburg Road: A Tragedy of the Apache Wars*. College Station: Texas A&M University Press.

Skinner, Woodward B. 1987. *The Apache Rock Crumbles: The Captivity of Geronimo's People*. Pensacola, FL: Skinner Publications.

Smith, Paul Chaat. 2009. *Everything You Know About Indians Is Wrong*. Minneapolis: University of Minnesota Press.

Sonnichsen, C. L. 1986. "From Savage to Saint: A New Image for Geronimo." In *Geronimo and the End of the Apache Wars*, edited by C. L. Sonnichsen, 5–34. Lincoln: University of Nebraska Press.

Sontag, Susan. 1977. *On Photography*. New York: Farrar, Straus and Giroux.

Spivak, Gayatri Chakravorty. 1994. "Can the Subaltern Speak?" In *Colonial Discourse and Post-Colonial Theory*, edited by Patrick Williams and Laura Chrisman, 66–111. New York: Columbia University Press.

Starr, Arigon. 1997. "About Geronimo." Starrwatcher Online. www.arigonstarr.com, accessed 3 September 2005.

Stedman, Raymond William. 1982. *Shadows of the Indian: Stereotypes in American Culture*. Norman: University of Oklahoma Press.

Steinbeck, John. (1939) 2006. *The Grapes of Wrath*. Reprint, New York: Penguin.

Sterngass, Jon. 2010. *Geronimo*. New York: Chelsea House.

Stimpson, Gordon. 1896. "A True Story about Geronimo." *American Field*, February, 104–5.

Stockel, Henrietta. 1991. *Women of the Apache Nation: Voices of Truth*. Reno: University of Nevada Press.

———. 2004. *Shame and Endurance: The Untold Story of the Chiricahua Apache Prisoners of War*. Tucson: University of Arizona Press.

Sullivan, George. 2010. *Geronimo: Apache Renegade*. New York: Sterling.

Sutton, Royal. 1972. "Introduction." *The Face of Courage: The Indian Photographs of Frank A. Rinehart*. Fort Collins, CO: Old Army Press.

Sweeney, Edwin R. 1991. *Cochise: Chiricahua Apache Chief*. Norman: University of Oklahoma Press.

———. 1998. *Mangas Coloradas: Chief of the Chiricahua Apaches*. Norman: University of Oklahoma Press.

———. 2007. "Geronimo and Chatto: Alternative Apache Ways." *Wild West*, August, 30–38.

———. 2010. *From Cochise to Geronimo: The Chiricahua Apaches, 1874–1886*. Norman: University of Oklahoma Press.

Symes, Ronald. 1975. *Geronimo: The Fighting Apache*. New York: William Morrow.

Thompson, Gerald. 1994. "Hollywood and History: *Geronimo: An American Legend*, A Review Essay." *Journal of Arizona History* 35: 205–12.

Thrapp, Dan L. 1964. *Al Sieber: Chief of Scouts*. Norman: University of Oklahoma Press.

———. 1967. *The Conquest of Apacheria*. Norman: University of Arizona Press.

———. 1969. "Geronimo's Mysterious Surrender." *Western Brand Book, Los Angeles Corral* 13: 17–35.

———. 1973. *Juh: An Incredible Indian*. El Paso: Texas Western Press.

———, ed. 1979. *Dateline Fort Bowie: Charles Fletcher Lummis Reports on an Apache War*. Norman: University of Oklahoma Press.

———. 1980. "Foreword." In *Indeh: An Apache Odyssey*, by Eve Ball, with Nora Henn and Lynda Sanchez, xiii–xvi. Provo, UT: Brigham Young University Press.

———. 1988. *Encyclopedia of Frontier Biography*. Glendale, CA: Arthur H. Clark.

Titla, Mary Kim. 2009. "Remembering Geronimo 100 Years after His Death." *Indian Country Today*, 4 March, 6–7.

Tohe, Laura. 2004. "See Real Indians." In *Beyond the Reach of Time and Change: Native American Reflections on the Frank A. Rinehart Photograph Collection*, edited by Simon Ortiz, 160–63. Tucson: University of Arizona Press.

Tomlinson, Edward T. (1920) 2010. *The Pursuit of the Apache Chief*. Memphis, TN: General Books.

Tomlinson, Rawdon. 2007. *Geronimo after Kas-ki-yeh: Poems*. Baton Rouge: Louisiana State University Press.

Trennert, Robert A., Jr. 1987a. "Fairs, Expositions, and the Changing Image of Southwestern Indians, 1876–1904." *New Mexico Historical Review* 62: 129–50.

———. 1987b. "Selling Education at World's Fairs and Expositions, 1893–1904." *American Indian Quarterly* 11: 203–20.

———. 1993. "A Resurrection of Native Arts and Crafts: The St. Louis World's Fair, 1904." *Missouri Historical Review* 87 (3): 274–93.

Tsinhnahjinnie, Hulleah J. 2003. "When Is a Photograph Worth a Thousand Words?" In *Photography's Other Histories*, edited by Christopher Pinney and Nicolas Peterson, 40–52. Durham, NC: Duke University Press.

Tunney, Tom. 1994. "*Geronimo: An American Legend*." *Sight and Sound* n.s. 4 (11): 47.

Turcheneske, John A., Jr. 1973. "The Arizona Press and Geronimo's Surrender." *Journal of Arizona History* 14: 133–48.

———. 1997. *The Chiricahua Apache Prisoners of War: Fort Sill, 1894–1914*. Niwot: University Press of Colorado.

Turner, Frederick W. 1996. "Introduction." In *Geronimo: His Own Story*, edited by S. M. Barrett, 3–35. New York: Penguin.

Turner, Katharine C. 1951. *Red Men Calling on the Great White Father*. Norman: University of Oklahoma Press.

Van Orden, Jay. 1989. "C. S. Fly at Cañon de los Embudos: American Indians as Enemy in the Field; A Photographic First." *Journal of Arizona History* 30 (Autumn): 319–46.

———. 1991. *Geronimo's Surrender: The 1886 C. S. Fly Photographs*. Museum Monograph 8. Tucson: Arizona Historical Society.

Vaughan, Alden T. 2006. *Transatlantic Encounters: American Indians in Britain, 1500–1776*. Cambridge: Cambridge University Press.

Vaughan, Thomas. 1989. "C. S. Fly: Pioneer Photojournalist." *Journal of Arizona History* 30: 303–18.

"Verse of the Year: Part One." 1893. *Overland Monthly* 22: 440–47.

Von Drehle, David. 2011. "Death Comes for the Terrorist." *Time*, 20 May, 14–21, 25–29.

Wellman, Paul I. 1936. *Broncho Apache*. New York: Macmillan.

Wesling, Donald. 1985. "Introduction." In *Internal Resistances: The Poetry of Edward Dorn*, edited by Donald Wesling, 1–12. Berkeley: University of California Press.

Whissel, Kristen. 2002. "Placing the Spectator on the Scene of History: The Battle Re-enactment at the Turn of the Century, from Buffalo Bill's Wild West to the Early Cinema." *Historical Journal of Film, Radio and Television* 22: 225–43.

"The Wives of Geronimo." 1973. *El Scribiano* 10 (3): 83–89.

Wood, Norman. 1906. *Lives of Famous Indian Chiefs from Cofachiqui, the Indian Princess, and Powhatan; Down to and Including Chief Joseph and Geronimo*. Aurora, IL: American Indian Historical Publishing Co.

Woodsum, Jo Ann. 1993. "'Living Signs of Themselves': A Research Note on the Politics and Practice of Exhibiting Native Americans in the United States at the Turn of the Century." *UCLA Historical Journal* 13: 110–29.

Wyatt, Edgar. 1952. *Geronimo: The Last Apache War Chief*. New York: McGraw-Hill.

Films and Sound Recordings

Aldrich, Robert, dir. 1954. *Apache*. Metro-Goldwyn-Mayer.

Altman, Robert, dir. 1976. *Buffalo Bill and the Indians, or Sitting Bull's History Lesson*. Lion's Gate Films.

Bennet, Spencer Gordon, dir. 1952. *Son of Geronimo: Apache Avenger*. Columbia Pictures.

Correll, Charles, dir., and Stan Hough, prod. 1990. *Gunsmoke: The Last Apache*. CBS Entertainment.

Costner, Kevin, dir. 1990. *Dances with Wolves*. Orion Pictures.

Craig, Dustinn, Sarah Colt, and Sharon Grimberg, dir. and prod. 2009. *We Shall Remain: Geronimo*. American Experience, in association with NAPT.

Curtis, Edward S, dir. 1914. *In the Land of the Head Hunters*. Seattle Film Company.

Cyrus, Billy Ray, Keith Hinton, and Don Von Treese. 1994. "Geronimo." *Storm in the Heartland*. Mercury, compact disc.

Dalton, Dan, prod. 1991. *The Great Indian Wars, 1840–1890*. Dan Dalton Productions.

Daves, Delmer, dir. 1950. *Broken Arrow*. 20th Century Fox.

Ford, John, dir. 1939. *Stagecoach*. United Artists.

———. 1964. *Cheyenne Autumn*. Warner Brothers.

Foster, Lewis R., dir. 1951. *The Last Outpost* (a.k.a. *Cavalry Charge*). Paramount Pictures.

Goodwin, Neil, dir., Lena Carr, prod., and Judy Crichton, prod. 1988. *Geronimo and the Apache Resistance*. WGBH Educational Foundation and Peace River Films.

Hathaway, Henry, dir. 1935. *The Lives of a Bengal Lancer*. Paramount.

Hausman, Sid. 1994. "Geronimo's Land." *Geronimo's Land*. Blue Bhikku Records, compact disc.

Hawks, Howard, dir. 1948. *Red River*. United Artists.

Hibbs, Jesse, dir. 1956. *Walk the Proud Land*. Universal-International.

Hill, Walter, dir. 1993. *Geronimo: An American Legend*. Columbia Pictures.

Hoffman, John, dir. 1950. *I Killed Geronimo*. Jack Schwarz Productions.

Kater, Peter. 1993. "Geronimo's Surrender." *How the West Was Lost* (soundtrack). Silver Wave Records, compact disc.

Lasar, Mars. 1993. "Geronimo." *The Eleventh Hour*. Real Music, compact disc.

Laven, Arnold, dir. 1962. *Geronimo*. Bedford Pictures/United Artists.

Levin, Tony. 2002. "Geronimo." *Pieces of the Sun*. Narada Music, compact disc.

Lixey, Bruce, and Robert Hecules, dir. and prod. 1995. *America's Great Indian Leaders*. Questar Video.

Marshall, George, dir. 1942. *Valley of the Sun*. RKO Radio Pictures.

Marvin, Hank. (1963) 1995. "Geronimo." *The Shadows: The First Twenty Years at the Top*. EMI, compact disc.

McIntyre, Kitty. 2003. "Geronimo." *The Cat Came Back*. Self-issued, compact disc.

Modern Talking. 1986. "Geronimo's Cadillac." *In the Middle of Nowhere*. Hansa, compact disc.

Murphy, Michael Martin. 1972. "Geronimo's Cadillac." *Geronimo's Cadillac*. Raven, compact disc.

Nazarro, Ray, dir., 1952. *Indian Uprising*. Columbia Pictures.

Nelson, Ralph, dir. 1970. *Soldier Blue*. AVCO Embassy Pictures.

Penn, Arthur, dir. 1970. *Little Big Man*. Cinema Center Films.

Sherman, George, dir. 1952. *The Battle at Apache Pass*. Universal-International.

Sirk, Douglas, dir. 1954. *Taza, Son of Cochise*. Universal Studios.

Sirota, Ted. 1999. "Geronimo's Free." *Propaganda*. Naim, compact disc.

Sloane, Paul, dir. 1940. *Geronimo!* Paramount Pictures.

Spearman, Glenn. 1997. "Geronimo's Song." *Let It Go*. Red Toucan Records, compact disc.

Starrett, Jack, dir. 1979. *Mr. Horn*. Lorimar Productions.

Witney, William, dir. 1954. "Geronimo." *Stories of the Century*. Republic Pictures.

Young, Roger, dir. 1993. *Geronimo*. Turner Pictures.

Newspapers

Albuquerque (NM) Journal

Anaconda (MT) Standard

Arizona Daily Citizen (Tucson)

Arizona Republican (Phoenix)

Arkansas Democrat-Gazette (Little Rock), formerly *Arkansas Gazette*

Army and Navy Journal (New York)

Atlanta (GA) Constitution

Boston Herald

Buffalo (NY) Evening News

Buffalo (NY) Sunday Morning News

Casa Grande (AZ) Dispatch

Chicago Mail

Chicago Times-Herald

Chicago Tribune

Chilicothe (MO) Constitution Tribune

Commercial-Appeal (Memphis, TN)

Constitution Democrat (Lawton, OK)

Daily Chief (Perry, IA)

Daily Kennebec (ME) Journal

Daily News Republican (Lawton, OK)

Daily Record (Oklahoma City, OK)

Daily Review (Decatur, IL)

Daily Tombstone (AZ)

Davenport (IA) Daily Republican

Deming (NM) Headlight

Denver (CO) Times

Des Moines (IA) Weekly Leader

Fresno (CA) Bee

Galveston (TX) Daily News

Harper's Weekly (New York)

Havre (MT) Daily News

Herald (Delphos, OH)

Hoof and Horn (Prescott, AZ)

Indian Country Today (New York)

Indiana (PA) Democrat

Indiana (PA) Weekly Messenger

Kansas City (MO) Journal

Kansas City (MO) Star

Kerrville (TX) Daily Times

Kerrville (TX) Mountain Sun

Las Vegas (NM) Daily Optic

Le Grand (IA) Reporter

Los Angeles Times

Mansfield (OH) Daily News

Mobile (AL) Register

Modesto (CA) Morning Herald

Morning Oregonian (Portland)

Nebraska State Journal (Lincoln)

Nevada State Journal (Reno)

New Orleans (LA) Times-Picayune

New Oxford (PA) Item

New York Evening World

New York Times

News (Frederick, MD)

North Adams (MA) Transcript

Omaha (NE) Daily Bee

Omaha (NE) World-Herald

Pensacola (FL) Daily News

Philadelphia (PA) Inquirer

Piqua (OH) Daily Call

Portsmouth (OH) Times

Prescott (AZ) Miner

Reno (NV) Evening Gazette

Rocky Mountain News (Denver, CO)

Salt Lake City (UT) Herald

Sandusky (OH) Daily Register

Sandusky (OH) Star-Journal

San Francisco Chronicle

Santa Fe New Mexican

Seattle (WA) Times

Semi-Weekly Robesonian (Lumberton, NC)

Silver City (NM) Enterprise

Socorro (NM) Bullion

Spokane (WA) Spokesman-Review

Stars and Stripes (Washington, D.C.)

St. Louis (MO) Globe Democrat

St. Louis (MO) Post-Dispatch

Times (London)

Times Democrat (Lima, OH)

Titusville (PA) Herald

Tucson (AZ) Daily Citizen

Tucson (AZ) Weekly Star

Washington Critic

Washington Post

Waterloo (IA) Daily Reporter

Weekly Gazette (Colorado Springs, CO)

Weekly New Mexican Review and Live Stock
    Journal (Santa Fe)

Winners of the West (Saint Joseph, MO)

Index